The SENCO HANDBOOK

The SENCO HANDBOOK

LEADING PROVISION AND PRACTICE

Sarah Martin-Denham & Steve Watts

CORWIN

Corwin
A SAGE company
2455 Teller Road
Thousand Oaks, California 91320
(800)233-9936
www.corwin.com

SAGE Publications Ltd
1 Oliver's Yard
55 City Road
London EC1Y 1SP

SAGE Publications India Pvt Ltd
B 1/I 1 Mohan Cooperative Industrial Area
Mathura Road
New Delhi 110 044

SAGE Publications Asia-Pacific Pte Ltd
3 Church Street
#10-04 Samsung Hub
Singapore 049483

Editorial Arrangement © Sarah Martin-Denham and Steve Watts 2019
Introduction, Chapters 1, 2, 4, 6, 7, 8, 9, 10, 11, 12
© Sarah Martin-Denham 2019
Chapters 3, 5 and 15 © Steve Watts and Sarah Martin-Denham 2019
Chapter 13 © Helen Benstead 2019
Chapter 14 © Steve Watts 2019

First published 2019

Apart from any fair dealing for the purposes of research or private study, or criticism or review, as permitted under the Copyright, Designs and Patents Act, 1988, this publication may be reproduced, stored or transmitted in any form, or by any means, only with the prior permission in writing of the publishers, or in the case of reprographic reproduction, in accordance with the terms of licences issued by the Copyright Licensing Agency. Enquiries concerning reproduction outside those terms should be sent to the publishers.

Library of Congress Control Number: 2019931379

British Library Cataloguing in Publication data

A catalogue record for this book is available from the British Library

Editor: Delayna Spencer
Assistant editor: Catriona McMullen
Production editor: Martin Fox
Copyeditor: Clare Weaver
Proofreader: Sharon Cawood
Indexer: Silvia Benvenuto
Marketing manager: Dilhara Attygalle
Cover design: Wendy Scott
Typeset by: C&M Digitals (P) Ltd, Chennai, India
Printed in the UK

ISBN 978-1-5264-6570-2
ISBN 978-1-5264-6569-6 (pbk)

At SAGE we take sustainability seriously. Most of our products are printed in the UK using responsibly sourced papers and boards. When we print overseas we ensure sustainable papers are used as measured by the PREPS grading system. We undertake an annual audit to monitor our sustainability.

Contents

Areas of SEND	xi
About the Authors and Contributors	xiii
Acknowledgements	xv
Online Resources	xvii
List of Acronyms	xix
Glossary	xxiii

1 Introduction — 1
Sarah Martin-Denham

The purpose of this book	2
The National Award for Special Educational Needs Co-ordination (NASENCO): Learning outcomes	2
Closing remarks	3

Part I – Professional Knowledge and Understanding — 5

2 The Statutory and Regulatory Context — 7
Sarah Martin-Denham

Legislation and regulation	8
Disability	10
Self-evaluation tools	11
SEN information report	11
The local offer	15

The four broad areas of need	15
SEN support	17
SEN register	19
Education, health and care plans	25
Funding models	30
Mediation and disagreement resolution arrangements	32

3 Leading in the SENCO Role — 33
Steve Watts and Sarah Martin-Denham

The role of the Special Educational Needs Coordinator (SENCO)	34
The characteristics of highly effective team leadership	35
Self-analysis of your own leadership	37
Supporting change in schools	39
Working alongside other professionals	41
Preparing for Ofsted	42

4 Best Practice in Collecting and Using Data — 45
Sarah Martin-Denham

What is data and why do we collect it?	46
Ofsted	47
What to do when children are not making expected progress	48
Provision management	49
Data presentation	50
Comparative data	52
Teacher accountability	57
Data sharing	58

5 Practitioner Enquiry — 61
Steve Watts and Sarah Martin-Denham

Origins of practitioner enquiry and action research	62
Teachers as action researchers	62
Origins of action research	63
What is action research?	63
Different approaches to action research	64
Planning an action research project	65
Research methods to support action research	66
Mixed methods	70
Using pilots	70
Reflective diary	71
Ethical considerations for action researchers	71
Ethical considerations for Sarah's practitioner enquiry	72
Interviewing children	73
Analysing data	76
Sharing the outcomes with senior leaders and governors	76
Recommended reading	77

Part II – Leading and Coordinating Provision — 79

6 Adverse Childhood Experiences — 81
Sarah Martin-Denham

What are adverse childhood experiences (ACEs)?	82
The ACE survey	82

Issues with the ACE survey	83
The impact of childhood adversity	83
The biology of stress	84
The impact of ACES across the life course	85
ACE-informed approaches	91

7 Meeting the Needs of Looked After and Permanently Placed Children — 95
Sarah Martin-Denham

Categories of care	96
Reasons children enter the care system	97
Trauma and loss	98
Attachment	102
Stages of attachment formation	102
Outcomes	104
The role of virtual school heads	106
The role of designated teachers	107
Trauma-informed approaches	108
Care approaches	109

8 Social, Emotional and Mental Health Difficulties — 115
Sarah Martin-Denham

Definition of mental health	116
What are social, emotional and mental health needs?	116
The role of the designated senior lead for mental health	117
Ill mental health in children	118
General indicators of social, emotional and mental health difficulties	119
Health and Wellbeing Agenda	120
Children and Young People Service (CYPS)	121
Generic assessment tools for SEMH	121
Evidence-based interventions and approaches	122
Self-reflection activity	122
The range of social, emotional and mental health difficulties	123

9 Neurodiversity — 161
Sarah Martin-Denham

Neurodiversity	162
Working memory	163
Systematic reviews	164
Essential source	165
General learning and teaching approaches for neurodiversity: Evidence based	165

10 Learning and Physical Disabilities — 189
Sarah Martin-Denham

The United Nations Convention on the Rights of People with Disabilities (UNCRPD)	190
Models of disability	190
Learning disability	192
Moderate Learning Difficulties	194
Sensory and/or physical needs	195
Assistive technologies	200
What is a risk assessment?	201
Supporting transitions	202

Individual healthcare plans	203
Equality Act 2010	205
Disability discrimination	209
Accessibility plans	210
Promoting disability equality	210

11 Preventing School Exclusion — 213
Sarah Martin-Denham

Types of exclusion	214
What are permanent exclusions?	214
What are fixed-term exclusions?	215
Alternative provision	215
How many children are excluded from school and why?	215
What happens once a child is excluded?	216
Informing caregivers about exclusions	218
Effective school policies to promote positive behaviour	218
Evidence-based approaches	219
Children who display Challenging, Violent or Aggressive Behaviour (CCVAB)	220
Debriefing processes following an incident	220
Types of debrief	221
SNAP (Special Needs Assessment Profile) online	224

Part III – Personal and Professional Conduct — 227

12 Person-Centred Approaches — 229
Sarah Martin-Denham

Person-centred approaches	230
Capturing the voice of the child	230
Whole-school approaches	233
Family leadership	234
Supporting transitions	237

13 Managing and Working with Support Staff — 243
Dr Helen Benstead

Exploring effective management of support staff: A model of good practice	244
Education Endowment Foundation: 7 principles of effective practice in deploying TAs	246
TA standards	247
Modes of working associated with support staff: how to identify and utilise them	248
Good practice approaches to leading an intervention group	253

14 Coaching and Mentoring — 257
Steve Watts

Investing in staff development	258
What is mentoring?	258
Modern mentoring	259
What is coaching?	260
What are the similarities and differences between mentoring and coaching?	261
What is government policy on mentoring and coaching?	261

Implications of recent government policy	263
What are the benefits of mentoring and coaching?	264
Creating a coaching and mentoring culture	266
Coaching and mentoring children	267
Leading in coaching and mentoring	269
Collaborative and alternative coaching and mentoring approaches	271
Coaching and mentoring code of ethics	273
Useful reading	273

15 Leading on Professional Learning — 275
Steve Watts and Sarah Martin-Denham

The nature of professional learning	276
Reflective learning for professional development	276
Reflective journals as professional development tools	277
Appraisal and target setting	278
The psychological contract	278
How to share information with teams	279
Leading on and utilising CPD for improvement	280
Recording CPD	281

Appendix – SEND: Assessment and Checklist Templates	285
References	307
Index	325

Areas of SEND

Anxiety	124
Attention Deficit Hyperactivity Disorder (ADHD)	178
Autism	182
Bereavement and loss	147
Bipolar Disorder	136
Deafblindness	200
Depression	133
Developmental Coordination Disorder (DCD) / Dyspraxia	175
Diabetes	195
Dyscalculia	172
Dyslexia	165
Eating disorders	144
Epilepsies	197
Foetal alcohol spectrum disorder (FASD)	197
Grief	148
Hearing loss	199
Irlen Syndrome	171
Obsessive Compulsive Disorder (OCD)	127
Post-traumatic Stress Disorder (PTSD)	131

Psychosis	138
Sectioning	159
Selective mutism	129
Self-harm	140
Sensory Processing Disorder (SPD)	186
Sight loss	198
Substance misuse (drugs)	155
Suicide	142

About the Authors and Contributors

Lead Author: Sarah Martin-Denham

Sarah Martin-Denham is a Senior Lecturer, Researcher and Programme Leader for the 'Post Graduate Certificate National Award for Special Educational Needs Coordination' and a Masters short course 'Supporting Children with Social, Emotional and Mental Health Needs' at the University of Sunderland. Sarah is a Senior Fellow of the Higher Education Academy, a Vice Chancellor Teaching Fellow, Chair of an independent SENCO network and a Convenor of an interdisciplinary research network for developing knowledge, understanding and approaches for supporting children who are experiencing adverse childhood experiences. She has extensive knowledge of learning and teaching in the North East of England in a variety of settings, ranging from early years to higher education. Sarah began her career as an infant school teacher in Sunderland then taught from entry level to foundation degree level study in a college. For the last eleven years Sarah has successfully developed and led four programmes and research projects in the School of Education at the University of Sunderland. Through her work with children and families over the last twenty years and her own neurodiverse abilities, she has developed a particular interest in special educational needs and disabilities.

Sarah's recent publications include:

Martin-Denham, S. (Ed.) (2015) *Teaching Children with Special Educational Needs and Disabilities 0–25 years*. London: SAGE.

Martin-Denham, S. and Stewart, C. (2017) *SENCO magazine: 'Ports in a Storm'*. Teach Primary.

Martin-Denham, S., Saddler, H., Ripley, S. and Donoghue, J. (2017) *The prevalence of special educational needs and disabilities identified in children 3–16 years.* School of Education, University of Sunderland.

Martin-Denham, S. and Donaghue, J. (2019) *An investigation into the factors that impact upon social and emotional wellbeing of children and young people from 3–16 years in Sunderland Local Authority which may lead to exclusion from school.* School of Education, University of Sunderland.

Co-author: Steve Watts

Steve Watts is the Head of the School of Culture at the University of Sunderland. He began his teaching career in schools in Northumberland. Following a successful career as Head of Humanities, Head of Year and SENCO, Steve moved to the University of Sunderland as a Senior Lecturer in the School of Education, eventually becoming a Principal Lecturer in secondary education. In 2011 Steve successfully led the Secondary ITE Team through an Ofsted inspection to Grade 1 Outstanding.

Steve became a Head of Department in 2011 and Head of School in 2016. During this time he wrote, developed and taught the Mentoring and Coaching module on the MA Education programme. The module was delivered to students studying from around the world as part of an independent distance learning course. Steve contributes to the NASENCO programme at the University of Sunderland. In addition to coaching and mentoring, Steve's interests include ethnography and action research where he has been involved in working with teachers, both in the UK and across the globe.

Website: www.wattscoaching.co.uk
Email: wattscoaching@talktalk.net

Contributor: Dr Helen Benstead

Helen has worked in central and local government, as a Youth Policy Advisor at the Cabinet Office, and for the Mayor of London's Education and Youth Team at Greater London Authority. She is the Founder and Director of Inclusive Classrooms and leads the MA Education programme in her role as Senior Lecturer at the University of Sunderland.

Acknowledgements

Lead author: Sarah Martin-Denham

I would like to give my sincere thanks to my true love Ben and my best friend and sister Lucy, who have supported me wholeheartedly in writing this book: without you both it would never have happened. To my lovely children Emily and William: thank you for understanding that I was writing a book and for giving me time to write – you mean the absolute world to me. To Maggie dog: thank you for the company and many paws as I wrote. Thank you to Steve for his enduring support and encouragement: you will always be my mentor. I would also like to thank all the reviewers for the book: your support and suggestions have been greatly appreciated.

Co-author: Steve Watts

My thanks go, first, to Sarah for inviting me to join her in writing this Handbook and for her faith in me. Second, thanks to all the colleagues, children and students who have joined me on my journey over the last 40 years and for everything that they have taught me. Finally, thanks to my wife, Ann, who, during the writing of this book, has waited on so many occasions for me to 'just finish this last paragraph'.

We would also like to thank Delayna Spencer at Sage for her ongoing support and encouragement. Further thanks to the following people who have been critical friends in reviewing chapters and providing support to this book project:

Dr Karen Horridge: Consultant paediatrician and clinical coordinator

Dr Wendy Thorley: Director, Children experiencing loss and trauma

Lou Mitchell: Adopter

Faye Waterhouse: SENCO

Philip Tebbs: SENCO

Claire Hornsby: SENCO

Laura Reynolds: SENCO

Vicki Tough: SENCO

Jacob Donaghue: University of Sunderland

Noah Chisholm: University of Sunderland

Online Resources

Head online to **https://study.sagepub.com/education/special-education/martin-denham-and-watts-the-senco-handbook** to download and print various resources from the book!

List of Acronyms

ACE	Adverse Childhood Experience
AD(H)D	Attention Deficit Hyperactivity Disorder
ARBD	Alcohol Related Birth Defects
ARND	Alcohol Related Neurodevelopmental Disorder
AP	Alternative Provision
ASD	Autism Spectrum Disorder
BAD	Bipolar Affective Disorder
BERA	British Educational Research Association
BILD	British Institute of Learning Disabilities
CAMHS	Child and Adolescent Mental Health Services
CBT	Cognitive Behaviour Therapy
CCVAB	Children who display Challenging, Violent or Aggressive Behaviour
CDSR	The Cochrane Database of Systematic Reviews
CPD	Continuing Professional Development
CUREE	Centre for the Use of Research Evidence in Education
CWMT	Cogmed Working Memory Training
CYPS	Children and Young People Services
DCD	Developmental Coordination Disorder
DfE	Department for Education

DoH	Department of Health
DPO	Data Protection Officer
DSG	Designated School Grant
DSM-5	Diagnostic and Statistical Manual of Mental Disorders
EHCP	Education, Health and Care Plan
EMDR	Eye Movement Desensitisation and Reprocessing
EYFS	Early Years Foundation Stage
FASD	Foetal Alcohol Spectrum Disorder
FE	Further Education
FIES	Food Insecurity Experience Scale
FSM	Free School Meals
GDPR	General Data Protection Regulation
GP	General Practitioner
HI	Hearing Impairment
HIV	Human, Immunodeficiency Virus
IASS	SEND Information, Advice and Support Service
ICD-10	International Classification of Diseases
IHCP	Individual Healthcare Plan
IPSEA	Independent Parental Special Education Advice
ITE	Initial Teacher Education
LA	Local Authority
LAIT	Local Authority Interactive Tool
MLD	Moderate Learning Difficulty
MSI	Multi-Sensory Impairment
NC	National Curriculum
NCTL	National College for Teaching and Leadership
NHS	National Health Service
OCD	Obsessive Compulsive Disorder
Ofsted	Office for Standards in Education
ONS	Office for National Statistics
PBS	Positive Behaviour Support
PECS	Picture Exchange Communication System
PFAS	Partial Foetal Alcohol Syndrome
PMLD	Profound and Multiple Learning Difficulties
PRU	Pupil Referral Unit
PTSD	Post-traumatic Stress Disorder
SEN	Special Educational Needs
SENCO	Special Educational Needs Coordinator
SEND	Special Educational Needs and/or Disability
SLCN	Speech, Language and Communication Needs
SLD	Severe Learning Difficulty
SMART	Specific, Measurable, Achievable, Realistic, Time bound
SMI	Severe Mental Illness
SPD	Sensory Processing Disorder
SpLD	Specific Learning Difficulty

List of Acronyms

SSRI	Selective Serotonin Reuptake Inhibitors
TA	Teaching Assistant
UNCRPD	United Nations Convention on the Rights of People with Disabilities
UNODC	United Nations Office on Drugs and Crime
VI	Visual Impairment
YOT	Youth Offending Team

Glossary

Active Listening: Focusing entirely on what the child is saying, understanding the emotions and feelings underlying the message

Alternative Provision: For children of compulsory school age who do not attend mainstream or special schools

Amphetamines: A group of amphetamine-type stimulants that includes amphetamine and methamphetamine

Annual Review: The review of an EHC Plan, which the Local Authority must make as a minimum every 12 months

Care Pathway: The route a person takes through healthcare services

Child Protection Plan: A plan drawn up by social care services to protect a child who they feel is suffering, or is likely to suffer, significant harm

Children in Need: A child within social care services who doesn't meet the threshold for being 'looked after' but is receiving intervention from social care services

Cocaine Salt: Cocaine hydrochloride

Cognitive Behavioural Therapy: A range of behavioural and cognitive behavioural therapies to achieve specific treatment goals

'Crack' Cocaine: Cocaine base obtained from cocaine hydrochloride through conversion processes to make it suitable for smoking

Dependence: Occurs when the body adapts to prolonged use of a drug and where the person experiences withdrawal in its absence

Depression: Where an individual usually suffers from depressed mood, loss of interest and enjoyment, and reduced energy, leading to increased fatigability and diminished activity

Designated Teachers: Champions the educational attainment of looked-after and permanently placed children

Diabetes Mellitus: A metabolic disease where the body is not able to regulate blood sugar levels due to an inability to produce insulin

Diagnosis: The process of identifying an illness by carrying out tests or by studying the symptoms

Dual Diagnosis: Co-existence of two illnesses or conditions

Dysphoria: An emotional state characterised by malaise, anxiety, depression or unease

Dysthymia: A chronic depression of mood

Early Years Foundation Stage: The framework for the learning, development and care of children from birth to five years

Education Health and Care Plan: Details the education, health and social care support that is to be provided to a child with SEN and/or disabilities

Effectiveness: The extent to which a specific intervention does what it is intended to do

Epilepsies: Convulsive attacks due to disordered electrical activity in the brain

Exogenous Stressors: Stress which derives from outside the body such as life-event stress

Family Therapy: Sessions based on systemic, cognitive behavioural or psychoanalytic principles

Graduated Response: A model of action and intervention to support children who have SEN

Healthy Child Programme: Supports pregnancy and the first five years of a child's life, focusing on universal preventative services with screening, immunisation, health and development reviews

Joint Strategic Needs Assessment: Information, advice and support services for children and caregivers with SEN or disabilities

Local Authority: Leading integration arrangements for children with SEND

Local Offer: Local Authority information about provision they expect to be available across education, health and social care for children in their area who have SEND

Maintained School: Schools which are maintained by a Local Authority

Methodology: Describes how research is carried out, including how information is collected and analysed, and why a particular method or methods have been chosen

Mild Depression: Four depressive symptoms as defined by the ICD-10

Moderate Depression: Five or six depressive symptoms as defined by the ICD-10

National Curriculum: Statutory entitlement to learning for all children from 5–16 years

NHS England: An independent body, to improve health outcomes for people in England

Official Exclusions: These are recorded with central or local government and include temporary fixed period exclusions or permanent exclusions

Ofsted: Responsible for the inspection of all schools in England

Opioids: A generic term applied to alkaloids from opium poppy (opiates), their synthetic analogues (mainly prescription or pharmaceutical opioids) and compounds synthesised in the body

Prevalence: How common a type of exceptionality is within a population, either at a point in time or over a given period of time

Prognosis: The medical assessment of the future course of events and probable outcome of an illness

Pupil Referral Unit: Provides education for children who would otherwise not receive suitable education because of illness, exclusion or any other reason

Reliability: The ability to get the same or similar result each time a study is repeated with a different population or group

Schizophrenia: A severe mental health disorder which is characterised by a loss of reality

SEN Support: Extra or different support that is provided in addition to the school's usual curriculum

Severe Mental Illness: Refers to those with psychological problems that are so debilitating that their ability to engage and function is severely challenged

Special Educational Needs: A child has SEN if they have a learning difficulty or disability which calls for special educational provision to be made

Special Educational Needs Coordinator (SENCO): A qualified teacher in a school or maintained nursery school who has responsibility for coordinating SEN provision

Severe Depression: Seven or more depressive symptoms as defined by the ICD-10

Social Care: All forms of personal care and other practical assistance for children who need extra support

Special Educational Provision: Provision that is different from or additional to that normally available to children with SEN to enable them to access and participate in learning

Specialist School: A school which is specifically organised to make special educational provision for children with SEN

Stakeholder: An organisation/individual with an interest in a topic, including public sector providers and commissioners of care or services

Statutory Duty: A duty that must be complied with

Unofficial Exclusions: These are not recorded as exclusions in the national data and include managed moves to a different school; a move into some form of alternative provision offsite; or illegal exclusions

Watchful Waiting: An intervention in which no active treatment is offered

Young Person: A person over compulsory school age (the end of the academic year in which they turn 16) to the age of 25

1
Introduction
Sarah Martin-Denham

The purpose of this book

The aim of this book is to enable SENCOs and aspiring SENCOs to develop their knowledge and understanding of how to strategically lead provision embedding evidence-based practices for children with special educational needs and disabilities (SEND). The book's chapters have been written to support you and your colleagues in becoming reflective practitioners who can critically evaluate provision to ensure truly inclusive practice with children and caregivers at the heart of decision-making. To achieve this, there needs to be a shift in thinking across provisions from 'what is wrong with this child?' to 'what is the reason for...?' and 'how can we best support them and their families?'. To achieve this, there needs to be understanding of each child's needs through thorough identification and assessment from highly trained staff who can then agree and plan support with the child and their caregivers. Where colleagues access high-quality training relevant to their role and those they teach, it is more likely that barriers to learning will be overcome.

The content of the book has been created through knowledge and understanding gained as programme leader and tutor for the Post Graduate Certificate National Awards for Special Educational Needs Coordination (NASENCO). It also reflects personal experiences and summation of extensive literature searches to draw upon and share current evidence-based practices. The book doesn't include all of the research, approaches, interventions or guidance that is available, but it does attempt to draw together the most useful sources.

Where possible, I have not used terms such as disorder, delay, impairment, condition, syndrome – unfortunately, these words are still used across services to name a particular need a child has been diagnosed with. As someone with a 'label' I hope for a move away from these, as I believe they detract from the child's needs and can lead to exclusion, stigma and discrimination. We are in a situation where labels are being applied to children without robust evidence to support the judgement; 'moderate learning difficulties' (MLD) is an example of this. As argued by Norwich et al. (2014), the concept of MLD is not clearly understood in both the definition and general use. I would suggest that children can be assigned a label without other reasons for their learning challenges being explored. I would encourage you, as SENCO, to analyse the SEN register to identify the validity and reliability of the label.

It is important to recognise that this handbook is a starting point and cannot prepare you to meet the needs of every child with SEND; in light of this there are links to further information signposted within chapters. I would advise that you join as many networks as you can, whether these are on social media or in local groups, so that you can share good practice and be supported in your role. I can be followed on twitter @BlogSENCO.

The National Award for Special Educational Needs Co-ordination (NASENCO): Learning outcomes

The chapters are mapped against the NASENCO learning outcomes to support those of you who are currently studying towards your NASENCO (NCTL, 2014). SENCOs appointed after 1 September 2008, who have not previously been the SENCO at that or any other school for more than 12 months, must achieve the NASENCO within three years of appointment. The learning outcomes are structured in three parts:

Part A: The ***professional knowledge and understanding*** that SENCOs need of the legislative context for SEN and theoretical concepts that underpin leadership and practice

Part B: The expertise and capabilities that SENCOs need to ***lead and coordinate provision*** effectively

Part C: The ***personal and professional qualities*** that SENCOs need to make a positive impact on the ethos and culture in schools and other settings

For ease of reading, the term:

- 'Children' will be used to refer to those from 0–25 years
- 'Caregiver' will be used to refer to birth parents, foster carers, adopters, kinship carers and legal guardians
- 'School' will be used to refer to all educational establishments where children receive education
- 'Code' will be used to refer to the Special Educational Needs and Disability Code of Practice (DfE, 2015a).

Closing remarks

There have been extensive reductions to funding across education, health and social care in recent years and this is having a detrimental impact on the health and wellbeing of school staff, children and caregivers. Due to this, SENCOs are under increasing pressure to be 'experts' in all areas of SEND and to take on duties beyond those as part of their prescribed role; this is not realistic or fair. The pathways within the health services in some local areas can be slow to meet the needs of children, particularly around mental health and wellbeing. High-quality provision and practice need to be driven by strong leadership, with a core vision which places children and families at the heart of systems, processes and learning and teaching experiences.

Part I

Professional Knowledge and Understanding

Part 1

2
The Statutory and Regulatory Context

Sarah Martin-Denham

→ NASENCO outcomes: The statutory and regulatory context for SEN and disability equality and the implications for practice. To challenge senior leaders and governors to understand their statutory responsibilities towards children with SEND. Identify children who may have SEND. Engage with the Local Offer to develop effective working partnerships with professionals in other services and agencies, including voluntary organisations, to support a coherent, coordinated and effective approach to supporting children with SEN and/or disabilities.

→ Read alongside: Chapter 10: Learning and Physical Disabilities; Chapter 12: Person-Centred Approaches

Chapter overview

The purpose of this chapter is to ensure you understand your legal duties as SENCO and as a school. It will provide an overview of relevant legislation, regulations and policy and suggest good practice in terms of compliance. All schools are at different stages in the provision and practice they offer and in how embedded processes and systems are. The self-evaluation tools will provide a useful starting point in strategically planning, monitoring and reviewing your provision and practice.

Legislation and regulation

The Children and Families Act (CAFA) (2014) part 3 is statute law and provides the most recent legislation for children with Special Educational Needs and/or Disabilities (SEND) aged 0–25 years in England. It is based on principles in the government's vision to reform services for children with SEND by embedding principles of inclusivity, agency and equality, as set out in the DfE (2011a) Green Paper, *Support and Aspiration: A new approach to SEND*. The Green Paper was a response to frustrations held by families and professionals who felt that there needed to be an explicit focus on early identification and assessment, with caregivers having greater control over the processes. CAFA (2014) sets out a legal duty for health, education and care to work collaboratively as a joined-up approach, for the benefit of families and children. It is legally binding, so schools and Local Authorities (LAs) must comply with the duties. The SEND regulations (2014) are the main set of regulations that underpin CAFA (2014). The Act is explicit that all children are entitled to an appropriate education that is suited to their needs and promotes high standards and the fulfilment of potential, to enable them to:

- achieve the best possible educational and other outcomes
- become confident individuals living fulfilling lives
- make a successful transition into adulthood.

The Act is set out and clarified in the statutory Special Educational Needs and Disability Code of Practice (herein referred to as the 'Code') (DfE, 2015a). It sets out the legal framework governing SEND and provides advice and guidance to LAs and schools. The key changes are:

- a 0–25 age range (previously it was 2–19)
- children and caregivers having a greater say in decisions that affect them
- a strong focus on high aspirations and providing the 'best possible' educational outcomes rather than 'adequate'
- guidance for LAs in meeting their joint planning and commissioning arrangements for services (to establish joint working between education, health and care)
- introducing guidance on the local offer
- replacing Statements of SEN with Education, Health and Care Plans (EHCPs)
- a graduated approach to SEN through assess, plan, do and review
- four new broad areas of need, including the addition of Social, Emotional and Mental Health Difficulties (SEMH)
- the right to a personal budget for caregivers
- new guidance on supporting children in youth custody.

If the Code states a school, college or Local Authority (LA) **'must'** do something then it is a compulsory obligation. It provides the legal requirements that must be followed without exception and the statutory guidance that you must follow unless there is good reason not to. It explains the duties of all stakeholders including LAs, health bodies, schools and colleges; as SENCO it is imperative that you understand your duties as you will have most of the day-to-day contact with children and an overview of the provision, practice and interventions in school. The CAFA (2014) enshrines the duty to:

- jointly commission services across education, health and care
- have a clear and transparent 'local offer' of services across education, health and social care, with children and caregivers involved in the preparation and review
- assess for education, health and care needs with the option of personal budgets for families and children who would like them
- name a particular college on an education, health and care plan (EHCP) and a right to appeal to the 'first-tier tribunal'
- have a strong focus on preparing for adulthood, and on planning for transition to employment and independent living and from children's to adult services.

The following principles in the CAFA (2014) are of paramount importance:

- Taking into account the views of children and their caregivers.
- The child and their caregivers participating as fully as possible in decisions and in being provided with the information and support needed to enable them to participate.
- The need to support the child and their caregivers to facilitate development to achieve the best possible educational and other outcomes, preparing them effectively for adulthood.
- To identify the needs of children and to provide high-quality provision.
- To focus on inclusive practice and removing barriers to learning.

Children with SEND can be subject to both direct and indirect discrimination; the Equality Act (2010) strengthens the rights of children and provides the legal duties schools have towards these children. For further information on equality duties, see Chapter 10. The relevant laws and regulations are as follows:

The Equality Act (2010): statute law which replaced all previous equality legislation such as the Sex Discrimination Act 1975, the Race Relations Act 2000 and the Disability Discrimination Act 2005

Equality Act (2010) (Disability Regulations) 2010: regulations which include provisions which support the definition of disability

The Special Educational Needs and Disability Regulations (2014): regulations which underpin the CAFA and are legally binding

The Special Educational Needs (Personal Budgets) Regulations (2014): these also deal with direct payments

Special educational needs (SEN):

- A child or young person has a learning difficulty or disability which calls for special educational provision to be made for him or her.
- A child of compulsory school age or a young person has a learning difficulty or disability if he or she:
  - has a significantly greater difficulty in learning than the majority of others of the same age, or
  - has a disability which prevents or hinders him or her from making use of facilities of a kind generally provided for others of the same age in mainstream schools or mainstream post-16 institutions.

DfE (2015a)

Some children with SEN will require additional or different provision as a result of their thinking, understanding, physical or sensory needs, speech language and communication needs, or emotional and behavioural difficulties. As SENCO, you will need to meet with the child's teacher(s) and caregivers to consider a range of evidence including their progress, national data and predictions of how they should be achieving, their strengths and interests, and to gather their views. Once the outcomes for the child have been agreed, there needs to be agreement on how to provide the necessary support through adapting what is already available or whether something additional is required. This is known as Special Educational Provision (SEP) as it is different to that which is normally available; the intention is that it supports children to access learning. The Code is explicit that 'high quality teaching, differentiated for individual children, is the first step in responding to children who may have SEN' (DfE, 2015a: 99).

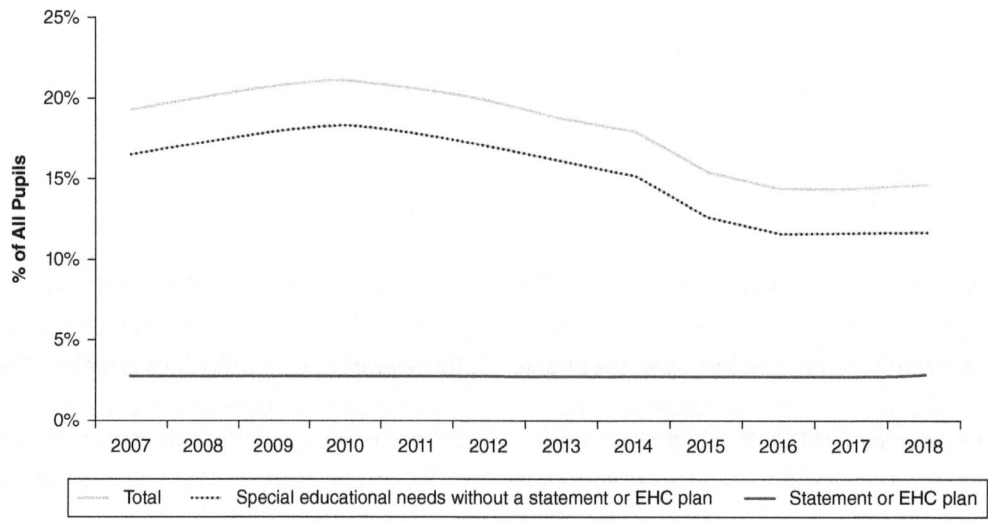

FIGURE 2.1 Time series showing the percentage of children with SEN
Source: DfE (2018a)

The DfE produces statistical first releases from school census data about children with SEN and information about the provisions they attend. As the time series in Figure 2.1 illustrates, the number of children with SEN rose for the second year from 14.4% to 14.6% of the total school population in January 2018. The percentage of children identified as needing SEN support rose from 11.6% in 2016 and 2017 to 11.7% in January 2018. For EHCPs, there has been an increase from 2.8% to 2.9% of the total population of children (DfE, 2018a).

Disability

The Code shares a definition of disability, which draws upon the Equality Act (2010). This explains that children have a disability if they present with 'a physical or mental impairment which has a long-term and substantial adverse effect on their ability to carry out normal day-to-day activities' (p. 135). This definition provides a relatively low threshold for disability and includes more children than many realise: 'long-term' is defined as 'a year or more' and 'substantial' is defined as 'more than minor or trivial'. The following needs are automatically treated as a disability under the Equality Act (2010): cancer, Human Immunodeficiency Virus (HIV), multiple sclerosis, severe disfigurement and if you are certified blind or have severe challenges with your sight as confirmed by a consultant ophthalmologist. For other physical and mental health conditions, it depends on the effect on daily life and includes:

- sight or hearing
- heart disease and asthma
- learning disabilities
- learning differences such as dyslexia and dyspraxia
- autism
- depression, schizophrenia, bipolar affective disorders, eating disorders, obsessive compulsive disorders
- difficulties due to brain injury.

There are difficulties that are not recognised as a disability regardless of the effect on daily life, such as stealing, starting fires, physical or sexual abuse of others, hay fever or addiction to drugs or alcohol. In these cases it is only classified as a disability if there are illnesses caused by those addictions, such as liver disease or depression. If a child with a disability also requires SEP they will be covered by the SEN definition. When a health service identifies a child under school age with a SEN or disability, they must inform the child's caregivers and the LA where appropriate (Ko, 2015).

Self-evaluation tools

The self-evaluation tools have been produced to support you as SENCO in identifying areas where you need to update systems, processes and procedures. These tools may also be useful for a discussion with senior leaders and governors to make explicit some of the legal requirements and regulations you need to adhere to and to inform your school development/improvement plan.

SEN information report

The SEND regulations (DfE, 2014a) require schools to have a SEN information report which must be published on the school's website. The report needs to include information on the kinds of SEN for which provision is made at the school; this is a statutory duty, unlike having a SEND policy. The document will be updated following any changes as they occur during the year. Depending on the quality of your report, it may be useful to look at SEN information reports from other schools in your area.

TABLE 2.1 Self-evaluation: Legal and regulatory duties

Self-evaluation: Legal and regulatory duties

SENCO is a qualified teacher working at the school and has the NASENCO within 3 years	CAFA (2014)	• SENCO has QTS • SENCO is currently on the NASENCO programme at the University of Sunderland	SENCO due to complete NASENCO Nov 2020	Nov 2020
School must inform the caregiver that SEP is being made through SEN support and record it in school systems	CAFA (2014)	• All caregivers are written to and invited into school to collaborate on SEN support/EHCP processes • Facetime discussions for those who cannot attend	**Action:** Audit to check all attend	Ongoing
Schools must ensure that SEP is made for those who need it	CAFA (2014)	• Provision management • Support plans • Lesson observations and book scrutiny	Continue to audit	Ongoing
The school must enable the child to take part in activities of the school as far as practicable	CAFA (2014)	• Risk assessments • Meeting records • Reasonable adjustments agreed with caregivers • Visit records	No action needed	Complete
Where a school is named in an EHCP it must admit the child	CAFA (2014)	• Admissions records	No action needed	Complete
SEN Information Report includes all legally required information	CAFA (2014)	• School website and approved by LA, SEND link governor and staff teams	**Action:** Update 2019	Dec 2019
Evidence-based intervention is quickly put into place and schools use their best endeavours to secure SEP needed by a child	Equality Act (2010) CAFA (2014)	• SEND policy and SEN Information Report • Provision Management records • Records of meetings with caregivers, support plans	**Action:** Continue termly audit of training needs for support staff and teachers	July 2020
There must be regard to the views, wishes and feelings of the child and their caregivers, with them participating as fully as possible in decisions and being provided with information to participate in decisions to achieve best possible outcomes	CAFA (2014)	• Minutes of meetings • One-page profiles • Learning plans • Survey monkey questionnaires, interviews and focus groups • Suggestion box/open door events • Child voice, graffiti wall, mind maps pilot, imovie and photographs • Targets led by child and caregiver • EHCP and reviews • Appraisals/performance management for teachers and support staff include review of person-centred approaches	**Actions:** **Children** SENCO to lead a practitioner enquiry into effectiveness of learning environment for children with autism Mind mapping to be rolled out across year groups to gather child voice	Ongoing
Schools must provide an annual report for caregivers on child's progress	SEN regulations (2014)	• Termly meeting for SEN support and EHCP • Annual review meeting EHCP	**Action:** To check all caregivers sign to say they have received report	January 2020

			Action	
How the school evaluates the effectiveness of provision	SEN regulations (2014)	• Provision management • SEND link governor report • Ofsted (2019) • SENCO audit, blink observations, learning walks (with children) and data analysis to review and monitor provision • SEN Support and EHCP review meetings • Data Tracking systems (achievement and attainment)	**Action:** A 'practitioner enquiry' model to be introduced as part of their appraisal process examining an aspect of SEND provision and/or practice	Ongoing
Schools must make reasonable adjustments to procedures, criteria and practices and by the provision of auxiliary aids and services and make physical adjustments	Equality Act (2010)	• One-page profiles include reasonable adjustments to prevent 'substantial disadvantage'. Compliance checks are carried out in teaching sessions through lesson observations and learning walks	**Action:** Staff training to take place termly and compliance checks carried out as lesson observations and appraisal system	Termly review
Schools must publish information about admission arrangements	Equality Act (2010)	• School website • Application history from caregivers of children with SEN		Ongoing
Everyone knows the SEND profile of the school (children with SEN support and EHCP)	Ofsted (2017a) Inspection Framework	• Ofsted Report 2019 • School level data available which is shared in staff meetings • SEND profile displayed in staffroom • Lesson observations	**Action:** SENCO to audit	Termly review
Inspectors will examine the impact of funded support for them on removing any differences in progress and attainment	Ofsted (2017a)	• Provision management • Ofsted Report 2019 • NC attainment (Tracking and monitoring reports and responses)		Half-termly review
SEN leads to additional or different arrangements being made	Ofsted (2017a)	• Provision management • SEN register and evidence of children leaving register over last 3 years • Lesson observations and children's progress	**Action:** CPD needed on Moderate Learning Difficulties, identification and support	Dec 2019
Differences between the progress and attainment in resource-based provision and those with similar starting points with SEND in the main school	Ofsted (2017a)	• Data analysis comparing progress between the two provisions	**Action:** Staff training in data tracking and intervention	Ongoing
Evaluation of the children's learning and progress relative to their starting points at particular ages	Ofsted (2017a) Inspection Framework	• Chronology of individual children showing prior progress and individual needs • Assessment and progress records for individual children with SEND	**Action:** Produce data showing national comparison for 2019	Termly review

Professional Knowledge and Understanding

The report must comply with CAFA (2014), which includes:

- the arrangements for the admission of children with disabilities
- the steps you have taken to prevent those with disabilities from being treated less favourably than other children
- the facilities you provide to help those with disabilities to access the school
- the accessibility plan you have prepared in compliance with paragraph 3 of schedule 10 to the Equality Act (2010).

TABLE 2.2 The SEN and Disability Regulations (2014) Part 3 Duties on Schools*

Self-evaluation: SEN Information Report	
Requirement	Included
1. The kinds of SEN for which provision is made at the school	
2. Information about the school's policies for the identification and assessment of children with SEN	
3. Information about the school's policies for making provision for children with SEN, whether or not children have EHCPs, including:	
(a) How the school evaluates the effectiveness of its provision	
(b) The school's arrangements for assessing and reviewing the progress of children with SEN	
(c) The school's approach to teaching children with SEN	
(d) Adaptations to the curriculum and learning environment for children with SEN	
(e) Additional support for learning that is available to children with SEN	
(f) How the school enables pupils with SEND to engage in the activities of the school (including physical activities) together with children who do not have SEN; and	
(g) support that is available for improving the emotional, mental and social development of children with SEN	
4. In relation to mainstream schools and maintained nursery schools, the name and contact details of the SENCO	
5. Information about the expertise and training of staff in relation to children with SEND and about how specialist expertise will be secured	
6. Information about how equipment and facilities to support children with SEND will be secured	
7. The arrangements for consulting caregivers of children with SEND about, and involving them in, the education of their child	
8. The arrangements for consulting children with SEND about, and involving them in, their education	
9. Any arrangements by the governing body or the proprietor relating to the treatment of complaints from caregivers of children with SEND, concerning provision at the school	
10. How the governing body involves other bodies, including health and social services bodies, Local Authority support services and voluntary organisations, in meeting the needs of children with SEND and in supporting the families of such children	
11. The contact details of support services for the caregivers of children with SEND	
12. The school's arrangements for supporting children with SEND in a transfer between phases of education or in preparation for adulthood and independent living	
13. Information on where the Local Authority's local offer is published	

*see Appendix and online resources for assessment template

The local offer

The local offer was formed due to the requirement in CAFA (2014) for Local Authorities (LAs) to publish and make accessible a local offer. The intention of the local offer is that it sets out, in one place, the information about provision they expect to be available across education, health and social care to support children who have SEN or disabilities. The purpose of the local offer is two-fold:

1. To provide clear, comprehensive, accessible and up-to-date information about the available provision and how to access it, and
2. To make provision more responsive to local needs and aspirations by involving children with disabilities and their caregivers in development and review.

The SEND regulations (2014) Part 4 state the statutory obligations on LAs in terms of the information to be included in the local offer:

- Special educational, health and social care provision for children with SEND, including online and blended learning
- Other educational provision, for example sports, arts and other clubs available in the area
- Travel arrangements to and from schools
- Transition guidance to support children between phases of education
- The process for resolving disagreements and/or mediation.

REFLECTIVE ACTIVITY

Imagine you are a caregiver and your son, age 3, has just been given a diagnosis of autism with additional mental health needs. Use the local offer to see what services are available across education, health and social care.

How useful would the local offer be in supporting you, your child and your family?

The four broad areas of need

This section outlines the four broad areas and provides an overview of the range of needs that should be planned for (DfE, 2015a). Many children will present with challenges in more than one of the four areas, some children will have difficulties in all and in many cases their needs will change over time. There are a multitude of reasons why children present with difficulties; many live in challenging circumstances which impact on their ability to develop, thrive and learn (see Chapter 6). Following the assessment and identification process, you will be able to plan the action you need to take as a school to respond to their needs.

Communication and interaction

Children identified with Speech, Language and Communication Needs (SLCN) may display difficulties in communicating with others, saying what they want to do, understanding what is being said, or being unable to interpret social rules of communication. They may have challenges with one, some or all of the different aspects of SLCN at different times of their lives. Children who are identified with autism are likely to present specific difficulties with social interaction and language, communication and imagination, which can impact on how they relate to others.

The Communication Trust provides 'speech, language and communication progression tools', the purpose of which is to support teachers in identifying children who may have SLCNs from the ages of 3–16. It is not a diagnostic resource but it will give you information to decide whether the child would benefit from targeted intervention or if they need specialist assessment and support. In addition, the tool can be used to track progress over time.

Cognition and learning

This category includes general learning difficulties and disabilities which impact on learning across the curriculum, such as Moderate Learning Difficulties (MLD), Severe Learning Difficulties (SLD) or Profound and Multiple Learning Difficulties (PMLD), where children are likely to have severe and complex learning challenges as well as physical disability or sensory needs. This area also includes specific learning difficulties (SpLD), also known as children who are neuro-diverse, who encounter more specific difficulties with aspects of learning such as literacy (Dyslexia), numeracy (Dyscalculia) or motor coordination (Developmental Coordination Disorder – DCD).

Social, emotional and mental health difficulties

This category represents a radical change in SEND policy, as it acknowledges mental health needs as a SEN for the first time. The Code (DfE, 2015a) explains that children may experience a wide range of social, emotional and mental health (SEMH) difficulties throughout their childhood and adolescence, which can manifest in different ways. This may include becoming withdrawn or isolated, as well as displaying challenging, disruptive or disturbing behaviour. These behaviours may reflect underlying mental health difficulties, such as anxiety or depression, self-harming, substance misuse, eating disorders or physical symptoms that are medically unexplained. Other needs that fall under the broad area of SEMH may include Attention Deficit Disorder, Attention Deficit Hyperactivity Disorder and Attachment Disorder.

Sensory and/or physical needs

In this broad area of need, children are identified with a disability which prevents or hinders them from making use of the educational facilities. The Code (DfE, 2015a) explains that these difficulties are often age-related and can fluctuate over time. Many children with a Visual Impairment (VI), a Hearing Impairment (HI) or a Multi-Sensory Impairment (MSI) will require specialist support and/or equipment to access their learning. Children identified with a Physical Disability (PD) often require additional ongoing support and equipment to access all of the opportunities available to their peers.

REFLECTIVE TASK

In your procedures within school, how do you record the child's primary and secondary needs? How are these then used for provision planning and to direct pastoral support?

SEN support

As SENCO, you will be central to decisions about whether or not a child needs special educational provision. You will need to consider all available evidence including their baseline data, progress over time, formative and summative assessments, and other assessments internal and external to the school to judge whether they need SEN support or if their needs require consideration for an EHC needs assessment. When it is agreed that a child is identified as having SEN, the school needs to take action to remove barriers to learning and to put in place effective special educational provision (DfE, 2015a: 100). If you are new to the role, it can be difficult to know how best to support these children; in recent years, there has been a vast increase in the available research evidence on learning and teaching approaches and interventions.

The graduated approach

The Code specifies that high quality teaching with differentiation and personalised support needs to be the first reaction to possible SEN; if there continues to be concerns then the graduated approach must be followed. For this process to be effective, there needs to be a clear understanding of the child's strengths, challenges and needs and the caregivers and the child must be at the heart of the process. The response will only be effective in achieving good outcomes for the child if teachers have high aspirations for them and if the plan of action is specific to their needs. The Code has a strong emphasis on early identification for SEN. It is anticipated that, in many cases, assessment takes place in the early years, though in reality this is not the case as children are identified throughout their school years.

The Code outlines the graduated approach cycle (sometimes referred to as the graduated response), through which earlier decisions and actions are revisited, refined and revised, leading to a growing understanding of the child's needs and what supports them in making progress and securing good outcomes (DfE, 2015a). There are four distinct stages to the graduated response, which rely on effective practice in meeting the needs of children identified as needing SEN support. These stages are:

- **Assess:** Teacher and internal assessments/experiences/knowledge of the child, screening tests, specialist assessments, curriculum attainment with comparison to peers and national data, behaviour records, caregiver and child's views and experiences and external advice from support services (where appropriate).
- **Plan**: Caregivers and child involved in deciding the evidence-based intervention(s) and support, reasonable adjustments for children with disabilities now need to be in place and a review date agreed and recorded.
- **Do**: Teacher is responsible for leading, planning and assessing the impact of the interventions; SENCO needs to provide support with guidance on further assessments where appropriate.

- **Review:** Evaluation to determine if the support has been effective and to review the impact on the agreed outcomes. The caregivers and children feed back into the cycle to decide if further assessments are needed and to modify outcomes or to remove the child from SEN support.

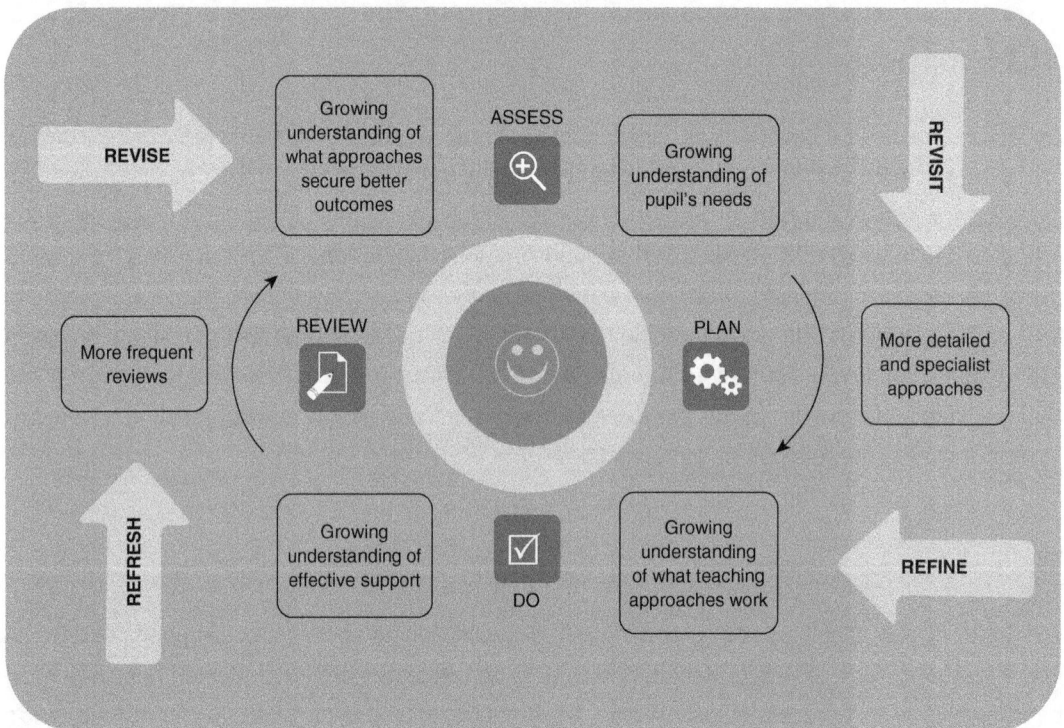

FIGURE 2.2 The spiral of support
Source: NASEN (2014: 16)

There will need to be a structured process in school for teachers and support staff to share concerns when they identify that a child is not making expected progress or where they are regressing and it is felt they may have a SEN. This is sometimes called a 'short note', 'monitoring' or 'cause for concern' and is a means of alerting the SENCO and colleagues to possible SEN. During this process, high-quality teaching must be targeted at the child's area of difficulty; observations, behaviour logs and individual assessments should be recorded to inform the graduated approach.

This is an information-gathering stage and will include an early discussion with caregivers and children about concerns. At this stage, the child is not on the SEN register; they are being monitored. Local Authorities will have an 'early help' process, which is based on early intervention and can be requested from pre-birth to adulthood. Early help is available to support families when they are unable to manage a child or meet the child's needs on their own. It is a multi-agency approach that intends to meet the child's needs early to prevent them escalating into greater concerns.

SENCO ACTIVITY

Find out about the 'early help' offer in your local area.

TABLE 2.3 Example of a short note*

Short note		
Name	Date of birth	Date
Current attainment	Status: Looked after, English as an Additional Language, Pupil Premium	Attendance
Child's area(s) of strength and difficulties		
Child's views		
Caregivers' views/concerns		
Agreed outcomes		
Next steps		
Review date and time		
Caregiver and teacher's signatures		

*see Appendix and online resources for assessment template

SEN register

If it is felt the child needs targeted provision different or additional to what is usually provided, with caregivers' agreement they will then move on to the graduated approach and be entered on the SEN register. At this point, formal assessment takes place to allow the teacher to be able to create expected outcomes and to plan the most suitable provision and intervention. The SEN register can be kept in any format but it needs to include the SEN status, the primary needs of the children and which of the four broad areas of need they have difficulties within. It is good practice to record additional (secondary) needs, as this will show you understand the holistic development and learning needs of this group of children and it will allow you to plan effective provision. Remember, caregivers must be notified if children are receiving special educational provision and are being added to the SEN register. Your school management system will be able to keep your SEN register secure – SIMS appears to be popular as this is where most schools will have their census data collected from by the LA.

SEN register status

Only the SENCO should have access rights to change the SEN status of a child. This should be done following review meetings so that the register is always up to date.

- E – Education, Health and Care Plan (EHCP)
- K – SEN support
- N – No SEN (this should only be used for the first census after a child is taken off the register).

In addition to the SEN register, you should keep and share with colleagues the following:

- a medical/disability register (with up-to-date individual healthcare plans)
- a short note, cause for concern or monitoring register.

As SENCO, you will need to work closely with colleagues with responsibility for looked after and permanently placed children, English as an additional language, pupil premium, safeguarding and attendance as some of these children may have unmet learning and mental health needs.

Assess

The Code clarifies that when a child is identified as needing SEN support, the teacher working with the SENCO should carry out a clear analysis of the child's strengths and needs (DfE, 2015a). Wedell (2017) discussed the issue of the term 'clear analysis', proposing that this understates the complexity of achieving this. It is also the case that there can be limited tools available for SENCOs to identify needs accurately or reliably at school level, or it may be that your school has insufficient funds to buy in any specialist assessments. The purpose of this stage is to gain an in-depth understanding of the child's needs to be able to effectively plan teaching approaches, to provide the most suitable provision and to inform any adjustments that need to be made. To identify the barriers to learning, you may need to access individualised identification tools; screening tools are widely available for neurodiversity and can be found in Chapter 9. Hearing and sight checks should be carried out as a matter of process through the GP or opticians, to eliminate any underlying physical needs before any SEN are explored. Glue ear can cause a child to appear as though they are not paying attention or concentrating and is easily resolved by treatment.

Initial and ongoing assessments should be reviewed regularly to ensure that support is tailored to meet individual needs. Where there is little or no improvement in the child's progress, more specialised assessment may be required from specialist teachers or from health, social care or other agencies beyond the setting. A consultant paediatrician will refer a child on to the most appropriate pathway based on their assessments; for example, for attachment difficulties, Attention Deficit Hyperactivity Disorder (ADHD), autism and physical and/or sensory needs. Where professionals are not already working with the setting, the SENCO should contact them, with the caregivers' agreement, for advice and guidance. Once the information is collated, there needs to be an early discussion with caregivers and the child so there is a shared understanding of the child's strengths and suggested outcomes to be achieved through a plan.

REFLECTIVE ACTIVITY

What systems and processes are in place for you to share the outcome of health assessments with teachers and support staff so they can use them to inform learning and teaching approaches?

Plan

In whatever form the school decides to create a SEN support plan, it must focus on the child's individual needs, not their SEN or disability label. The label itself will not be sufficient to explain their barriers to learning due to the variance of the impact on different children. The language used should be child-centred and the outcomes written in such a way that they can understand what they are expected to achieve. It is good practice to ask the child to explain each outcome to you to check they have processed the information and to see if any adjustments need to be made. Most schools will identify three to four outcomes, which focus on supporting their wellbeing, not just developing academic skills. They should be personalised and agreed by all parties.

The child, teacher and caregiver need to agree:

- the outcomes they are seeking to meet the identified need(s)
- the interventions, strategies and support to be put in place (based on robust evidence of effectiveness)
- the expected impact on progress, development or behaviour
- a date/time for review.

An outcome can be defined as 'the benefit or difference made to an individual as a result of an intervention' (DfE, 2015a: 163). It should be personal and not expressed from a service perspective and it should be something that those involved have control and influence over. So, an outcome is a change that you want to achieve; this can be in relation to learning, behaviour, skills or attitudes. There is not a dictated format for you to use for 'the plan' – some schools call them SEN support plans, Individual Education Plans (IEPs), learning plans, pupil passports or something else.

Plans must take into account:

- the views of the child and caregivers
- any reasonable adjustments, when the child has a disability.

We know from research that not all interventions have the same impact on children's wellbeing and progress. Any intervention provided should be based on reliable evidence of effectiveness, and be provided by staff with sufficient skills and expertise (DfE, 2015a).

REFLECTIVE ACTIVITY

What is the evidence base that assures you that your teaching approaches and interventions have a positive impact on wellbeing, development and progress of children with SEND?

Evidence-based SEN support plan

To support you in developing your SEN support plans, two differing exemplar plans have been created (see Tables 2.4 and 2.5). Remember, there is no set format but you are required to record outcomes sought, support and teaching strategies or approaches. To do this effectively:

- focus on the individual needs of the child, not their SEND
- use easy-to-access language
- highlight their strengths
- capture child and caregiver voice and aspirations
- only use evidence-based approaches.

The second plan below is more child-centred and captures a greater amount of information on the child's views, wishes and aspirations. The child should be encouraged to present their views in whatever format they prefer, including drawings, photographs or using technology.

TABLE 2.4 Example 1: SEN support plan

Name: Jose	DoB: 05/05/2011	Year group: 5	Review date: July 2020	Current attainment: Expected level in all areas
Strengths: Excels in all sports, empathetic and kind to others		**Child's views:** I like my teacher but I get distracted by others and it makes me anxious because I can't concentrate on my work		
		Child's aspirations: To be an athlete and compete in the Olympics		
Challenges: Cognition and learning: specific to handwriting skills and concentration		**Caregiver's views:** Jose is enjoying year 5 but has no interest in English, he doesn't enjoy writing, maybe he would if it was related to sport		
		Caregiver's aspirations: For Jose to follow his dream of being an athlete		

Agreed outcomes

Outcome	Target	Start date	How often it will happen	Teacher	Intervention/ Resource	Outcome achieved Y/N/ Partial
To develop social skills within a small group	Jose will build a project collaboratively with 3 friends performing set roles within 6 weeks	Immediate	2 x 45 minutes a fortnight	Mrs New	Lego therapy	
To develop coping skills in school	Jose will use breathing techniques every time he feels anxious in literacy	Immediate	Every literacy lesson	Mrs New	FRIENDS for Life	
To regulate anxiety	Jose will use a short mindfulness activity such as 5, 4, 3, 2, 1 to regulate his emotions within 6 weeks	Immediate	As and when needed	Mrs New to support	FRIENDS for Life	

TABLE 2.5 Example 2: SEN support plan*

Name: DoB: Attendance:	All about me: (In child's voice) My strengths: My interests: My aspirations:	
What is important to me	What is important to my family	
What is working well for me	What I would like to change What I need	
Planned support/intervention How long for		
My targets	What we hope I will achieve	What I will need
1.		
2.		
3.		
Date of review:	Child's/caregiver's signature/comments: SENCO/Teacher signature comments:	

*see Appendix and online resources for assessment template

There are companies such as Edukey Provision Map that have the online capability to create a learning plan (a type of IEP). Although you can use a bank of targets provided externally, it is best practice to create your own as these can be individualised to the needs of individual children.

At this stage it is good practice to create a school passport (also known as a 'pupil passport') with the caregiver and child. This is particularly important in secondary and Further Education (FE) when the child has multiple teachers. The passport is usually one page of A4 and includes the following:

- A photograph of the child
- Information about the child (I would like you to know that…)
- How they learn (I learn best when I can…)
- What they find hard (I find it difficult to/when…)
- What supports them (It would help me if…)
- How they help themselves (I will do this if…)
- It should also give the name of their key worker/form tutor/pastoral contact, any access arrangements and external support they are currently receiving.

....**INSET ACTIVITY**

The following questions are useful for you to explore with colleagues and senior leaders to ensure the graduated approach is effectively implemented.

For senior leaders:

How do we know that teachers and support staff have, access and use the information on the specific learning and wellbeing needs of children in their everyday teaching?

How is this tracked and monitored?

(Continued)

(Continued)

For teachers and support staff:

> How well do I understand specialist assessments from external agencies?
>
> So I differentiate my teaching for children with SEN, how do I know this is effective in improving their outcomes and wellbeing?
>
> What are my training needs?

Do

This stage is the implementation of the actions as agreed on the SEN support plan. The teacher remains responsible for working with the child on a daily basis and for monitoring the impact of interventions and support, whether or not the child is working with support staff. The SENCO can support the teacher in assessing the child's response to the actions taken, in problem solving and advising on the effective implementation of support. The teacher will need to reflect on the progress of the child so they can refine their learning and teaching approaches. Children should not be withdrawn from lessons they enjoy and, where possible, they should remain alongside their peers. If it is clear that the outcomes are not suitable or if they are achieved quickly, the review date should be brought forward to decide next steps with the caregiver.

Review

The Code explains that regular reviews of the effectiveness of support provided and its impact on the child's progress should occur, at least three times a year, so it can feed into the next planning phase of the graduated approach (DfE, 2015a). The impact and quality of the support should be evaluated by the teacher and the SENCO and reported to the child and their caregivers in a review meeting, which should include the sharing of evidence. Agreement should be reached on any changes to the outcomes and support for the child in light of the child's progress and development.

Key questions to explore in a review meeting

- How is the child's mental health and wellbeing?
- Has the child met expected progress? If not, why not? (attendance, concentration, seating plan)
- What are the child's views?
- Are they on track to meet targets?
- What progress have they made?
- Is the attainment and progress gap narrowing?
- What are the caregivers' views?
- Does the child need to remain on the SEN register?

Caregivers should have clear information about the impact of the support provided and be involved in planning next steps, whether that is to complete another cycle of the graduated approach, to remove the child from the SEN register or to apply for an Education, Health and Care needs assessment.

> **Case study**
>
> Kerry has a diagnosis of dyscalculia; she is 15 years old and is about to begin Year 11. She was entered on the SEN register in Year 10 following a private diagnosis from an educational psychologist. Her mother was concerned that she had not made progress in Mathematics since Year 7, and this was confirmed by the data within school. The school realised they had not provided special educational provision for a year so decided to give her 2 hours a week of intervention where she would be supported with homework across subjects.
>
> - What should have happened when Kerry was in Year 7?
> - Why do you think the lack of progress since Year 7 was not identified sooner?
> - What assessments could have taken place?
> - Is the intended intervention appropriate?
> - What should happen next?

Education, health and care plans

A school or caregivers can consider applying for an Education, Health and Care (EHC) needs assessment when the child has not made expected progress against the expected outcomes through cycles of the graduated approach for SEN support (most LAs would expect at least two evidenced cycles). Other agencies involved with the child, including nursery staff, health and social care professionals, and Youth Offending Teams (YOT), can also request an EHC needs assessment. The Education, Health and Care Plan (EHCP) is a legal document and was introduced with the principle of a person-centred approach to supporting children aged 0–25 years who need more support than can be provided through SEN support. The EHCP is a single document that describes the child's strengths and needs in a multi-disciplinary and holistic way. The voice of the child and the caregiver is fundamental in the application for an EHCP; they must be co-creators in the process. They will need to be supported and scaffolded so that their views are well represented in a format they find accessible and that suits their range of needs. Section A of the EHCP must include the child's own perspective on their views, wishes and aspirations – this should relate to the child's characteristics and their relationships. It needs to include not only what they like and enjoy doing but also what they are good at.

What evidence will Local Authorities want to see?

The legal duty to carry out and issue an EHCP assessment lies with LAs. An EHC needs assessment can only be requested if it is believed a child 'may' have a SEN; it cannot be requested if there are only health and care needs, no matter how severe. The prime consideration will be that despite relevant and purposeful action by the school to 'identify, assess and meet the SEN of the child', they have not made expected progress. You should have evidence from the process of planning special educational provision in the graduated approach cycles. For children progressing to an EHC needs assessment, it will be the case that despite quality first teaching and the graduated approach they are not making the expected progress.

There is a range of evidence the LA will expect to see, including:

- the views, wishes and feelings of the child and their caregivers
- evidence of their attainment and rates of progress (or developmental milestones in younger children)
- information about the nature, extent and cause of their SEN
- evidence of a graduated approach with SMART (specific, measurable, achievable, realistic and time bound) targets and other action taken to meet their SEN
- evidence of the extent of the support that is different to or additional to that usually provided
- evidence of their physical, social, emotional and mental health needs with evidence from clinicians and other professionals and what they have done to meet those needs
- when they are over 18 years of age, the LA will need to consider if they need additional time to complete their education or training.

(DfE, 2015a: 146)

REFLECTIVE ACTIVITY

How are children's voices currently presented in Section A of the EHCP?

How much choice do the children have in how they share their views?

What methods are used to elicit their views?

Is the focus on their disabilities or abilities?

How could you improve this process?

If, following the referral meeting by the LA, it is decided to carry out an EHC assessment the caregivers will be asked to provide information outlining their child's needs. You will need to provide reports and, where relevant, assessments from health services.

The LA will advise the caregivers within 16 weeks whether an EHCP has been agreed upon. The caregivers have the right to request a particular school to be named on an EHCP. Some of the provisions specified in the EHCP can be procured by the caregiver or the young person through a personal budget. Where there is to be a direct payment to deliver provision on the school premises, the LA must have written agreement from the school.

EHCPs need to be accessible, so consider if wikis are a more suitable way to illustrate the EHCP. For some families, paper-based approaches may not be accessible – there may be a preference for platforms that use pictures, words, video and sound to capture the voice, skills and aspirations collectively; they are also easier to update. This allows everyone involved in the plan, including the child, to upload footage and to share what works well in meeting the child's needs, including achievements and progress. This can keep everything in one place and can be easily shared by those with the login details. Free wikis can be made on WordPress; alternatively, you can purchase subscriptions for wikis through companies such as RIX and Wikidot.

SMART outcomes

Writing SMART outcomes requires skill and training, as you need to take into consideration the views, wishes and feelings of the child and caregivers and the provision available (resources, physical space, specialism and availability of staff).

All outcomes, whether for SEN support or an EHCP, need to be SMART.

TABLE 2.6 Considerations for the writing of SMART outcomes

Specific	What do you want them to be able to do?
	Is it related to their needs, interests, skills and stage in the learning process?
	Is it child-centred and based on their wishes?
Measurable	How will you know they have achieved the outcome?
	Can it be observed?
	Can you give a yes/no response to 'have they achieved the target?'
	How will you measure the achievement of the outcome? Will you use quantity, quality, accuracy?
Achievable	Can the expected outcome be achieved given the child's difficulties?
	Does it need breaking down into smaller steps?
	Is the provision available?
Realistic	Is the outcome at the right level for the child?
	Is it feasible and manageable within the time frame?
	Does the child have the potential skills and knowledge to achieve the outcome?
Timebound	What is the time frame for them to achieve the outcome?
	When will interim progress be reviewed?

Outcomes should be child friendly; they need to state a planned outcome for the child in positive and easy-to-access language. Whatever the format, it must be recorded on the school information system.

The differences between broad and SMART outcomes are shown in Table 2.7:

TABLE 2.7 Broad and SMART targets

Broad outcomes (not measurable)	SMART outcomes (measurable)
To stay in his seat	William will use his 'help card' in lessons when he needs Mrs Keen, 4 out of 5 times, by Autumn half term 2019.
To follow instructions	Zizi will follow two verbal instructions from Mr Bee that involve moving from one side of the classroom to the other without having the instructions repeated and be successful 3 out of 4 times.
To develop PE skills	Esme will catch a large foam ball when it is carefully passed from 1 metre by the teacher, 2 out of 5 times, by May half term 2020.

As SENCO, you will be involved in the development and review of EHC needs assessments and plans to determine what can reasonably be provided from the school's resources and externally and the cost of this to supply. The format of the EHCP will be agreed by the LA. There are statutory sections, which **must** be labelled separately using the following letters:

Section A: The views, interests and aspirations of the child and his or her caregivers or the young person

Section B: The child or young person's SEN

Section C: The child or young person's health needs which are related to their SEN

Section D: The child or young person's social care needs which are related to their SEN or to a disability

Section E: The outcomes sought for the child or young person. This should include outcomes for adult life. The EHCP should identify the arrangements for the setting of shorter term targets by the provider

Section F: The special educational provision required by the child or the young person

Section G: Any health provision reasonably required by the learning difficulties or disabilities which result in the child or young person having SEN. Where an individual healthcare plan is made for them, the plan should be included

Section H1: Any social care provision which **must** be made for a child or young person

Section H2: Any other social care provision reasonably required by the learning difficulties or disabilities which result in the child or young person having SEN. This will include any adult social care being provided

Section I: The name and type of school to be attended by the child or young person

Section J: Where there is a personal budget, the details of how it will support particular outcomes, the provision it will be used for including any flexibility in the usage and arrangements for direct payments for education, health and social care. The SEN and outcomes that are to be met by any direct payment **must** be specified

Section K: The advice and information gathered during the EHC needs assessment **must** be attached

If the child is in Y9 or beyond the EHCP must include (in sections F, G, H1 or H2 as appropriate) the provision required by the young person to assist in preparation for adulthood and independent living.

(DfE, 2015a: 161–2)

The Council for Disabled Children (2017) provides exemplar EHCPs for SENCOs and advises the following as good practice for each section of the plan (Table 2.8):

TABLE 2.8 Good practice for EHCP section

Section of plan	Good practice
A	<ul><li>Children should be allowed to meet without caregivers so they can talk without influence</li><li>Children's views should be equal to those of professionals and caregivers</li></ul>

Section of plan	Good practice
B	• Each SEN should be detailed individually with provision needs against them
C	• Be specific, remember a label doesn't explain needs, as every child will be different • Explain the practical implications of health needs for their life and your provision • Keep the language simple
D	• Get as much information as possible from the range of health and social care personnel but also other teachers, youth workers or a social worker
E	• Outcomes should follow on from the child's aspirations
F, G, H	• Set out what is going to happen, who by, with what skills, qualifications and training they need from F (education), G (health) and H (social care)
I	• Name and type of school to be attended
J	• If there is a personal budget, detail how this will support the outcomes, and arrangements for any direct payments for education, health and social care
K	• Attach advice and information gathered during the EHC needs assessment

Source: Council for Disabled Children (2017)

Supporting caregivers

Caregivers will have differing levels of knowledge of the SEN system; the majority will need support and guidance to access the process and to have the confidence to contribute their thoughts. To support them you should:

- Explain the EHC process including the referral meeting, paperwork that is needed and their role in the process
- Give a copy of acronyms and key terms and give them your email address
- Discuss the support the child already receives and the impact it is having on their holistic development and progress, and be positive
- Ensure they are listened to and are updated throughout the process
- Provide timelines for the EHC process and the role of all stakeholders
- Share the support available through the local offer and other organisations
- If they are unsuccessful you will need to support them with disagreeing with the decision to not carry out an assessment, or to create an EHCP, or to challenge the school named in the EHCP through the SEND tribunal.

The outcomes specified in the plan must relate to the child's SEN and to the views, wishes and feelings of the child and those of their family.

SENCO ACTIVITY

How do you ensure all colleagues who teach or support a child have read and understood the EHCP?

How do you monitor the progress towards the EHCP outcomes? Do you hold termly meetings with the teacher, caregiver and child?

How do you support colleagues with training to allow them to meet the child's needs?

Professional Knowledge and Understanding

Leading an EHCP review meeting

There is a legal obligation for the EHCP to be reviewed every twelve months. LAs can require schools to convene the meeting. The focus of the review meeting is to discuss the child's progress towards achieving the specified outcomes and to consider whether the outcomes are still appropriate and to set interim targets for the coming year. As with all SEN processes, the review needs to be carried out in collaboration with the child and their caregivers and they must be notified of the meeting four weeks in advance. The review will:

- gather and assess information to support the child's progress and access to learning and teaching
- review the effectiveness of the special educational provision made for the child
- review the effectiveness of the health and social care provision
- consider the appropriateness of the EHCP in light of their progress the previous year and agree any changes in outcomes, provision, establishment for schooling and whether or not to continue the plan
- set new interim targets and agree new outcomes
- review any interim targets set by education.

(DfE, 2015a)

It will be the SENCO's role to organise the review meeting, which is usually held at the school with the child attending as this is the most familiar environment to them. If you have several children with an EHCP it would be advisable to schedule in all the review meetings at the start of the year, taking into consideration what works best for the family around their other commitments. You will only need to invite specialists from health and social care if there have been significant changes in the child's life or health; all parties will need at least six weeks' notice of the meeting.

The meeting is a time for reflection; the atmosphere needs to be relaxed and supportive with the room set up in an informal layout. Provide refreshments, pens, post-its and an iPad for sharing ideas about what is working and what needs to be changed. Pre-plan the structure of the meeting and share it with the child and caregiver so they know what to expect and who will be there. The suggestions below will support you:

The LA will have processes you need to follow for EHCP reviews, including how to send any documentation. There will be GDPR considerations so check your data management systems prior to sending anything electronically. If it is decided at the meeting not to continue a plan, the LA must notify the caregivers and inform them of their right to appeal.

> **Housekeeping**: Share where the toilets are, notify of any planned fire drills and provide refreshments.
>
> **Introduction:** Introduce everyone and their roles and responsibilities. Provide name badges or names on folded card; maybe younger children could make these.

Funding models

The government can and does make changes to the way that funding is allocated to schools. As SENCO, you need to know the SEN budget and collaborate with senior leaders to ensure it is being used as intended to fund special educational provision. The Designated Schools Grant (DSG) is broken down into three elements: schools, early years and high needs block.

Element 1: Funding based on the number of children in a school; a core budget for general provision including those with SEN.

Element 2: An amount of money to help schools make special educational provision to meet the needs of children with SEN, also known as the notional SEN budget. Currently this is £6,000 worth of provision to meet a child's SEN, and this is not ring-fenced money. It is intended to support the raising of standards attainment, early intervention, equal opportunities, reasonable adjustments and safeguarding the right of entitlements for children with SEN.

> **Discussion**: Start with the positives – write or record everyone's comments about what they admire about the child, and have a range of formats including some that don't require reading or writing. Find out what is important to the child, what their needs are, what they find difficult and how they can best be supported. Review the plan, try to use a shared document so everyone can contribute and discuss changes as they are made.
>
> **Close:** Summarise what has been agreed and ask people to sign to agree, explain the next steps and gather caregivers' and child's views on the process. Have an informal conversation with caregivers and the child once other professionals have left the room to check on their wellbeing.

Element 3: For high levels of need, where provision is more than £6,000. The intention of high needs funding is to provide appropriate support packages for children with SEN, taking into account the choices of children and their caregivers. Children who receive high needs funding usually have an EHCP but this is not a legal requirement. LAs decide how much to set aside from their high needs budget, which has two main components: core funding and top-up funding (sometimes known as element 3). Most high needs places are costed at £10,000 per year though it varies depending on the provision.

Personal budgets

A personal budget is an amount of money identified by the LA set out in an EHCP where the caregiver is involved in securing the provision. The use of a personal budget is optional; the obligation is on the LA to prepare one for special educational, health and social care provision when requested. Each LA will have a policy which sets out the funding available, the eligibility criteria and the decision-making process, which must be published on the local offer.

The delivery of the personal budget can happen in four ways:

1. Direct payments: where the caregiver receives the money to contract, purchase and manage services themselves
2. An arrangement: where the LA, school or college holds the funds and commissions the support on behalf of the caregiver
3. Third-party arrangements: where the direct payments are paid to and managed by an individual or organisation
4. A combination of the above.

(DfE, 2015a: 179)

Mediation and disagreement resolution arrangements

Mediation is offered when there is a decision by a LA not to carry out an EHC assessment, not to draw up an EHCP, after a final EHC is received or an amended plan, following a decision not to amend a plan or a decision to cease an EHCP. Mediation is specifically linked to decisions about EHC needs assessments and will be led by an independent adviser. If caregivers are not satisfied after this process they can progress to tribunal but only when they have accessed the mediation process. Further information on this can be found in the Code (DfE, 2015a: 244–72).

Disagreement resolution arrangements are designed to resolve disagreements about the performance of duties, SEN provision, disagreements over health and social care provision, health commissioners and LAs.

Chapter summary

- The Children and Families Act (2014) extended the SEN system from birth to 25 years, giving children and caregivers greater control and choice in decisions that affect them
- Schools have to publish a SEN information report on their website
- The Equality Act (2010) protects children and adults from discrimination, harassment and victimisation
- The 'local offer' is intended to outline universal services across education, health and social care, which every Local Authority is required to publish and review
- The graduated approach is a process of assess, plan, do and review
- An EHCP is a 20-week process and there is no guarantee a LA will issue one
- Schools receive funding for children with SEN as part of the DSG
- Caregivers can request a personal budget from a LA

3

Leading in the SENCO Role

Steve Watts and Sarah Martin-Denham

- NASENCO outcomes: The principles and practice of leadership in different contexts. To work strategically with senior colleagues and governors to advise on and influence the strategic development of a person-centred and inclusive ethos, policies, priorities and practices.
- Read alongside: Chapter 2: The Statutory and Regulatory Context; Chapter 4: Best Practice in Collecting and Using Data; Chapter 12: Person-Centred Approaches

Chapter overview

The purpose of this chapter is to explore the role of a SENCO within the requirements of current legislation and the expectations of what is considered to be good practice. Theories and models of leadership and management will be explored, along with practical exercises, to support you in evaluating where you are in your leadership and management roles, where you need to go next and how to get there. Consideration will be given to managing change, working with other professionals and preparing for Ofsted.

The role of the Special Educational Needs Coordinator (SENCO)

The Code requires governing bodies of maintained mainstream schools and the proprietors of academy schools (including free schools) to ensure that there is a qualified teacher designated as SENCO (DfE, 2015a). The National Award for Special Educational Needs Coordination (NASENCO) is a mandatory award, of which 50 per cent is made up of preparing the SENCO to become a leader. Your role is strategic, overseeing the day-to-day operation of the SEND policy, coordinating provision, supporting colleagues with professional guidance, advocating for caregivers and children and being the point of contact for external agencies.

REFLECTIVE ACTIVITY

Do the SEND policy, behaviour policy and safeguarding policy complement each other in effectively supporting children with SEND? If not, what amendments need to be made?

Done et al. (2016) discuss the shift in the SENCO role over recent years and suggest that instead of functioning as an 'in-house expert' to whom responsibility for inclusion could be delegated, the SENCO is now more likely to be engaged in whole-school organisational-level initiatives, including performance evaluation, data tracking and the identification and leading of continuing professional development (CPD). The reality is that the SENCO role varies from context to context, due to a range of factors, such as numbers of children with SEND, Ofsted ratings, Senior Leadership Team priorities and the willingness of colleagues to reflect upon and improve provision and practice. Unfortunately, there are no statutory requirements in terms of the amount of time a SENCO should have to carry out the role effectively, only that 'the school should ensure the SENCO has sufficient time and resources to carry out their functions' (DfE, 2015a). This should include administrative support and time away from teaching to fulfil responsibilities expected as part of the role.

The SENCO role includes the following duties:

- Overseeing the day-to-day operation of the school's SEN policy
- Coordinating provision for children with SEN
- Liaising with the relevant designated teacher where a looked after pupil has SEN
- Advising on a graduated approach to providing SEN support
- Advising on the deployment of the school's delegated budget and other resources to meet children's needs effectively
- Liaising with caregivers of children with SEN
- Liaising with other schools, educational psychologists, health and social care professionals, and independent or voluntary bodies
- Being a key point of contact with external agencies, especially the LA and LA support services
- Liaising with potential next providers of education to ensure a young person and their caregivers are informed about options and a smooth transition is planned
- Working with the headteacher and school governors to ensure that the school meets its responsibilities under the Equality Act (2010) with regard to reasonable adjustments and access arrangements
- Ensuring that the school or maintained nursery keeps the records of all children with SEN up to date.

DfE (2015a)

SENCO audit

Often, SENCOs are overstretched because colleagues are unclear or have misconceptions about their role. If not clarified, this can lead to an increase in your workload and stress, impacting on your health and wellbeing. The following checklist (Table 3.1) can serve as a reminder of your role to colleagues and could be useful to discuss with senior leaders to develop an action plan for provision, practice and training.

TABLE 3.1 Audit for provision, practice and training*

Theme	RAG rating	Action
How well do colleagues understand their responsibilities to children with SEND?		
How well do colleagues understand the school's approach to identifying and meeting the needs of children with SEND?		
Do colleagues understand the process of how to raise causes for concern to the SENCO and caregivers? Do they have the confidence to initiate early intervention?		
How confident are staff in implementing the graduated response: assess, plan, do and review cycle?		
How well are children with SEND learning and making progress? Are outcomes good in all year groups with all members of staff?		
How well supported and trained are all staff employed by the school? Is the process for the induction of new staff and supply staff effective?		
How closely engaged are caregivers and how is their information/suggestions/concerns responded to?		
How well does the school liaise with external agencies and is this supportive to the SENCO in their role?		

*see Appendix and online resources for assessment template

The characteristics of highly effective team leadership

As can be seen from the discussion above, the SENCO holds many responsibilities, to the staff, the children, the governors, caregivers, external agencies and so on. In order for this 'team' of key stakeholders to function effectively, they need to be given clear direction by the SENCO, which is supported by senior leaders. This direction will emanate from the strategic overview of the current educational environment, both internal and external, that the SENCO will provide.

Thus, SENCOs are both leaders and managers. They are leaders of people and managers of resources. The roles are very different, but both equally important. Essentially, a leader provides vision, direction, motivation and strategic overview, while a manager implements the strategy by drawing upon the resources, both staffing and physical, that are available.

Definitions of leadership and management:

> Leading is about vision and strategy and providing inspiration to the people working in the organisation so that the aims of the organisation can be achieved. Managing is about putting the vision into practice and enabling the organisation to function. (Kydd et al., 2002: 1)

There are many models of leadership, but one that should resonate with readers is the transactional/transformational leadership model. In its crudest form, it positions leaders at either end of a continuum and while we can all probably give examples of leaders we have known at both ends of the spectrum, most leaders adopt approaches that draw upon a range of strategies across the continuum.

TABLE 3.2 Leadership models

Transactional leadership model	Transformational leadership model
Compliance is achieved through the use of reward and punishment	Built on motivation and connecting emotionally with colleagues; leaders show appreciation and provide support to others
Ensures others follow the vision	Ability to design/create and articulate a shared and long-term vision
Respect achieved through compliance	Mutual respect and admiration for skills, knowledge and understanding of others
Manages day to day to ensure tasks are being completed	Motivates others to work beyond expected levels
The leader wants assurance that delegated tasks will be completed and orders obeyed	Allows for creative solutions to challenges
Colleagues understand what needs to be done and when by so can be productive	Colleagues trust and support the leadership team
Can cause stress if the demands are unrealistic	This model increases staff morale and reduces stress

Source: Adapted from Hayes et al. (2014: 156)

Experienced leaders tend to draw upon a range of approaches, according to the context in which they are working. To reflect this, Hersey and Blanchard developed the situational leadership model during the 1970s and 1980s (Hayes et al., 2014). The premise of the model is that there is no single effective style of leadership; leaders adapt their leadership style to the context in which they are attempting to lead. Blanchard later developed the model and renamed it the situational leadership II (SLII) model (Northouse, 2016).

The situational leadership II model provides the flexibility to support leaders according to the 'situation' in terms of the task and the readiness of the colleague to undertake the work. The skill of the leader is in determining which approach to use in which context, ranging from directive to supportive behaviours:

S1 – Telling/Directing: This style is based on one-way communication through which the leader defines the role and provides the direction so that the followers know what, how, when and where to carry out the tasks

S2 – Selling/Coaching: This style is based on two-way communication through which, even though the direction is largely coming from the leader, they are attempting to get buy-in to the decisions that have been made

S3 – Facilitating/Counselling: This style involves two-way communication through which the leader and follower share the decision making and where the leader facilitates the process because the follower has the knowledge and ability to complete the task

S4 – Delegating: Here the leader delegates since the followers are in high readiness, have the ability and are willing to take responsibility for directing their own behaviour

Leading in the SENCO Role

REFLECTIVE ACTIVITY

Using the four behaviour types identified above, consider occasions when you have been in a position to draw upon them in different situations. Reflecting on these, is there one behaviour over all others that is predominant? Is this because the 'situation' requires such behaviour on your account or is it because it is your default position when leading?

The advantage of the SLII model is that it has been widely used on training and development programmes for 30 years and is instantly recognisable. Indeed, the authors suggest that it has been used by more than 400 of the Fortune 500 companies (Northouse, 2016: 98). It is practical, flexible, easy to interpret and apply. The model provides solutions for leaders who are facing challenges because it directs the leader to one of the four quadrants and indicates how the leader should behave. Most of all, it reminds us that our workforces are not homogenous groups, but rather collections of individuals with their own skills, motivation and autonomy levels. In such situations we cannot apply a one-size-fits-all approach, but instead differentiate according to context.

The SLII model is not without its critics: the empirical evidence that the model is based on is limited, with recent studies attempting to replicate the model not being able to find any basis to support it as an approach. Other limitations include the lack of reference to different populations, such as those based on age, gender, education and experience. Evidence by Northouse (2016) suggests that female workers prefer more supportive approaches, while male workers expressed a preference for a more directive style. The weaknesses highlight how a model, which is a simplified representation of reality, cannot always address every eventuality. Notwithstanding its shortcomings, the model serves to remind us that leaders need to be flexible in their approach. When leaders treat all their employees the same way and discover that, for example, the directing style has demotivated those who have high levels of competence, skill and motivation then the model is helpful in explaining (a) why it has happened and (b) what to do about it.

Self-analysis of your own leadership

There are many self-analysis tools available for leaders to draw upon to enable them to reflect on their leadership qualities. Ramsden (1998) identifies seven key leadership attributes, and while these relate to higher education, they are relevant because, unlike 'generic' models, Ramsden's list makes reference to teaching and research. These are outlined below with a space for self-reflection (see Table 3.3). What is important is that having completed the self-analysis you develop an action plan to further your development. Identify a coach or mentor to guide you through this process.

When working with the table on the next page you could add a Likert Scale to the reflection column and score your self-analysis against a scale of 1–5 or 1–10. Those attributes with low scores could be added to an action plan. This could be shared with a coach or mentor and progress monitored at regular sessions and a full review completed from time to time with a revised score. Such development could also, in theory, form part of a practitioner enquiry into your own leadership practice through an action research project.

TABLE 3.3 Self-analysis of key leadership attributes*

Attribute	Explanation	Reflection
Fair and efficient management	Do you manage resources effectively and maintain fairness and openness in decision making?	
Development and recognition	Do you recognise the contribution of others and support colleagues to develop their full potential?	
Interpersonal skills	Do you communicate clearly and give constructive feedback? Are you clear with your expectations and honest in your dealings?	
Strategy and vision	Do you work to create a shared vision and welcome new thinking?	
Transformational and collaborative leadership	Do you encourage participation, welcome questions, encourage the sharing of ideas and learn positively from mistakes?	
Leadership for teaching	Do you inspire respect as a teacher, and bring new ideas about evidence-based approaches to learning and teaching?	
Leadership for research	Do you encourage others to research and reflect on their own practice, to share their findings and experiences and engage in CPD?	

*see Appendix and online resources for assessment template

What makes an effective manager?

Pedler et al. (2007) identify from their research eleven qualities of an effective manager. They argue that the eleven qualities fall into three distinct groups from the foundational level (1), skills and attributes (2) and the meta level (3). They suggest that qualities are more appropriate than competencies in describing the eleven skills and attributes, though they recognise that competencies is the more often-used term in organisations. They feel that recognising an employee as 'competent' limits the fact that they might be exceptional. Equally, if you are not competent then the implication is that you are incompetent. Thus, these seemingly crude terms do not provide for useful measures. Using a Likert Scale in your reflection will support you to identify those management qualities you possess in strength, as well as those you might want to work on to further develop. Working with a coach or mentor would be beneficial and, as in the discussion about leadership above, a practitioner enquiry into your management qualities could be an appropriate way forward. The eleven qualities of an effective manager are:

A. Foundation level:
   1. Command of basic facts
   2. Relevant professional knowledge

B. Skills and attributes:
   3. Continuing sensitivity to events
   4. Analytical, problem-solving and decision/judgement-making skills
   5. Social skills and abilities
   6. Emotional resilience
   7. Proactivity – inclination to respond purposefully to events

C. Meta qualities:
   8. Creativity
   9. Mental agility

10. Balanced learning habits and skills
11. Self-knowledge

Source: Pedler et al. (2007)

To be a highly successful and efficient manager then the higher, meta, levels outlined above need to be achieved. More and more evidence is confirming that balanced learning habits and skills and self-knowledge are what make the difference between good managers and exceptional managers. Indeed, Pedler et al. (2007) argue that the ability to learn is the key hallmark of an exceptional manager and the detail surrounding these qualities is worth following up. They suggest that exceptional managers demonstrate the following hallmarks:

- They use a range of different learning approaches.
- They are more independent as learners.
- They are capable of abstract thinking.
- They possess a wider view of the nature of skills.

Source: Adapted from Pedler et al. (2007)

Working with a coach or mentor, consider your approaches to learning, using the four prompts above to reflect and monitor over time.

Supporting change in schools

Anybody working in education will confirm that change is a feature of everyday life. Those who have been involved in education for several years will say that the pace of change is accelerating; it is often cited as one of the reasons why so many teachers leave the profession. To paraphrase Darwin, it is not strength or intelligence that ensure survival, but the ability to adapt to changing circumstances with ourselves and our teams. This section seeks to examine two issues. First, how do we manage introducing change and second, how do we as a profession manage ourselves as it impacts on our professional and, increasingly, personal lives?

Change comes from a multiplicity of sources, both internal and external. External sources (as in external to the self) include government legislation, school policies, Ofsted schedules and national agendas. The danger with externally imposed change is that quite often it is resisted. Internal change (as in internal to the self), which is owned by the practitioner and is in response to their reflection on and evaluation of their own practice, or in collaboration with others, is more likely to succeed because there is a personal investment. As a SENCO it is inevitable that you will be asked to introduce change to systems and processes at some point in your career. It might be a change you have identified is needed and which might attract resistance. Mohanna (2007: 55) suggests that there are three steps to managing effective change:

- Understanding barriers – a key part of the process is to understand the barriers to change that exist and to recognise that sometimes barriers are put in place deliberately to prevent the change from happening. There could be occasions when the barriers cannot be removed and drawing in support from other colleagues becomes essential.

- Enabling transition – the transition phase is key to successful change and needs to be managed carefully, especially as those involved could be at different stages in accepting the change. Patience and encouragement are key during this phase.
- Sustaining developments – once change has been successfully implemented, the process has not ended and it is important to ensure that the change is embedded. This can be achieved by recognising success, encouraging perseverance and continuing to evaluate the change.

In considering the process above, it is worth remembering that not all colleagues affected by the change will accept it straight away. Rogers (1995) suggests that as the change 'diffuses' into the organisation, there is growing acceptance by colleagues (Table 3.4).

TABLE 3.4 Acceptance of change (Mohanna, 2007)

Colleagues	%	Explanation
Innovators	2.5	Those colleagues who take risks and can cope with high levels of uncertainty
Early adopters	13.5	These colleagues are opinion leaders, serving as role models, who are more integrated into the team than the innovators. They are respected and their acceptance of the change can act as a catalyst for others who place confidence in their judgements
Early majority	34	These colleagues tend to spend more time deliberating before completely adopting the idea. They follow others into the change, but rarely lead on the change
Late majority	34	These colleagues have come to the conclusion that they need to take the change on board, perhaps for the sake of their work and also possibly because of peer pressure
Laggards	16	These colleagues tend to be deeply suspicious of innovations and change agents. They need to be fully reassured that the change will not fail and is here to stay before accepting it

Once we are aware of the steps necessary to plan for change and have understood that not all colleagues will accept the changes immediately, we are better prepared to plan for and manage the process of change.

Case study

Sui had recently been appointed SENCO following the current SENCO taking on a new role in another school. She noticed that not all children on SEN support had a learning plan, the plans that were in place did not have any input from the child or the caregiver and there were no clear processes in place for tracking the review of the graduated approach. On checking, the SENCO discovered that not all the caregivers were aware that their child was on the SEN register; some learning plans had not been reviewed in a year.

What does Sui need to prioritise in this situation?

What are the key issues?

Who should Sui consult with to manage this situation?

How would you manage this situation as SENCO?

As SENCO, you need to have a clear understanding of what you want to change/achieve and the rationale for it. Consider the following:

- What do you hope to achieve and why?
- How are you going to share your vision/strategy with the senior leaders and governors?
- How are you going to motivate/inspire others to support you?
- How will you decide who to involve?
- How will you monitor and review the new strategy/approach/intervention?

Working alongside other professionals

As SENCO, you can involve specialists at any time for advice on meeting a child's needs or to support early identification. This can involve early help support, or the implementation of the graduated approach, or when data analysis is showing the child is making little or no progress or there are concerns about their mental health and wellbeing. Using the expertise of specialists is required when a child makes less than expected progress, despite evidence-based support and intervention or you suspect the child may have a disability or learning need that requires full assessment (DfE, 2015a). If caregivers provide consent you can take a child to an appointment with other agencies (if the caregiver can't) or accompany the caregiver and the child. Schools can involve specialists at any point for advice; ensure the caregivers are involved in any decision to involve external agencies and that agreement is recorded. Such specialists may include:

- Consultant paediatricians
- Occupational therapists
- Physiotherapists
- School nurse
- Educational psychologists
- Child and Adolescent Mental Health Services (CAMHS)
- Children and Young People Services (CYPS)
- Social workers
- Specialist teachers (for example, for children with hearing and visual challenges)
- Therapist (speech and language, play, occupational and physio)
- LA school improvement officers.

The Code clarifies that 'the SENCO and class teacher, together with specialists, and involving caregivers, should consider a range of evidence based and effective teaching approaches, appropriate equipment, strategies and interventions in order to support the child's progress' (DfE, 2015a: 103). As SENCO, your role is to coordinate the support across the school and to liaise with external agencies. Provision management tools need to be used to keep up-to-date records of all contacts, emails, letters, telephone calls, meetings, assessments, reports and reviews from external agencies.

Depending on the external specialist, they will provide support in different ways – some will come into school and lead staff training, whilst others will discuss strategies and approaches over the telephone with you. Others will observe children at home, school, hospital or assessment centres to carry out a formalised assessment of need and teach you some approaches for use in school.

> **Case study**
>
> Jacob had been SENCO for a year and was in his third year of teaching. A teacher requested a meeting to discuss concerns about Lucy in Year 3. She had become increasingly violent and aggressive towards him, the other children and the teaching assistant (TA), which resulted in the TA being signed off on long-term sick following a kick to her stomach. In the school records there wasn't any previous involvement with professionals outside of school or any formal diagnoses of any sort. Lucy was currently working at reception level, both academically and developmentally, and was not able to concentrate for more than 2 minutes at a time on a task that wasn't chosen by her. With caregiver agreement Jacob had kept a log of behaviours for two weeks but was unable to identify any patterns of when she would be most likely to bite, hit, kick, throw chairs or run out of the classroom. Her mother also reported an escalation of dangerous behaviours at home such as trying to climb out of upstairs windows.
>   Questions for Jacob to consider:
>
> What is the priority?
>
> What do the child, caregiver and teacher need support with?
>
> Who is the best person to give advice external to the school?
>
> What outcome is needed for the child and family?

Preparing for Ofsted

The aim of this section is to prepare you for capturing the essential evidence for an Ofsted inspection. It is advisable to complete the self-evaluation tools in Chapter 2 with accompanying evidence for discussion with the inspection team.

Recent focus area/requests by Ofsted inspectors in relation to SEND

- To evidence the SEN register, how were individual children identified and assessed?
- From the SEN register, certain children were selected for the SENCO to present their SEN support and EHC plans.
- Evidence of review meetings for SEN support and questions about how outcomes and next steps were communicated to all staff.
- During teaching observations, staff were asked to evidence from their planning how they had incorporated the information from the SEN support plans into their teaching approaches.
- Teachers were asked to show differentiation in the children's books for children on SEN support and EHC plans.
- SENCOs were asked to show progress in provision and practice for SEND since the last inspection; a grid has been produced to track this (Table 3.5):

TABLE 3.5 SENCO audit: Progress since last Ofsted inspection

Date	Comments from last inspection	SENCO response	Impact
Leadership and management	A lack of communication between staff about the SEND of children, particularly in KS4	Provision management tool to be implemented across school with assessments shared with relevant staff Learning plans for all children on SEN support	Staff all have access to external assessments evidenced in their differentiation in lessons
Quality of teaching, learning and assessment	Teacher planning shows varied focus on differentiation	CPD for all staff on quality first teaching for SEN	CPD evaluations show learning and observations show evidence-based strategies in place
Personal development, behaviour and welfare	Pastoral system works well for most children	Have a system to debrief and monitor in school exclusions Strengthen child voice	Exclusions reduced by 60% since introduction of debrief process
Outcomes for pupils	Children with SEN join the school below expected levels of attainment Children made less progress in 2017/18 than in 2016/17 Progress 8 scores are significantly below average of -0.63 in 2017/18	Improve transition documentation with feeder primary schools to target provision and booster classes in Year 7 Heads of subjects to provide exam/revision strategies and after school support for pupils with SEN LSA targeted support	Termly data for 2019 shows increase in outcomes for Y7 within 12 weeks Initial data shows IDL literacy intervention is improving reading ages in both KS3 and KS4

Chapter summary

- The role of the SENCO is a legal requirement for schools
- The role of the SENCO is significant in schools as part of the SLT
- SENCOs are leaders and, as such, one of their key roles is to provide the strategic leadership necessary to influence learning and teaching approaches for children with SEND
- SENCOs are also managers who have responsibility to deploy resources, both in terms of human and physical resources, and associated budgets, as effectively as possible
- SENCOs can audit and develop their leadership and management skills, ideally with the support of a coach or mentor
- A key facet of the SENCO's role is change management and it is important that any new systems or processes implemented are planned carefully in advance
- All schools are inspected and the SENCO plays a crucial role in the preparation for Ofsted

4
Best Practice in Collecting and Using Data

Sarah Martin-Denham

- NASENCO outcomes: To establish systems to collect, analyse and interpret data to inform policy and practice and to set challenging targets. To record and review the progress of children with SEND. To make effective use of data to evaluate and report upon the effectiveness of provision and its impact on progress and outcomes. Relevant guidance on data protection, accountabilities and confidentiality.
- Read alongside: Chapter 3: Leading in the SENCO Role

Chapter overview

This chapter will support you in effectively tracking and using data to review provision and practice and to identify when children need additional support.

What is data and why do we collect it?

Schools are increasingly accountable for children's progress and are required to have in place robust tracking and monitoring systems to record the development and attainment of all children (Ofsted, 2017a). This needs to include the details of any SEND, outcomes, teaching strategies and the involvement of specialists. These systems must have the capability to track progress, target set and to identify any children who are not making the expected levels of attainment so that evidence-based interventions can be put in place. Collection and analysis of data needs to be firmly embedded in school processes and practices so that the quality of learning and teaching can be reviewed. The data will be used by governors and senior leaders to:

- review the progress of individual and groups of children in relation to expected outcomes
- identify patterns and trends for particular groups, such as SEN support, those with an EHCP, pupil premium, looked after and permanently placed, individual classes and key stages.

In 2013, the government removed National Curriculum (NC) levels to report children's attainment and progress; they were not replaced. The intention was that schools would have the freedom to decide how to teach the curriculum and track progress. The DfE (2014b) produced a set of core assessment principles to guide schools: these state that schools are expected to demonstrate children's progress, to keep caregivers informed, to enable governors to make judgements about school effectiveness and to inform Ofsted inspections. Overall, the focus is to give reliable information to caregivers and to drive improvement. In addition to the removal of NC levels there has been the introduction of pre-Key Stage 1 and 2 standards. These were for use in 2018/19 onwards as a statutory assessment of children engaged in subject-specific study who are working below the overall NC standards but above P scale 4. These were introduced following the recommendations of the Rochford Review (2016), which examined the statutory assessment arrangements for children in primary school who were working below the standard of NC assessments.

Assessment is the collection, analysis and interpretation of information to give an insight into learning. It should give teachers and schools knowledge of what children know and understand over a period of time; this can only happen if the data generated is valid (measures what is intended) and reliable (consistent over time). For example, a mathematics assessment should focus on mathematical ability rather than ability to read a question as this would disadvantage children who encounter challenges with reading. Schools should not be only assessing academic skills but also analysing progress in other areas – for example, social, emotional, communication and behaviour – as difficulties in these areas will impact their ability to participate and learn. An example of a tool that tracks and measures progress in social, emotional development and behavioural difficulties is SNAP-B (see Chapter 11).

The data collected by schools either as a baseline assessment or as part of interim or end of year reviews should be used to judge whether:

- children are making progress in comparison to their peers
- there are underlying primary and secondary needs
- children are not making progress in line with expectations
- there are quality first teaching and effective interventions taking place
- there are training needs in the school.

Best Practice in Collecting and Using Data

REFLECTIVE ACTIVITY

- What entry, interim and exit data do you collect at school, class and child level?
- How is the data used?
- Who is the data for?
- What purpose does it serve?
- How useful and reliable is the data?
- How does it improve and influence provision and practice?

Ofsted

The Department of Education clarified that Ofsted does not expect performance and tracking information to be presented in a particular format, and this is unlikely to change with the introduction of the new inspection framework in 2019 (Ofsted, 2017b). Inspectors will consider performance information, data and analysis in whatever format the school uses. It will be expected that you can show what your children know, understand and can do and what you are doing to narrow any gaps.

It is evident from training SENCOs over a number of years that Ofsted inspection can be an extremely stressful and worrying time and not just for those new to the role. Ofsted is predominantly interested in the progress of the children and less interested in the day-to-day aspects of provision and practice. It is advisable to ensure your data is ready to present to inspectors in a format you can understand and discuss with them and which is General Data Protection Regulation (GDPR) compliant. Think about what works best for you – if you are not technically able, have an A4 folder, in sections, with all the information you need; others may have school storage systems or use 'Box' or 'Google drive'. Some areas of consideration are given in Table 4.1:

TABLE 4.1 Information for school inspection (Ofsted, 2017a)

School inspection handbook	SENCO evidence
Consider the progress of children with SEND compared to national and those with similar starting points	Provide up-to-date school data on outcomes with comparisons to the local, regional and national picture
Examine the impact of funded support on removing differences in progress and attainment	Provide rigorous evidence of monitoring and the impact of any SEN support across the child's time in school in achieving outcomes
Check identification of SEN and additional or different arrangements made as a result and improvement in progress	Show SEN information report, evidence-based interventions, targets and next steps for children with SEN support, with evidence of caregiver and child involvement
Consider differences between progress and attainment of children in resource-based provision and those in the main school	Provide school data (historic and current) across provisions
For children where attainment is unlikely ever to rise above 'low', the judgement will be based on an evaluation of the child's learning and progress relative to their starting point and any assessment the school holds	School-level data from baseline to date Evidence from graduated approach, EHCP and review
Consider the progress of children who attend off-site alternative provision and the school's own records of the progress of these children	Provision management Provide school data

Professional Knowledge and Understanding

What to do when children are not making expected progress

There will be some children who are not making sufficient progress despite targeted quality first teaching. The Code (DfE, 2015a) is explicit that 'in deciding whether to make special educational provision, the teacher and the SENCO should consider all of the information gathered from within the school about the child's progress'.

Identifying children who are making less than expected progress is characterised by progress which:

- is significantly slower than that of their peers starting from the same baseline
- fails to match or better the child's previous rate of progress
- fails to close the attainment gap between the child and their peers
- widens the attainment gap.

(DfE, 2015a: 95)

Where there are concerns there needs to be an assessment of needs, as set out in the graduated approach of assess, plan, do and review outlined in Chapter 2. You will need to formally gather evidence (including the views of the child and their caregiver) and during this time additional teaching and intervention needs to be put in place immediately as you await the outcome. There can be many reasons for children not making progress, being disruptive or withdrawn; it does not always mean they have a SEN. As discussed in other chapters, there can be underlying learning disabilities, learning differences, bereavement, communication and mental health needs; all of these factors will impact on wellbeing and, therefore, engagement with learning. The starting point is to work with colleagues to decide on the aims and objectives.

If a child is giving cause for concern and is not achieving expected levels of progress, you need to gather information on:

- the child's current and previous attainment, learning and development
- observations of participation in learning, social interaction, behaviours and external assessments, specialist advice
- caregivers' views and any concerns they have (recent bereavements, separation, sleep patterns, changes within the family circumstances)
- the child's wishes, views and feelings, their strengths and what they find difficult.

Aims: Statements of intent, your overall purpose written in broad terms, setting out what you hope to achieve at the end of the process, for example 'to develop social skills'.

Objectives: Specific statements that define measurable outcomes, e.g. the steps to be taken to achieve the desired outcome. Objectives must be SMART: Specific; Measurable; Achievable; Realistic and Time constrained, for example 'Ben will share with another child for five minutes with only one adult prompt by Autumn half term'. Further examples of SMART targets can be found in Chapter 11.

An underlying principle of the Code (DfE, 2015a) is that evidence-based practice is used to inform and deliver interventions with children in the plan/do and review phase of the graduated approach. Monitoring progress will allow you to understand if a child is meeting expected milestones; this is different to evaluating an intervention. Evaluation of intervention is crucial as you reflect on how effective it was to decide if it should be continued. As you monitor progress and evaluate interventions you will then

Best Practice in Collecting and Using Data

have an evidence base to inform teaching practices and to examine what is and is not working. As SENCO, you need to use this information to strategically plan provision and practice for the child.

REFLECTIVE ACTIVITY

What is your evidence base that the strategies, approaches and interventions are the best response to children who are not achieving expected levels of attainment?

Provision management

The Code advises that provision management is an efficient way of showing all the provision in a school that is additional to and different from that which is offered through the curriculum. It adds that provision maps can support SENCOs in maintaining an overview of the programmes and interventions used with different groups of children and their impact on outcomes and progress (DfE, 2015a: 105). The information can be presented in any format – paper based, an Excel document or a purchased programme, such as Edukey. You will need to include details of any SEN and disabilities, intervention and staffing costings, outcomes, teaching strategies and the involvement of specialists. Teachers should be writing and evaluating their own provision maps which you oversee for quality assurance. When effective, these records will contribute to school improvement by identification of provision needs, highlighting where training is needed and evaluating the impact on children with SEN.

Provision Map by Edukey is an online resource that can be used to strategically monitor special education provision, to show how you have implemented the graduated approach in your school and evaluated its effectiveness in terms of children's progress and outcomes. The resource offers a central store for EHCPs, SEN support plans, passports/profiles, provision costings, frequency and outcome measures, reports, medical plans, behaviour support plans and meeting records.

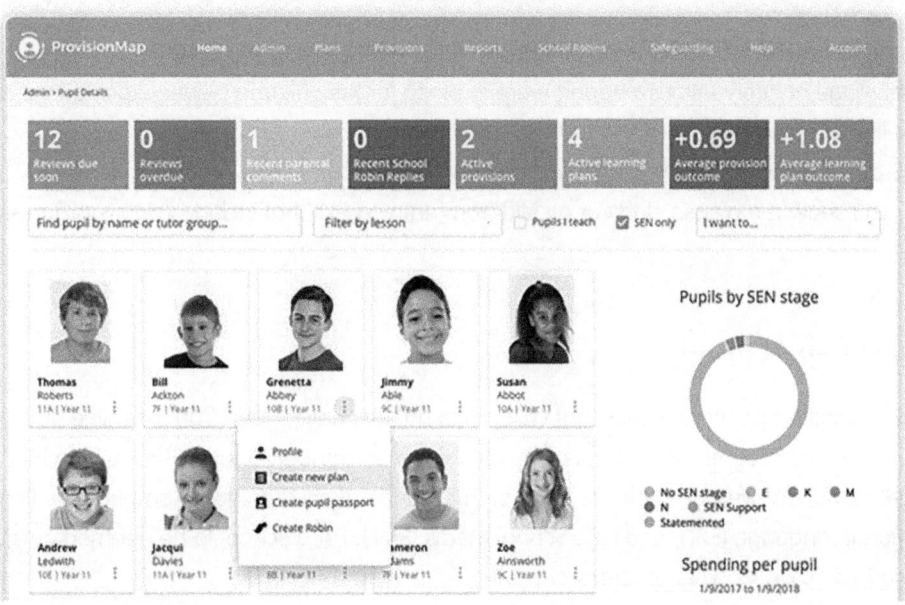

FIGURE 4.1 Edukey provision map

Source: www.edukey.co.uk

The tools in this software can be linked to your school management information system so the data only has to be entered once; there is also a transfer of information capability for when children move to a new school that also uses the software. It also provides reminders when reviews are due to take place. Caregivers can access and view the plans for their child and there is a messaging system for communication.

Data presentation

The next section provides examples of how you can present data on attainment and progress.

Nursery: Exit to entry data

TABLE 4.2 Nursery: Exit to entry data

Theme	Entry Baseline (62 children, 10 SEND)			Exit Summer Data		
	Below	Achieving	Exceeding	Below	Achieving	Exceeding
Making relationships	100%				67%	33%
Reading	100%			7%	63%	30%
Writing	100%				88%	12%
Numbers	100%			5%	62%	33%

Data presentation provided by Faye Waterhouse, SENCO

Ofsted may ask the following questions:

- Tell me about the 7% below expectations in reading by the end of nursery.
- What range of interventions/support were in place for the children below expectations at the baseline assessment?
- How do your chosen interventions narrow the gaps?
- Can you show me a case study of a child from entry to exit that includes points progress?

Nursery: Points progress

This grid exemplifies points progress that children in nursery have made from baseline data to leaving nursery. Points progress is calculated by counting the number of levels that each child makes then working out an average score for each of the groups of children; for example, SEN, English as an Additional Language (EAL), and Free School Meals (FSM). For a school to be deemed outstanding they need to achieve 4 points progress or more.

Table 4.3 is based on 51 children (including 8 SEN and 2 with disabilities) in the early years.

TABLE 4.3 Illustration of points progress from baseline to leaving nursery

Aspect of learning	All	SEN	Disability
Communication and language	6.2	5.2	4.3
Physical development	6.5	6.1	3.8
Literacy	5.5	5.9	5.7
Mathematics	5.3	5.5	6.1

Ofsted may ask the following:

- How does this compare with last year's data?
- Which of these children are also early years pupil premium?
- Are there any trends?
- How have you narrowed the gaps for different groups?

Spiky profiles

A child who exceeds in some areas of the curriculum yet is working well below expectation in others is known to have a spiky profile. Children all have different strengths, abilities and challenges and these reflect in their development and academic attainment profiles. This can be due to ability in areas of the curriculum but difficulties in communication and co-existing challenges which impact on their ability to access and participate in learning. Any child can have a spiky profile, although these are particularly common in children with SEN and disabilities. Table 4.4 shows an assessment profile for a child with autism who has a spiky profile; the data illustrates their baseline and exit data.

TABLE 4.4 Spiky assesment profile

Broad Areas of Need		Phase 0–11 months			Phase 16–26 months			Phase 22–36 months			Phase 30–50 months			Phase 40–60+ months		
		E	D	S	E	D	S	E	D	S	E	D	S	E	D	S
Personal, Social and Emotional	Making relationships		Baseline						Exit								
	Self-confidence and self-awareness								Baseline			Exit					
	Managing feelings and behaviour					Baseline			Exit								
Communication and Language	Listening and attention				Baseline				Exit								
	Understanding				Baseline				Exit								
	Speaking						Baseline		Exit								
Physical Development	Movement and handling											Baseline	Exit				
	Health and self-care								Baseline	Exit							

Key

E Emerging
D Developing   Baseline
S Secure   Exit

As you can see, on entry to nursery, as shown by the dotted blocks, the baseline shows the child is working well below national expectations, particularly in communication and language. For this child, having autism impacts on his ability to use communication and language and also on his personal, social and emotional development; however, he excels in numeracy. This profile was used by Faye and the nursery team to identify the support needed to enable him to access the curriculum and learning environment. Daily activities targeted to his areas of need, strategies such as the use of 'first and then' board and daily routine timetables, Picture Exchange Communication System (PECs) and speech and language therapy intervention all enabled the child to participate in learning opportunities and progress. This was achieved by identifying the child's motivators, strengths and challenges to enable staff to narrow the gaps in his learning alongside 1:1 support. The striped blocks on the profile show the exit data for the child as he left the nursery to start school. The child was exceeding some national expectations in areas of development due to the interventions put in place and he continued to excel in numeracy.

Comparative data

The data you collect should come from a number of sources: national tests, in-house assessments, photographic evidence, observations and examples of the child's work. Over time, the various sources will build a picture of the child's holistic development and progress, which will support you in reviewing SEN support or EHCPs, the impact of interventions and approaches to learning.

Types of comparative data that can be used in school

1. Centrally provided data, Analyse School Performance (ASP), national statistics from the Department for Education, league tables, and the LAIT (Local Authority Interactive Tool) which draws data from a range of sources (how to access this is shown below)
2. Teacher assessments (formative and summative).

> **Case study**
>
> Tom was made SENCO in his second year of teaching; there was no handover as the previous SENCO had retired due to ill health. He found there was no tracking and monitoring of data beyond the school-level data. How could Tom compare his school data to the local/national picture?

How to compare school-level data to the local and national picture

This section will support you as SENCO and your Senior Leadership Team in benchmarking data against the LA, statistical neighbours, the region and nationally. There are many resources available to use and some are briefly explored in this section.

Best Practice in Collecting and Using Data

Find and compare schools in England: This website allows comparisons to be made across schools both locally and nationally, on a range of performance measures including: reading, writing and mathematics progression, attainment scores, Ofsted ratings and school absences. The website is accessible via www.gov.uk/school-performance-tables.

Local Authority Interactive Tool: This tool allows for regional and national benchmarking, using a wide range of public data. A brief step-by-step guide is given below using fictitious schools and LA:

1. Visit: www.gov.uk/government/publications/local-authority-interactive-tool-lait and download the LAIT tool
2. Open the Excel document
3. Click 'Enable Editing' and 'Enable Content'

You should now be able to view the contents page, where you can access a range of information from Ofsted Judgements, Office of National Statistics (ONS) data and further interactive and comparative tools.

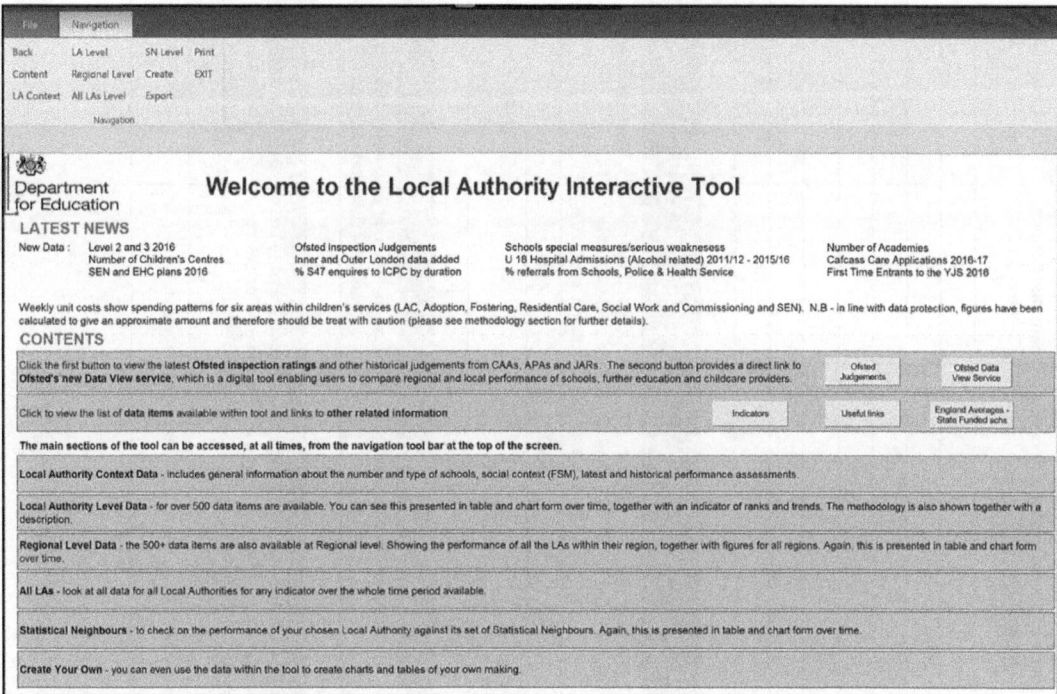

FIGURE 4.2 The Local Authority Interactive Tool

Source: www.gov.uk/government/publications/local-authority-interactive-tool-lait

4. To view an educational overview of your local area, click on the LA context button on the navigation pane (top left) and select your LA. You should see a series of tables similar to the ones below (Figure 4.3).

Gevan Local Authority Context View

Schools Information:

LA Maintained	Number of Pupils (January 2018)	Number of Schools (January 2018)	CTCs (January 2018)	Sure Start Children's Centres (July 2018)	Schools requiring Special Measures (June 2018)	Schools with serious weaknesses (June 2018)	Academies/Free Schools - Number of Academies (inc Free Schools) (July 2018)	Academies/Free Schools - Schools requiring Special Measures (June 2018)	Academies/Free Schools - Schools with serious weaknesses (June 2018)
Nursery									
Primary									
Secondary									
Independent									
Special									
PRU									
Total									

Social Context:

	Primary FSM Eligibility 2018 (inc. Nursery)	Secondary FSM Eligibility 2018	Primary First language other than English 2018	Secondary First language other than English 2018	Index of Multiple Deprivation 2015 - Average Score	Index of Multiple Deprivation 2015 - Rank of Average Score	LA Engagement - Intervention (Sept 2018)	School Improvement Inspection - Publication Date	School Improvement Inspection - Assessment
Percentage	20.10	21.30	5.90	4.80	29.73	31*	Yes	-	-
Rank	128	133	25	31	*- 1 being most deprived				
England %	13.70	12.40	21.20	16.60					

Inspection of Local Authority Children's Services (ILACS)

Publication Date	Type of Inspection	Overall Effectiveness	Experiences and progress of children in need for help and protection	Experiences and progress of children in care and care leavers	Impact of leaders on social work practice with children and families
-	-				-

Inspection of Services for Children in Need for Help and Protection, Children Looked After and Care Leavers and Review of the Effectiveness of the Local Safeguarding Children Board

Publication Date	Overall Judgement	Children who need help and protection	Children looked after and achieving performance	>> Adoption Performance	>> Experience and Progress of care leavers	Leadership and governance	Effectiveness of the Local Safeguarding Children Board
20/07/2015 & 25/07/2018	Inadequate	Inadequate	Requires Improvement	Good	Requires Improvement	Inadequate	Inadequate

FIGURE 4.3 The LAIT overview of your local area

Source: www.gov.uk/government/publications/local-authority-interactive-tool-lait

5. To benchmark your LA against others, click on the LA Level button on the navigation pane and select your LA, topic and indicator.

A table and graph will be created as a result. All information can be exported and/or printed using the navigation tools.

6. To export the data and use it to make comparisons with your school, click on 'export'. You will be prompted to save a version of the file to your hard drive.
7. Once you have opened the new file, you will be able to select and copy the data into another spreadsheet to customise it.

The tables and figures below were created using the LAIT to benchmark a series of fictional schools against regional and national data.

Nursery

Table 4.5 and Figure 4.4 present the percentage of children registered as SEN achieving a good level of development at the end of the Early Years Foundation Stage (EYFS).

TABLE 4.5 % Good level of development achieved – children with SEN, without statement of SEN/EHCP

Local Authority, Region and England	2014	2015	2016	2017	2018	2019	Change from previous years
Cherry Tree Nursery	11.00	12.00	18.00	27.00	35.00	36.00	1.00
Gevan Local Authority	12.00	24.00	23.00	26.00	30.00	31.00	1.00
Region	14.00	20.00	24.00	29.00	30.00	31.00	1.00
Statistical Neighbours	13.70	16.70	20.70	23.00	24.90	25.00	0.10
England	16.00	21.00	24.00	26.00	27.00	28.00	1.00

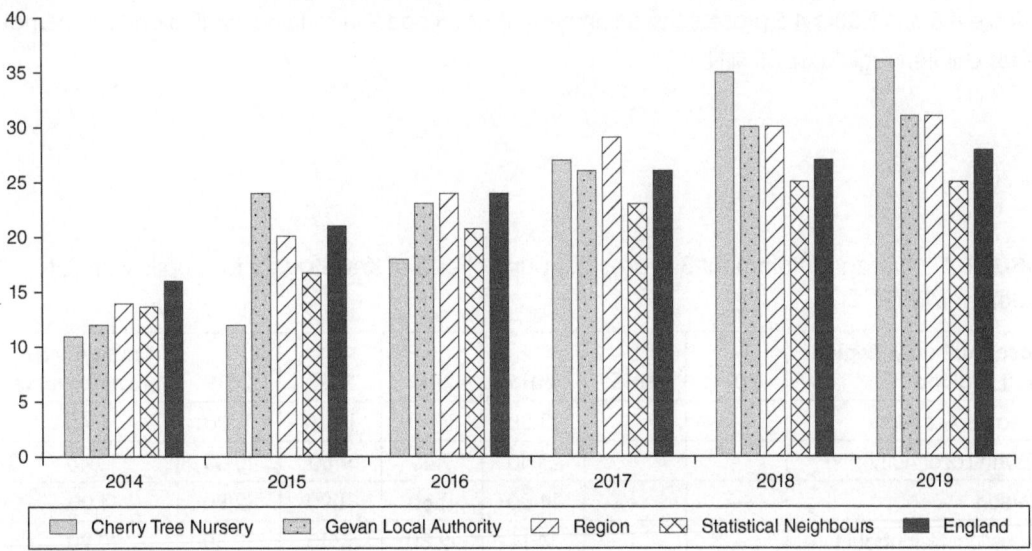

FIGURE 4.4 % Good level of development achieved – pupils with SEN, without statement of SEN/EHCP

Primary

TABLE 4.6 Attainment of Key Stage 2 (RWM) for children registered as SEN

Local Authority, Region and England	2014	2015	2016	2017	2018	2019	Change from previous years
Fig Lane Primary	-	-	22.00	27.60	25.00	21.00	−4.00
Gevan Local Authority	-	-	21.00	23.00	25.00	26.00	1.00
Region	-	-	19.00	24.00	24.00	25.00	1.00
Statistical Neighbours	-	-	17.88	22.11	23.00	24.00	1.00
England	-	-	16.00	21.00	26.00	25.00	−1.00

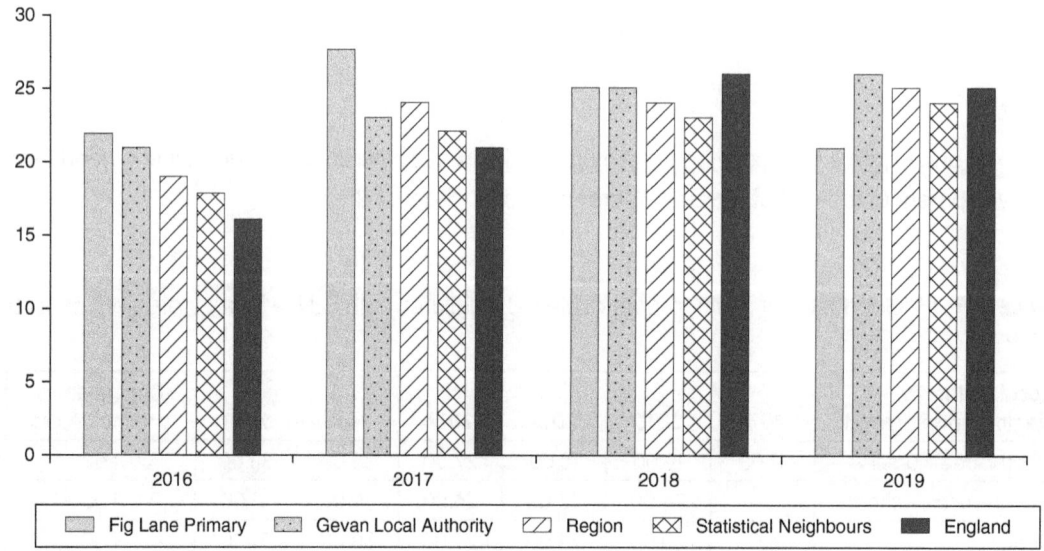

FIGURE 4.5 Attainment of Key Stage 2 (RWM) for pupils registered as SEN

Table 4.6 and Figure 4.5 present the attainment at Key Stage 2 in reading, writing and mathematics for children registered as SEN.

Secondary

TABLE 4.7 Average Attainment 8 Scores per pupil at end of Key Stage 4 for pupils with SEN Statement/EHCP

Local Authority, Region and England	2014	2015	2016	2017	2018	2019	Change from previous years
St Jacks Academy	-	-	13.90	10.10	10.60	11.00	0.40
Gevan Local Authority	-	-	15.40	9.40	9.60	10.00	0.40
Region	-	-	14.00	11.60	11.90	12.90	1.00
Statistical Neighbours	-	-	14.14	12.80	12.10	12.80	0.70
England	-	-	17.00	13.90	14.80	15.00	0.20

Table 4.7 and Figure 4.6 show the average attainment 8 scores of children registered as SEN Statement/EHCP. The attainment 8 score measures children's achievement from Key Stages 2 to 4 against the national average attainment 8 for all children who had a similar prior attainment score.

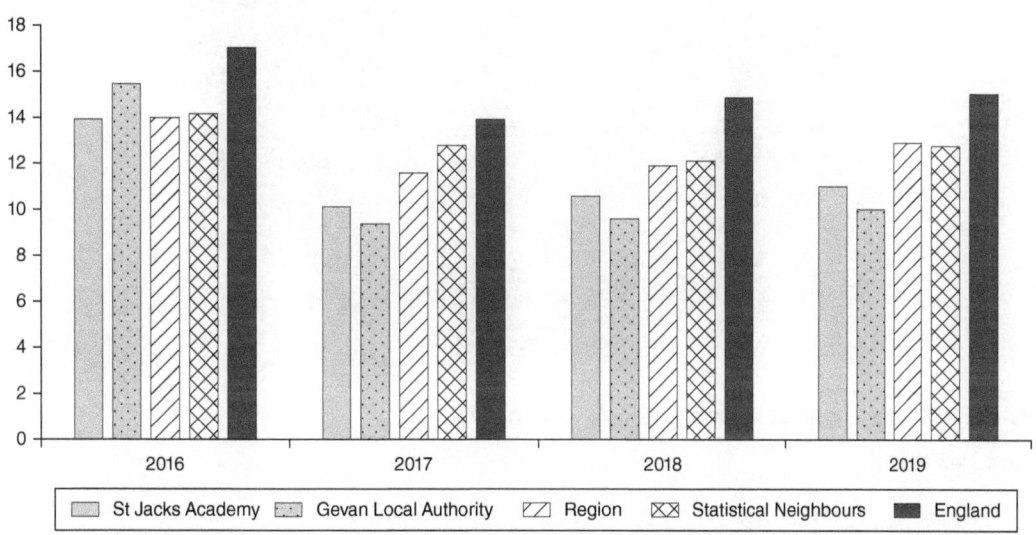

FIGURE 4.6 Average Attainment 8 Scores per pupil at the end of Key Stage 4 for pupils with SEN statement/EHCP

National statistics: The Department for Education publishes a 'statistical first release' with data from the school census. This contains extensive information about children with SEND in England and is used in the LAIT data sets. It separates data into type of SEN and disability, age, national curriculum year group, gender, ethnicity and EAL and free school meal eligibility.

SENCO ACTIVITY

Create an improvement plan by analysing the current attainment and progress of children with SEND. Consider the factors for differences locally, regionally and nationally and the realistic steps you can take to address these.

Devise an action plan, stating clear aims and objectives.

Teacher accountability

Teaching standard 5 (DfE, 2011b: 11) states that teachers must adapt teaching to respond to the strengths and needs of all children; they must be able to use and evaluate distinctive teaching approaches to engage and support them. As illustrated below (Figure 4.7), the responsibility and accountability for development and progress of children with SEND lies with teachers, not the SENCO or support staff.

Professional Knowledge and Understanding

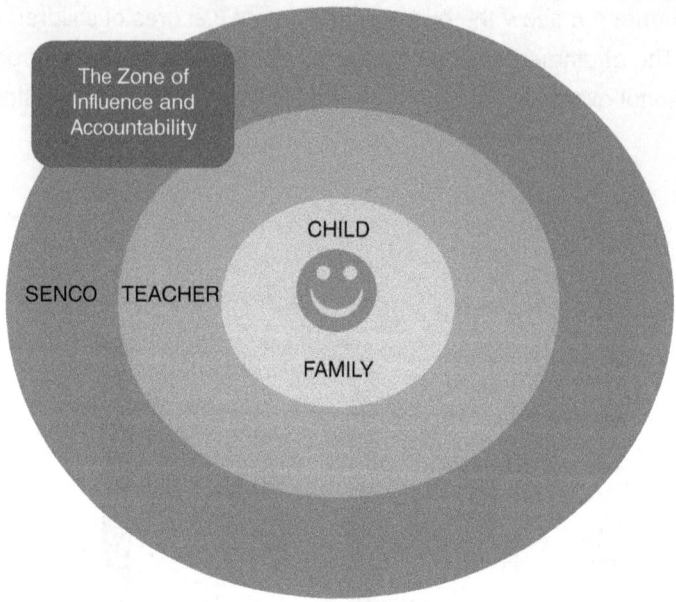

FIGURE 4.7 The Zone of Influence and Accountability
Source: NASEN (2014)

The Code adds that teachers:

- are responsible and accountable for the progress and development of the children in their class, including where children access support from support staff or specialist staff
- should remain responsible for working with the child on a daily basis, even when interventions involve group or one-to-one teaching away from the main class or subject teacher
- should work closely with any teaching assistants or specialist staff involved, to plan and assess the impact of support and interventions and how they can be linked to classroom teaching
- working with the SENCO, should revise the support in light of the child's progress and development, deciding on any changes to the support and outcomes in consultation with the caregiver and child.

(DfE, 2015a: 99, 101, 102)

REFLECTIVE ACTIVITY

- How are teachers informed of the individual SEN and disabilities of children?
- What is the process for teachers informing you about children falling behind, not making expected progress or excelling?
- What processes are in place to monitor the effectiveness of learning and teaching?
- How does feedback to children improve their learning?

Data sharing

The General Data Protection Regulation (GDPR) dictates safeguards regarding the use of personal data and applies to schools. Schools have extensive data on children's attainment, medical needs and other personal information. They also hold data on staff, governors, caregivers and volunteers. If a school holds data, those it affects have the legal right to know the types of data being held, how, why, and to whom it may be communicated. Every school or group of schools must designate a Data Protection Officer (DPO). To support the transition to these new data regulations, the DfE (2018b) produced guidance 'privacy notices', which are useful for schools to adopt as they explain in user-friendly language the use of personal information.

Considerations for SENCOs:

- How is data transferred between systems and to any third parties?
- When a new system or subject-specific software is introduced, what is the process of gaining DPO approval?
- Do you know the process for reporting a data breach? (For example, emailing the wrong caregiver or losing personal information.)
- Is your technology and that of your colleagues (phones, laptops, tablets, computers) password protected and adequately encrypted?
- Don't hold any data on USB sticks as they are easily lost or stolen.

Chapter summary

- It is important to evaluate the validity and reliability of assessments used in schools
- The purpose of assessment is to support learning
- Schools can create and use their own tracking and monitoring systems for data
- Ofsted will question you about your data and the development and attainment of the children in your school
- GDPR has implications for SENCO; you need approval from your DPO to ensure the use and transfer of any data is safe

5
Practitioner Enquiry

Steve Watts and Sarah Martin-Denham

→ NASENCO outcomes: To draw upon relevant research and inspection evidence about teaching and learning in relation to children with SEND. To improve practice and to undertake small-scale practitioner enquiry to identify, develop and rigorously evaluate effective practice in teaching children with SEND.

→ Read alongside: Chapter 4: Best Practice in Collecting and Using Data; Chapter 14: Coaching and Mentoring

Chapter overview

The purpose of this chapter is to explore the origins of practitioner enquiry, its purpose and how it can be applied to teachers' and SENCOs' contexts. Guidance will be provided on how to conduct a practitioner enquiry through action research, including approaches to participatory and collaborative methods. The ethical issues to be considered when carrying out a research project will be addressed, as well as the processes involved in writing up the project. Finally, the implications of findings, their evaluation and dissemination will be considered.

Origins of practitioner enquiry and action research

The idea that practitioners should enquire into their own practice could be said to originate with John Dewey nearly a century ago in the USA (Dewey, 1933). Dewey's notion of reflective practice introduced the idea of teachers thinking about, and reflecting upon, their practice in a systematic way in order to improve. He stated that reflective thinking fosters the development of three attitudes that further the 'habit of thinking in a reflective way':

- open-mindedness (freedom from prejudice)
- wholeheartedness or absorbed interest
- responsibility in facing consequences.

These three attitudes are still relevant today and serve to remind us that, when reflecting, we have a responsibility to ourselves and those situations that we are reflecting upon.

More recently in the UK, interest in teachers using their reflections as a way to improve practice emerged in the 1970s. Instrumental in this movement were, among others, Stenhouse (1975) and Elliott (1978). The emphasis here was on practitioners' intrinsic concerns, rather than researchers' external concerns (McAteer, 2013: 15).

Practitioner enquiry has also variously been called practitioner research, practitioner learning, practitioner action research and so on. While practitioner enquiry can draw upon a range of research methodologies, the main process for a practitioner to research their own practice is usually the action research cycle. This chapter will focus on action research for practitioner enquiry.

Teachers as action researchers

Teachers are natural action researchers, even though they probably don't realise it. Thinking like an action researcher is a skill they bring to the role intuitively and which develops over time to become instinctive. Every time a teacher plans a lesson or an intervention, or they walk into a classroom or sit down with a child, they are action researchers. This is because everything a teacher does is based on a hunch or theory that what they propose to do will work for that particular child or set of children. They draw upon their entire professional knowledge, including their understanding of their needs, to ensure that what they plan will support them in achieving the best possible outcomes. Thus, a teacher might think 'this child needs this intervention, so I'm going to implement it and evaluate its success and adjust my materials and approach in the light of my findings'.

All research is based on a hypothesis waiting to be tested or a foreshadowed problem that needs further exploration and this process is essentially replicated in the classroom. The process of action research formalises this through a structured approach that reflects what teachers do intuitively. By thinking of it this way, we can begin to demystify the term action research and locate it as a central activity in a teacher's daily classroom practice. Thus, action research is not about the children, but about the teacher – what they planned, how they delivered it and what results they achieved.

Origins of action research

Action research is a process that originated in the USA during the 1930s and 1940s as a way of approaching and analysing problems. The term was coined simultaneously, though independently, by two colleagues, Kurt Lewin and John Collier. The emphasis from the very beginning was on social change for social justice (McNiff and Whitehead, 2011: 41). Collier, who was US Commissioner for Indian affairs, is generally credited as identifying the concept first. Lewin, a refugee from Berlin who arrived in the USA in 1933 and worked as a social psychologist, is usually credited with developing Collier's concept (Adelman, 1993). He believed that action research must include the active participation of those who are involved. The process he conceived of involved identification of the problem, a subsequent investigation, leading to group decisions about adjustments, and monitoring and regular reviews to determine when the strategy had been completed, leading to further cycles (Adelman, 1993).

What is action research?

Action research is sometimes called practitioner enquiry because it can be carried out by practitioners, from any profession. In this sense, as McNiff and Whitehead (2011) suggest, it is an empowering process because practitioners own it. In this way, it can be carried out as a private, solo, enquiry by a practitioner with a query or question about their practice. It can also be led by a group of professionals enquiring into shared concerns. It can be kept internal and in-house, or it can be shared with a wider audience, submitted as part of an accredited course and sometimes published.

> **Definition:** 'Action research is a form of enquiry that enables practitioners to investigate and evaluate their work. They ask, "What am I doing? Do I need to improve anything? If so, what? How should I improve it? Why should I improve it?"' (McNiff and Whitehead, 2011: 7).

In contrast to social scientists who carry out research on others (outsider research), action research is carried out on our own practice (insider research). Thus, social scientists usually stand outside of the research process looking in, while action researchers see themselves as very much part of the process. Action researchers tend to follow a cyclical process, which may proceed through several cycles before completion.

McNiff and Whitehead (2011) propose an action-reflection cycle based on the following process (Figure 5.1):

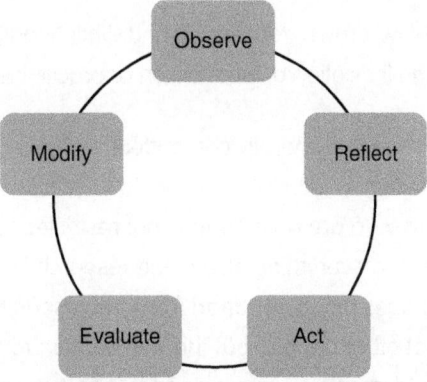

FIGURE 5.1   The Action Research Cycle

Different approaches to action research

There is considerable controversy surrounding action research; this is because certain schools of thought do not recognise it as legitimate research. The 'interpretive' action research school advocates the research being carried out by an 'external' researcher who watches and reports on what the practitioner is doing. The other main school of thought, often called 'self-study' action research, believes that a practitioner is capable of offering explanations for what is happening. In this book, the emphasis will be on 'self-study' action research.

McNiff and Whitehead (2011) set out assumptions that clarify the underpinning principles that drive action research. These assumptions are extremely important because they serve to remind us that action research is about the researcher and is not something that is done to others. It is subjective and value laden, focusing on how the researcher can improve themselves in relation to other professionals; about how the action researcher can learn; and about how the researcher needs to hold themselves accountable for their educational influence and how, by following these processes, they can improve society. Once we come to think about these principles we begin to see (a) how powerful action research is for personal and professional transformation and (b) how by being accountable for our own practice we begin to contribute to a better and fairer society.

> **Case study**
>
> On a tour of school facilities after school when the building was empty, given by a headteacher to members of the governing body, many expressed surprise that every classroom was different in terms of its layout, wall displays, where the teacher's desk was located, the prominence or otherwise of children's work and the general atmosphere that all the above factors created. The governors had not realised that each classroom represented a statement by the teacher about their personal values in terms of how children learn, the importance given to children's work and what their subject has to offer society. The teachers involved in the school may never have carried out a formal action research study, but their classrooms revealed how each day they put into practice their personal values, modifying them after intuitive reflection and evaluation in order to continue to learn about themselves and their contribution to the school's and wider society's culture.

The assumptions outlined below, drawn from McNiff and Whitehead (2011: 39), confirm that what the governors saw on their tour is an indication of what action or practitioner research seeks to exemplify:

- Action research is value laden and morally committed, which is different to the assumption that research can be value free.
- It aims to understand what I/we are doing and is not restricted to what 'they' are doing.
- The researcher is in relation to everything else in the research field, both influencing and being influenced by others, and does not stand apart from the research.
- The object of enquiry is not other people, but the 'I' in relation to other 'I's'.
- Knowledge is uncertain and answers are created through negotiation.
- Knowledge is the property of individuals so it is often subjective and biased.
- Action researchers do not do research on others, but do it on themselves in company with others.

- Action research aims to improve workplace practices through improving learning.
- Practitioners evaluate their own work in relation to their values; they do not need 'external' evaluation, though they do understand the need for stringent testing.
- Practitioners need to learn how to change their thinking in order to improve their practices.
- The capacity of individuals to think for themselves and to hold themselves accountable for their educational influence can act as the grounds for the creation of good societies.

These are profound assumptions, but in many ways, as the case study of the governors' visit above indicates, they are nothing more than the formalisation of what the empty classrooms conveyed. Imagine how much more powerful it would have been if they could have seen the teachers and children interacting and, as part of that process, constantly constructing and reconstructing their understanding through social interaction. The action research process seeks nothing more than to formalise what is happening naturally in classrooms and schools every day, with a view to improve learning and wider society.

REFLECTIVE ACTIVITY

Look at the teaching spaces you spend time in. What do they say about you as a teacher or the teacher whose room it is? Sit in the room when it is empty and take a 360-degree view and identify what 'messages' the room conveys about the personal beliefs of the teacher or yourself. Try the activity again with children present and repeat the exercise. Does the interaction of those in the room reflect the messages that the empty room conveyed?

Planning an action research project

With the assumptions outlined above in mind, there is a cyclical process that action researchers follow. McNiff (2013: 90) identifies several general principles in planning a piece of action research below (Table 5.1):

TABLE 5.1 The Principles of the Action Research Cycle

Principle	Explanation
We review our current practice	In reviewing our current practice, is there something that we would like to review to improve practice?
We identify an aspect we wish to investigate	Make explicit the issue that you wish to review, perhaps by phrasing it as a question because this initiates the need for a response
We ask focused questions about how we can investigate it	Identify how the issue can be investigated, for example by observation, analysis of children's work or behaviour or their responses to tasks
We imagine a way forward	Here we envisage how we will carry out the investigation, identifying the processes and steps to be taken
We try it out and take stock of what happens	This is the stage where we implement the idea and monitor what happens
We modify our plan in light of what we have found and continue with the action	As we receive feedback about the new process, we modify the action and continue

(Continued)

TABLE 5.1 (Continued)

Principle	Explanation
We evaluate the modified action	Drawing upon the data we have collected during the process, such as pupil work, observations, interviews, etc., we evaluate the action
We then reconsider what we are doing in light of the evaluation – this can then lead to …	We identify the key learning points emerging from the evaluation which may then trigger a further cycle of action research
… a new action-reflection cycle	Repeat above process

Research methods to support action research

Waring (2017: 15) suggests that all researchers 'need to understand that their research is framed by a series of related assumptions' based around four key questions.

The first question concerns 'ontology.' Ontological assumptions form the starting point of all research. In essence, ontological assumptions form a continuum from 'realism' to 'constructivism'. In realism, the ontological assumption is that there is a single objective reality that exists independent of individuals' perceptions of it. At the other end of the spectrum, the ontological assumption is that there is no objective reality, but rather multiple realities that are 'constructed' by individuals (Waring, 2017: 16).

Establishing the researcher's ontological assumptions leads to the next question about epistemology. Waring (2017: 16) states that epistemology relates to knowledge and the researcher should ask the question 'how can what is assumed to exist be known?' There are two positions along the continuum, named positivism and interpretivism. Working with a 'realist' ontology, 'positivism sees it as possible to achieve direct knowledge of the world through direct observation or measurement of the phenomenon being investigated' (2017: 16). At the other end of the continuum, interpretivists do not believe that direct knowledge is possible. Waring (2017: 16) argues that 'it is the accounts and observations of the world that provide indirect indications of phenomena, and thus knowledge is developed through a process of interpretation'.

Once the ontological and epistemological assumptions of the researcher are made explicit, the research methodology should be identified. Waring (2017: 16) suggests that 'methodology asks what procedures or logic should be followed'. A realist ontology/positivist epistemology would draw upon nomothetic and experimental methodologies, which seek to generate general scientific laws, while a constructivist ontology/interpretivist epistemology would draw upon ideographic and dialectical methodologies which focus on the individual.

The fourth question refers to the methods that will be adopted to gather the data. The methods will usually be congruent with the ontological and epistemological assumptions of the researcher, though Waring (2017: 16–17) suggests that this is not always the case. Thus, a researcher who holds the constructivist ontological assumption that there is no objective reality and the epistemological assumption that knowledge is developed through a process of interpretation will adopt qualitative methods such as interviews, questionnaires and observations.

In terms of the methods available to practitioners in order to conduct their enquiries, the toolkit of methods is wide-ranging and extensive. The key issue is to select the most appropriate method available in order to collect the data that is needed to answer the research question.

The literature review

While most are agreed that conducting a review of the literature around the issue being investigated is important, there exists disagreement about the best time to do this. Those who adopt a grounded theory approach and believe that theory emerges from the analysis of the data, would argue that exploring the literature would occur after the data has been collected and explored, so as not to influence it. Traditionalists would argue that one of the first things a researcher should do after identifying their research question is to explore the literature (McAteer, 2013: 89).

> **Definition of the literature review:** 'Anything that represents the results of research or scholarship on a subject.' (Thomas, 2009: 30)

Whatever approach the researcher takes, it is important to survey the literature in the field of study. This is because it is very likely that your research question has been asked before, perhaps many times, and so in reading the work of other researchers you will be better placed to locate the findings of your study within the wider research community.

For those taking their action research project further through either internal or external publication, or as part of an accredited course, the following four points are particularly relevant, because they highlight the four key functions of a literature review, which are to:

1. Provide background on the issue being investigated
2. Locate the social, political, economic, educational and environmental context of the investigation
3. Consider what has already been written within the area of the investigation, looking particularly at the similarities and differences between studies
4. Discuss the relevance of any existing research to the area being investigated.

(Adapted from: Burton and Bartlett, 2009)

The literature to be reviewed can come from a multitude of sources, such as books and journal articles, but also from government reports and policy, charity research and best practice guides and so on. More recently, the use of information from websites has become more acceptable, but as with any text, either virtual or hard copy, the source of the material must be substantiated.

Observation

One of the most accessible approaches to gathering data is through observation. Practitioners spend their working day observing their children and constantly revise their understanding of how they are progressing with their learning as a result of what they see and hear. In research terms there are two types of observation: participant and non-participant. Most practitioners will be engaged in participant observation because they are immersed in the classroom, participating in the interactions between themselves and their children, as well as between the children, as they teach. To be a non-participant observer requires the practitioner to step back from the class and be a detached observer. This can only be done by observing from the edges of the classroom and deliberately stepping back and disengaging from the class while a colleague teaches. The advantage of this approach is that the observation can be focused and less likely to cause distractions.

Using participant observation as a method for collecting data, while easy to fit into the school day, presents particular challenges when it comes to recording the observations.

> **Case study**
>
> As a practitioner researcher, Steve used the following approaches in order to capture data during participant observation:
>
> 1. Carry a notebook/tablet around during the lesson and record brief notes or aide memoires that would trigger deeper notes after the lesson.
> 2. Create a classroom plan so notes and observations can be annotated next to individual children.
> 3. Write up the notes made as soon as possible after the lesson while they are still fresh in your mind.
> 4. Where possible, choose a class that is being observed so that there is a break, lunchtime, non-contact time or end of day immediately afterwards which will thus provide an opportunity to write up the observations straight away rather than dashing to the next lesson.
> 5. It might be possible to video or audio tape the lesson/group work so that it can be analysed alongside the written notes (permission would need to be sought for this to happen).
> 6. Ask a colleague to observe for you, perhaps giving them a particular focus to concentrate on.

The key issue here is finding the opportunity to write up the notes as soon as possible while they are still fresh in your mind. The notes don't need to be recorded in prose, but can be bullet points, notes, annotations, tables and so on. Even if the observation is being recorded it is still important to keep notes because what is important is not just what you see when observing, but how you interpret what you see.

Interviews

Interviews are another common way of gathering data though, as with observations, it is not easy to find the time and an appropriate location in a busy school to conduct interviews. There are essentially three types of interview – structured, semi-structured and unstructured. A structured interview involves the creation of a pre-interview set of questions, which when asked, tend to be adhered to without deviation so that the experience across the interviews is as similar as possible for each interviewee, which makes analysing the responses more straightforward.

Semi-structured interviews also involve the creation of a list of questions prior to the interview, but when the interview is being conducted the interviewer and interviewee are able to digress if an interesting point emerges that is worthy of further exploration, even though it may not be fully related to the original question. The interviewer exercises their discretion about what to pursue and probe into further.

With unstructured interviews, the interviewer will have a set of pre-prepared topics that are to be explored, and the participant is free to roam wherever the discussion goes. The advantage of this approach is that what might emerge is what the interviewee feels is important, rather than being tied to the interviewer's questions. The data is likely to be richer, but also more difficult to analyse in relation to the data emerging from other unstructured interviews.

Interviews are usually sources of very rich data and the less structured they are, the richer the material. Children can be interviewed, as can other colleagues and professionals, along with caregivers. One would only interview if there was a compelling reason to do so and when preparing for interviews the ethical guidelines should be referred to.

Focus groups

A useful and time-efficient way of gathering rich data is to lead a focus group. One reason for this is that interviewing children one-to-one can be quite intimidating for the child, but creating a group of children provides an element of security. It also has its challenges, of course, because it can be equally intimidating contributing to a focus group, particularly when there are confident characters who want to lead the conversation. The facilitator/researcher will need very specific enabling skills for the group to work collaboratively to share their views. It can work well to have 'child researchers' where they take the lead in asking and recording responses; with this approach you will be more likely to gather their authentic voice, as there are no adults present to influence responses.

A key issue with focus groups is similar to the difficulties with participant observation in that it is difficult to both be the facilitator and to record notes. Other ways of addressing this include, as mentioned above, asking a colleague to either act as scribe or the lead so you can manage the recording of responses.

> **Case study**
>
> A SENCO came to see me frustrated that a focus group she had created was not providing useful data. The children were quite reticent to speak and detailed responses were not emerging. She decided to set up an internal Mahara discussion forum (Mahara is a free e-portfolio system that is popular in educational institutions) for the focus group to contribute to and she was astounded by the response that she received. The children opened up and contributed regularly, interacting with each other and the practitioner. It was clear that the children were used to engaging with each other online through social media such as Facebook, WhatsApp, Instagram and so on, but were less comfortable with the face-to-face nature of a focus group. In analysing the data the practitioner observed that in the face-to-face focus group the teacher's presence was too prominent and that seemed to inhibit discussion, but on Mahara it was as if the teacher was not present, even though the children could see the teacher contributing to the discussion.

It is quite possible that such online fora already exist in your organisation, in which case both children and staff will be familiar with its use, but if not and you'd like to consider setting up an online discussion forum then the organisation's protocols for the use of such digital media will need to be followed. Use of an internal learning platform would be appropriate, but it would be advisable not to use social media, such as Facebook, even though they offer a closed group facility.

Questionnaires

Questionnaires are a popular way of gathering data because they can be administered quickly to large populations and can provide data that is easily analysed. As with interviews, questionnaires come in various versions. The most straightforward are closed questionnaires that require single responses to each question, which are easy to collect and analyse. Such questionnaires can collect factual information, such as age, ethnicity, gender and so on and responses on a continuum of values, such as those provided by the Likert Scale or through the use of visual representations such as emojis. Closed questionnaires are a valuable way of collecting such details, but are limited in providing explanations or feelings – for example, using the Likert Scale of 1–10 with ten being the highest score for 'how interesting did you find the lesson?' This will give instant feedback, but it won't tell you why the lesson attracted such a high or low score. Thus, questionnaires are sometimes written in a semi-structured way so that after a question requiring a score there is a supplementary question asking why. Adding the reasons provides richer data but also takes longer to analyse, especially if you have distributed many questionnaires.

Questionnaires have a notoriously low return rate, so large numbers have to be distributed in order to get a reasonable response; using an online resource such as SurveyMonkey will save you time and will do some analysis for you. When gathering data internal to the school it is easier because the audience is already in situ, but it should be remembered that both staff and children have the right not to participate. Before progressing with preparing a questionnaire, it is best to consult the ethical guidelines because there are concerns not just with permission, but also with secure storage of the data (BERA, 2018).

Mixed methods

The use of mixed methods when researching educational settings has increased in popularity over the last two decades. Biesta (2017: 159) confirms that 'in its most basic form mixed-methods research entails a combination of qualitative and quantitative approaches, with the ambition to generate a more accurate and adequate understanding of social phenomena'. One of the advantages of adopting a mixed-methods approach is greater opportunity for triangulation of data. Triangulation of data is important because using more than one method or approach means that the researcher is able to cross-reference data about the same phenomenon, derived from different approaches or methods. He suggests that there are two approaches to adopting a mixed-methods approach – the concurrent and the sequential. In a concurrent mixed-methods approach both quantitative and qualitative methods are used simultaneously, citing the example of a study of a school where quantitative data about student performance is collected at the same time as interviews with staff are conducted to build up a picture of the school. In a sequential mixed-methods approach, quantitative data about student performance may be analysed first in order to identify the most pertinent questions to ask in teacher interviews (Biesta, 2017: 161).

Using pilots

When constructing questionnaires and interview questions, it is advisable to carry out a pilot. The purpose of this is to check to make sure that the questions being asked are appropriate in terms of eliciting the information required. Pilots are usually carried out on a small representative sample of the population to be surveyed. The whole process, including the experience of carrying out the questioning, is reviewed after the pilot has been completed, with a view to making adjustments to the questions and process, where necessary, before continuing with the rest of the data gathering. The findings of the pilots are usually discarded before commencing the actual survey or interviews.

Reflective diary

The 'reflective diary' can come under a variety of names including 'learning journal', 'research journal' and so on. What is important is that some form of journal or diary is kept. There are many reasons for this, including the following:

- It provides a focus for the research.
- It slows the process down.
- It provides a thinking space.
- It provides a feeling of ownership of the research.
- It provides a place for recording the unstructured and spontaneous aspects of the research.
- It encourages learning through the process of writing.

(Moon, 2006)

What is important is that the researcher writes in their diary/journal regularly, and ideally daily, in order to keep the research question at the forefront of their mind. The entries do not need to be extensive or discursive; brief notes and bullet points are valuable, alongside key dates, times and locations, with a code for participants so they cannot be identified. The entries must be factual and objective and could include records of emotions, reactions, reflections, observations and prevalent points.

Case study

Steve was reflecting on his students' learning, but despite classroom observations, questionnaires and interviews, he was unable to fully elicit why some of the students were not connecting with the learning. Then, in an unguarded moment during breaktime and away from the more formal teaching and research settings, a student suddenly burst out in a long verbal stream of consciousness all her frustrations with the tasks she'd been asked to complete. Steve quickly reached for his research journal and recorded the words verbatim. This incident provided the evidence needed to explain the difficulties the students were experiencing, but was outside the formal setting, totally spontaneous and unscripted.

As Steve's experience above reminds us, the research moment may present itself at any time and the practitioner researcher must always be ready to capture such revealing and rich data.

Ethical considerations for action researchers

As part of your National Award for Special Educational Needs Coordination (NASENCO) part B of the NASENCO outcomes (NCTL, 2014: 7) you are required to show you can 'critically evaluate evidence about learning, teaching and assessment in relation to pupils with SEN to inform practice and enable senior leaders and teachers to: Undertake small-scale practitioner enquiry to identify, develop and rigorously evaluate effective practice in teaching pupils with SEN and/or disabilities'. To be able to do this effectively you need to have knowledge and understanding of how to lead a practitioner enquiry; once you are confident, you will be able to mentor your colleagues in adopting this approach as part of school improvement processes.

The British Educational Research Association (BERA) (2018) suggests that educational researchers aim to extend knowledge and understanding in all areas of educational activity and from all perspectives, including those of learners, educators, policymakers and the public.

Guidance on how to ethically lead research with adults and children is available from a variety of organisations, two of which are highlighted below:

BERA (2018) *Ethical Guidelines for Educational Research.* London: BERA.

National Society for the Prevention of Cruelty to Children (NSPCC) (2012) *NSPCC Research Ethics Committee: Guidance for Applicants.* London: NSPCC.

These documents are essential to ensure you fully understand the ethical requirements and the importance of informed consent. The NSPCC document provides guidance and principles for interviewing children.

This section of the chapter will guide you through the ethics process that Sarah followed for her practitioner enquiry for her NASENCO.

Case study

Sarah was on the NASENCO programme and was planning her practitioner enquiry; she was interested in understanding the factors that led to the increase of 65% in fixed-term exclusions in her school in the last academic year. She hoped to find out if there were any underlying factors that led to the exclusions so she could share suggested changes to systems and processes with the Senior Leadership Team (SLT) and governors to address this issue.

Ethical considerations for Sarah's practitioner enquiry

TABLE 5.2 Ethical considerations for Sarah's practitioner enquiry

Steps	Process
Step 1: Choose your theme	You need to decide what you want to investigate, analyse and investigate. Some examples are given below
Some examples:	
What are the factors that lead to children receiving fixed-term exclusions?	
What is the knowledge of staff of the impact of adverse childhood experiences on children and their ability to learn in school?	
How effective is a 10-week intervention programme when used with nursery-aged children to improve their speech, language and communication development?	
Step 2: Gain initial permission to carry out the enquiry from the SLT and the NASENCO training provider on your preferred area of focus	There may be some sensitivities, so check with the SLT to discuss your preferred theme and inform them of the likely participants (4 excluded children, 2 colleagues in pastoral support and 2 caregivers)

Steps	Process
Step 3: Once step 2 is agreed, complete ethics paperwork from the NASENCO provider, attaching examples of information sheets, consent forms, gatekeeper's permission (agreement from the headteacher or principal) and your enquiry questions	You will need written consent from the gatekeeper of the school to evidence they are happy for your enquiry to proceed Gain consent from all participants
Step 4: Once all consents and approvals have been gained, the enquiry can begin	Plan your data management, how you will keep data secure and how long you will store it for Ensure all data is anonymised, and no personal information is shared or noted
Step 5: Analyse the data	You will use your coding system and data analysis to identify key trends using quantitative and qualitative approaches
Step 6: Data presentation and key findings	Relate your finding to the literature review you have undertaken. Do your findings correlate with the literature? What are the key issues you have evidence for?
Step 7: Conclusions	What have you discovered? Refer back to your question: have you found out the factors that lead to fixed-term exclusions? What are the next steps/ solutions?

Interviewing children

A principle of the CAFA (2014) and Code (DfE, 2015a) is the importance of partnerships with children and caregivers. As SENCO, at a strategic level and as part of your role, you will be required to develop and monitor the SEND policy and provision in the school; interviewing and observing children as part of your enquiry can give you rich data to lead to school improvement.

The NSPCC (2012) has identified five principles that underpin its policy and these should be taken into account when carrying out research with children.

Principle 1: Voluntary participation based on valid informed consent

As SENCO, you will observe and speak to children on a daily basis; this is a key part of your role. However, if you are carrying out a practitioner enquiry it is important that you and your colleagues are fully informed around issues of informed consent. Children, their caregivers and the 'gatekeeper' of the school all need to consent to you carrying out research. The gatekeeper is consenting to you having access to the participants and they need to have a clear understanding of your intentions. The caregivers also need to consent to their child taking part and they will need to have the research aims and processes fully explained to them. In addition, the child needs to consent to participating (if under the age of 16) (NSPCC, 2012). Should the gatekeeper and the caregiver consent but not the child, then the child cannot under any circumstances take part. It is advised not to observe or interview any children who are looked after due to the complexity of gaining consent. The process of consent is ongoing: the child may consent prior to the research happening but change their mind, so you need to check to ensure they continue to be happy to participate and withdraw them and their data if they request you to do so.

To gain consent from a child to participate you need to provide information to them about your enquiry. This needs to be in a format that they can access, with a reader if necessary. It is advisable to show them the information on the research and give them time to think about whether or not they want to take part; a week should suffice. For example, a comic strip can be a good way of getting all the information across to a child in an understandable format that avoids jargon and technical terms.

For consent, emojis can be a useful way of gaining verbal consent and should be used alongside the words, not sure, yes and no, for those who are unable to identify with visual representations of emotions. An example of a consent form from Sarah's study can be found below (Figure 5.2*):

FIGURE 5.2 Consent form

*see Appendix and online resources for assessment template

Gaining verbal consent and the child indicating consent on a form like this show you have taken appropriate steps to explain your intentions to the child. Ensure the child has time to reflect on their decision. No research can begin until all consent is received.

Principle 2: Enabling participation where possible and avoiding the systematic exclusion of particular sections of society

As SENCO, you will need to ensure access and consider any mobility issues, literacy difficulties and learning difficulties to ensure all children taking part can access your research. Likely adjustments will ensure that:

- Your information sheets/comic strips are age and developmentally appropriate
- The language that you use is easy to access and understand
- Access to the room is considered prior to any research taking place.

Principle 3: Avoidance of personal and social harm to participants

Taking steps to avoid personal and social harm is a key aim when planning to carry out any research. Any risks of such harm happening must be identified and appropriate steps taken to reduce the risk. Key risks that the NSPCC identifies include:

- Vulnerable individuals can find participating in research stressful
- 'Reawakening' old feelings or memories
- Uncovering hidden or suppressed feelings
- The child may be concerned about what they have shared.

(NSPCC, 2012: 11)

Principle 4: Non-disclosure of identity and personal information

Participants' identities and personal information must not be disclosed. As professionals, it is perfectly acceptable to share information about the children in classes with colleagues and other professionals, but in a research context we would behave differently. This is even more important if the findings from the research are to be shared outside of the school. With the passing of the Data Protection Act 2018, which contains the General Data Protection Regulation (GDPR), we now have a duty to keep any data derived from the research safe. You are advised to seek guidance from the SLT in your organisation and comply with the systems and policies in place. Given that you will be collecting data there are four data processing principles that it would be wise to follow:

1. Be compliant with the law.
2. Only collect data for a specific purpose.
3. Record what is said accurately; don't presume what participants mean.
4. Data should be stored for only as long as necessary and needs to be kept secure.

Principle 5: Ethical application and conduct of research methods

This principle reminds us about the importance of adopting appropriate research methods and conducting the research in an ethical and transparent way, so that findings are not skewed with the potential to mislead, misinform and cause harm. SENCOs should ensure that their research design is fit for purpose and will derive data that is relevant to the research question. For example, questions should be designed to collect data specific to the research question.

Example interview questions for children

1. What do you enjoy about school?
2. What don't you like about school?

3. Is there anything you find hard/difficult about school?
4. Why do you think you find it difficult?
5. When you are in class, who do you work with?
6. What could we do to make school better?
7. Who do you like to talk to when you feel worried or frustrated?
8. What makes a good school?

Analysing data

As we have seen, data can come from a wide range of sources. It can include secondary sources, such as school policy documents, government legislation, guidance briefings from charities and so on. There is also data that you as a SENCO will have collected from primary sources, such as interviews, observations, questionnaires and attainment data. Some of this data could be quantitative in nature, such as test scores, examination grades, SAT levels and so on, while some of it (usually the majority) will be qualitative data.

The first principle to consider is that we gather data to generate evidence and that generating evidence involves analysing data (McNiff and Whitehead, 2011: 147). Given that most of the data is likely to be qualitative, one approach to analysis is coding. This involves careful reading of the data item by item in order to identify key themes. If your investigation is examining why there is a rise in fixed-term exclusions you might code/highlight the responses from the children as:

Red: relates to being angry about an aspect of school rules

Blue: refers to negative home life and childhood adversity

Green: refers to challenges with friendships

Purple: relates to being unable to access learning or teaching approaches

The coding makes it easier to identify patterns, as it is a visual method. You will also analyse your results in relation to the literature you have read as part of your NASENCO.

REFLECTIVE ACTIVITY

Do your findings from the practitioner enquiry echo or dispute what has been found in research publications? What changes, if any, need to be made to provision, practice, staff training and child/caregiver relationships?

Sharing the outcomes with senior leaders and governors

The essence of practitioner enquiry is that it is about yourself for yourself and the main purpose is to improve your own practice, both for your own learning and the learning and experiences of those you teach. Following your practitioner enquiry there needs to be a process of sharing the findings so that you can strategically develop provision and practice to actively improve the school. For greatest impact you need to share your findings with the SLT, staff and governors, with an action plan to be agreed that includes agreement of the planned next steps. In the earlier example of Sarah's study, the actions included:

- A change to the SEND policy and behaviour policy to remove the 'zero tolerance' approach as due to some children's needs it was not supporting them to stay in school but instead meant sanctions for low-level behaviours were not exploring any underlying causes
- The development of safe spaces for children at risk of exclusion to go when they feel stressed and frustrated by the showing of a card to their teacher
- The creation of a caregiver forum to develop a process whereby they can report concerns about their child's wellbeing and mental health for early intervention through schools and health services support
- To embed practitioner enquiry as part of the appraisal process for all to improve provision and practice for children with SEND.

Case study

Steve organised a shared and paired reading project for children with low confidence in reading. He monitored progress very carefully, noting improvements he could make in terms of his own approach, as well as how to improve the support and opportunities for the children. The outcomes were beyond all expectations for all involved so the decision was made to share and celebrate the successes with the caregivers of the children involved. The findings were also shared with the school's SLT and governors, with the result that the school changed its policy towards the way it supported children with their reading, increased the budget for the library and reviewed its policy for home and school partnership. A video was made showing caregivers how to carry out paired and shared reading at home.

The case study above shows how the findings of practitioner enquiries can influence policy and practice in school and be used to celebrate success. This stemmed from a small-scale practitioner enquiry based on the question 'how can I better support children's reading development and encourage reluctant readers and those with low reading ages?' One unintended outcome was with the reading mentor children who volunteered to support those children who were unable to receive support at home. As is often the case with mentoring projects, the mentors ended up benefiting as much as, if not more than, their mentees. This was especially so in their levels of confidence and leadership, as well as the skills necessary to support and mentor their peers.

McAteer (2013: 152) points out that in her experience of supervising action research projects the outcome that strikes her most 'is the very real and deep changes that people experience in both their own professional lives and practices, and the impact that action research has on their colleagues'. She goes on to explain that almost all 'universally talk of the ways in which they have exposed their assumptions and practice to critical questioning, how unanticipated insights have caused them to re-conceptualise their relationships with pupils, and with colleagues, and how these processes have helped them articulate their own beliefs and values, and more fully live them in practice'.

Recommended reading

McNiff, J. and Whitehead, J. (2011) *All You Need to Know About Action Research*. London: Sage.

Chapter summary

- The most common approach to practitioner enquiry is action research
- Practitioner enquiry is a process that teachers do informally every day as they reflect on their practice and make adjustments
- There are ethical processes to be followed when planning, carrying out, analysing and sharing research findings
- Practitioner enquiry is essentially 'insider' research for teachers to improve their practice
- Action research, first developed in the USA in the 1930s and 1940s, essentially involves a series of cycles of plan-do-review
- There are many ways to generate data from which theory emerges through a process of induction
- The data is analysed using a coding process intended to identify themes
- While the outcomes of action research projects are intended for the practitioner, they also provide an evidence base for approaches to learning and teaching; sharing the outcomes can be a powerful way to both change colleagues' practice and influence school policy and home–school liaison

Part II

Leading and Coordinating Provision

6
Adverse Childhood Experiences

Sarah Martin-Denham

- NASENCO outcome: How SEN and disabilities affect children's participation and learning and the breadth and complexity of the causes of underachievement.
- Read alongside: Chapter 7: Meeting the Needs of Looked After and Permanently Placed Children; Chapter 8: Social, Emotional and Mental Health Difficulties

Chapter overview

The purpose of this chapter is to develop your knowledge and understanding of how Adverse Childhood Experiences (ACEs) can affect how children respond to stress, their resilience, capacity to develop long lasting relationships and life outcomes. It will provide you with some ACE-informed approaches that can be used to support the wellbeing of children and their families.

What are adverse childhood experiences (ACEs)?

The original study into ACEs was conducted by Felitti et al. (1998) – there were 17,000 participants who were patients responding to a variety of questions under ten key themes about childhood experiences and any adversity within their experience as a child including: family dysfunction, current health status and behaviours. The study introduced the findings as ACE scores, which is a cumulative index combining childhood stressors from neglect or abuse (physical, emotional and sexual abuse, physical and emotional neglect) to challenges in the household (caregiver being treated violently, divorce or separation, parental incarceration, substance abuse and a member of the household living with mental illness). The questions measure the total number of ACEs that have been experienced within the first 18 years of life. The implications following the first ACE study have led to duplications of the research internationally. In follow-up surveys the initial questions used were reduced to the ten most common themes rather than the full survey that has shown repeatedly that adversity in childhood does relate to later adult health and life choices. A more recent study by Bellis et al. (2014) found, from a study of 3,885 adults in England, that almost half had experienced one adverse childhood experience and 9% had experienced four or more.

The ACE survey

The ACE survey is shown below (Table 6.1). Note that this is for adults over the age of 18 and is not to be used with children. If this is used as part of staff training, the following is good practice:

- Remember that these are risk indicators and not an outcome and that poor outcomes may not occur.
- It is not a diagnosis in any shape or form and must never be used as one.
- It is not an assessment indicator and should never be used as one.
- Make it explicit that it is voluntary; not everyone had a happy childhood and not everyone has to take part.
- Ask that scores are not shared as this may make some people uncomfortable.
- Allow individuals to complete the survey privately.
- Have a break after the survey is completed so staff can talk to each other but not about their own result, and allow staff to seek support should they need to.
- If those with a high ACE score are concerned about their mental or physical health, you/or someone else will need to provide support if you are qualified to do so. Colleagues need to be supported to see their GP or to access other health services.

'While you were growing up, before the age of 18...'

TABLE 6.1 ACE survey

ACE	Question
Caregiver separation	Were your caregivers or significant person ever separated or divorced or did they die when you were a child?
Domestic violence	How often did your caregivers or adults in your home slap, hit, kick, punch or beat each other up?

ACE	Question
Physical abuse	How often did a caregiver or adult in your home ever hit, beat, kick or physically hurt you in any way? This does not include gentle smacking for punishment.
Verbal abuse	How often did a caregiver or adult in your home ever swear at you, insult you, humiliate you or put you down?
Sexual abuse	Did an adult at least 5 years older than you ever… touch or fondle you or have you touch their body in a sexual way? Or attempt to or actually have oral, anal or vaginal intercourse with you?
Emotional neglect	Did you often or very often feel that no one in your family loved you or thought you were important or special? Or your family didn't look out for each other, feel close to each other or support each other?
Neglect	Did you often feel you didn't have enough to eat, had to wear dirty clothes and had no one to protect you?
Mental illness	Did you live with anyone who was depressed, mentally ill or suicidal?
Alcohol/drug misuse	Did you live with anyone who was a problem drinker, alcoholic, or who used street drugs or prescription medication?
Incarceration	Did you live with anyone who served time or was sentenced to serve time in prison or a young offenders institution?

Source: Adapted from Felitti et al. (1998) and Bellis et al. (2014)

Issues with the ACE survey

As reported by Bellis et al. (2014), the ACE survey is prone to issues as it relies on accurate recall and willingness to report ACEs; recollection of issues in childhood may be limited due to the impact of the trauma. Some children will have multiple vulnerabilities, such as those who are neglected are more likely to have speech, language and communication challenges. In addition, the ACE survey does not include other important predictors such as violence outside of the home, peer rejection, low socioeconomic status and academic performance at school. There needs to be a move away from agencies identifying and intervening with one characteristic and instead exploring and responding to children's holistic needs. In the UK there is discussion to make this part of GP and primary health services.

The impact of childhood adversity

Felitti et al. (1998) concluded that as the number of ACEs increased so did the association with chronic disease, high-risk behaviours, mental health problems and premature death. Since 1998, the research base continues to show associations between ACEs and poor health, including asthma, cancer, cardiovascular disease, hypertension, chronic obstructive pulmonary disease and diabetes (Slack et al., 2017). Shonkoff et al. (2012) examined how early life experiences and environmental influences leave a lasting impact on the genetic predispositions that affect emerging brain architecture and long-term health. They argue that human development is driven by ongoing, inextricable interaction between biology (genetics) and ecology (the social and physical environment). These findings establish the need for developing knowledge and understanding of the impact of ACEs on children's mental health and wellbeing so that schools can begin to apply evidence-based prevention and intervention.

The biology of stress

Exposure to maternal stress in the prenatal stage can influence future stress responses as it alters the developing neural pathways shaping the development of the brain. The plasticity of the young brain means it is particularly sensitive and responsive to chemical influences which, if exposed to elevated stress levels, can alter the neuronal architecture of the amygdala, hippocampus and prefrontal cortex and lead to functional differences in learning, memory and aspects of executive functioning (Shonkoff et al., 2012). Exposure to stress can result in children being hypervigilant as they prepare for further trauma; this can present as anxious behaviours and a heightened emotional state, leading to an increased risk of anxiety and depression. Healthy brain architecture relies on loving and consistently positive interactions with caregivers; if this is not the case then brain development will be disrupted, as the brain does not receive the positive stimulation it needs.

Toxic stress is a term developed by Shonkoff et al. (2012), who discuss that healthy development can be hindered by excessive or prolonged activation of the stress response systems in the brain and body. This can happen due to exposure to abuse and neglect, growing up in households with domestic violence or adults with substance misuse problems, or in environments where there is a high level of criminal activity or sense of hopelessness. Long-term, toxic stress can impact on the structure and function of the brain and therefore the ability to participate and engage in learning. It can activate the flight, fight and freeze responses, which may be misinterpreted as disruptive, aggressive or challenging behaviour. Looked after and permanently placed children as well as those who have experienced trauma in their environments, such as natural disasters or terrorism, are more likely to have neurodevelopmental challenges and to encounter and display toxic stress responses.

TABLE 6.2 Types of stress response

Type of stress response	Physiological response	Potential cause	Protective effect
Positive stress response	Brief increase in heart rate and slight elevation in hormone level	First day at school Forgotten homework Going to the dentist Vaccination	Availability of a supportive, caring and responsive adult or peer
Tolerable stress response	Excessive activation of stress response systems which can lead to physiological harm and long-term consequences for health and learning	Death of a family member Not passing an exam Serious illness or injury Divorce Natural disaster	Adult and peer relationships that facilitate the child's adaptive coping and sense of control which reduce the physiological stress response
Toxic stress response	Disrupted development of the brain architecture and circuitry and other organ and metabolic systems, increased risk of mental health challenges across the life course	Prolonged, frequent adversity such as: child abuse, neglect, a caregiver with mental health challenges or parental substance misuse	Adult, peer relationships may be sufficient if there is a strong, established, safe and available relationship. This would normally require a caregiver in addition to school staff

Source: Adapted from Shonkoff et al. (2012)

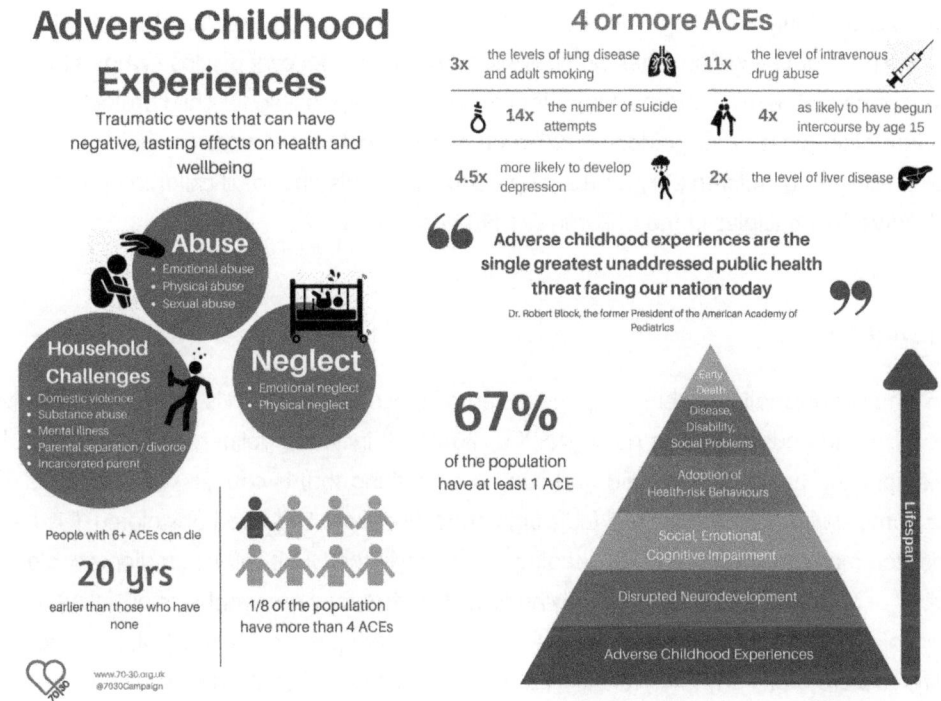

FIGURE 6.1 Adverse childhood experiences
Source: 70/30.org

....**SENCO ACTIVITY**
Carry out an audit to find out the knowledge and understanding of colleagues of childhood adversity and the impact of toxic stress.
....

The impact of ACES across the life course

ACEs can affect people across the life course, which has implications for children, young people and adults, as when they are exposed to adverse and stressful events these impact on their ability to think, to interact with others and to process information and learn. The infographic above (Figure 6.1) shows the impact of ACES on health and wellbeing in terms of risk and should not be seen as things that 'will happen' but that 'may happen'.

The following part of this chapter focuses on the ten thematic areas within the ACE survey and their impact on the child's wellbeing. Bereavement, loss and substance misuse are discussed in Chapter 8.

Abuse

If you are worried a child is being abused, neglected and/or exploited you need to be observant for any unusual behaviours such as: aggression, being withdrawn, being anxious, being clingy, taking unusual risks, suddenly behaving differently, obsessive behaviours and school absence. The indicators of any type of abuse will not often be obvious; children may not ever disclose what is happening or has happened to them. The Department for Education is responsible for child protection and sets out the legislation, policy and guidance in this area. The most recent statutory guidance, *Working together to safeguard children* (DfE, 2018c), applies to all schools and to all children up to the age of 18 and follows the principles of the Children Act 1989 and 2004.

Emotional abuse

Children who suffer emotional abuse experience emotional neglect, which is also known as psychological abuse and causes serious harm (NSPCC, 2018a). It includes deliberately trying to frighten, humiliate, ignoring or isolating a child and can be something that is caused within schools rather than the home environment if the child feels frightened, humiliated, ignored or isolated. It is the second most common reason for children needing protection in the UK; it can occur alone or alongside other types of abuse: 'it may involve conveying to a child that they are worthless or unloved, inadequate, or valued only insofar as they meet the needs of another person' (DoH, 2015). It can be difficult to identify, as there aren't any physical signs; also, changes in emotional state are to be expected as part of growing up.

Indicators of emotional abuse or neglect

TABLE 6.3 Indicators of emotional abuse or neglect

Babies/Early Years	Older children
Are overly affectionate towards strangers	Use language and actions which you wouldn't expect them to know
Lack confidence and are wary or anxious	Are unable to control emotions and have extreme outbursts
Don't seem connected to their parent(s)	Seem isolated from their parents
Show aggression towards children and animals	Lack social skills and have few, if any, friends

Source: NSPCC (2018a)

Physical abuse

This is when a child is deliberately hurt, causing injuries such as bruises, burns, broken bones or cuts. These injuries are not accidental and include being hit, kicked, poisoned, slapped, burned or having objects thrown at them and should be recognised when bullying occurs in school as well as at home. When a baby is shaken or hit the result can be non-accidental injuries, which can result in death. Fabricated or induced illness is when a caregiver makes up or creates symptoms in a child to gain attention; an example of this is overdosing a child with salt or medicines. There can be a multitude of reasons why adults physically abuse children including: addiction to substances, anger, frustration, they were exposed to abuse as a child, issues with their physical and mental health and an inability to manage their child's behaviour.

Adverse Childhood Experiences

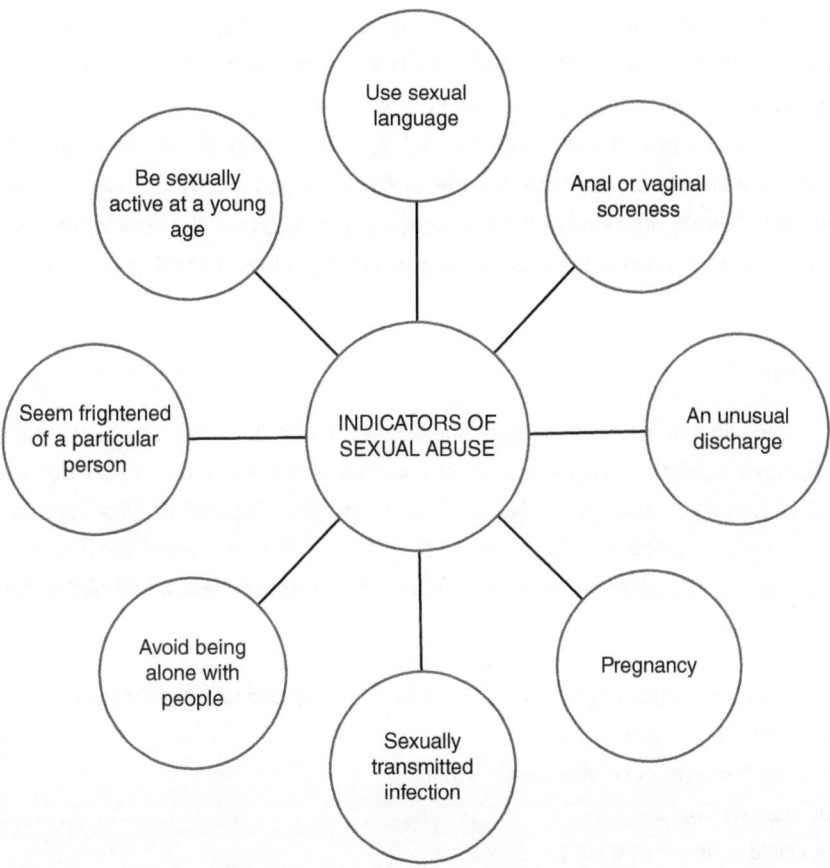

FIGURE 6.2 Indicators of sexual abuse

Sexual abuse

A child is sexually abused when they are forced or persuaded to take part in sexual activities; it does not have to be physical contact and can happen online. The NSPCC (2018b) reports that 1 in 20 children in the UK have been sexually abused.

Violence including domestic violence

UNICEF (2008) stated that children who are exposed to violence in the home may suffer a range of severe and lasting effects including emotional stress and harm to the development of the brain. The NSPCC (2018c) reports that abusive behaviour can occur in any relationship, from either party, and it can continue once the relationship ends but it can also occur from children towards siblings or adults in the home. These children are also more likely to have problems with school work, poor concentration, lower reading abilities and mental health needs such as depression and suicidal tendencies. The Children's Commissioner (Longfield, 2018) reported that these children will often have to take care of themselves, their siblings and the caregiver who is being abused. She added that they often miss school, are unable to complete homework, are tired and may deliberately misbehave to get attention.

It is likely that these children will be fearful of being at home and to cope will be keen to do after-school activities. These children are less likely to disclose what is happening as they know it will cause further anger in the family home, resulting in them being taken into care.

A child witnessing domestic violence is recognised as being at significant harm in law, unless this violence is caused by a child to an adult (see children with challenging, violent and aggressive behaviours). It can be difficult to identify domestic violence is happening as it is usually in the family home; for some children, they will have to move out of their home which disrupts their friendships and education.

Case study

Simone, 11, lived with her mother and her mother's new partner. The couple were often arguing, particularly after drinking alcohol, and her mum had frequently contacted the police but would never press charges. One evening, Simone was woken up by swearing, shouting and things being smashed. She rang the police who arrested the man, who had beaten her mother badly and she had to be taken to hospital. As Simone was taken to stay with her uncle, she could see there were holes in the wall and blood on the kitchen table.

- What range of emotions might Simone feel prior to, during and after the incident?
- What might Simone worry about?
- How could this experience affect her in school?
- What support might she need?
- What would your school do in this situation?

Support organisations

National Domestic Violence Helpline: Partnership between Women's Aid and Refuge

Website: www.nationaldomesticviolencehelpline.org.uk   **Helpline:** 0808 2000 247

Men's Advice Line

Website: www.mensadviceline.org.uk   **Helpline:** 0808 801 0327

Email: info@mensadviceline.org.uk

Hunger

Since 2010, social policy in the UK has been dominated by welfare reform and austerity, which has had a detrimental effect on household income. The reality is that many families don't have enough money to buy essentials, such as food, heating and clothing for everyday living. Foodbanks are playing an increasing role in feeding the most vulnerable due to reduced welfare state support, illness, disability, family breakdown and/or the loss of employment. The Trussell Trust is the largest foodbank organisation, providing 1,332,952 emergency three-day food supplies to those in crisis, an increase of 6% on 2016–2017. The Trust cites the main reasons for referral to foodbanks as low income, benefits, not earning, benefit delay or change, or debt.

The Food and Agriculture Organization of the United Nations (2016) estimates that food insecurity occurs due to a number of factors and that as money to buy food is restrained anxiety arises. Furthermore, diets become less balanced, more monotonous and portion sizes are reduced or meals are skipped.

The FIES (Food Insecurity Experience Scale) measures the ability to access food at a household or individual level over the last 12 months. There are eight questions, which refer to food-related behaviours and experiences.

The eight questions, because of a lack of money or other resources:

1. You were worried you would not have enough food to eat?
2. You were unable to eat healthy or nutritious food?
3. You ate only a few kinds of foods?
4. You had to skip a meal?
5. You ate less than you thought you should?
6. Your household ran out of food?
7. You were hungry but did not eat?
8. You went without eating for a whole day?

Talking about these themes with caregivers will require established and secure relationships. It is likely to be more appropriate to provide signposting to foodbanks or to apply for funding for breakfast clubs to support those families you identify as being at risk of hunger.

REFLECTIVE ACTIVITY

Would the FIES be a useful tool for your school? How could it be used?

How does your school identify and support those with food insecurity?

What do you put in place to prevent children going hungry during school holidays?

Parental divorce, separation or death

Children will need time to adjust and grieve when caregivers separate or when someone close to them dies. This can take many years and they will need ongoing support to enable them to cope with their emotions and the changes in their lives. Their emotions will vary and are likely to include being:

- upset
- angry
- frustrated
- rejected
- confused
- sad.

For some children, prior to a separation or divorce there may have been significant conflict for a number of months or years. Barumandzadeh et al. (2016) evaluated 2,017 children aged 11 to 12 to examine the frequency of conflict in their homes. They found that in a number of cases where caregivers had separated, the conflict was not lessened because arguments were significantly

> **Support organisation**
>
> **The Trussell Trust:** You can search for the nearest foodbank by postcode and the process for getting vouchers is clearly explained
>
> **Website:** www.trusselltrust.org **Telephone:** 01722 580 180
>
> **Email:** enquiries@trusselltrust.org

> **Support organisation**
>
> **Relate:** The UK's largest provider of relationship support. There is a useful section on supporting children who have caregivers who are separating
>
> **Website:** www.relate.org.uk **Helpline:** 0808 2000 247
>
> **Email:** relate.enquiries@relate.org.uk

more numerous, but children felt them less intensely. Rauh et al. (2016) evaluated a ten-week French programme for high-conflict separating families, 'Giving Children Hope', which aimed to support families and their children to prevent the triggering of childhood depression, stress and emotional difficulties. The adult component focuses on decreasing conflict and improving parenting while the children's element builds resilience to parental conflict. The outcome of the Rauh et al. (2016) study was that through directed mediation children reported feeling supported and safe and that they were able to have fun during a difficult time, and the caregivers reported being less stressed, having less anger and that the children had fewer behavioural difficulties.

Prison

It is well known that children who have caregivers in prison experience stress prior to, during and on their release from incarceration. They are more likely than any other group of children to experience childhood adversity such as abuse or mental health issues within the household, poverty and drug and alcohol misuse (Turney, 2018). Jones et al. (2013) shared the outcomes of a European report, which examined the health and educational outcomes of children of prisoners. They described the stigma of having a caregiver in prison, which can cause children to be labelled and rejected by peers, to withdraw from social contexts and to be likely to have low self-esteem. One of the key findings of the research was that children with a caregiver in prison were found to have a significantly greater risk of mental health challenges compared to the general population, particularly when they are 11 years +. There are many factors that will impact on the child's response, depending on whether they witnessed the illegal act, what it was and how the parent was arrested (was it confrontational/violent); the child may not know what happened, just that the caregiver has disappeared.

In most cases, a caregiver going to prison will have a detrimental impact on a child's emotional and social wellbeing as they experience feelings such as hopelessness, sadness, isolation, fear, anger, disappointment, frustration and emotional instability. Jones et al. (2013) advocate that for most children regular contact with the imprisoned caregiver is crucial for the child's wellbeing, whether this is direct (face to face) or indirect (letters and phone calls); this is obviously dependent on the offence committed. Schools need to be mindful that having an imprisoned caregiver will likely result in increased demands on older children to contribute to the household. Also, the outcome of the research was that children cope better when they understand the truth about where their parent is and what they did as this prevents them imagining scenarios, as shown below (Figure 6.3).

FIGURE 6.3 Impression of a prison cell

An 8-year-old thought his father's bed was a cage to prevent his escape and described as being under constant observation.

Source: Jones et al. (2013)

Children will also need significant support once a caregiver is released from prison.

Case study

Lara was an only child who lived with her father and uncle. She was 9 when her father was arrested in the family home and subsequently imprisoned for actual bodily harm, burglary and fraud. The school did not know about this for 4 weeks until another child mentioned it in class.

What should the school's response be to this?

What information do they need to find out?

What might the impact be on Lara?

What support could be offered to Lara and her uncle?

ACE-informed approaches

Bellis et al. (2014) conducted a national study of 3,885 English residents aged 18–69 to categorise the number of ACEs they had experienced. They concluded that a stable and protective childhood is the most critical factor in the development of resilience to health-harming behaviours. Nurturing and positive childhood environments are needed to allow children to become resilient to pressures from peers, school and their lived environment. NHS Scotland (2017) recommends early intervention through peer mentoring as a way to share lived experiences through an understanding and nurturing approach. To achieve this, the building of resilience from the early years and supporting families to break the cycle of intergenerational ACEs are fundamental.

Couper and Mackie (2016) advocate that resilience is a positive and adaptive response, which can transform 'toxic stress' into 'tolerable stress'. They add that evidence from research shows that children who do well despite adversity have had at least one stable and committed relationship from either a supportive caregiver or another adult; this could even be a strong relationship with a peer. In addition, children need adults to be vigilant and notice when they are unhappy, stressed or anxious. It is believed that a supportive community may change the likelihood of ACEs continuing into future generations.

Communities and schools are well placed to begin to reduce or prevent ACEs for life long benefits across generations. The community where a child lives will affect their exposure to ACEs; for example, a lack of services, low socio-economic status and access to drugs and alcohol. Schofield et al. (2018) carried out research with 451 two-parent families to examine the intergenerational continuity of ACEs and found that community cohesion is a protective factor in reducing ACEs across generations.

Many caregivers have financial barriers to daily living so schools need to consider the impact of expecting them to contribute to school finances – remember, state education is free for all children. The Department for Education has confirmed that schools cannot require a caregiver or child to pay for, or to have to supply, any equipment for the purposes of their education.

Below are some approaches to addressing adversity and building supportive communities (Table 6.4):

TABLE 6.4 Approaches to addressing adversity and building supportive communities

Theme	ACE approach
School policies	No shouting policy
	Inclusion rather than isolation rooms/places/workplaces
	Relationship-based behaviour policies with reasonable adjustments, de-briefs, understanding and empathy
	Behaviour is telling you a story and staff need to be trained to listen
	Zero tolerance behaviour policies do not allow for this
Staff	Smile and welcome each child by name as they arrive to class
	Positive body language
	Friendly voice tones
	Active listening
	Use of praise
Staff training	For all staff, volunteers and governors on the impact of ACEs
	INSET tasks to discuss useful ACE approaches to be adopted
Reducing toxic stress	Provide supportive relationships to buffer the physiological effects of toxic stress
	Consistent staffing and seating plans
	'Serve and return' conversations with eye contact where the adult is responsive to child
Building community connections	Find out what services, organisations and community groups exist in your local area that would like to work in partnership with your school. My community (www.mycommunity.org.uk) is funded by the Department for Communities and Local Government and gives information and advice to make communities better places to live
Tackling school holiday hunger	There are approximately 170 non-school days where children don't have free school meals. The Trussell Trust can give advice on setting up a holiday club so children have breakfast and lunch; this includes signposting to funding

Theme	ACE approach
Eliminate costs to caregivers for:	Request donations from caregivers when their children have grown out of dress-up/costumes
Costumes for school plays/productions	Community organisations and residents make costumes (e.g. multi-residence housing, nursing/retirement homes, community groups, local community, Women's Institute)
Reducing costs to caregivers	Children all make a Christmas end of year card/gift in school
	Communities/ex-students donate dresses/suits if children request a formal prom
	School bus to take all students to prom
	Local colleges to do hair and nails
Private music tuition in school	Teaching of musical instruments to all children to prevent disadvantage to those who cannot afford the fees
Compulsory purchase of IT equipment, e.g. iPads	Free iPads for low-income families or for children with siblings in school; these must be available for both home and school use. You cannot require a caregiver or child to purchase equipment for school
School trips	School-led trips are free or at a much lower cost than those led by 'leader'. English Heritage and the Forestry Commission provide free, self-led school visits
	Useful website: www.ukschooltrips.co.uk
Collaborative learning techniques	A teacher-led approach for group work which promotes 'talk' and empowers children to work together, nurturing emotional and social development; very good also for children with English as an Additional Language
	Useful website: www.collaborativelearning.org

Further approaches are given below:

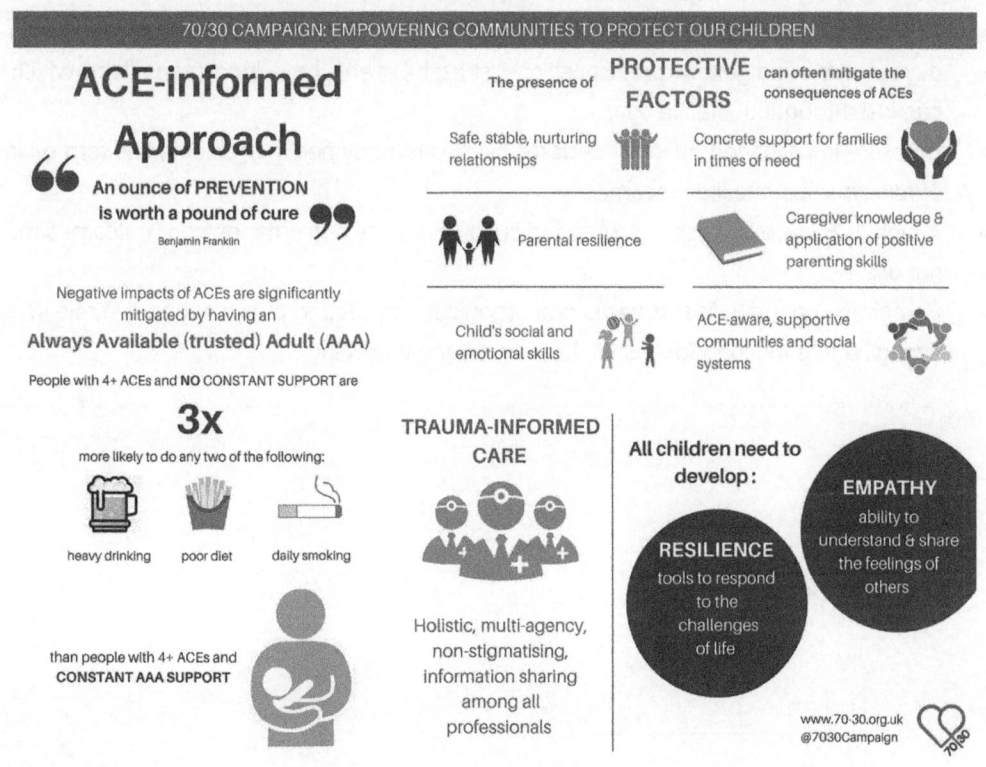

FIGURE 6.4 ACE-informed approaches

Source: www.70-30.org.uk

> **Useful resources**
>
> **CEL&T (Children Experiencing Loss and Trauma):** Provides information for anyone who wants to know about loss and trauma and the impact on children. They offer online eLearning units with CPD hours recognised on certificate of completion and lead ACEs Network North East in collaboration with University of Sunderland, Interdisciplinary Research Network and partner organisations.
>
> **Website:** www.celandt.org   **Email:** celandt@celandt.org
>
> **Beacon House:** They have a particular focus on repairing the effects of trauma and attachment disruption. The resources section on the website is particularly useful as it includes free materials that can be used to develop your own knowledge base and create trauma and attachment strategies for use in the classroom.
>
> **Website:** https://beaconhouse.org.uk   **Email:** admin@beaconhouse.org.uk
>
> **Inner World Work:** A free support resource centre provides a collection of creative works in different formats to support caregivers and professionals working with children who have experienced trauma.
>
> **Website:** www.innerworldwork.co.uk   **Email:** helen@innerworldwork.co.uk

Chapter summary

- ACES are common, with approximately half of those in a recent study having experienced at least one ACE (Bellis et al., 2014)
- It is widely recognised that early experiences and environmental influences shape brain development and genetic predispositions; stressful events have long-term effects which can last throughout the life course
- Exposure to childhood adversity is associated with many health problems, the formation of relationships and life outcomes
- A high ACE score is a risk indicator and is not a definite outcome, as poor outcomes may not occur
- Caregivers, communities, services and organisations need to play a supportive role in strengthening the foundations of child health and wellbeing

7

Meeting the Needs of Looked After and Permanently Placed Children

Sarah Martin-Denham

→ NASENCO outcomes: Strategies for improving outcomes for children with SEN and/or disabilities. To select, use and adapt approaches, strategies and resources to personalise provision for children with SEN and/or disabilities. Inform all staff about the learning needs, emotional, social and mental health needs and achievement of children.
→ Read alongside: Chapter 6: Adverse Childhood Experiences; Chapter 8: Social, Emotional and Mental Health Difficulties

Chapter overview

The intention of this chapter is for you to reflect on the particular needs of looked after children (LAC) and those who are permanently placed, to understand the impact that early life experiences can have on their life course and development. The underlying message is that we need to focus on care, exploring and responding to any developmental gaps while providing a secure base. As SENCO, you need to understand the chronology to relate to the circumstances these children have been exposed to and that have shaped the way they think and respond to school. This chapter will also discuss how to nurture teachers' emotional resilience as they deal with complexities in children's lives.

Leading and Coordinating Provision

Categories of care

The term 'looked after' was introduced under the 1989 Children Act for England and Wales and refers to children to whom the Local Authority (LA) has a set of specific legal duties, which can include accommodating the child and legally obtaining parental responsibility. Children in need is a term used to describe children where there has been a referral to children's social care; an assessment is carried out to determine if they are in need of services. This can include services for family support, leaving care support and adoption support of children with disabilities. Some looked after children no longer live with their birth parents and will not return to their caregivers' home due to state intervention and will reside in foster care, residential care, secure care or in kinship care, as a long-term placement option; other arrangements are as follows:

- Voluntary agreements are where the parents retain legal responsibility for the child.
- Family and friends or kinship care refers to the care of children by a relative, family friend or connected person; the child will usually continue to maintain contact with their birth parent(s) and the Local Authority (LA) may retain legal responsibility depending on which care order is in place for the child, if any.
- Special guardianship was introduced in 2005 as a permanent arrangement without ending the child's ties to their birth parents; it is usually extended family who take on this role as a response to need until the child reaches adulthood; however, a special guardianship can be arranged if the child's parents have died and a guardian is appointed.

The Children Act 1989 states that a child is looked after by a LA if they are provided with accommodation for more than 24 hours. These children can also be subject to a care order (made by the court) or a placement order (a court order which permits a LA to place a child for adoption in a long-term environment). A Fostering for Adoption (FfA) placement is when a looked after child is placed in a foster placement with foster carers who are approved prospective adopters and where adoption is likely to become the outcome; however, this cannot be guaranteed as the child may be returned to their birth family. Concurrent planning refers to situations where the LA is trying to rehabilitate the child with the birth parents, but is also planning for adoption in readiness for the rehabilitation failing.

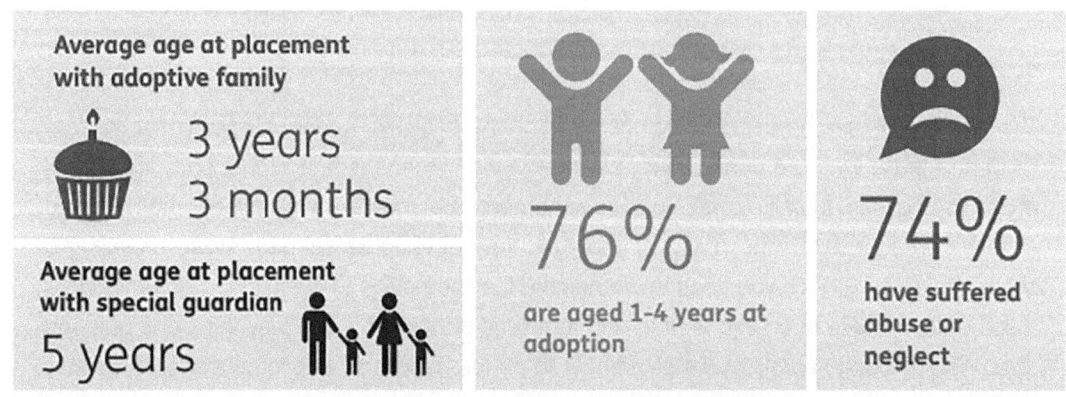

FIGURE 7.1 Statistics for looked after and permanently placed children
Source: PAC-UK (2017) www.pac-uk.org

The number of looked after children has steadily increased over the last nine years. The statistics share that on 31 March 2017 there were 72,670 looked after children in England (DfE, 2017a); however, it must be remembered that more children may enter and leave care during the period of 1 April–31 March in any given year and they will not be counted within the official Office of National Statistics (ONS) data as this only calculates those in 'Care' on 31 March in any given year. It can be seen from the infographic above (Figure 7.1) that the average age of adoption is around the time children begin nursery and school, with an average wait of up to 2 years; however, changes in current policy seek to place children within 26 weeks if adoption is agreed as the best outcome for the child(ren).

Reasons children enter the care system

The chart below (Figure 7.2) shows that following assessment by children's social care, the most prominent primary need for being looked after is abuse or neglect at 62%.

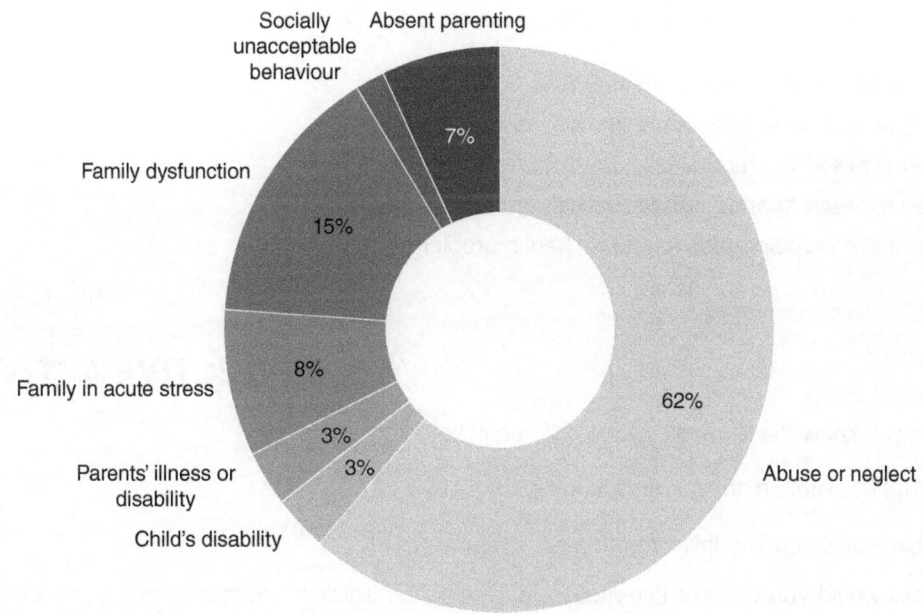

FIGURE 7.2 Chart 1: Proportions of looked after children by category of need
Source: DfE (2017a)

> **Case study**
>
> Monika, age 14, was taken into care aged 2 following systemic abuse within the family, thought to include sexualised abuse though this was unproven. Following the breakdown of four foster placements, Monika was moved out of area and has had a further 13 placements; the current placement is also at risk of failing due to her unpredictable and volatile behaviour towards other adults and peers. The behaviour includes biting, spitting, fighting and criminal damage. She has also begun to display sexualised behaviour towards other children such as exposing herself and encouraging others to abscond for sex.
>
> *(Continued)*

> (Continued)
>
> What could be the reasons for Monika's behaviour?
>
> What is the communication behind the behaviour?
>
> What are the reasons behind the repeated placement breakdown?
>
> What measures could be put in place to reduce the risk of placement breakdown?
>
> How could Monika be supported in developing resilience and appropriate coping strategies?

The designated teacher for looked after and permanently placed children should work alongside you and advise of any changes in children's circumstances, which may impact on their mental health and wellbeing. It is widely believed that permanently placed children and those in other types of placements such as kinship care will need extensive support as they adapt to changes in their circumstances and deal with any childhood adversity; such support needs to be seen in the context of the child's history rather than presumed to be the case. For example, some children may have:

- lost significant relationships in their lives
- experienced some form of neglect and/or maltreatment
- been exposed to prenatal drug and/or alcohol abuse
- been exposed to poor maternal health and/or nutrition
- inherited a predisposition to mental health problems.

(Thomas, 2013)

REFLECTIVE ACTIVITY

Do you know the 'life story' of the children in your context?

What information do you need to know and why?

How would you find this information?

How would you use this information to inform staff training needs and to support individual children?

Trauma and loss

The American Psychological Association (2008: 1) defines a traumatic event as one that threatens injury, death or the physical integrity of self or others and also causes horror, terror or helplessness at the time it occurs. Traumatic events can include sexual abuse, physical abuse, domestic violence, community and school violence, medical trauma, motor vehicle accidents, acts of terrorism, war experiences, natural and human-made disasters, suicides and other traumatic losses.

Trauma and loss in the early years is particularly harmful as it is during this time that the brain is laying down fundamental pathways and connections (www.pac-uk.org). During stressful experiences, the child's body is flooded with stress hormones including high levels of cortisol, and prolonged exposure to this can damage the 'plasticity' of the hippocampus, which is required to adapt to new learning. This can then result in lifelong challenges with working memory and other cognitive functions if intervention is not provided (Simmons and Douglas, 2018). In addition, high levels of stress hormones can impact on immune systems, increasing vulnerability to infections and chronic illness, as seen in adverse childhood experience studies (e.g. Perry and Pollard, 1998). Children who are exposed to violence, abuse or trauma can operate in survival mode if they feel they are under threat; this is an instinctive function and not one of choice, as the brain triggers stress responses commencing in the amygdala, affecting the child's ability to think, retrieve information and manage their behaviour.

Due to what they have experienced prenatally or in childhood, adopted and permanently placed children may have difficulties in some or all of the following areas:

- forming trusting relationships with adults
- developing social skills and relationships with peers
- managing and understanding their feelings
- executive functioning skills, such as planning, organising, remembering, inhibiting their impulses, focusing their attention and initiating tasks
- speech and language
- learning difficulties or disabilities
- coping with transitions and change.

(www.pac-uk.org)

The brainstem is responsible for basic functions such as digestion, heart rate, breathing, hormone regulation and how we respond to stress. This system is divided into the sympathetic nervous system, which is commonly known as the fight/flight/freeze response, while the parasympathetic nervous system is for rest and digest. Rest and digest operates when there is no perceived threat. The brainstem is responsible for managing our survival and functions in the face of threat; in children who have experienced loss and trauma, the stress response activates the instinct to flight, fight or freeze automatically as a survival response to what the child sees as threatening. Overuse of the brain stem comprises the developing prefrontal cortex; this is the area of the brain responsible for empathy, logic, cause and effect and reasoning (Bomber, 2007). Bomber explains that the survival response(s) of flight, fight, freeze are initiated by the amygdala, located in the limbic region of the brain – when there is a perceived or real threat, the child will be overwhelmed as the body is flooded with hormones.

Below are some possible signs that the child is no longer feeling safe (Table 7.1).

TABLE 7.1 Typical responses to flight, fight, freeze and submit

	Flight	**Fight**	**Freeze/submit**
Response	Inability to process information, instructions or discipline		
Physical	Large and darting eyes, restless legs, fidgety, turning/running away, hyperactive, clumsy, disruptive, disrespectful, vigilant, increased heart rate, tense muscles, sweating	Move forward, hitting out, kicking, biting, flexed jaw, grinding teeth, snarling, glaring, argumentative, unable to follow rules, confrontational, loud and noisy	Speechless, shocked, cold, numb, pale skin, holding breath, increased heart rate
Emotional	Restless, anxiety, trapped, manic, aggressive, overwhelmed, terrified, worthless, ugly, not belonging	Anger, rage, tense, terrified, unable to cope, faint, dizzy, worthless	Dread, shutting down, unhappy, withdrawn, anxious, quiet, passive

Leading and Coordinating Provision

Schools need to find ways to support children to understand what is happening in their bodies; in an age-appropriate way these responses need to be explained to them so that they move from 'what is wrong with me' to 'what happened to me' (in terms of the response not reliving their past). When children experience flight/fight/freeze response(s) you and your colleagues will need to support them when they feel unsettled and dysregulated; some of these approaches may be useful:

- breathing exercises
- changing activity or focus (distraction)
- when regulated, ask the child what they do to relax and use this in school; not all children will want to and this needs to be respected
- make a plan with the caregiver so the same approaches are used for consistency or ask the caregiver what works at home and use the same in school.

Brodovsky and Kiernan (2017) provide some useful scripts to support children in making sense of trauma and loss and the fight/flight/freeze response(s) they have. They recommend being engaged in play or informal conversation during the process to make it easier for children to take in the information. An example is given below for talking to children in the fight response (Figure 7.3).

Look at the picture together:

FIGURE 7.3 Discussion prompt

Source: Wikimedia Commons

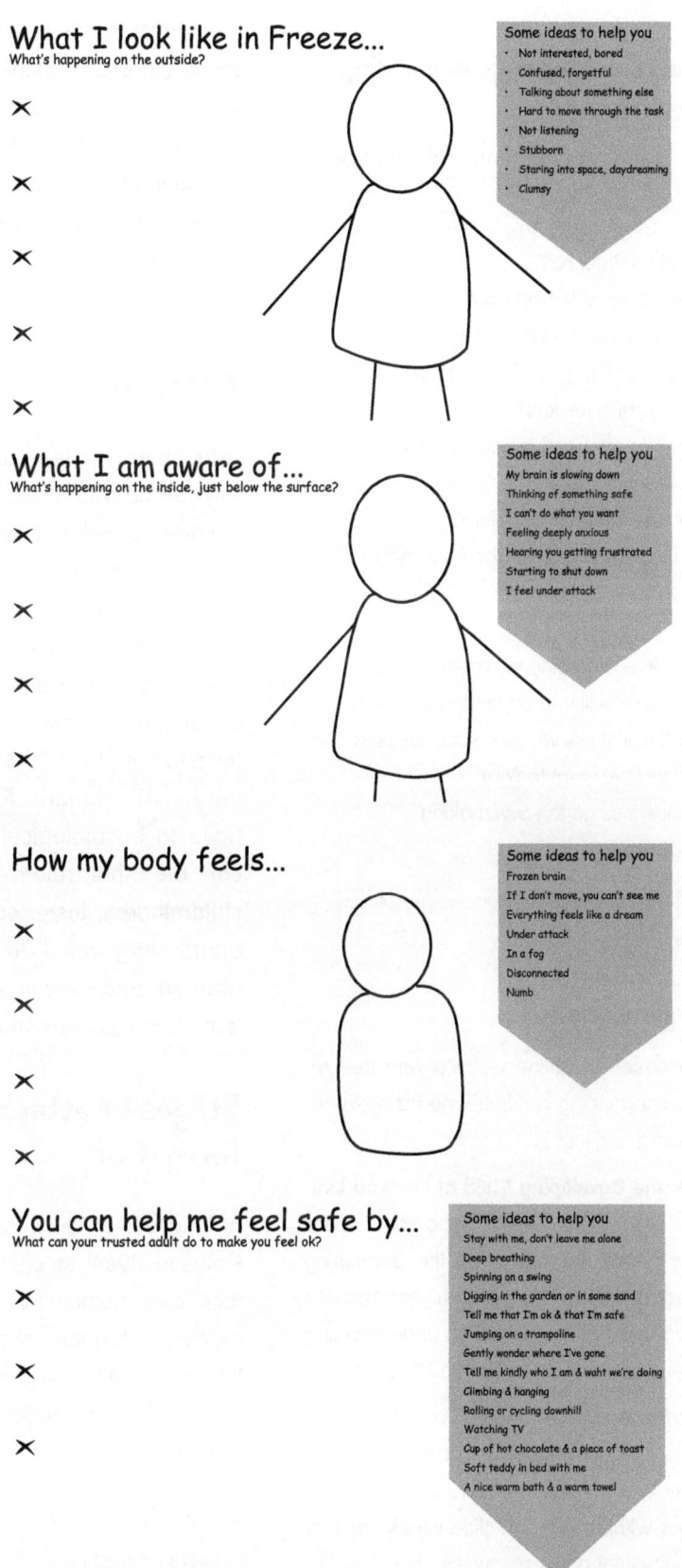

FIGURE 7.4 Discussion task

Source: Townsend (2017)

> **Activity questions (change depending on the age of the child)**
>
> Imagine you are a tiger fighting with another tiger:
>
> - How would the tiger run?
> - What would it do with its claws?
> - Would it roar? (child and adult roar)
> - Notice your breathing, is it fast or slow?
> - How do your muscles feel?
> - Can you tell if your heart is beating fast?
> - How does your body feel?
> - Have you ever felt like this before?
> - How will the tiger feel after the fight, how will his body change? (heart rate, breathing, muscles)
> - Introduce some breathing exercises and talk about what it was like to pretend to be the tiger, how it is just like when we are stressed or scared and we want to fight.
> - For other activities go to www.makingsenseoftrauma.com.

> **Support organisations**
>
> **Beacon House:** An online website with free resources on supporting children who have experienced trauma and loss.
>
> **Center for the Developing Child at Harvard University:** Extensive resources including short videos that show clearly the impact on the developing brain. The director, Jack Shonkoff, is highly regarded in this area and has developed an understanding of the difference between 'stress' and 'toxic stress'.
>
> **Child Trauma Academy:** Provides a library of videos and reading developed by Dr Bruce Perry – internationally respected for his work in this area – their videos within the seven slide series are very short but very informative resources.
>
> **Children Experiencing Loss and Trauma:** www.celandt.org.uk: Provides training across education,

Inner World Work has a useful document, 'What survival looks like for me' – all children who need one of these should have one created with their preferred member of staff and their caregiver. Three images from the resource are shown above (Figure 7.4).

Attachment

Attachment is a term used to describe the dependency relationship that children develop towards their primary caregivers. Children form multiple relationships to 'attachment figures' who provide physical and emotional care, with continuity and consistency, and are emotionally invested in the child's life (Pearce, 2017). Attachment figures do not have to be biological parents, they can be other relatives or siblings, childminders, foster carers or neighbours; they need to be available, attuned and responsive so that a 'safe base' is consistently provided.

Stages of attachment formation

A longitudinal study by Schaffer and Emerson (1964) studied 60 children in their own homes for a period of 18 months. Through observations and interviews with caregivers, they developed an attachment sequence as follows:

- Asocial 0–6 weeks: infants enjoy social and non-social stimulus
- Indiscriminate attachments: 6 weeks to 7 months: human company is enjoyed, smiles are given to regular caregivers

- Specific attachment: 7–9 months: Preference for attachment figures for security and comfort, fear of strangers and upset when separated from caregivers
- Multiple attachment: 10 months+: Can form and sustain multiple attachments.

Bomber (2007) identified some examples of risk factors, which may impact on the quality of attachment to caregivers; these are outlined below (Table 7.2):

> health, care and other services to raise awareness of the impact of adverse childhood experiences across the life course and CPVA and resilience.
>
> **Inner World Work:** An online support and resource centre for caregivers who are supporting traumatised children; it has free whole-school and classroom resources to support professionals.
>
> **NAVSH:** National Association of Virtual School Headteachers is very supportive of schools.
>
> **PAC-UK:** National adoption support for children, families and schools with an education advice line.

TABLE 7.2 Risk factors

Pre-birth stress, mother self-harms or has experience of domestic violence	Born prematurely	Substance misuse during pregnancy
Medical complications in utero	Ante- or post-natal depression	Caregivers with mental health needs
The baby has a disability	Abuse or neglect	Abandonment
Family bereavement	Home instability	Multiple home and school placements

The Department for Education (2018d) concludes that looked after and permanently placed children start with the disadvantage of their pre-care experiences and, often, have special educational needs. Bowlby (1969, 1988) used the concept of 'good enough' parenting – this is where a baby has a positive experience of having their holistic needs met and satisfied consistently, allowing for a secure attachment to be formed. While some children who are looked after, permanently placed or in kinship care will have adapted well to changes in their lives, for others this will not be the case.

The physical survival needs, which include nourishment, protection and warmth, lie alongside the emotional needs to form secure connections with the primary caregivers through their response to a child's communication and interaction. These are essential for children to go on to form other relationships during their lives. Attachment styles describe how a child relates to a 'significant other', and we know that children will relate to others based on the quality of care they received in their early years (Bomber, 2017). However, it is now widely acknowledged that children can form secure and stable attachments later in life despite difficult early experiences if supportive interventions are provided. Within the literature, four attachment styles are identified: secure, avoidant, ambivalent and disorganised; children can have any combination of these.

Securely attached: These children show a preference for contact with the attachment figure(s) but can engage with strangers – if there is no anxiety shown from their caregiver, they have a sense of trust. They have a positive world view and are mostly able to regulate their emotions and explore the world around them with curiosity and confidence.

Insecure avoidant attachment: These children appear to cope with separation from attachment figure but lack a strong emotional connection so appear to have no clear preference for their attachment figure or a stranger. They seem to enjoy solitary activities and appear disinterested in attachment figure following a separation.

Insecure ambivalent attachment: These children are excessively clingy and distressed during separation from their caregiver. When reunited they can be inconsolable, showing obsessive behaviour and even anger.

Insecure disorganised attachment: These children have a need to be in control of everything as they don't want to risk being dependent as it makes them vulnerable. These children are often in survival mode and forming relationships and learning are difficult. They will be hypervigilant, continuously looking for threats, which will be exhausting.

Disorganised/disoriented: These children have no consistent or organised attachment behaviours and display contradictory responses to separation and being reunited.

> ### Case study
>
> Zen, age 11, has a number of diagnosed learning difficulties, and displays a number of indicators of autism, although there is no formal diagnosis. He was taken into care aged 9 following a substantiated disclosure of prolonged physical and sexual abuse in the family home, perpetrated by his father and grandfather. After three placements broke down, he was placed with a specialist care team and was in a stable long-term children's home placement, which was meeting his many needs. In the run-up to Christmas, he was asked to help clear the dishes following tea, after which the house would sit and watch a film. Zen immediately became highly dysregulated and aggressive, he began swearing and shouting, throwing plates and physically assaulted another young person and a member of staff. He was restrained to prevent him from hurting himself or others until he regulated his emotions. Subsequently, it was discovered that his grandfather used a very similar phrase before he abused him, a fact previously unknown to professionals.
>
> - What were the causes of Zen's rapid dysregulation?
> - Why did he present such behaviours?
> - How can colleagues prepare for unknown triggers without compromising the quality of care?

Outcomes

Trauma and loss impact on a child's ability to develop and learn, form relationships and function day to day as they believe the world to be a threatening, intimidating and unpredictable place to be. The impact of their lived experiences is likely to influence their ability to achieve to their full potential, particularly when there isn't a trauma-sensitive school environment. Sebba et al. (2015) argue that these children are disadvantaged educationally compared to the rest of the population and have increased risk of school absence and exclusion.

In the UK, children who have been in care achieve poorer educational outcomes compared to those who were not (DfE, 2018d).

However, what needs to be remembered is that these children may also have SEN or disabilities, in which case it may well be that their performance outcome is a reflection of their learning and

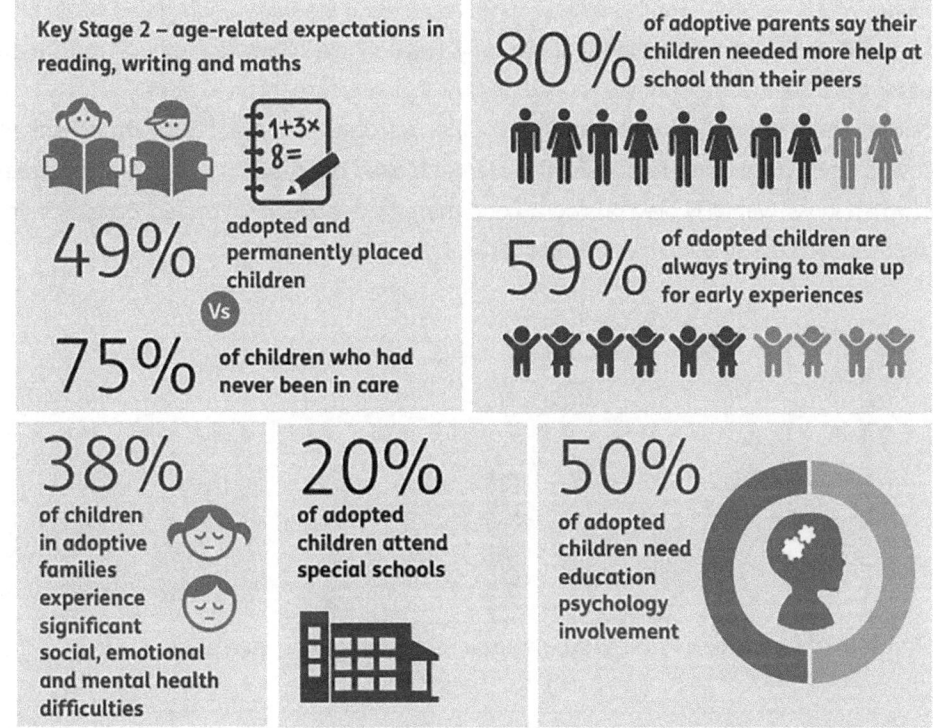

FIGURE 7.5 Key Stage 2 – age-related expectations in reading, writing and maths
Source: PAC-UK (2017) www.pac-uk.org

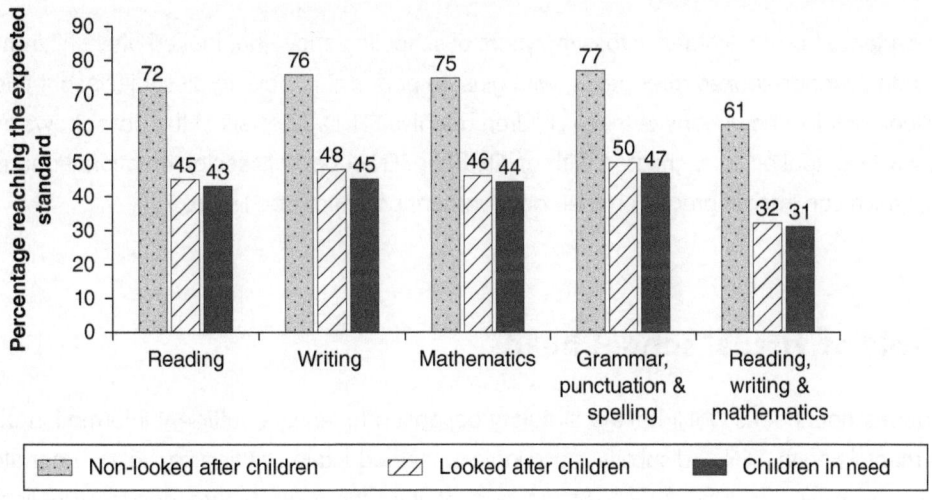

FIGURE 7.6 Percentage reaching the expected standard in Key Stage 2
Source: DfE (2018e)

physical needs rather than their adoptive or looked after status, which was not considered in the PAC-UK infographic (Figure 7.5).

The national data by DfE (2018e) highlights that looked after children perform slightly better than children in need, in achieving expected standards in Key Stage 2; however, both these groups attain much lower than non-looked after children, as shown in Figure 7.6, but again this does not reflect those looked after children who have SEND. For this reason, while recognising the issues highlighted within the statistics, we need to also recognise that these do not provide the whole information schools require, such as the focus on the child, their legal status (looked after) or their educational need (SEND).

National data in England reports that in 2017 the average attainment 8 score for looked after children was much lower than for those who are not looked after (see Figure 7.7); the difference is reduced when those with SEN are considered and more so if those who are looked after with SEND are recognised within SEN data rather than simply 'looked after' data.

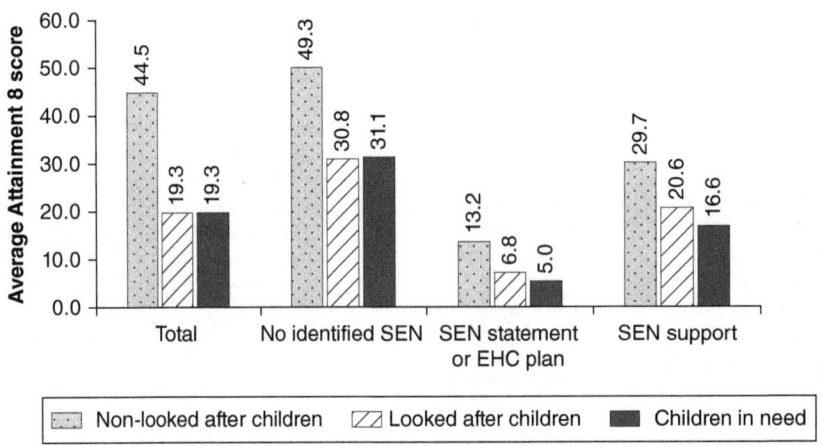

FIGURE 7.7 Average Attainment 8 score

Source: DfE (2018e)

The evidence from outcomes across the years of schooling show that looked after children attain lower than their non-looked after peers, with girls outperforming boys in all subjects, but this does not include detail of how many of these children are also SEND. Analysis of the data shows that the primary SEN for looked after children with an EHCP or SEN support is social, emotional and mental health, which can impact greatly on their achievement potential (see Figure 7.8).

The role of virtual school heads

The virtual school heads (VSH) have a statutory obligation to 'ensure sufficient information about a child's mental health, SEN or disability is available to their education setting so that appropriate support can be provided' (DfE, 2018d: 8). As part of this, the VSH, where possible/applicable in conjunction with an officer, are responsible for making links with mental health services and should work with designated teachers to ensure:

- schools are able to identify signs of potential mental health issues and know how to access further assessment and support where necessary
- schools understand the impact that issues such as trauma and attachment difficulties and other mental health issues can have on looked-after and permanently placed children, and are 'attachment aware'.

(DfE, 2018d)

Meeting the Needs of Looked After and Permanently Placed Children

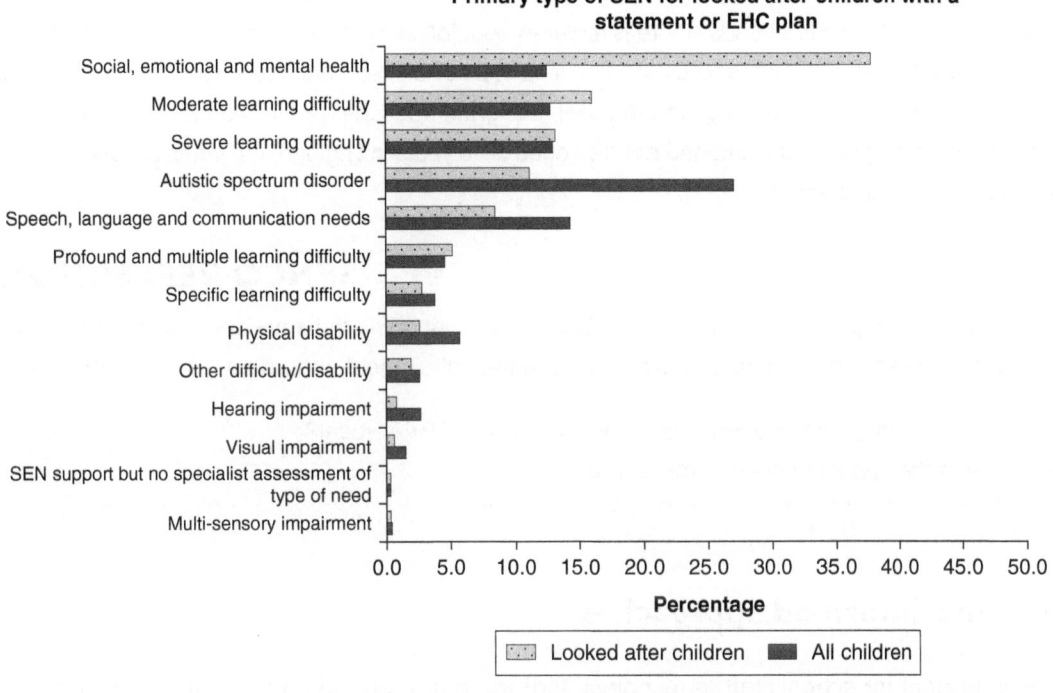

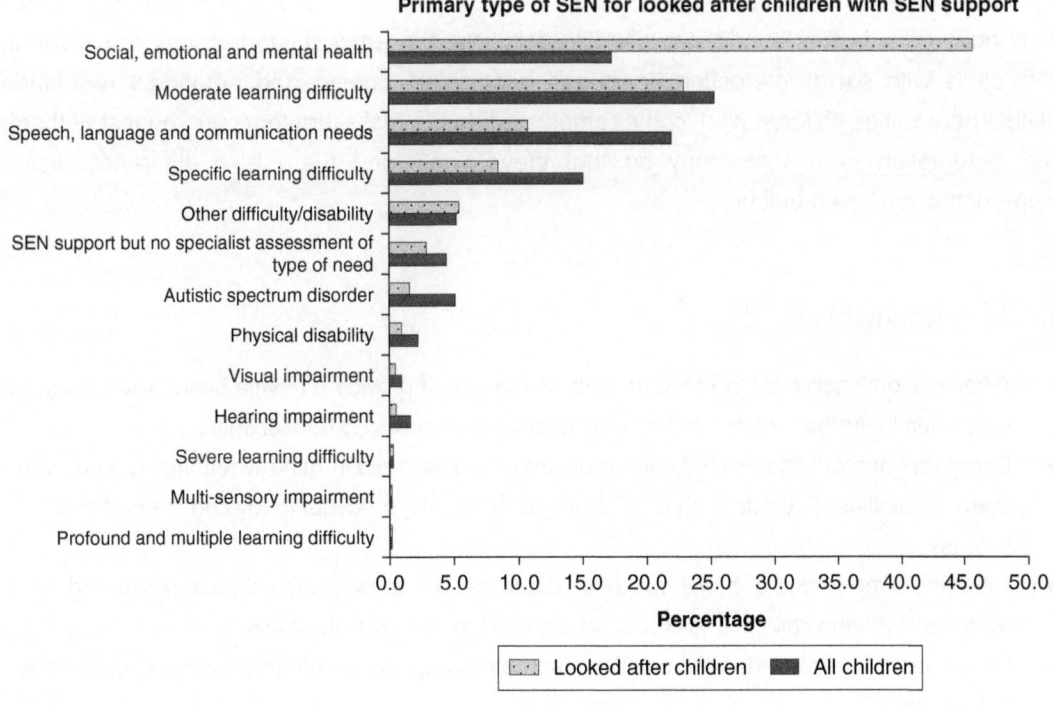

FIGURE 7.8 Looked after children by primary SEN in 2017

Source: DfE (2018e)

The role of designated teachers

The DfE (2018e) states that the statutory role of the designated teacher is to undertake responsibilities within the school to promote the educational achievement of looked after and permanently placed children and in doing so they should have trauma and attachment training to complete their role.

The designated teacher will need to work closely with the SENCO to plan effectively how to assess and provide for the child's needs. There is statutory regulation for the education of LAC and permanently placed children which applies to all teachers, such as Personal Education Plans (PEP), Pupil Premium Plus (PP+) and working with the VSH, designated teacher or LAC coordinator. The PP+ is additional funding for disadvantaged children aged 5–16 years in England; the funds should be used to narrow the attainment gap.

SENCO REFLECTION

The intention of Pupil Premium Plus is that it is spent on supporting the emotional, social and education needs of permanently placed children to raise their attainment and address their wider needs.

- How are caregivers involved in decisions about how PP+ is spent?
- How is the impact of the PP+ measured?

Trauma-informed approaches

It is important for school staff to recognise that trauma or loss in early childhood impacts on the development of the child as they have not had their holistic needs met. Due to this they may have gaps in the foundations usually established in early childhood; this can result in difficulties with social interaction, language acquisition, coping and emotional regulation skills. There will be children who *'can't'* comply and do the tasks that teachers request of them; the assumption from some may be that they *'won't'* and there is a difference. Some approaches are given below.

Build relationships

- A key person (chosen by the child) to take on the role of providing a 'safe base'. This should be supported by further adults who develop positive and enduring relationships.
- Caregivers and adults to let the child know they hold the child in mind when they are not with them – transitional objects such as a photograph, scents, or favourite toy can support this process.
- Following a reprimand at home or school, adults need to seek out the child to repair and reconnect with the child; this is crucial for the child to reduce toxic stress.
- Use of supportive phrases such as: 'You found the group work a bit hard today, what can I do to help you?'

Structure and routine

- Use of visual timetables, now and next boards, colour-coded timetables at home and school; let the child know in advance of any changes to routines.
- When a new staff member will be joining the class, give the child a photograph so they become familiar with who is arriving and when.

Coping with feelings

- Create an ability age-appropriate safe space which is available with a familiar adult, and allow the child a 'pass' card or similar to show when they are beginning to feel overwhelmed so they are allowed to go to the safe space without telling the whole class. The safe space needs monitoring to see if there are particular times, days or lessons that children are finding more difficult to enable effective intervention to be planned and reduce the frequency of use. Children need to discuss this so they know it is not an opt-out for a particular lesson. There needs to be a member of staff present to support and monitor the child who can paint/colour/read or just sit quietly until they feel they can return to class.
- Find out what helps to relax and calm them; this could be listening to music, smells, feeling textures, yoga, running or squeezing a toy. Items could be stored in a box in the safe place so they are readily available for the child.
- Mindfulness techniques to ground and settle their anxiety; this could include a listening walk, weighted blanket or breathing exercises.

Nurture groups

- Provide a family-like environment to build early foundations, which may have been missed in the early years, such as reading with an adult, exploring outdoors and sharing a meal/snack. Lego therapy is often used in nurture groups.

Supportive transitions

- Share changes in advance such as room/staff changes, supply cover, trips, menu changes, school closure days; share these on a visual schedule.
- Visit new schools in advance and after school hours; consult the child and family about how to manage and prepare for transitions.

(Adapted from Beacon House and Inner World Work)

Care approaches

Pearce (2017) provides a CARE approach – 'consistency, accessibility, responsiveness and emotional connectedness' – to support children by creating environments to support the development of positive attachments (see Table 7.3).

We need to create environments that are responsive to the needs of those who have experienced childhood trauma.

Colleagues need to:

- understand the impact of trauma and how it affects children through ongoing training
- recognise the signs of trauma and the varying ways it can present

Leading and Coordinating Provision

- understand the implications of childhood adversity
- buy into the need to support and regulate traumatised children
- connect with the child and repair relationships
- have effective practices and procedures that inter-play in all aspects of school life and culture
- understand that challenging and other behaviours may occur as a result of trauma
- ask 'What has happened to this child to shape these behaviours?'

These ideas have been simplified into a useful diagram (Figure 7.9) to illustrate the importance of supporting children to learn, think and reflect, through following the simple sequence of 'the three Rs' to reach the learning brain.

TABLE 7.3 Care approaches

CARE approach	Experience of care	Protective factors	Risk factors
Consistency	• Consistent response to cues, signals and behaviours through a stable environment	Good parenting Positive relationships with schools and other professionals Positive attitudes Empathy Training of staff	Mental health of the caregiver Domestic violence Substance misuse Inadequate parenting Lack of staff knowledge and understanding of attachment and trauma
Accessibility	• Consistent staff who knows their needs • Staff present and available both physically and emotionally • Offer comfort to buffer stress		
Responsiveness	• Knowing the child's signals • Responding with understanding		
Emotional connectedness: 'affective attunement'	• Attachment figures tuned into expressed emotions by reflecting the same or similar emotions back through tone of voice, facial expressions and gesture		

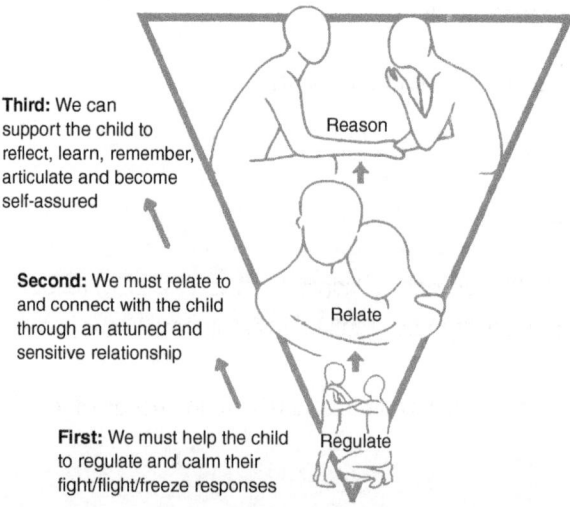

Third: We can support the child to reflect, learn, remember, articulate and become self-assured

Second: We must relate to and connect with the child through an attuned and sensitive relationship

First: We must help the child to regulate and calm their fight/flight/freeze responses

FIGURE 7.9 The three 'Rs'
Source: Beacon House Therapeutic Services Team and Bruce Perry

Case study

The following section is written by 'Lou' who adopted two boys, who share their views on the perfect school.

The children

Alfred is 12, in Year 8 in a mainstream comprehensive, and he has avoidant attachment disorder. His brother Jacob is 9, in Year 4 in a mainstream primary school, and has ambivalent attachment disorder. They have been part of our family for 6.5 years and prior to joining us they spent 15 months in foster care, having been removed from their birth parents by social services. Their background is one of severe neglect and possible physical abuse, known domestic violence witnessed by Alfred, potentially by Jacob. There was a history of drug abuse by birth father and birth mother struggled with mental health issues.

The perfect school would:

- Understand and meet the individual needs of the boys, and would acknowledge that age is not a factor in their behaviour. Alfred may be 12 on the outside, but on the inside, he is about 8
- Recognise that length of time in placement does not magically make the attachment issues disappear
- Encourage open dialogue with us as caregivers, we can be your best resource in knowing our child and how to reach them and make them feel safe when they enter survival mode
- Understand what survival mode means to my child; what they look like, what they are aware of, what their body feels like and what is happening in their inner world

The children's views

In a perfect world my teacher will:

Alfred

- Nurture me
- Help me understand my feelings, by asking 'I wonder if you are....?' (name the feeling)
- Allow me to work in small groups with different children each time
- Praise me regularly, I fear failure
- Know I cannot cope being centre of attention, do not single me out in class, I might freeze
- Not ask me in front of the class for my homework, I worry it will be wrong
- Know that I am easily bullied, but will tell you everything is alright

Jacob

- Give me a visual timetable and instructions
- Give me a consistent and structured routine
- Explain tasks in small steps
- Say hello to me as I come into class and bye when I leave
- Give me a quiet space I can go to
- Help me with friendships and sorting out problems
- Help me when I am anxious and stressed

(Continued)

(Continued)

You need to know:

- What I am good at (maths, drawing, helping others, listening)
- What I find hard (being told I am wrong, being told no – I see it as rejection)
- What I look like when I am struggling (I won't ever admit I find something hard, that admits failure)

Lou's wishlist

- To call a child by their chosen name (not their legal name if different), which should be agreed prior to the child starting at the school
- To have one consistent teacher who understands attachment
- To not judge behaviour but focus on their needs
- To care about their wellbeing and that of the wider family
- To talk to all children about different families (stonewall resources)
- To work together throughout the year and not just when things go wrong
- To be accessible, have one point of contact who knows the child and caregiver so you don't have to tell the story again and again
- To have a SEN plan, pupil profile or working together plan (see Chapter 11) written with child and caregivers (begin with strategies which are based on them feeling safe/secure)
- To give him transitional objects: 'look after this for me, whilst we…'
- To notice him and keep him in mind: 'I thought of you when…'
- To give him extra support in transitions (day to day if outside of the classroom)

To conclude this chapter it is important to consider how best to support colleagues with their mental health and wellbeing. Below you will find the contact details for Education Support Partnership, an organisation which provides a range of services including factsheets, blogs, counselling, a free stress test and financial advice.

Support for teachers' mental health and wellbeing

Education Support Partnership: www.educationsupportpartnership.org.uk: The UK's only charity providing mental health and wellbeing support services to all education staff and organisations.

Telephone: 08000 562 561

Support organisations for schools and caregivers

Beacon House: www.beaconhouse.org.uk: An online website with free resources on supporting children who have experienced trauma and loss.

Children Experiencing Loss and Trauma: www.celandt.org.uk: Provides training across education, health, care and other services to raise awareness of the impact of adverse childhood experiences across the life course as well as CCVAB and resilience.

Inner World Work: www.innerworldwork.co.uk: An online support and resource centre for caregivers who are supporting traumatised children, it has free whole-school and classroom resources to support professionals.

Center for the Developing Child at Harvard University: https://developingchild.harvard.edu/resources has extensive resources including short videos that show clearly the impact on the developing brain. The director, Jack P. Shonkoff, M.D. is highly regarded in this area and has developed an understanding of the difference between 'stress' and 'toxic stress'.

Child Trauma Academy: http://childtrauma.org/cta-library provides a library of videos and reading developed by Dr Bruce Perry – internationally respected for his work in this area – their videos within the seven slide series are very short but very informative resources.

Chapter summary

- Flight, fight and freeze responses occur when the nervous system is overwhelmed and disconnects the body and mind
- The term 'attachment' is used to describe the relationship of dependency between a child and their caregiver(s)
- Children can have more than one attachment figure and it may not be an immediate family member. It will be someone who has an emotional investment in the child's life
- Attachment develops through early experiences and there are different types of attachment depending on the dimensions of CARE the child has received
- Positive attachments are needed to develop resilience to adversity and your colleagues will need to understand this through high-quality training
- Traumatic events impact on a child's sense of the world and their behaviours
- Symptoms of trauma can resurface until they are processed and understood by the child
- One committed adult at school can make a positive difference to a child and their family

8

Social, Emotional and Mental Health Difficulties

Sarah Martin-Denham

- NASENCO outcome: How children's development is affected by SEN and/or disabilities, including mental health needs.
- Read alongside: Chapter 6: Adverse Childhood Experiences; Chapter 7: Meeting the Needs of Looked After and Permanently Placed Children; Chapter 9: Neurodiversity; Chapter 10: Learning and Physical Disabilities

Chapter overview

The intention of this chapter is to support SENCOs in providing appropriate support and intervention for children and adolescents experiencing a range of mental health challenges, as you wait for assessment, diagnosis and guidance from health services.

Definition of mental health

Parkinson (2012: 12) argues that mental health is a much-debated concept, with no universally accepted definition or consistency in use of terminology. She further discussed complexities over the use of language, as education professionals will often refer to social and emotional wellbeing and resilience whereas health colleagues use the term 'mental health'. For the purposes of this chapter, the term 'mental health' will be used and includes 'social and emotional wellbeing'. The World Health Organization (WHO) (2018: 12) defines mental health as 'a state of wellbeing in which the individual realises his or her own abilities, can cope with the normal stresses of life, can work productively and fruitfully, and is able to contribute to their community'. Mental health difficulties encompass a wide range of mental and behavioural difficulties described in the World Health Organization International Statistical Classification of Diseases (ICD) and Related Health Problems (10th and upcoming 11th edition, ICD-10 and ICD-11); psychiatrists will tend to use this system to diagnose mental health needs. These include: depression, BAD, schizophrenia, anxiety, substance misuse, and intellectual disabilities and developmental and behavioural difficulties that typically arise from childhood through adolescence, including autism. DSM-5 is also used to diagnose mental illness and is broadly based on the ICD classification, providing clear definitions and patterns of symptoms. Within DSM-5 Asperger's Syndrome was removed as a separate diagnosis and is replaced with 'Autism Spectrum Disorder'.

What are social, emotional and mental health needs?

Social, emotional and mental health difficulties are one of the four broad areas of need as set out in the Code (DfE, 2015a: 98). There are children who are more susceptible to developing mental health challenges, including those who are looked after, previously looked after, victims of abuse or exploitation, those with disabilities or long-term health needs and those within the criminal justice system (The Mental Health Taskforce, 2016). These difficulties will vary in duration, intensity and in the impact they have on the child, their needs and behaviours and the extent to which they will impede their ability to participate and learn in school. It is important to note that, as SENCO, you are not qualified to diagnose any mental health needs that children present with. There will be co-existence, for example if a child self-harms they may be depressed and/or have anxiety and/or suicidal thoughts and may have other health or learning needs. Mental health needs can lapse and return or remain throughout childhood into adulthood and if not addressed are linked to a higher probability of school drop-out/exclusion, teenage pregnancy, unemployment and criminality (Beecham, 2014). Furthermore, ill mental health can manifest in challenging or concerning behaviours, which could be a result of a child being unable or reluctant to effectively communicate their needs. It is important you consider that in some cases their mental health needs could be due to another underlying factor, such as undiagnosed autism, a learning disability or unidentified learning needs.

The DfE (2015a) Code outlines that children may experience a wide range of social and emotional difficulties, which manifest themselves in many ways. These may include becoming withdrawn or isolated, as well as displaying challenging, disruptive or disturbing behaviours. These behaviours may reflect underlying mental health difficulties such as anxiety or depression, self-harming, substance misuse, eating disorders or physical symptoms that are medically unexplained. Other children may have other challenges such as Attention Deficit Disorder (ADD), Attention Deficit Hyperactive Disorder (ADHD) or Attachment Disorder. In an ideal world we would have the resources and training across the disciplines of health, education and care to identify early and intervene when a child is in need of support to prevent more serious difficulties arising. Sadly, due to pressures on health services, this is not the case, so it is becoming increasingly the role of the SENCO and school staff to 'use their best endeavours' to begin to meet the needs of these children and to support their peers who witness or who are exposed to their ill mental health. In order to do this well, we first need to understand why most children develop or have mental health difficulties. There needs to be a shift in thinking from 'What is wrong with this child?' to 'What has happened to this child?' and how we can best support them. To do this, you will need to develop a mental health policy (see whole-school approaches in the section on depression).

Longfield (2017) provided the government response to the consultation on transforming the mental health and wellbeing of children. She suggested the following areas of good practice:

- Every child benefits from teaching and a school environment which helps them build emotional resilience.
- Any child who needs it can access early support when problems begin to emerge.
- Children with serious needs can access high-quality, specialist support within clear waiting time standards.
- With in-patient care that children access this without delay, as close to their home as possible and for no longer than is necessary.
- To integrate in-patient services with community services.

As part of the mental health and wellbeing reforms, the DoH and DfE (2017) have shared three key elements (pillars) to tackling early signs of mental health issues:

1. Schools will be incentivised to have a designated senior lead for mental health and wellbeing who will be the link for schools and colleges for rapid advice, consultation and signposting.
2. New mental health support teams, supervised by NHS staff, will provide additional capacity for early intervention and ongoing support; this will be managed jointly with schools.
3. There will be a trial for a 4-week waiting time for access to specialist NHS mental health services.

The government has confirmed that it will support schools through whole-school approaches, commitment from senior leaders and support externally through mental health awareness training.

The role of the designated senior lead for mental health

It is anticipated the role will include:

- oversight of the whole-school approach to mental health and wellbeing, including its reflection in behaviour and curriculum policies, how staff are supported and how children and caregivers are engaged
- supporting the identification of 'at risk' children

- having knowledge and links with local mental health services and referring children to them when appropriate
- oversight of any interventions being delivered in the school
- supporting staff who are in contact with children with mental health needs
- overseeing the outcomes of interventions for children's education and wellbeing.

REFLECTIVE TASK

Consider the provision you have in place to support all children as a preventative measure for ill mental health:

- What universal strategy and approaches are in place for all children?
- What bespoke or group provision is in place?
- Who decides who accesses the provision and what are the criteria?
- How is the impact of the provision evaluated?
- How could the provision be further developed?

Ill mental health in children

NHS England (2017) reports that 1 in 10 children aged 5–16 have a diagnosable mental health need. We know that adverse childhood experiences compound the risk of anxiety and depression. The infographic below (Figure 8.1) illustrates that mental health challenges often develop early.

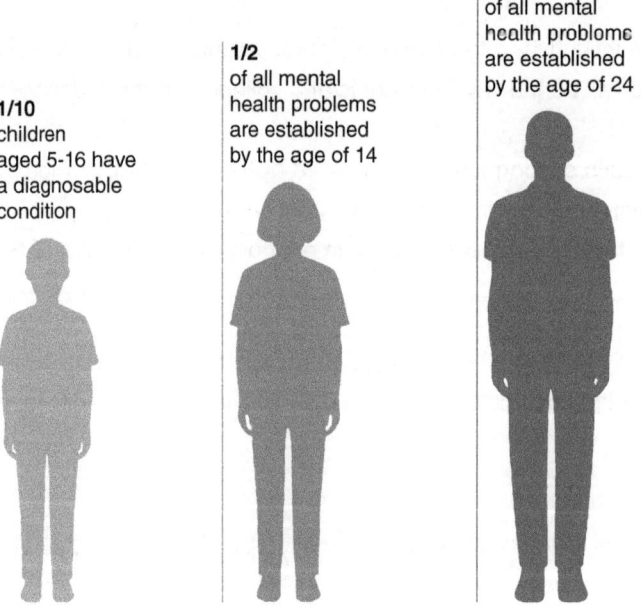

FIGURE 8.1 Prevalence of ill mental health

Source: The Mental Health Taskforce (2016)

The Department of Health (DoH, 2015) advises that these mental health needs range from short spells of depression or anxiety through to severe and persistent conditions that can isolate, disrupt and frighten those who experience them. Severe Mental Illness (SMI) is when psychological challenges are so great that the person is unable to function in activities; schizophrenia and BAD are often referred to as an SMI (Public Health England, 2018). It adds that poor physical health is common in people with SMI as is a premature death from health conditions (estimated to be 15–20 years sooner than the general population).

The DoH and DfE (2017) share that the prevalence of mental health needs varies by age, gender, ethnicity, sexuality and exposure to childhood adversity. Adversity and multiple disadvantages in childhood, as well as abuse and neglect, and caregiver mental health problems, are some of the factors associated with an increased risk of mental health problems in both childhood and adulthood. The Mental Health Taskforce (2016) recommends that local communities work together to raise awareness of good physical and mental health support to challenge the stigma around ill mental health.

REFLECTIVE ACTIVITY

We all have mental health in the same way we have physical health.

How do you start conversations about mental health with children, caregivers and colleagues?

How does your school challenge the stigma and discrimination of ill mental health?

General indicators of social, emotional and mental health difficulties

The grid below (Table 8.1) outlines some key indicators of ill mental health; it is important to note that children will experience stress and anxiety and this is a normal part of growing up. Childline (2018) states that if negative or stressful thoughts happen all the time and these thoughts start to affect daily life, there may be a mental health issue. As SENCO, you and your colleagues need to focus on the needs of the individual child and understand that there is variance; it is good practice to develop Individual Healthcare Plans to ensure systems are in place for those causing concern (see Chapter 9). As SENCO, you need to promote whole-school approaches to mental health and wellbeing as being 'everybody's business'. This will involve working in partnership with governors, senior leaders, teachers and all school staff as well as caregivers, health services and the wider community.

TABLE 8.1 Key indicators of ill mental health

Younger children	Older children	All ages
Become irritable, tearful or clingy	• Lack the confidence to try new things or seem unable to face simple, everyday challenges • Find it hard to concentrate	• Are prone to angry outbursts without a known reason • Start avoiding everyday activities, such as seeing friends, going out in public • Reduced school attendance • Withdrawn
Have difficulty sleeping, start wetting the bed	• Have problems with sleeping or eating	
Wake in the night, have bad dreams	• Have negative thoughts going round and round their head, or keep thinking that bad things are going to happen	

Source: NHS Scotland (2017)

Health and Wellbeing Agenda

The National Association of Head Teachers (2018) reported that 45% of school leaders have found it difficult to commission mental health support for their children. The key findings of the research based on responses from 655 school leaders, published by Place2Be, was that 44% of the respondents claimed that knowing what type of support was needed was a barrier to providing mental health support as was funding. Longfield (2017) highlights the discrepancy between child and adult mental health services, showing local areas spend on average 6% of their budget on children despite them making up around 20% of the population. Crenna-Jennings and Hutchinson (2018) examined the demand for children's mental health services: who was referred for support and how many weren't accepted. Their findings were:

- The number of referrals to specialist CAMHS has increased by 26% over the last five years.
- Between ⅕ and ¼ of those referred to specialist services are not deemed appropriate for specialist services (approximately 55,800 children).
- Limited or no follow-up after a referral was deemed inappropriate.
- Self-harm is not always sufficient to trigger access to specialist services.
- The average waiting time in 2017–18 was 34 days to assessment and 60 days to treatment.

The NHS (2017) has set out its ambition over the next five years, which is to support Clinical Commissioning Groups to work with partners to build effective, evidence-based, outcome-focused Child and Adolescent Mental Health Services (CAMHS), working in collaboration with children and families. CAMHS support children who have challenges with their emotional, behavioural and mental health difficulties with a team usually consisting of psychologists, psychiatrists, social workers, nurses, support workers, occupational therapists, psychological therapists, link workers and specialist substance abuse workers (NHS, 2017). Due to waiting times for appointments, there is increased pressure on pediatricians in clinics to support children and families. In spite of this, school staff are at the frontline of supporting children with SEMH needs, often with little or low quality training. Longfield (2017) reported survey results from headteachers found over half thought CAMHS services were poor and 65% were unable to secure support for their children who needed it. There is also regional variation: in one area 75% of referrals are turned away for assessment or treatment, and the average waiting time for 'life-threatening conditions' is 16 weeks. Although there is funding from government for a teacher in every school to be trained in mental health first aid through a two-day programme, this cannot prepare for the number and range of SEMH issues that present in children. Furthermore, this does not qualify those trained to identify mental health needs but instead to offer initial support and to signpost to support services to address the underlying causes. As Pienaar and Johnston (2018) state, schools are excellent at pastoral care but this is often a reactive response as mental health challenges arise whereas what we need to be doing is early identification in addressing the root causes that affect children's wellbeing.

When a child or young person is experiencing difficulties and there is a concern about their mental health they are usually identified within 'Tier 1' services. This would include SENCOs and teachers; the concerns could be identified by the school or through caregivers. There can then be a referral for assessment and intervention can be made to CAMHS.

Services (Tiers 1–4) are listed below. Referral times and processes will vary between local authorities.

Tier 1: Universal provision, by non-specialists in settings such as schools. It includes early intervention and preventative programmes aimed at improving wellbeing and resilience.

Tier 2: Child and adolescent mental health services relating to workers in primary care including clinical child psychologists, paediatricians with specialist training in mental health, educational psychologists, child and adolescent psychiatrists, child and adolescent psychotherapists, counsellors, community nurses/nurse specialists and family therapists.

Tier 3: Specialised child and adolescent mental health services for more severe, complex or persistent disorders including child and adolescent psychiatrists, clinical child psychologists, nurses (community or inpatient), child and adolescent psychotherapists, occupational therapists, speech and language therapists, art, music and drama therapists, and family therapists.

Tier 4: Child and adolescent mental health services such as day units, highly specialised outpatient teams and inpatient units. A child can be sectioned and kept in hospital under the Mental Health Act 1983, if their own health and/or safety are at risk, or to protect other people.

Children and Young People Service (CYPS)

This is a single service provided for children, usually 0–18 years, who are presenting with mental health difficulties. In some NHS trusts or Local Authorities, this service was formerly known as CAMHS, and in other areas both CAMHS and CYPS exist, so find out which model is used in your own local area.

Generic assessment tools for SEMH

There is a range of assessment tools available for use in schools. They all have benefits and limitations in their use, and it is recommended that these are not used in isolation as a sole measure, as formalised identification and assessment must be via health services.

The Boxhall Profile is a resource for the assessment of children's social, emotional and behavioural development (from 3–16 years). It involves the completion of a two-part checklist by staff, which identifies the levels of skill the children have to access learning. It supports early identification, assessment, individualised target setting, intervention and tracking of progress.

The Strengths and Difficulties Questionnaire (SDQ) is widely used worldwide by researchers, mental health practitioners and education professionals to assess the mental health needs of children aged 2–17 years. The questionnaire asks about a child's psychosocial attributes (positive and negative behaviours), with caregivers and teachers each completing independently. The questions are grouped into five sub-scales: four measure difficulties and the other pro-social behaviour, and the responses to these give an overall difficulty score ranging from 0–40. The thresholds were created by comparing SDQ scores with psychiatric judgements of interviews with 10,000 caregivers of children in the UK (Goodman et al., 2000).

Evidence-based interventions and approaches

Evidence-based practice is when professionals use knowledge and understanding gained from research evaluations of interventions to improve their pedagogical approaches. O'Reilly and Parker (2013: 16) state that the concept of evidence-based practice has become synonymous with robustness and quality.

SENCO ACTIVITY

Consider the range of interventions you use in your context to support those with mental health needs. What is the evidence base that suggests they are effective and have a positive impact on children's emotional wellbeing?

Self-reflection activity

TABLE 8.2 Relevance of intervention/teaching approach checklist*

Consideration	Evidence base/notes	Action
➢ What is the evidence base that the intervention is necessary?		
➢ What is the evidence base that the intervention or approach has a positive impact?		
➢ Are colleagues including senior leaders supportive of a new intervention?		
➢ What additional training is needed prior to beginning the intervention?		
➢ How and when will you evaluate the impact of the intervention? Are monitoring systems in place and are they fit for purpose?		

*see Appendix and online resources for assessment template

The Education Endowment Fund (EEF) (2019) provides accessible summaries of international educational research based on children aged 5–16 years within the teaching and learning toolkit. These are useful for SENCOs and Senior Leadership Teams when looking at outcomes of interventions versus costs. The EEF (2019) breaks down the social, emotional learning interventions into three broad categories:

1. Universal programmes which generally take place in the classroom
2. More specialised programmes, which are targeted at students with particular social or emotional problems
3. School-level approaches to developing a positive school ethos, which also aim to support greater engagement in learning.

The EEF evaluates projects and research in terms of the cost and the impact; for example, 'Magic Breakfast'. The aim of the project was to improve attainment outcomes by increasing the number of children who ate a healthy breakfast. The schools in the project were schools in England with a relatively high proportion of disadvantaged children. Schools were provided with free food, support from a Magic Breakfast school change leader and a £300 grant towards up-front costs (see Table 8.3).

TABLE 8.3 Cost and progress comparison

Group and outcome	Number of schools	Estimated months progress	EEF cost rating
Year 2: KS1 maths	102	+2	£££££
Year 2: KS1 reading	102	+2	£££££

Evaluation of 'Magic Breakfast' schools shows that schools should consider breakfast clubs as a cost-effective way to raise pupil attainment. By clicking on the 'big picture' section on the EEF website you can filter interventions by 13 themes, including behaviour, literacy, mathematics, parental engagement and character and essential life skills.

The range of social, emotional and mental health difficulties

This section will explore a range of mental health challenges children encounter, and at the end of each section you will find a list of useful websites, books and resources. There are also outlines of whole-school and classroom approaches, where you will see that these are good practice for all children regardless of individual needs. Children with learning disabilities are particularly susceptible to ill mental health as often their needs are not recognised as the focus is on their behaviour not the cause; 1 in 3 or 36% of children with learning disabilities will have a diagnosable psychiatric need (Youngminds, 2019). When a child has a learning disability the following changes in behaviour may indicate a mental health difficulty:

- loss of skills or needs more prompting to use skills
- social withdrawal
- irritability
- avoidance
- agitation
- loss of interest in activities they usually enjoy.

(NICE, 2016a)

The increased risk of having a mental health need is across all types of psychiatric difficulties for children with learning disabilities; this is worsened for those where there are greater levels of support needed and who have challenges communicating feelings or distress. Children with learning disabilities are:

- 33 times more likely to have autism
- 8 times more likely to have ADHD
- 4 times more likely to have emotional difficulties
- 3 times more likely to experience schizophrenia.

(Youngminds, 2019)

Anxiety

Definition

The National Institute for Health and Care Excellence (NICE) (2011) defines generalised anxiety disorder (GAD) as one of a range of anxiety disorders that includes panic disorder (with and without agoraphobia), post-traumatic stress disorder, obsessive compulsive disorder, social phobia, specific phobias (for example, of spiders) and acute stress disorder. Anxiety disorders can exist in isolation but more commonly occur with other anxiety and depressive disorders.

Causes

The NHS (2018a) explains that the exact cause of anxiety is not fully understood, though several factors play a role, such as overactivity in areas of the brain involved in emotions and behaviour. Also, there is an imbalance in the brain chemicals serotonin and noradrenaline, which regulate mood. It adds that genetics increase the likelihood of developing anxiety and that a history of stressful or traumatic experience, such as child abuse or bullying, is a factor.

Prevalence

The Department of Health (2015) reports that 3.3% or about 290,000 children have an anxiety disorder; however, recent indicators point to this being as high as 60% in secondary schools during exam periods. Anxiety disorders are particularly common in children with learning disabilities who have Autism, as they are more likely to have difficulty coping with adverse events or communicating their needs (NICE, 2016a).

Indicators

The NHS (2018a) lists the signs of anxiety as:

- finding it hard to concentrate
- not sleeping, or waking in the night with bad dreams
- not eating properly
- quickly getting angry or irritable, and being out of control during outbursts
- constantly worrying or having negative thoughts
- feeling tense and fidgety, or using the toilet often
- always crying
- being clingy
- complaining of tummy aches and feeling unwell.

Separation anxiety is common in younger children, whereas older children and teenagers tend to worry more about school or have social anxiety. It is worth remembering that many of the indicators are also normative age-stage development for teenagers, which makes anxiety harder to identify in this age group.

Assessment/diagnosis

NICE (2011) outlines that a formal diagnosis using the DSM-IV classification system (the universal authority for psychiatric diagnosis) will occur through the NHS and requires two major symptoms (excessive anxiety and worry about a number of events and activities, and difficulty controlling the worry) and three or more additional symptoms from a list of six. Symptoms should be present for at least six months and should cause clinically significant distress in social, occupational or other important areas of functioning.

Treatment

The NHS (2018a) suggests counselling can help children understand what's making them anxious and allow them to work through the situation. This can take different forms and should be based on an assessment of the best approach for the child. Cognitive Behavioural Therapy (CBT) is a talking therapy that can help the child manage their anxiety by changing the way they think and behave. However, it is well documented and recognised that if the child's anxiety is due to neglect or abuse presenting as post-traumatic stress disorder (PTSD), attachment difficulties or similar, CBT does not work and neither does counselling, and can cause further anxiety for the child. Anxiety medication may be offered if the anxiety is severe or doesn't get better with talking therapies and is not recommended for children under the age of 11. It is usually only prescribed by doctors who specialise in child and adolescent mental health. The most common range of medication is the range of Selective Serotonin Reuptake Inhibitors (SSRIs); however, these drugs do not come without risk and are therefore not used in the first instance until therapeutic interventions have been tried; if prescribed the risk needs careful consideration and close monitoring is required.

Whole-school and classroom evidence-based approaches

FRIENDS resilience: A suite of evidence-based, social and emotional skills programmes which are designed to build lifelong resilience (fun FRIENDS 4–7 years, FRIENDS for life 8–11 years, my FRIENDS youth 12–15 years and adult resilience for 16+ years). The programmes are endorsed by the World Health Organization as best practice for the prevention and treatment of anxiety and depression. Murphy et al. (2017) attempted to systematically compare the largest school-based mental health programmes and concluded that this intervention had significant and measurable positive effect on the emotional, behavioural and academic outcomes of children and adults. Similar results on effectiveness were shared by Barrett (2010) and Higgins and O'Sullivan (2015).

Mindfulness: The NHS (2018b) describes mindfulness as 'paying more attention to the present moment – to your own thoughts and feelings, and to the world around you'. Mindfulness is recommended by NICE (2018) as a way to prevent depression as evidence suggests benefits to health and wellbeing.

THRIVE: This practical all-age approach can be used as a whole-school strategy or as an intervention for individual and groups of children with social and emotional needs. It does this by training those involved in the education and care of children, including caregivers, to understand and meet their developmental needs. It is based on research from neuroscience, attachment and child development theory and research on the role of creativity and play. This approach supports children in gaining control through achieving self-regulation and building relationships. Thrive has six strands: 'being' (3rd trimester to 6 months), 'doing' (6 to 18 months), 'thinking' (18 months to 3 years), 'power and identity' (3 to 7 years), 'skills and structure' (7 to 11 years) and 'interdependence' which is 11 years to adulthood. There are two sections – the training and Thrive-online. Thrive-online is an assessment, action-planning tool to measure progress, which allows you to identify where the child may have early interruptions in their social and emotional development. It then provides the licensed practitioner with activities and strategies to meet earlier unmet needs through schemes of work.

Growth Mindset: Schmidt et al. (2017) describe that your beliefs about whether ability is fixed or malleable is also known as fixed or growth mindset. The outcome of this research is that growth mindset interventions impact on short- and long-term attainment because they change the way that students engage with academic content.

> ### Case study
>
> Zak was in Year 2 and began to have disturbed sleep, which escalated into getting out of bed many times a night complaining of his 'worry tummy'. His mother told the school who said they would 'talk to him'. His class teacher rang and said that he was finding school stressful as he found the work hard and they would keep an eye on him. At home he was consistently sent back to bed but the situation did not improve and he was getting out of bed up to 25 times a night. His mother arranged an appointment with the GP as she was concerned that there may be something physically wrong with his stomach, but after careful examination this was ruled out. The GP spoke to Zak about his worries and he said 'Year 2 is a really important year for me, I have SATS and they will affect my whole career and I need to get better at my handwriting.' That night Zak slept through for the first time in 3 months; he was diagnosed with anxiety due to pressures at school.

TABLE 8.4 Recommended books

Age Phase	Title	Strengths
Early Years/KS1	Evans, J. (2016) *Little Meerkat's BIG PANIC: A story about learning new ways to feel calm.* London: Jessica Kingsley Publishers.	This book is suited to young children aged 2–6 years of age to talk about anxiety and emotions. It explains how the brain works and gives useful ways to feel calmer in child-friendly language and explains how adults can best support children.
Upper primary to FE (10+)	Collins-Donnelly, K. (2013) *Starving the Anxiety Gremlin: A cognitive behavioural therapy workbook on anxiety management for young people.* London: Jessica Kingsley Publishers.	This book is similar in layout and style to the 2–6 years book above, though is suited to older children aged 10+. It supports young people in understanding and managing types of anxiety, including generalised anxiety and obsessive compulsive disorder.
Secondary to FE	Knowles, S., Gallagher, B. and McEwan (2018) *My Anxiety Handbook: Getting back on track.* London: Jessica Kingsley Publishers.	This book is for young people aged 12–18 years with anxiety. The intention is to support the child in recognising and managing their anxiety.
All ages	Time to change resources: www.time-to-change.org.uk	Time to Change is led by Mind and Rethink Mental Illness and provides mental health resources for schools and caregivers.

Obsessive Compulsive Disorder (OCD)

Definition

The NHS (2018c) states that OCD is a common mental health condition in which a person has obsessive thoughts and/or compulsive behaviours, which affect them on a daily basis.

Causes

The cause is not known but the following factors play a role (NHS, 2018c):

- Genetic factors: other family members with a history of OCD.
- Areas of unusually high activity in the brain or low levels of serotonin.
- It is more common in those who have experienced bullying, abuse, neglect or a bereavement.
- Personality: neat, meticulous and methodical people are more likely to develop OCD including those who are quite anxious.

> **Support organisations**
>
> **No panic:** This charity helps people who experience panic attacks, phobias, obsessive compulsive disorders and other related anxiety disorders. They offer support for those who care for people who have anxiety disorders.
>
> **Website:** www.nopanic.org.uk **Youth Helpline:** 13–20-year-olds: 03300 606 1174 (3pm–6pm charges apply).
>
> **The Mix:** This is a UK-based charity that provides free, confidential support for young people under 25 on a range of issues including mental health, via online, phone, email, webchat, social and mobile.
>
> **Website:** www.themix.org.uk **Freephone:** 0808 808 4994 (1–11pm daily).

Overview

Some develop OCD around puberty but usually it is during early adulthood. OCD-UK (2019) classifies OCD as a serious anxiety-related condition with 50% of cases being classified as severe.

- An obsession is an unwanted or unpleasant thought, image or urge that repeatedly enters your mind, causing feelings of anxiety, disgust or unease.
- A compulsion is a repetitive behaviour or mental act that the person feels driven to perform.

Prevalence

OCD-UK (2018) reports that 1.2% of the population, from young children to adults, are affected by OCD. However, NICE (2005) reported a prevalence of 2–3% and explains that those with depression, anxiety, alcohol and substance misuse and eating disorders are at a higher risk of OCD.

Indicators

- Repetitive physical behaviours, actions or mental thought rituals that are performed over and over again to relieve the anxiety (compulsions).
- Some behaviours are observable such as physically checking, unlike obsessively repeating phrases in their minds.
- Poor attention (as they may be obsessing or performing mental rituals).
- Prolonged toilet visits.
- Repetitive hand washing.
- Worrying excessively about handwriting or neatness of schoolwork, excessive rubbing out.
- Counting as they complete tasks (this may not be out loud).

(NICE, 2005; OCD-UK, 2018)

Assessment/diagnosis

Advise the parents to take their child to the GP who will refer to a local psychological therapy service if deemed necessary (NHS, 2018c). OCD-UK (2018) advises that OCD is diagnosed when the child is over 8 years of age and the obsessions and compulsions consume excessive amounts of time (an hour or more), cause significant distress and anguish and interfere with daily functioning at school and home.

Treatment

It is unlikely that the child will recover without treatment which is usually in the form of cognitive behaviour therapy (CBT) in groups or individually, or medication (anti-depressants). The NICE (2005) guidelines do recommend that mental health services have specialist OCD multi-disciplinary teams offering age-appropriate care, though this will vary by Clinical Commissioning Groups (CCGs).

Whole-school and classroom evidence-based approaches

NICE (2005) advocates that the children and families should receive verbal and written information about OCD, the likely causes and its treatment; schools should also request a copy of this. Health services should liaise with other professionals involved in the child's life to give advice and guidance.

OCD-UK (2018) recommends the following approaches:

- Put in place the same methods as the caregivers and other agencies for consistency.
- Have a home/school diary to update caregivers on the child's day.
- Allow the child to type up schoolwork if they are obsessing over their handwriting.
- Be aware in mathematics they may have issues with certain numbers being 'bad', or 'unlucky'.
- Check on the child's wellbeing during times of high pressure.
- Make the student aware of the daily routine and any changes to prevent anxiety.
- Don't try to physically stop a behaviour, instead talk to the child about why they need to do it.

Selective mutism

Definition

'Selective mutism (SM) refers to selectivity of speaking in children, in some situations such as home, where a child may have age-appropriate speech but not in others, usually school, where they can be completely silent' (Smith and Sluckin, 2015: 369).

Causes

The NHS (2018d) proposes that SM is a fear/phobia of talking to certain people. The cause isn't always clear, but it's known to be associated with anxiety with other individualised contextual factors, which need to be explored (Oon, 2010). The child will usually have inherited a tendency to experience anxiety and have difficulty taking everyday events in their stride. Research by Muris and Ollendick (2015) has also indicated that there is a familial/genetic link (9% of fathers and 18% of mothers who had children with SM also had SM as a child).

> **Support organisations**
>
> **OCD Action:** This charity provides support and information to anybody affected by OCD.
>
> **Website:** www.ocdaction.org.uk   **Helpline:** 0845 390 6232
>
> **Email:** support@ocdaction.org.uk
>
> **OCD-UK:** OCD-UK is the leading national charity, independently working with and for almost 1 million children and adults whose lives are affected by OCD.
>
> **Website:** www.ocduk.org   **Helpline:** 03332 127 890 (10–4pm most days)
>
> **Email:** support@ocduk.org

Prevalence

Prevalence rates are known to be between 0.18 and 1.9% of the population (Muris and Ollendick, 2015). The NHS (2018d) translates this into 1 in 140 children. The typical onset of SM is between the ages of 3 and 5 years.

Indicators

The NHS (2018d) provides the following signs of selective mutism:

- Nervous, uneasy or socially awkward
- Rude, disinterested or sulky
- Clingy
- Shy and withdrawn
- Avoid eye contact
- Stiff, tense or poorly coordinated
- Stubborn or aggressive, having temper tantrums when they get home from school, or getting angry when questioned by caregivers.

Assessment/diagnosis

A diagnosis cannot be made in the first month (DSM-5) (Muris and Ollendick, 2015). The parents need to take the child to the GP and the school can also make a referral to speech and language therapy. It is crucial that early intervention is in place – the child should not be left to 'grow out of it'.

Treatment

Behavioural and cognitive therapies and interventions:

- Usually involves 12–20 sessions with child, parent and teacher
- Creates speaking situations where the therapist models, shapes and reinforces speech
- Use of feelings chart; create a talking ladder
- Exposes child to speech and interaction.

(Muris and Ollendick, 2015)

- Provide a controlled small environment where they communicate and add more people one at a time
- Use caregiver as 'safe base' and then add teacher and classmates
- Use shaping strategy (first communicate non-verbally, then make certain sounds, then whisper, then speak a word to a sentence).

(Hung et al., 2012)

- When psychosocial therapies are ineffective: pharmacotherapy (Fluoxetine – improvement for 76% of the children)
- Phenelzine – moderate side-effects of weight gain, low blood pressure and constipation.

(Muris and Ollendick, 2015)

Whole-school and classroom evidence-based approaches

SMIRA (2019) highlight the importance of early intervention; remember, children with SM want to speak but are physically unable to do so due to their heightened levels of anxiety. Add to this a formal learning context and a transition to a new class or context.

Systematic desensitisation, also known as 'graduated exposure therapy', is an intervention where the child learns to cope with and overcome fear in small steps, which allows them to take greater steps to mitigate or extinguish stress and fear responses in specific situations (Hung et al., 2012).

Stimulus fading, also known as 'sliding in technique', is where the child is brought into a controlled environment with someone they are comfortable with and who they will communicate with (a parent or sibling, for example). More people are added one at a time (peers, teacher).

Shaping or the 'vocalisation ladder' is a process where the child is slowly encouraged to communicate non-verbally, then to vocalise certain sounds, then whisper and finally speak a word to a sentence (Oon, 2010).

Additional approaches are activities such as art and play therapy to facilitate communication. Bork et al. (2014) suggest that play is an obvious place to start, as it is important in a child's experience; it is a useful window for assessing development and is an important way to provide an intervention. Some learning activities that involve play are outlined below (Table 8.5):

TABLE 8.5 Learning activities

Severity of selective mutism	Activity	Benefits
No eye contact or sound ↓ No sound but relaxed and are ready to risk speech	1. Play with puppets (chosen by the child)	Through play children may lose themselves as they believe it is the puppets speaking not them. Pair the child with a friend and start with a silent character, gradually building on this
	2. Sign language and/or symbolic language	Teach everyone some basic sign language and use alongside speech and a symbol system such as communicate and print. This will ensure the child can communicate basic needs
	3. Imitate animal sounds	Using a book such as *Where the Wild Things Are*, use play to imitate animal sounds; these may be less intimidating than talking
	4. Turn off the lights	This strategy can be used to build confidence. Check all the children are happy for the lights to be off. Teacher spells a word, which the children repeat such as light, sun, candle, lamp, star, and slowly raises the lights.

Source: Adapted from Bork et al. (2014)

Post-Traumatic Stress Disorder (PTSD)

Definition

Post-Traumatic Stress Disorder (PTSD) is a psychological disorder that can occur after a traumatic event (American Psychiatric Association, 2013). The NHS (2018e) defines PTSD as an anxiety-related disorder.

> **Support organisations**
>
> **Selective Mutism Information and Research Association (SMIRA)**
>
> The charity supports families with selectively mute children. They also provide information to health and education professionals.
>
> **Website:** www.selectivemutism.org.uk
>
> **Facebook and Twitter Support:** SMIRA

Causes

The NHS (2018e) clarifies that PTSD is caused by stressful, frightening or distressing events. Youngminds (2019) argue that PTSD can happen after you experience something such as violence, abuse, neglect, rape or a life-threatening situation; it can also be as a result of witnessing a serious accident or natural disaster.

Prevalence

PTSD is believed to affect 1 in 3 people who have a traumatic experience. It can happen immediately or occur weeks, months or years later (NHS, 2018e).

Indicators

- Flashbacks or nightmares about what happened
- Vivid memories
- Avoidance and numbing, where you try to keep busy and avoid thinking about it
- Heart palpitations and anxiety
- Being tense and on guard in case it should happen again
- Difficulty sleeping
- Difficulty concentrating
- Feelings of isolation, irritability and/or guilt
- Not speaking
- Anger

(Youngminds, 2017; NHS, 2018e)

Assessment/diagnosis

An initial assessment can be made by the child's GP who will usually refer to mental health specialists for further assessment and treatment (NHS, 2018e).

Treatment

PTSD can be successfully treated even when it develops many years after the traumatic event, though treatment will vary depending on the severity of the symptoms. There may be a period of watchful waiting to see if the child improves or deteriorates without treatment (this should only be the case where symptoms are mild and have been present for less than four weeks). Psychotherapy, CBT, EMDR (Eye Movement Desensitisation and Reprocessing) and/or anti-depressants may also be recommended. Caregiver support is crucial though this can be difficult for them to provide, particularly if they too are distressed.

Whole-school and classroom evidence-based approaches

- Create a safe environment; if possible, let the child choose where they sit as certain seating may elevate anxiety (such as back to the door)
- Have collaborative activities so the child can build connections with others
- Promote safe, predictable and consistent relationships
- Give high rates of praise
- Inform the child in advance of any changes in the school day
- Teach relaxation skills, mindfulness
- Use peer tutoring, aiming to give the child a leadership role
- Have awareness of your tone of voice, don't shout
- Break teaching into small steps with interactive modelling and clear explanations
- Empower the child to share their voice and give choices during support
- Celebrate and share successes

Depression

Definition

According to NICE (2017a) depression is a broad diagnosis that can include different symptoms in different people. However, depressed mood or loss of pleasure in most activities are key signs of depression. The guidelines add that depressive symptoms are frequently accompanied by symptoms of anxiety, but may also occur on their own.

Causes

The NHS (2018f) advises that there is a trigger for depression, such as life-changing events. Also, those with a family history of depression are more likely to experience it.

Overview

During adolescence there is a period of biological, neurocognitive and social change and during this time the prevalence of emotional problems, in particular depression, increases (Thapar et al., 2012).

Prevalence

The prevalence of childhood depression has been estimated to be 1% in pre-pubertal children and around 3% in post-pubertal young people. It is experienced by twice as many adolescent females as males (NICE, 2017a). The Department of Health (DoH, 2015) shares that 0.9% or nearly 80,000 children are seriously depressed.

Indicators

- Persistent sadness or low mood (may present as irritability)
- Loss of interest or loss of pleasure (anhedonia)
- Fatigue/low energy

(NICE, 2017a)

If any key symptoms are present, the presence of other, associated symptoms should be determined:

- Poor quality of, or increased need for, sleep
- Poor concentration or indecisiveness
- Low self-confidence
- Poor or increased appetite
- Agitation or slowing of movements
- Guilt or self-blame
- Withdrawal for social situations
- Suicidal thoughts or acts

Assessment/diagnosis

Family context, previous history and the degree of associated difficulties are all important in the assessment of depression. Because of this, it is important to assess how the child or young person functions in different settings (for example, at school, with peers and with family), as well as asking about specific symptoms of depression (NICE, 2017a).

For a diagnosis of depression in children aged 5–18 years, symptoms should be present for at least 2 weeks and every symptom should be present for most of the day (NICE, 2017a). The International Statistical Classification of Diseases (ICD-10) uses an agreed list of 10 depressive symptoms, and divides depression into 4 categories: not depressed (fewer than 4 symptoms), mild depression (4 symptoms), moderate depression (5 to 6 symptoms), and severe depression (7 or more symptoms, with or without psychotic symptoms). It is important to note that the SENCO can make a referral to CAMHS or CYPS with caregiver consent.

Depression has been divided into the following categories as defined by the ICD-10/DSM-5:

Mild depression: Few, if any, symptoms of depression in excess of the 5 required to make the diagnosis, and symptoms result in only minor functional impairment, according to DSM-5 (American Psychiatric Association, 2013).

Moderate and severe depression: Symptoms of depression or functional impairment are between mild and severe.

Severe depression with psychotic symptoms: Most symptoms of depression, according to DSM-5, markedly interfere with functioning. Can occur with or without psychotic symptoms.

Treatment: The SENCO and other colleagues should encourage the caregivers to make an appointment with their GP (General Practitioner) for support and referral to other health services.

Mild depression: Antidepressant medication should not be used for the initial treatment of children with mild depression. For children with diagnosed mild depression who do not want an intervention or who, in the opinion of the healthcare professional, may recover with no intervention, a further assessment should be arranged normally within 2 weeks – known as 'watchful waiting'. Following 'watchful waiting' for a period of up to 4 weeks, all children should be offered supportive therapies such as talking therapy, guided self-help or group cognitive behavioural therapy (CBT). If there is no response after 2–3 months to these therapies, the child should be referred to a tier 2 or tier 3 CAMHS team (NICE, 2017a).

Interventions for mild depression: NICE (2017a) clarifies that there is no good-quality evidence that one type of psychological therapy is better than the others.

Moderate to severe depression: Children with moderate to severe depression should be reviewed by a CAMHS tier 2 or 3 team and offered a specific psychological therapy (individual CBT, interpersonal therapy, family therapy or psychodynamic psychotherapy) that runs for at least 3 months (NICE, 2017a). In addition, they should not be offered antidepressant medication unless it is in combination with a concurrent psychological therapy.

For young people aged 12–18 years there can be combined therapy (fluoxetine and psychological therapy) for the initial treatment of moderate to severe depression, as an alternative to psychological therapy followed by combined therapy. Fluoxetine is the only medication that should be offered to children, as it is the only one with clinical evidence to suggest the benefits outweigh the risks (NICE, 2017a).

REFLECTIVE ACTIVITY

If you have a young person newly prescribed an antidepressant in your context, they need to be closely monitored by health teams for the appearance of suicidal behaviour, self-harm or hostility. What systems do you have in place in your context to monitor young people in this situation? How is this information shared with parents and carers and health professionals? Do you need to make any modifications to your processes and procedures in school to record and report this information?

Children prescribed antidepressants

Specific arrangements must be made for careful monitoring of adverse drug reactions, as well as for reviewing mental state and general progress; for example, weekly contact with the child or young person and their parent(s) or carer(s). In the event that psychological therapies are declined, medication may still be given, but as the young person will not be reviewed at psychological therapy sessions, the prescribing doctor should closely monitor the child or young person's progress on a regular basis and focus particularly on emergent adverse drug reactions (NICE, 2017a).

Whole-school and classroom evidence-based approaches

The Charlie Waller Memorial Trust (2017) has a useful guide to writing a mental health and wellbeing policy, *Depression – Let's get talking*. This advocates assigning a mental health lead or champion in your school; this does not need to be the SENCO, designated teacher or safeguarding person but colleagues need to have an identified member of staff. You could also consider that the mental health lead wears a different coloured lanyard so they are clearly identifiable by both children, caregivers and colleagues.

Depression: Recommended books

TABLE 8.6 Depression: Recommended books

Age Phase	Title	Strengths
Early years/ primary	Tan, S. (2001) *The Red Tree*. Sydney: Lothian Children's Books.	This is a picture book that can be used to talk to children about emotions and the power of hope. Individual pages could be used to discuss how the child in the story is feeling and how she overcomes these thoughts.
Across the age ranges	Rosen, M. and Blake, Q. (2004) *Michael Rosen's Sad Book*. London: Walker Books.	This book is suitable across the ages as it explores how experiencing a loss can make you really sad. The illustrations are suitable for all ages and will allow discussion about how the character is feeling.
For colleagues	Johnstone, M. (2008) *I Had a Black Dog*. London: Robinson.	The author takes the reader through his journey of depression, externalising it as a 'black dog'.

Bipolar disorder

Definition

Bipolar disorder was formerly known as manic depression (NHS, 2018g). NICE (2014) defines bipolar disorder as a potentially lifelong disabling condition which is characterised by episodes of mania (abnormally elevated mood or irritability and related symptoms with severe functional or psychotic symptoms for 7 days or more) or hypomania (abnormally elevated mood or irritability and related symptoms with decreased or increased function for 4 days or more) and episodes of depressed mood.

> **Support organisations**
>
> **Black dog animation on YouTube:** www.youtube.com/watch?v=XiCrniLQGYc
>
> **Samaritans:** Provides confidential non-judgemental emotional support 24 hours a day to people who are experiencing feelings of distress or despair, including those that could lead to suicide.
>
> **Website:** www.samaritans.org **Helpline:** 116 123 **Email:** jo@samaritans.org
>
> **Young Minds:** Is committed to improving the emotional wellbeing and mental health of children and young people, providing information to professionals and caregivers.
>
> **Website:** www.youngminds.org.uk
> **Helpline:** 0808 802 5544 **Email:** parents@youngminds.org.uk

Causes

The exact causes remain unknown; however, the NHS (2018g) shares that there are a number of factors that can trigger an episode; these are believed to be extreme stress, overwhelming problems, life-changing events, genetic and chemical factors.

Overview

Bipolar disorder often coexists with other difficulties such as anxiety, substance misuse, personality disorder and attention deficit hyperactivity disorder (ADHD) (NICE, 2014). The guidance suggests peak onset at 15–19 years. The nature of bipolar is that the person will move between high and low states, which can be so extreme they impact on everyday life (NHS, 2018g).

Prevalence

Bipolar I disorder (mania and depression) is estimated to be 1% of the population, and bipolar II (mania and depression) is understood to affect 0.4% of adults. Bipolar disorder in children under 12 years is considered to be very rare (NICE, 2014).

Indicators

- Feeling very happy, elated, overjoyed, full of energy
- Talking quickly, full of ideas and having important plans
- Easily distracted, irritated or agitated
- Impulsive, talkative, distracted

- Withdrawn, unmotivated, difficult to engage
- Crying for no apparent reason
- Explosive, lengthy and often destructive rages
- Rapidly changing moods changing in minutes or days
- Delusional, having hallucinations and illogical thinking
- Not feeling like sleeping or eating
- Separation anxiety
- Defiance of authority
- Cravings for certain foods
- Excessive involvement in multiple projects and activities

(CABF, 2007; NHS, 2018g)

Assessment/diagnosis

Assessment of bipolar can be complicated due to the overlap with ADHD; a referral should be made to CAMHS where the child is under the age of 14. For young people over 14 it is recommended by NICE (2014) that they are referred to specialist early intervention for psychosis or CAMHS with expertise in the assessment and management of bipolar disorder. The diagnosis will only be made following intensive, longitudinal monitoring from health care professionals or a multi-disciplinary team trained in this area (NICE, 2014). A diagnosis will involve the following being present:

- Mania
- Euphoria (for most days, for most of the time, for at least 7 days).

Treatment

- A psychological intervention
- A high-intensity psychological intervention (CBT) or interpersonal therapy
- Medication which can cause slurring, speech and memory recall difficulties

Whole-school and classroom approaches

- Produce visual timetables to share the structure of the day which includes break times
- Provide positive reinforcement and use of praise
- Stay calm and resolve conflict in a non-confrontational manner
- Reduce distractions by not having overstimulating displays or lots of clutter on tables
- Use a range of teaching approaches to keep the child engaged
- Provide opportunity for the child to move around the classroom and use technology
- Consider your seating plan carefully, placing the child next to a child who isn't easily distracted, preferably near the teacher
- Offer ear defenders to reduce noise
- Provide a safe place where the child can go if they are feeling overwhelmed

> **Support organisations**
>
> **Bipolar UK:** Bipolar UK is the national charity dedicated to supporting individuals with bipolar, their families and caregivers.
>
> **Website:** www.bipolar.org **Helpline:** 0333 323 3880 **Email:** info@bipolar.org
>
> **MIND:** The bipolar section of their website explains what bipolar disorder is, what kinds of treatment are available, and how you can help yourself cope. Also provides guidance on what friends and family can do to help.
>
> **Website:** www.mind.org.uk

Psychosis

Definition

'Psychosis is a mental health problem that causes people to perceive or interpret things differently from those around them. This might involve hallucinations or delusions' (NHS, 2016).

Causes

For the NHS (2016) it is sometimes possible to identify the cause of psychosis as a specific mental health condition, such as:

- Schizophrenia – a condition that causes a range of psychological symptoms, including hallucinations and delusions
- Bipolar disorder – a mental health condition that affects mood; a person with bipolar disorder can have episodes of low mood (depression) and highs or elated mood (mania)
- Severe depression – some people with depression also have symptoms of psychosis when they're very depressed

Overview

People with a history of psychosis are more likely than others to have drug or alcohol misuse problems, or both. Some use these substances as a way of managing psychotic symptoms. However, substance abuse can make psychotic symptoms worse or cause other problems and have a higher than average risk of self-harm and suicide.

Psychosis can also be triggered by:

- a traumatic experience
- stress
- drug misuse
- alcohol misuse
- side-effects of prescribed medication
- a physical condition – such as a brain tumour.

The NHS (2016) clarifies that how often a psychotic episode occurs and how long it lasts can depend on the underlying cause.

Prevalence

NICE (2016b) suggests the prevalence of psychotic disorders in children aged between 5 and 18 years has been estimated to be 0.4%. Schizophrenia is very rare in pre-pubertal children but incidence increases significantly from 15 years onwards.

Indicators

The NHS (2016) gives the indicators as:

- hallucinations – where a person hears, sees and, in some cases, feels, smells or tastes things that aren't there; a common hallucination is hearing voices
- delusions – where a person has strong beliefs that aren't shared by others; a common delusion is someone believing there is a conspiracy to harm them.

The combination of hallucinations and delusional thinking can cause severe distress and a change in behaviour.

NICE (2016b) adds that the symptoms of psychosis are usually divided into 'positive symptoms', including hallucinations (perception in the absence of any stimulus) and delusions (fixed or falsely held beliefs), and 'negative symptoms' (such as emotional apathy, lack of drive, poverty of speech, social withdrawal and self-neglect).

Experiencing the symptoms of psychosis is often referred to as having a psychotic episode.

Assessment/diagnosis

There is no text to positively diagnose psychosis; a GP will ask the parent and child where appropriate about their symptoms and refer to relevant services.

Treatment

NHS (2016) treatment for psychosis involves using a combination of:

- antipsychotic medication – which can help relieve the symptoms of psychosis
- psychological therapies – the one-to-one talking therapy cognitive behavioural therapy (CBT) has proved successful in helping people with psychosis; family interventions (a form of therapy that may involve partners, family members and close friends) have been shown to reduce the need for hospital treatment in people with psychosis
- social support – support with social needs, such as education, employment or accommodation

If a person's psychotic episodes are severe, they may need to be admitted to a psychiatric hospital for treatment.

After an episode of psychosis, most people who get better with medication need to continue taking it for at least a year. Around 50% of people need to take long-term medication to prevent symptoms recurring.

Whole-school and classroom evidence-based approaches

- See approaches for anxiety and depression as children with psychosis are not likely to be attending school or are medicated.

Support organisation

Rethink Mental Illness: Provides free factsheets, online information and online webchat

Website: www.rethink.org

Leading and Coordinating Provision

Self-harm

Definition

MIND (2017) describes self-harm as when children hurt themselves as a way of dealing with very difficult feelings, painful memories or overwhelming situations and experiences.

Prevalence

The NHS (2018h) reports that self-harm is more common than many people realise, especially among younger people. It's estimated that around 10% of young people self-harm at some point.

Known causes

MIND (2017) shares that there are no fixed rules about why people self-harm; it is different for everyone. Self-harm can be linked to a specific experience and can be a way of dealing with something that is happening in a child's life or that happened in the past. Some children are unable to understand why they self-harm.

Reasons children self-harm (MIND, 2017):

- To express something that is hard to put into words
- To turn invisible thoughts or feelings into something visible
- To change emotional pain into physical pain
- To reduce overwhelming emotional feelings or thoughts
- Due to pressures at school
- Due to bullying
- To have a sense of being in control
- Due to difficult feelings, such as depression, anxiety, anger or numbness
- Due to sexual, physical or emotional abuse
- To escape traumatic memories
- To have something in life that they can rely on
- To punish themselves for feelings and experiences
- To stop feeling numb, disconnected or dissociated
- To create a reason to physically care for themselves
- Due to bereavement and loss
- To express suicidal feelings and thoughts without taking their own life
- To express something that is hard to put into words

TABLE 8.7 Indicators of self-harm

Physical signs (NSPCC, 2018d) (commonly found on head, wrists, arms, thighs and chest)	Further signs of self-harm (MIND, 2017)	Emotional signs of self-harm (NSPCC, 2018d)
Cuts	Cutting various parts of their bodies	Depression, tearfulness and low motivation
Bruises	Poisoning themselves	Becoming withdrawn and isolated

Physical signs (NSPCC, 2018d) (commonly found on head, wrists, arms, thighs and chest)	Further signs of self-harm (MIND, 2017)	Emotional signs of self-harm (NSPCC, 2018d)
Burns	Overeating or undereating	Unusual eating habits; sudden weight loss or gain
Bald patches from pulling out hair	Biting themselves	Low self-esteem and self-blame
	Picking or scratching at their skin	Drinking or taking drugs
	Burning their skin	
	Inserting objects into their bodies	
	Hitting themselves or walls	
	Overdosing	
	Exercising excessively	
	Pulling hair	
	Getting into fights they know they will lose	

Assessment/diagnosis

Psychosocial assessment through the NHS (NICE, 2017b).

Treatment

For NICE (2017b), the decision about referral for further treatment and help should be based upon a comprehensive psychiatric, psychological and social assessment, including an assessment of risk, and should not be determined solely on the basis of having self-harmed. Treatment packages will vary depending on level of need.

Whole-school and classroom approaches

The starting point for meeting the needs of children who self-harm is training for teachers to build their understanding and confidence in recognising indicators, providing school-based support and signposting to guidance from health services and charity organisations. As SENCO,

> **Support organisations**
>
> **Harmless:** A voluntary organisation that responds to the needs of children and young people who do or are at risk of self-harm. It provides a range of services including support, information and training.
>
> **Website:** www.harmless.org.uk   **Tweet:** @HarmlessUK
>
> **Email:** info@harmless.org.uk
>
> **NSPCC:** The helpline is recommended for young people to speak about self-harm. They're used to dealing with the effects of self-harm and calls can be made anonymously.
>
> **Website:** www.nspcc.org.uk **Helpline:** 0808 800 5000
>
> **Childline:** Has trained counsellors who can help children talk about the emotions they may be feeling and which may be their triggers to self-harm; available 24 hours a day.
>
> **Website:** www.childline.org.uk **Helpline:** 0800 1111

you should ensure there are whole-school approaches, procedures and protocols for responding to self-harm.

Safe, supportive and nurturing environments, which promote emotional wellbeing, are essential (Lee, 2016). In addition to this, there should be compulsory staff training from a local health service, such as educational psychologists, as the response of a member of staff when a child discloses self-harm can influence whether or not they seek help.

Suicide

Definition

The ONS definition of suicide includes all deaths from intentional self-harm for persons aged 10 and over, and deaths where the intent was undetermined for those aged 15 and over (Office for National Statistics, 2017).

Prevalence

Child Bereavement UK (2017a: 5) reports that each year around 6,000 families are bereaved by suicide. Their school information pack (2017b) adds that suicide rates for teenagers are on the increase, as one of the most common types of violent death in teenage boys, with 75% of suicides being carried out by males.

Use of language

Schreiber et al. (2017) discuss the complexity of language used when a person dies through suicide. In their journal article they share the story of a boy aged 11 during a 'Sharing Circle' at a residential camp for grieving boys. He introduced himself by saying, 'My dad committed suicide because he didn't want to be part of our family anymore.' The words used by the child to describe how his father died include the word 'committed', a word used to describe someone who commits sins or illegal acts. As Beaton et al. (2012) argue, using the word 'commit' within the context of suicide is not only unnecessary, it is also harmful. They recommend we use language which accurately and sensitively describes the experience, such as 'died by suicide' or 'ended his/her life'. As SENCO, you may wish to discuss the appropriateness and necessity of using this terminology as it can provoke both guilt and shame (Beaton et al., 2012).

Schreiber et al. (2017) discussed the impact on children when a parent dies by suicide. They suggest that these children experience a 'double whammy'. That is, the suicide itself carries stigma, which influences and is influenced by feelings of isolation, abandonment and a sense of responsibility on the child. The child may feel guilt and need to protect the memory of the lost parent while protecting and defending the lost parent.

As SENCO, alongside the SLT you will need to consider how you will support parents, carers, siblings and family members who lose a child to suicide. Child Bereavement UK offers group sessions for people bereaved by suicide; an example is given in Child Bereavement UK (2017a: 5) of a parent whose son took his own life – she said 'losing a child is the worst, worst possible thing that I think anybody has to deal with; in the early days I couldn't deal with life very easily'.

Indicators

Rethink (2018) provides the following indicators:

- anxious, irritable or confrontational
- mood swings
- acting recklessly
- sleeping too much or too little
- wanting to be alone
- being negative about themselves
- having problems with school work
- they may threaten to hurt or kill themselves
- talking/writing about death, dying or suicide.

Assessment/diagnosis

Screening tools used by health professionals.

Why do young people attempt suicide?

Child Bereavement UK (2017b) shares that young people often attempt suicide as they feel it is the only way they can take control. They might not want to die but cannot find a sufficient reason to keep living.

Whole-school and classroom approaches

A hope box: The child may choose an alternative name. The idea was created by PAPYRUS and is a personalised box to fill with objects (keepsakes from loved ones, notepad to write/draw feelings, photos, music, stress balls, hand lotion, soft cloth, beads, rubber bands to snap on wrists, colouring books, soft socks, touch stones, sweets, perfume) to make the child feel better when they are feeling upset, anxious or experiencing suicidal thoughts. Small pocket-sized versions are also recommended for children to have with them wherever they go.

A keep safe plan:

My keeping safe plan

This is what makes me worry

This is how it makes me feel

This is how you can help me feel safe

If I can't keep safe I will tell

This is what I need you to do to help me

Useful book

Age phase	Title	Strengths
Primary	Sands, D. (2010) *Red Chocolate Elephants: For children bereaved by suicide*. Sydney: Karridale.	This book and DVD provide a sensitive approach to engage with children about death through suicide for those supporting children in schools. To be read with an adult.

SENCO ACTIVITY

Think and reflect on your current policies, procedures and resources and how sufficiently they would guide, prepare and support you should the following situations occur:

- A child or young person is presenting as suicidal
- A child or young person loses a parent/carer through suicide

Eating disorders

Definition

Eating disorders are defined by the negative beliefs and behaviours they cause people to have about themselves and their eating, body shape and weight. They can cause people to adopt restricted eating, binge eating and compensatory behaviours (such as vomiting and excessive exercise).

The emotional and physical consequences of these beliefs and behaviours maintain the disorder and result in a high mortality rate from malnutrition, suicide and physical issues (such as electrolyte imbalances). This is most common in people with anorexia nervosa. There are also other physical complications (such as osteoporosis) and psychiatric needs (such as anxiety disorders) that affect the wellbeing and recovery of people with an eating disorder and raise the cost of treatment (NICE, 2017c).

Prevalence

From figures for UK hospital admissions from 2012 to 2013, the eating disorders charity BEAT estimated that there were over 725,000 people with an eating disorder in the UK, approximately 90% of whom were female. However, recent community-based epidemiological studies suggest that as many as 25% of people with an eating disorder are male. About 15% of people with an eating disorder have anorexia nervosa, which is also more common in younger people. Most people with an eating disorder meet diagnostic criteria for bulimia nervosa, binge eating disorder, or other specified feeding and eating disorder (OSFED) (NICE, 2017c).

The most common eating disorders are:

- **Anorexia nervosa** – when you try to keep your weight as low as possible by not eating enough food, exercising too much, or both
- **Bulimia** – when you sometimes lose control and eat a lot of food in a very short amount of time (binging) and are then deliberately sick, use laxatives (medication to help you poo), restrict what you eat, or do too much exercise to try to stop yourself gaining weight

- **Binge eating disorder (BED)** – when you regularly lose control of your eating, eat large portions of food all at once until you feel uncomfortably full, and are then often upset or guilty
- **Other specified feeding or eating disorder (OSFED)** – the most common disorder, when your symptoms don't exactly match those of anorexia, bulimia or binge eating disorder, but it doesn't mean it's a less serious illness

(NHS, 2018i)

CPD OPPORTUNITY

The NICE guidelines (2017c) explicitly state that education professionals working with people with an eating disorder should be trained and skilled in:

- Negotiating and working with family members and carers
- Managing issues around information sharing and confidentiality
- Safeguarding
- Working with multi-disciplinary teams.

Think about who would/should take the lead on this in your context and why

SENCO   Safeguarding officer   Pastoral team

Known causes

The NHS (2018i) states that we don't know exactly what causes eating disorders.

However, children are more likely to get an eating disorder if:

- a member of their family has a history of eating disorders, depression, or alcohol or drug addiction
- they have been criticised for their eating habits, body shape or weight
- they are concerned about being slim, particularly if they feel pressure from society, for example ballet dancers, models or athletes
- they have anxiety, low self-esteem, an obsessive personality, or are a perfectionist
- they have been sexually abused.

TABLE 8.8 Indicator checklist for concerns: Eating disorders

Indicate concern level: red ▨, amber ▨, green ▨, blue (for N/A/unsure) ▨	
An unusually low or high BMI or body weight for their age	red
Rapid weight loss	red
Dieting or restrictive eating practices (such as dieting when they are underweight) that are worrying them, their family members or carers, or professionals	red
Family members or carers report a change in eating behaviour	red
Social withdrawal, particularly from situations that involve food (lunchtimes, breakfast clubs)	red
Other mental health problems	green
A disproportionate concern about their weight or shape (for example, concerns about side-effects of the contraceptive pill)	blue
Problems managing a chronic illness that affects diet, such as diabetes or coeliac disease	blue

(Continued)

Leading and Coordinating Provision

TABLE 8.8 (Continued)

Menstrual or other endocrine disturbances, or unexplained gastrointestinal symptoms	⊠
Malnutrition, including poor circulation, dizziness, palpitations, fainting or pallor	▒
Compensatory behaviours, including laxative or diet pill misuse, vomiting or excessive exercise	▨
Whether they take part in activities associated with a high risk of eating disorders (for example, professional sport, fashion, dance or modelling)	▓

Source: Adapted from NICE (2017c)

The checklist in Table 8.8 will not give a diagnosis of an eating disorder; a full assessment will need to be carried out by a health professional or team of specialists. However, it will give you indicators that may be useful to share as concerns with the young person, parents and carers (where appropriate).

Assessment/diagnosis

Referral usually needs to be made to a General Practitioner (GP), who, if they have concerns, will then refer the young person on to an eating disorder specialist (BEAT, 2019). NICE (2017c) advocates young people with eating disorders should be assessed and receive treatment at the earliest opportunity. If an eating disorder is suspected after an initial assessment, immediate referral to a community-based, age-appropriate eating disorder service for further assessment or treatment should be made.

BEAT (2017) notes the two main systems used to diagnose mental health issues are the Diagnostic and Statistical Manual of Mental Disorders (DSM) and the International Classification of Diseases (ICD). Both cover eating disorders and are very similar in the criteria they use. The DSM is used more often in the USA, and the latest version, the DSM-5, was published in 2013 (American Psychiatric Association, 2013). The main eating disorders listed in the DSM-5 are anorexia, bulimia and binge eating disorder (BED).

Treatment

Early treatment is particularly important for those with, or at risk of, severe emaciation, and treatment for these children should be prioritised (NICE, 2017c). The NHS (2018i) states that children can recover from an eating disorder, but it may take time and recovery will be different for everyone. Specialist teams will discuss the support for individual children, depending on the type and extent of their eating disorder, which may include a treatment plan. The treatment will usually be in the form of an individual or group psychological therapy depending on the type of eating disorder.

Case study

From the age of 11, Sam developed insecurities about the way she looked. She felt overweight and ugly even though she was a size 10 and well liked by her peers. Also, she was dyslexic and was finding school very challenging, struggling in both English and Mathematics. Sam had school dinners – as both parents worked there was no time to prepare packed lunches. She would leave her school lunch,

Social, Emotional and Mental Health Difficulties

> making excuses to go to the toilet and not returning; controlling her eating felt good and with every meal missed there was a sense of satisfaction. Her parents often argued and she had little freedom as her parents would not let her out on evenings with her peers. Sam couldn't control her parents' arguing but she could control what she ate: she wanted the feeling of achievement from not eating. She wasn't aware she was losing weight and her family didn't notice as she wore baggy clothes.
>
> **Strategies to support Sam at lunchtimes**
>
> Agree in advance with her what she will be eating, including the portion size, to reduce anxiety about what the choices will be. The agreed meal must not change as this can cause heightened stress so discuss this with the kitchen staff.
>
> Check she has been to the bathroom prior to sitting down to eat.
>
> Keep any conversations away from food.
>
> After the meal have an activity or 'job' to do to take her mind off any compensatory behaviours such as exercising. Don't comment on what she has eaten as this may heighten feelings of guilt.
>
> You will need to address why Sam does not want to eat, refer to CAMHS and speak to the caregivers about your concerns.
>
> (Adapted from BEAT)

Bereavement and loss

Definitions

Natural bereavement: This is where a death is expected and can be emotionally prepared for.

Traumatic bereavement: Barlé et al. (2017) described that a death is considered to be traumatic if it occurs without warning and is untimely. It includes events where the death is witnessed, murder, accidents, drug and alcohol related deaths and suicides. They also reiterated that in most cases the impact of a traumatic loss is significantly more intense and prolonged than after a natural death.

Support organisations

Anorexia and Bulimia Care (ABC): With over 25 years of experience, ABC provides support and information for the eating disorder community throughout the UK.

Website: www.anorexiabulimiacare.org.uk

BEAT: Beat is the UK's leading charity for eating disorder recovery. Resources include peer support and regional projects to foster community awareness.

Website: www.beateatingdisorders.org.uk

National Centre for Eating Disorders (NCFED): The NCFED provides training for professionals and resources for those struggling with eating disorders.

Website: https://eating-disorders.org.uk

Overview

Child Bereavement UK (2017b) concludes that all children have difficulty with the concept and permanence of death. We know that for children with learning difficulties and for children with Autism understanding that someone has died can be particularly challenging. To grasp permanence they may need practical examples of dead and living things. Here are some examples given by the charity:

- Buy a dead fish and compare it to a live one. Put the dead fish in water, what happens? It will not move, swim, eat or breathe
- Replicate a burial with the dead fish
- Explain a cremation by burning leaves and mixing with earth
- Photograph the above activities so they can be a visual reminder for the child

There are many picture books available that have quite real examples of funerals, cremations and coffins that can be used to talk to children. If you know that a death is expected it would be worthwhile, with the agreement of caregivers, to also prepare the child in school.

Grief

Nyatanga (2018) discussed the link between loss, grief and bereavement. This is due to the attachments that people have with each other, which are lost when a loved one dies. Kennedy et al. (2008) explain that the grieving process following the loss of a spouse may negatively affect parenting as their grief impacts on meeting the child's needs. How the remaining parent copes influences the emotional health of the child. In addition, a child's loss of a parent may impact on their behaviour and performance at school (Graydon et al., 2010; Child Bereavement UK, 2017a). We know as adults that everyone grieves in their own way; it is not for us to judge others or assume a 'right way to grieve'. Children need opportunities to express their grief, as it is a normal and important part of the recovery process. School plays an important role during the grief process as it can offer a sense of security and continuity, particularly where at home others are struggling to deal with their grief (Child Bereavement UK, 2017b). As SENCO, you will need to have a selection of resources available for colleagues to introduce the concept of death; this should be discussed with family members so they know the support you are putting in place. There are some recommended books and a therapy pack at the end of this chapter.

Child Bereavement UK (2017b) acknowledges that children will mature at different rates so their understanding and response to a death will vary. The following is a useful guide:

2–5 years: They may not appreciate the finality of death and ask when the person is coming back. The use of language at this time needs to be final so don't say 'gone away' or 'gone to sleep'. They will need reminding they have died.

5–8 years: Most will realise dead people are different to those who are alive, that they cannot feel, hear, smell or speak. By age 7, the majority accept death is permanent and can happen to anyone; this can result in separation anxiety. Let them ask questions and give as much information to help them adjust, including about death rituals.

8–12 years: It is believed that their understanding of death almost matches that of an adult. They may become increasingly aware of their own mortality, which can make them fearful and insecure. They will ask for details and seek answers to specific questions.

Adolescence: A death can increase their anxiety about the future and they may experience depression. They might prefer to talk to a friend or adult than close family. This age group are more likely to have difficulty understanding their own mortality and therefore take part in high-risk behaviour. Anger is also more likely, which can be compounded by a sense of injustice.

Prevalence

The Childhood Bereavement Network (2019) has reported that up to 70% of schools will have a bereaved pupil on roll at any one time. This equates to 1 in 29 children who are experiencing the loss of a parent or sibling. Child Bereavement UK (2017a: 10) shares that a parent of children under the age of 18 dies every 22 minutes, leaving 111 children bereaved of a parent every day.

As SENCO, you need to reflect on how well your context meets the needs of these children, particularly those with an identified SEND. Although 1 in 29 children have been bereaved of a parent or sibling, 80% of teachers in a survey by Child Bereavement UK (2017a) said they had received no bereavement training.

Indicators (normal part of grief)

- Unnaturally quiet, withdrawn or unusually aggressive
- Anger at all ages
- Disturbed sleep and bad dreams
- Anxiety displayed through reluctance to separate from caregiver
- More easily upset than usual
- Difficulty concentrating, being forgetful and/or not with it
- Physical complaints, such as headaches, stomachaches and feeling run down

(Child Bereavement UK, 2017b)

REFLECTIVE ACTIVITY

TABLE 8.9 Self-assessment supporting children and families*

	RAG rating	Action to be taken
Self-assessment of knowledge and confidence of staff in supporting a child who has experienced bereavement. The second column to be used as an audit: Red (not in place and ineffective) Amber (in development) Green (in place and effective)		
There is an agreed procedure in place explaining processes the school will follow when a child is bereaved (including sudden bereavement)		
There is a named person responsible for the wellbeing and pastoral support of bereaved children		

(Continued)

Leading and Coordinating Provision

TABLE 8.9 (Continued)

1:1 in-school support is available for children and this person can be chosen by the child		
Staff have access to training on the complexities of grief and the impact of both natural and traumatic deaths on children (Archer, 2008; Attig, 2015)		
Support is available for the member of staff supporting the child and this is made explicit		
Peer support is available and the peers are chosen by the child		
There are age/culturally appropriate books in the library and classrooms which talk about bereavement and loss using appropriate terminology such as 'death' and 'dead' rather than 'lost' and 'gone'		
Bereavement and loss are part of PHSE		

Source: Adapted from Child Bereavement UK (2017b)

*see Appendix and online resources for assessment template

Managing a sudden death in the school community

In my experience of SENCOs who tell me about a child, parent, sibling or member of staff dying, no one was prepared or knew what to do. As Child Bereavement UK (2017a) reports, 10,061 babies and children (under the age of 25) died in the UK in 2016 – that is 28 every day. It is likely that some of the children who die will have siblings, cousins or friends and it is important that there is support in place to help them and their families rebuild their lives.

> ### Case study
>
> 'It was quite different to not have a mum and I remember I used to say "Why did it have to happen to us?" It is quite scary going into a new school when nobody really knows about the situation you are in. I got worried when people would say "Is your mum picking you up?" At the early stage I used to panic. I didn't tell many people for a while because I just found it hard to bring it up in conversation.'
>
> (Child Bereavement UK, 2017a: 3)

It also needs to be considered that some deaths attract condemnation which can isolate and stigmatise those left behind; for example, if a family member dies due to substance misuse or suicide (Valentine et al., 2016). For a child who is bereaved by suicide the reaction of guilt and anger is common, they may feel rejected and will be left wondering why the person left them. They will need professional help, so contact a bereavement organisation (Child Bereavement UK, 2017b). I would also advise that you find out if the child witnessed any part of the suicide or previous attempts; if they found the body you need to know this information to ensure vital support is in place.

As SENCO, in collaboration with colleagues and the SLT, it is essential to have a policy/procedure in place as once a situation occurs your ability to think through what needs to happen will be very difficult. Obviously, how you respond will need to vary depending on the circumstances and the wishes of the families of the deceased; for example, some will want funeral details shared and others will not. Fortunately, the charity Child Bereavement UK has a website to guide you through preparations, with seven clear and easy to navigate sections, which are:

Social, Emotional and Mental Health Difficulties

The first 30 minutes

Refer to your school policy, which should outline your processes and guide you through the process. Identify the team and clearly define roles and responsibilities. Inform any other agencies and the Local Authority. Prepare letters to parents in advance (samples adapted from Child Bereavement UK (2017b) are provided in Figure 8.2) and collect together in school resources to support the child.

Sharing the news with the community that a child has died

Note: Before sending a letter home to caregivers about the death of a child, permission must be gained from the caregivers agreeing the contents and the distribution list.

Dear caregivers,

Today we learned that Tobin in year 5 has died. He was playing outside after school and was hit by a car. The police are interviewing witnesses, please contact them if you have any information that will help their enquiries. Obviously we are all devastated by this news and are all trying to come to terms with what has happened whilst supporting the children in school.

We understand that many children and adults will be affected by this sad news. Please let us know if your child needs additional support and we will provide it for them. We have arranged for police road safety officers to visit the school to remind them of how to keep safe.

In the coming weeks we will be organising a special assembly and memorial with Tobin's family. For now, look after each other and know we are here for you.

Yours sincerely

Sample letter to caregivers on the death of their child

Dear Claire, Jack, Tom and Chloe,

We are so sorry to hear today that Tobin died last night. As a school community we want you to know that we are all thinking of you all during this heart breaking time. We wanted to let you know that Tobin will be missed, he was a special boy, kind, funny and one of the most talented singers we have had in our school. Tobin's class teacher is making a memory box with the children which we will give to you when you feel ready. If there is anything we can do to support you or your family, please just let us know.

Yours sincerely

Sample letter following the death of a staff member

Dear caregivers,

I am sorry to break the news to you that Mr Malton died yesterday. He had been unwell for some time but it is still a shock to the school community. The class teachers are supporting the children and talking about his time at the school. We will be making a memory box for his family, we are aware that he may have taught some of the children's parents and grandparents as he taught at the school for 31 years. If you would like to contribute to the box please just let the school know. The children have already added pictures, letters and photographs celebrating his time in school. The family have asked for privacy at this time and will be sharing funeral details next week.

Yours sincerely

FIGURE 8.2 Sample letters to parents

Source: Adapted from Child Bereavement UK (2017b)

Breaking bad news

This must be discussed with the family so they can contribute what they would like to be said; there may also be religious and cultural considerations you need to respond sensitively to. In the event a death has affected an individual child and it has been decided to inform the school community, ensure the child is involved in what is going to be said. Be factual and don't make any assumptions or repeat rumours. Ensure all staff, including those who are part-time, are informed and that support is available for those who need it. It is recommended that children are told by familiar staff; ensure you guide colleagues on the terms and manner in which they break the news – pre-prepared documents that everyone adheres to are the most effective. Consider if there are any children who will need additional support to understand the news, who have been previously bereaved or who may have witnessed the death. Send the letter to caregivers the same day.

Suggested words for a primary school assembly

I have some very sad news to tell you. Emma in Year 5 died on Saturday morning in a road traffic accident. An ambulance was called and she was taken to hospital. The doctors and nurses did all they could to try to save her life but her injuries were too severe and tragically she died. Her mum is not injured.

Emma was well known throughout the school for being a Manchester United fan and a very keen member of the football team. She was only nine years old and much too young to die but sadly, very occasionally, accidents do sometimes happen. Some of you may be feeling shocked at this news, some of you might be feeling rather frightened, some of you might be feeling nothing at all. All of these feelings are okay.

When you go to your classes after this assembly, you can spend some time thinking about what I have just told you. Your teachers will try to answer any questions that you might have.

We can all help Emma's family a little bit by drawing a picture of our favourite memory of her or just writing a card that we can send to let them know that we are thinking about them.

The school will be holding a special assembly next week for Emma when we can spend more time thinking about her, remembering her, and saying a special goodbye. When I have more details I will let you all know. If any of you have ideas for this or would like to take part, I would love to hear from you.

FIGURE 8.3 Suggested words for a primary school assembly

Leading a special assembly

Child Bereavement UK (2017b) recommends you have a clear beginning, middle and end and that it takes place just before a break so the children have time to reflect before going back to class.

Introduction: Explain the purpose of the assembly and remind the children of the circumstances of the death and when it happened. Remind them that everyone will react differently: some will be sad, others thoughtful and others will have different feelings.

Main element:

- Light a candle to remember them
- Play their favourite music or read out some of their school work
- Friends and staff can recount stories and memories
- Show photographs, though a large image can be too much, particularly if family members are attending or are children in the school
- Have a memory box to share and add items to
- Create a memory tree or collage for children to add their memories to; this could be part of the assembly
- Read a story (primary)

End: Blow out the candle and give items to pass on to the family. This could end with a tree/bulb planting by each class or as a school. Play uplifting music as the children leave and remind them what support is available.

Supporting a bereaved family

Signpost the family to their GP and charity organisations as they are qualified to give bereavement support; you can find relevant charities at the end of this chapter.

Supporting the school staff

Supporting anyone through a bereavement can be emotionally draining, but it is particularly challenging when it is a child. As SENCO, in collaboration with the SLT staff, you will need to support colleagues who are working with a child who has suffered a bereavement. Providing opportunities for staff to talk about their feelings and worries is important to ensure they are supported. The list of organisations at the end of this chapter will also be useful.

Traumatic deaths

A sudden and unexpected death means the event is unplanned. Children will need support to come to terms with what has happened.

Social media and media relations

This advises schools to ensure the accuracy of any publically shared information; agree with the families what is and is not to be made public.

Looking to the future

Plan ahead and provide training for staff on bereavement and loss. Children will need support across school years even though they 'appear' to be coping.

Whole-school and classroom approaches to support the grief process

The support for a child needs to be flexible and adapted to the child's cognitive understanding, communication style and needs (Tuffrey-Wijne, 2013). Furthermore, Child Bereavement UK (2017a, 2017b) advocates that someone from the school liaises with the family to ask them their views on what should happen.

Listening: Child Bereavement UK (2017b) advises that schools need to spend quiet time with a child to give them the opportunity to talk. Again, it is vitally important that you use the word 'death' – 'I am sorry to hear about the death of your mum…' They will need to be given time to adapt and cope with a death, which can take months or years, and will affect their ability to concentrate in class.

Breathing space: Give the child permission to leave the class through the use of an agreed item or card to find some personal space when they are upset. It is imperative that they are not just wandering but are going to a designated place/person (Child Bereavement UK, 2017b).

Memory boxes: Young and Garrard (2016) advocate the use of memory boxes as a person-centred approach, which allows the child to reflect on the one they have lost in a meaningful way. The child should be encouraged to gather a range of mementos to represent the loved one such as favourite perfumes, aftershaves and unwashed clothes. Malloch and Trevarthen (2009) suggest including objects, photographs, clothing, artwork, music and writings.

Child Bereavement UK (2017) adds that video clips are particularly useful for those who have a visual impairment. These approaches are believed to facilitate healing as the child can tell the story of each item, exploring memories. The child should be encouraged to decorate the box with a person with whom they have a secure attachment. This approach is understood to give children the time and opportunity to deal with a significant loss and to deal with the range of social, emotional and physical changes that occur; it will also benefit other family members who are involved in the process (Young and Garrard, 2016).

Multisensory storytelling: These have been used effectively to explore sensitive issues with those with complex needs. Young and Garrard (2016) support this approach as it allows the child to engage with sensitive issues.

Life story work: This therapeutic approach is where a book of photographs, pictures and texts are placed in chronological order to verbally explore the history of the lost person's life (Read and Bowler, 2007).

Support groups for adults: McClatchey (2018) in small-scale research with ten bereaved fathers with dependents found the benefits of support groups. She suggests peer-support groups in schools and health services would be helpful.

SENCO TASK

Use the example of a bereavement policy on the https://childbereavementuk.org website (in the schools tab, select primary/secondary schools) to develop one which is suited to your school.

Bereavement and loss: Useful books

TABLE 8.10 Bereavement and loss: Useful books

Age phase	Title	Strengths
Primary	Gibbs, C. (2015) *A Sky of Diamonds*. London: Jessica Kingsley Publishers.	This is a story for children about loss, grief and hope. This book tells the story of Mia whose mother dies unexpectedly. She asks questions about what has happened and this book supports you in leading discussions with a child as they are experiencing the range of emotions associated with the death of a loved one.
Upper primary to FE (10+)	Helbert, K. (2013) *Finding Your Own Way to Grieve: A creative activity workbook for kids and teens on the autism spectrum*. London: Jessica Kingsley.	Although this book suggests it is for children with autism, it is suitable for all children. The book explains death in clear terms and supports the exploring of feelings and emotions through writing, art and craft, cooking, movement, relaxation and remembrance activities.
For colleagues	Child Bereavement UK (2017) School Information Pack	This pack aims to provide you with support and information when a death occurs in the school community or if the school is facing an expected death. It is very useful as it contains information sheets, resources and examples you can use within your school to help support staff, children and the community at a difficult time. It also includes a bereavement policy.

Substance misuse (drugs)

Definition

The United Nations Office on Drugs and Crime (2017) defines problem drug use as those who engage in the high-risk consumption of drugs; for example, injecting drugs, using drugs on a daily basis and/or people diagnosed with drug use disorders (harmful use or drug dependence), based on clinical criteria as contained in the Diagnostic and Statistical Manual of Mental Disorders (fifth edition) of the American Psychiatric Association, or the International Classification of Diseases (tenth revision) of the World Health Organization.

Prevalence

The United Nations Office on Drugs and Crime (UNODC) (2017) reports that there is an estimated minimum of 190,000 premature deaths globally from drug use.

Assessment/treatment

There are international standards for the Treatment of Drug Use Disorders, which were prepared by the United Nations Office on Drugs and Crime and the World Health Organization (UNODC, 2015).

> **Support organisations**
>
> **Child Bereavement UK:** Provides support to families and professionals when a child dies or when a child is bereaved of someone important in their life.
>
> **Website:** www.childbereavementuk.org **Helpline:** 0800 02 888 40
>
> **Email:** support@childbereavementuk.org
>
> **Child Bereavement Network:** The Childhood Bereavement Network (CBN) is the hub for those working with bereaved children, young people and their families across the UK.
>
> **Website:** www.childhoodbereavementnetwork.org.uk/home.aspx
>
> **Helpline:** Support online only
>
> **Child Death Helpline:** A telephone helpline for anyone affected by the death of a child, from pre-birth to the death of an adult child, however long ago, and whatever the circumstances.
>
> **Website:** http://childdeathhelpline.org.uk
> **Helpline:** 0800 282 986/0808 800 6019
>
> **Email:** contact@childdeathhelpline.org
>
> **Winston's Wish:** Supports bereaved children up to the age of 18 through a whole range of activities including a helpline, group work, residential events and resources.
>
> **Website:** www.winstonswish.org **Helpline:** 08008 020 021
>
> **Email:** info@winstonswish.org

Why do young people take drugs?

Mind (2018) advises that addiction is linked to mental health difficulties that may begin as a way to cope with how people feel. The UNODC (2015) includes the following as the most powerful risk factors: biological processes, personality traits, mental health needs, family neglect and abuse, poor attachment to school and the community, and growing up in marginalised and deprived communities. It is important to note that all children can take drugs and that this spans all socio-economic groups and households; it may just be that they are curious and want to experiment.

Supporting caregivers and carers in talking to their child

The NHS (2018j) acknowledges that caregivers can find conversations about drug use difficult. Their advice when drugs are found is to remain calm and then discuss concerns with love and without anger. As SENCO, you may find out about a child's drug use from a parent. The guidance from the NHS (2018j) is that concerns should not be raised while the child is high but during a relaxed period in the household. Many teenagers will experiment with drugs but only a small proportion will then become dependent.

Which drugs are addictive?

The list of drugs that young people can become addicted to is extensive. This section will focus on cannabis, cocaine, ecstasy/MDMA, LSD and heroin. These drugs affect the brain and body in different ways as they impact stimulators in the brain (getting high, being stoned). Drugs are classified A–C, with Class A drugs being the most harmful; all drugs discussed in this section are illegal. The UNODC (2017) reports that those who inject drugs face the most severe health consequences including living with HIV (1 in 8) and hepatitis C (more than 50%).

Table 8.11 below is intended to develop your knowledge base of drugs so that you can identify/support the young person prior to them gaining support through the NHS or charity organisations.

The most common drugs used by teenagers

Key:

Class A: Illegal to have for personal use, to give away or sell

Penalty: Possession – up to 7 years in prison

Supplying – up to life in prison and/or an unlimited fine

Class B: Illegal to have for personal use, to give away or sell

Penalty: Possession – up to 5 years in prison

Supplying – up to 14 years in prison and a fine

Whole-school and classroom approaches

The UNODC (2015) advocates the use of preventative strategies based on scientific evidence with families, schools and communities to protect children. They add that the primary objective of drug prevention is to avoid or delay initiation into the use of drugs or, if they have started, to prevent dependence. They advise the focus in schools should be on engaging children in structured activities to give them opportunities to learn and develop personal and social skills.

The charity DrugWise recommends that drug education includes:

- Increasing knowledge and understanding of drugs, their use, dangers, the law and agencies who can provide support
- An exploration of views, to challenge attitudes and stereotypes
- Assertiveness training so they are enabled to say 'no'

TABLE 8.11 Overview of street drugs

Drug	Street names	Appearance	Classification/Law	Some effects	Risks
Cannabis: Can be smoked (in a spliff, joint or pipe (bong). Can be eaten when mixed in cookies or cakes	Weed, skunk, grass, green, solid, sensi, resin, puff, pot, hashish, hash, ganja, draw, dope, bud and bhang	Hash: black or brown lump. Grass/Weed/Skunk: dried herbs	Class B	Chilled out, happy, relaxed, suspicious, hungry, mood swings. Hallucination, altered senses. Lack of concentration, anxious. Whitey – feel light-headed/sick	Addiction. Affects brain function, can induce anxiety, panic attacks, hallucinations and paranoia. Reduced memory. Lung disease (when smoked). Feeling faint, sickness. Increased risk of psychotic illness
Cocaine: Smoked (in a pipe, glass tube, bottle or foil) or snorted (divided into lines)	White, wash, toot, stones, snow, rocks, percy, pebbles, freebase, crack, coke, ching, Charlie, chang, C	Coke: a white powder. Crack: is a form of cocaine made into small lumps or rocks	Class A	Wide awake, on top of the world, confident. Effects: immediate for smoking crack, peaking for around 2 minutes but lasting only 10 minutes. Effects: snorting coke takes longer to peak and lasts 20–30 minutes. Reduces hunger. Crash period/come down lasts days	Death from overdose and Speedballing (injecting cocaine and heroin can be fatal). Feeling invincible, risky behaviours. Increased heart rate, convulsions, heart attack/failure, damaged cartilage in nose, depression, ulcer, gangrene
Ecstasy: Chemical name MDMA. Swallowed but can be crushed, smoked, snorted or if powdered dabbed onto gums	XTC, superman, rolexes, pink superman, pills, Mitsubishis, MDMA, mandy, E, dolphins, crystal, cowies, brownies	Pure ecstasy is a powder of white crystals. Usually sold on the street as tablets in a range of colours, often with designs and logos	Class A	Feel energised, alert, talkative and alive. Can make music and colours seem more intense. Feeling love and affection for everyone around them. Anxiety, panic attacks, confusion, paranoia and psychosis. Dilated pupils. Tightening of jaw muscles	Comedown leaves people lethargic and depressed. Memory problems. Anxiety. Liver, kidney and heart problems. Overheating and dehydration. Those with heart/blood pressure problems, epilepsy or asthma can have a dangerous reaction. Death (670 between 1996 and 2014) (Frank, 2018)

(Continued)

TABLE 8.11 (Continued)

Drug	Street names	Appearance	Classification/Law	Some effects	Risks
LSD: Tabs (or pellets) are swallowed. Drops of liquid acid are dripped onto food, like a sugar cube and eaten	Windows, trips, tab, stars, smilies, rainbows, paper mushrooms, micro dot, lucy, liquid acid, lightening flash, L, hawk, flash, drop, dots, cheer, blotter and acid	Appearance varies as it is marketed in many forms with new substances emerging and disappearing (UNODC, 2017)	Class A	A trip: can take up to 20 minutes to up to 2 hours to take effect Can make users happy and relaxed with nice hallucinations. A bad trip can make them agitated and confused with scary hallucinations Speeding up and slowing down of movements and time Distortion of colour, sounds and objects Feeling tired, anxious, panicky and/or depressed	Flashbacks which can happen days, months or years later Harming themselves during a bad trip Can trigger mental health problems No evidence to suggest long-term damage to the body or long-term psychological damage No evidence that it is addictive
Heroin: Made from morphine, extracted from the opium poppy	Smack, skag, horse, H, gear, brown	Pure heroin is a white powder, but it can be cut with a range of substances so can be from brownish white to brown	Class A	Feeling of warmth and wellbeing It is a very strong painkiller with the effects lasting a number of hours	Highly addictive and sharing equipment increases risk of catching or spreading a virus such as HIV or hepatitis C Overdoses, coma and death as it can cause respiratory failure (where breathing stops) and inhaling of vomit due to sedation effects Gangrene and damage to veins and arteries

It is recommended that schools contact local services who support young people to find out their approaches and to get advice on what works best. The FRANK website has a facility where you can enter your postcode and find the services nearest to you alongside some national agencies.

Useful book

Age phase	Title	Strengths
Colleagues and children (check age suitability)	Taylor, C. (1992) *The House That Crack Built*. San Francisco: Chronicle Books.	This is a useful book for professionals, parents, families and teenagers as it illustrates the impact of the supply and taking of illegal drugs and the impact on babies born every day. The illustrations should be used as talking points as staff teams and where appropriate with young people.

Sectioning

There are different types of sections within the Mental Health Act 1983; this legislation covers assessment, treatment and rights of those with a mental health need. The decision to detain someone under this Act is usually made by two doctors and an Approved Mental Health Professional. In an emergency the police, a magistrate or doctor can also use powers within the Act for 72 hours. There are different rules on how long children can be detained in hospital (section 2 up to 28 days and section 3 up to 6 months). What happens to children when they are sectioned depends on their specific mental health needs and need for care and treatment and their personal circumstances. Being sectioned means you are admitted to hospital whether or not you agree to it, as the authority to admit comes from the law, not your consent. The reasons for sectioning a child are:

- they need urgent assessment and treatment
- their health is at risk of becoming worse if they do not receive treatment

> **Support organisations**
>
> **Childline:** A very useful and child-friendly site which includes clear overviews of mental health issues children may have. It provides helpful video clips on what happens when you visit a doctor.
>
> **Website:** www.childline.org.uk   **Helpline:** 0800 1111
>
> **1:2:1 online chat and email also available**
>
> **Change, Grow, Live:** Works with people who want to change their lives for the better. Their areas of expertise include substance misuse, children's services and family services. Within the 'get help' tab on the website you can enter your postcode to find the nearest support service; there is advice and information, self-assessment tools and online support.
>
> **Website:** www.changegrowlive.org   There is no direct email/phone number but an online form to complete for support.
>
> **FRANK:** Provides friendly, confidential drugs advice. There is a useful A–Z of drugs, frequently asked questions and detailed advice and guidance.
>
> **Website:** www.talktofrank.com   **Helpline:** 0300 123 6600
>
> **Text:** 82111   **Email and live chat** also available through the website
>
> **SchoolBeat:** A bilingual site from the All-Wales Liaison Core Programme, providing information and resources for teachers, children and parents.

Leading and Coordinating Provision

> The website has three main themes: drug and substance abuse, social behaviour and personal safety.
>
> **Website:** www.schoolbeat.org   There is email available through the website.

- their safety or the safety of others is at serious risk if they don't receive treatment quickly
- a doctor thinks they need assessment and treatment in hospital.

Longfield (2017) shares the promise made by the prime minister that by 2021 no child will have to travel 'out of area' to access in-patient mental healthcare. This is to address the 65% of children requiring a bed who this applies to.

Chapter summary

- 1 in 10 children have a diagnosable mental health need
- As SENCO, you cannot diagnose mental health but you can promote preventative approaches and support children and colleagues in school
- There is a national issue with timely early intervention, assessment and treatment for children with a range of SEMH challenges
- Mental health has not been as prioritised as physical health and there are ongoing issues with funding and staffing in the health services
- Public attitudes towards mental health are improving
- Schools will need to have a designated senior lead for mental health to establish a whole-school approach to mental health and resilience amongst children and staff
- Mental health challenges disproportionately affect those who have encountered childhood adverse experiences

9
Neurodiversity

Sarah Martin-Denham

- NASENCO outcomes: How development is affected by Special Educational Needs and Disability (SEND) and the teaching they receive, high incidence SEN and implication for teaching, learning, inclusive practice and removing barriers to participation and effective practice in including children with SEND. Plan and intervene to meet the needs of children with SEND; Theories of learning as the basis upon which to design an effective intervention.
- Read alongside: Chapter 8: Social, Emotional and Mental Health Difficulties; Chapter 12: Person-Centred Approaches

Chapter overview

The intention of this chapter is to develop your knowledge and understanding of neurodiversity, the strengths and challenges it can bring and to provide evidence-based approaches to provision and practice. There will be a focus on responding to the interests and needs of children to provide relevant school experiences that promote success and wellbeing. This chapter will allow you to reflect on how effectively we teach children who are neurodiverse and to explore some screening tools to provide indicators of individual needs.

Neurodiversity

The term 'specific learning difficulties (SpLD)' is used as an umbrella term for those who have specific rather than general learning differences, which are lifelong and affect the way information is learned and processed. They are neurological (rather than psychological), usually run in families, occur independently of intelligence and vary in severity. Zakopoulou et al. (2014) acknowledge that the term SpLD integrates a number of difficulties, such as dyslexia, dyspraxia, dysgraphia, autism, sensory processing disorder and attention deficit hyperactivity disorder (AD(H)D). The British Dyslexia Association (2017) agrees, adding that SpLD is a term used to cover a range of frequently co-occurring difficulties. A more recent term being used to describe SpLD is neurodiversity.

'Neurodiversity is an understanding that neurological differences are to be honoured and respected as with any human variation, including diversity in ethnicity, gender identity, religion and sexual orientation' (Armstrong, 2017: 10). This is a relatively new term and was coined by Singer, a social scientist in 1998 as a move away from the medical model of disability. It is the idea that there is not one 'typical' type of brain or mind, everyone is different and this should be celebrated; it is simply human variation. It is important to remember that every child who is neurodiverse will present differently; for example, a child with dyslexia may have greater challenges with planning and organisation but another child with spelling and decoding. Furthermore, secondary needs may have a greater impact on them than their primary need; they could have a diagnosis of autism but it is anxiety that is the barrier to learning and interaction. Both primary and secondary needs must be assessed and understood for there to be effective provision to meet needs. There will also need to be reasonable adjustments applied, as diagnosed needs in the neurodiverse range would be a disability in accordance with the Equality Act 2010. Interventions need to be chosen according to a full assessment of needs, with an acknowledgement that no single approach will be effective for all children. The co-existence of common diagnoses is illustrated below (Figure 9.1):

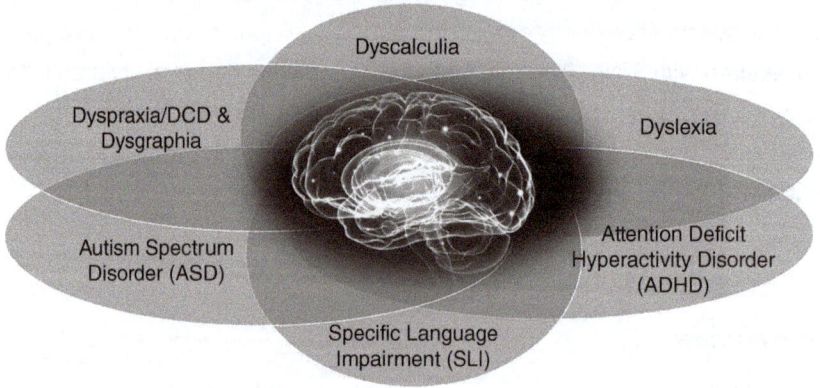

FIGURE 9.1 SpLD and neurodiversity

Source: Patoss and DfE (2018)

REFLECTIVE ACTIVITY

In this chapter, you will find the national prevalence for the neurodiverse range. You can use this as a comparison to the diagnosis rates in your school.

This will allow to you to:

Identify any under/over identification

Identify where you may need to carry out additional training for your colleagues

---

The implications of neurodiversity in education are that the mindset needs changing from 'Why can't they do that/cope with this?' to 'what are their strengths/how can I support them?' The needs of children who are 'neurodiverse' can be met by thinking about how we present learning experiences in classrooms to focus on what their skills are and how best to develop them.

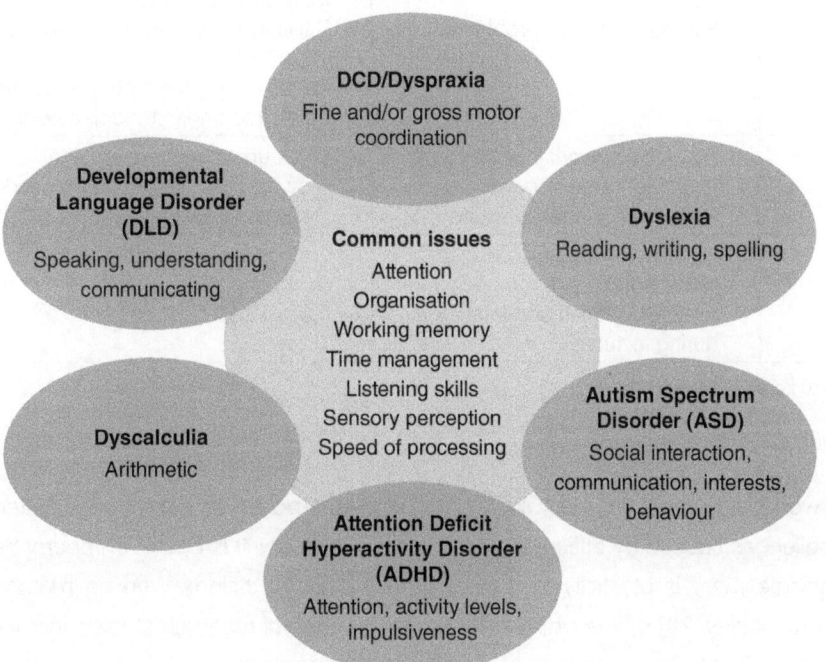

FIGURE 9.2 Neurodiversity

Source: Teaching for Neurodiversity: A guide to specific learning difficulties funded by the DfE (2018)

Working memory

Working memory is a term which was proposed by Baddeley and Hitch (1974) to describe separate but interconnecting temporary memory systems that are involved in maintaining and manipulating the information needed to carry out tasks such as learning, understanding and reasoning. It is a system for storing and processing information for short periods of time. Challenges with working memory are common in children who are neurodiverse and in children who have experienced a brain injury.

Alloway and Alloway (2015: 3–4) discuss two types of working memory:

- Verbal working memory (to remember instructions, learn language and complete reading comprehension)
- Visual-spatial working memory (linked to mathematics skills and remembering sequences of patterns, images and locations)

TABLE 9.1 Indicators for working memory intervention

Age	Working memory is crucial for...	Indicators that working memory needs exercise
Preschool	<ul><li>Learning the alphabet</li><li>Following short instructions</li><li>Repeating rhymes</li><li>Staying on task to complete independent activities</li></ul>	<ul><li>Unwilling to learn alphabet, numbers</li><li>Can't focus long enough to understand instructions</li><li>Can't recall even when repeated</li><li>Flits from one task to another</li></ul>
Primary school	<ul><li>Reading and comprehension</li><li>Mental arithmetic</li><li>Interaction and responding to others</li><li>Solving multi-step problems</li></ul>	<ul><li>Can read (decode) but not understand the material read</li><li>Problems with remembering mathematics facts such as number bonds</li><li>Difficulty waiting turns and taking part in group activities</li><li>Reads the problem but cannot break it down into understandable parts</li></ul>
Secondary school	<ul><li>Doing homework independently</li><li>Planning for an activity</li><li>Participating in team sports</li></ul>	<ul><li>Gives up without supervision</li><li>May pack but forgets items needed</li><li>Problems understanding/grasping the rules</li></ul>
College	<ul><li>Focusing on and following a conversation</li><li>Sustaining focus and interest during lectures</li></ul>	<ul><li>Changes topics suddenly, makes irrelevant comments</li><li>Falls asleep or 'zones out'</li></ul>

Source: Adapted from Cogmed (2018)

Cogmed working memory training (CWMT) is an evidence-based computer-based intervention for attention challenges caused by difficulties with working memory. It is based on neuroscientific findings that indicate there is plasticity in areas of the brain that include working memory capacity (Söderqvist and Nutley, 2016). It is claimed there are 80 original research studies that examine the positive effects of CWMT, including that it leads to improvements in:

- working memory from childhood to adulthood
- attention
- learning outcomes in reading and mathematics
- the brain's neurochemistry, in particular the dopamine receptors.

Below is an outline of common learning differences with definitions, national prevalence, causes, indicators, barriers to learning and evidence-based approaches to learning. The approaches to learning provided are good practice for all children, not just those who are neurodiverse. Some sections provide evidence from systematic reviews and others from singular pieces of research.

Systematic reviews

These provide the most reliable source of evidence to give assurance of effectiveness of an intervention. They are a systematic review of all available primary research in an area to establish the existing knowledge and evidence base; for example, on the effectiveness of a particular intervention, strategy or approach. Researchers will have clear aims and objectives and a set of eligibility criteria for the research studies they will include for analysis. The difficulty with evidence-based practice is understanding what this actually means; often the research can be limited to a few studies which may focus on differing skills that are gained from an intervention. It can also be the case that the benefits are short term, so it is useful to consider what works in meeting the individual needs of the child; you will find that different strategies and resources work effectively and you won't know the reason why. As the Code states, 'ensure the approaches used are based on the best possible evidence and are having the required impact on progress' (DfE, 2015a: 25). The purpose of this is to ensure that children are provided with interventions and practices, which are shown to be effective through research.

Essential source

The Cochrane Database of Systematic Reviews (CDSR) is the leading journal database for systematic reviews in healthcare but these are often highly relevant to education. It identifies, appraises and synthesises all empirical evidence that meets the pre-specified eligibility criteria to answer a specific research question.

Website: www.cochranelibrary.com

General learning and teaching approaches for neurodiversity: Evidence based

TABLE 9.2   General learning and teaching approaches for neurodiversity: Evidence based

Inclusive approach	Evidence/research base
Use of mathematics manipulatives to support children with disabilities	Bouck and Park (2018) **systematic review**
Equipment available without request including coloured overlays, writing slopes, counting frames, number squares, story frames, word mats and stationery	El Zein et al. (2014)
Support with sitting still through exercise balls, wobble boards, bean bags or standing desks	Goodmon et al. (2014)
Flipped learning models (teaching outside, child-led learning, teacher as a coach, collaborative approaches)	Altemueller and Lindquist (2017)
Consistent font, size and no underline agreed as a school	British Dyslexia Association Guidance (2018a, 2018b)

Dyslexia

Definition

According to the British Dyslexia Association (BDA) (2018a) the word 'dyslexia' is Greek in origin and means 'difficulty with words'; it is a lifelong difficulty. The International Dyslexia Association (2018)

adds that dyslexia 'is characterised by difficulties with accurate and/or fluent word recognition and poor spelling and decoding abilities.'

National prevalence

The BDA (2018a) estimates that 10% of children in the UK have dyslexia. However, as with all neuro-diversity, often it is undiagnosed so the numbers could be higher.

Co-existence

The International Dyslexia Association (2018) estimates that 30% of those with dyslexia have ADHD; they share difficulties with reading due to the attention and concentration it demands and the inability to maintain attention as they become tired or unstimulated so losing their place.

Known causes

There is no definitive cause identified due to a lack of consistent results from pathological and imaging studies (International Dyslexia Association, 2018).

Indicators

Dyslexia occurs across ethnicities, backgrounds and abilities, and varies from child to child: no two people will have the same strengths and challenges. Dyslexia occurs independently of intelligence and can affect learning and the acquisition of literacy skills. Dyslexia is not just literacy difficulties, it can affect:

- the ability to organise and plan effectively
- the ability to remember spoken information
- the retrieval of words from long-term memory
- concentration, coordination and numeracy skills
- the ability to remember multiple instructions
- reading comprehension
- self-confidence, causing feelings of isolation and exclusion.

Some common indicators of dyslexia are outlined below (see Table 9.3). These are not to be used to diagnose a child but to inform interventions, learning and teaching approaches that are designed to respond to their needs.

TABLE 9.3 Indicators of dyslexia across the age phases

Pre-school	Primary	Secondary
Family history of dyslexia/reading difficulties		
Poor concentration, confidence and self-esteem		

Pre-school	Primary	Secondary
Jumbled phrases (e.g. 'beddy tear')	Has particular difficulty with reading and spelling	Still reads and spells inaccurately
Use of substitute words (e.g. lampshade for lamppost)	Puts letters and figures the wrong way round	Difficulty planning and writing essays
Difficulty remembering nursery rhymes and rhyming words	Leaves letters out of words or puts them in the wrong order	Gets mixed up with long words such as preliminary and philosophical
Later than expected speech development and an inconsistent naming of objects	Can confuse 'b' and 'd' and words such as 'no/on'. Confuses left and right, days of the week and months of the year	Confuses places, times and dates and continues to confuse left and right, days and months
Difficulties dressing and putting shoes on correct feet	Difficulties dressing and tying shoe laces	Difficulty processing complex language or a series of instructions
Did not crawl	Still needs to use fingers or marks on paper to make simple calculations, remembering times tables and alphabet	
Enjoys reading but has no interest in letters or words	Has problems understanding what he/she has read	
Difficulty catching, kicking or throwing a ball, hopping and skipping	Takes longer than average to do written work	
Difficulty with clapping a simple rhythm	Problems in processing language at speed	

Source: Irving and Martin-Denham (2015); British Dyslexia Association (2018a)

Indicators specific to reading

- Difficulty in looking at written page
- Complaining of headaches or feeling sick
- Regularly turning away from written page, being unable to look at it for fixed periods of time
- Moving closer to or further away from the text when reading
- Rubbing eyes
- Complaining of eyes feeling itchy, tired and scratchy
- Commenting that the words appear to move
- Affected by different levels of light or glare of black print on white paper

(Irving and Martin-Denham, 2015)

Identification

An educational psychologist will be able to do a full assessment to identify dyslexia and learning needs. If the school does not have the funding or you need a first step approach to identifying the needs of children where you have concerns, free checklists have been produced – see Patoss: www.patoss-dyslexia.org. Go to the website and search 'neurodiversity'; it is not a diagnostic tool but will give you an indication of the areas to focus an intervention on. An example is given below (see Figure 9.3).

The guidance by Patoss recommends that for each behaviour you select the relevant response: **'not at all'**, **'sometimes'** or **'often'**. You should complete all checklists due to co-existence of needs;

Leading and Coordinating Provision

they are available as one document for dyslexia, dyspraxia, ADHD, autism, dyscalculia and sensory language needs. By examining the sometimes and often responses you will have an overview of the child's areas of difficulty. Teachers could use the completed checklist to discuss with you as SENCO the next steps and recommendations for adaptations to learning and teaching and to implement interventions as part of the graduated approach.

	For each behaviour, select not at all, sometimes or often	not at all	sometimes	often
Dyslexia	Other family members with similar difficulties			
	Problems recalling facts			
	Difficulty with recalling/following instructions			
	Difficulty remembering sequential information			
	Poor concept of time			
	Poor organisation skills			
	Difficulty with fluent, accurate reading			
	Continued difficulty with phonological awareness			
	Persistent difficulty with spelling			
	Poor structure/organisation of written work			
	Difficulty copying from the board			
	Has obvious good/bad days			
	Low self-esteem			
	Work avoidance tactics used			
	Poor comprehension skills			
	Slow speed of writing			
	Weak short-term and/or working memory			
	Slow speed of reading			

FIGURE 9.3 Indicator checklist for dyslexia

Source: www.patoss-dyslexia.org

> **Case study**
>
> Eleni was in her GCSE year and had a diagnosis of dyslexia, dyspraxia and dyscalculia. As part of her agreed 'reasonable adjustments' she was not required to read out loud in class as it made her anxious. For her English coursework she was required to take part in a role play, including reading from a script. The school, caregiver and Eleni agreed that she could instead have a structured conversation 1:1 with her key worker. Eleni would still demonstrate the same knowledge but in an alternative format.

Evidence-based programmes, apps and resources

The Dyslexia-SpLD Trust (www.thedyslexia-spldtrust.org.uk) (2018) has a website which provides an online tool to search for evidence-based interventions. You can filter the results as a list view or complete an advanced search, by school phase, the areas of difficulty and whether it is a teacher's, computer or other resource you need. Interventions for dyslexia vary in the number of sessions, how often they are delivered/accessed, group sizes and total number of hours; what is clear in the literature is that the best outcomes happen where there is early intervention in small groups, by well-trained staff (Griffiths and Stuart, 2013).

The IDL Literacy (https://idlsgroup.com) online programme by Ascentis is a multi-sensory, web-based and simple to use resource for both students and teachers, with the added benefit of the child choosing the background and font colour. This specialist dyslexia support software can be used with children showing dyslexic indicators, for children with EAL and for those with a low level of literacy ability. IDL Literacy is said to improve reading and spelling ages by an average of 11 months after just 26 hours' use, along with reports of improved self-esteem, confidence and engagement with school life in general (Scrase, 1998). Below is an example of a chart produced by the resource, which shows the increase in reading and spelling age following the intervention (Figure 9.4).

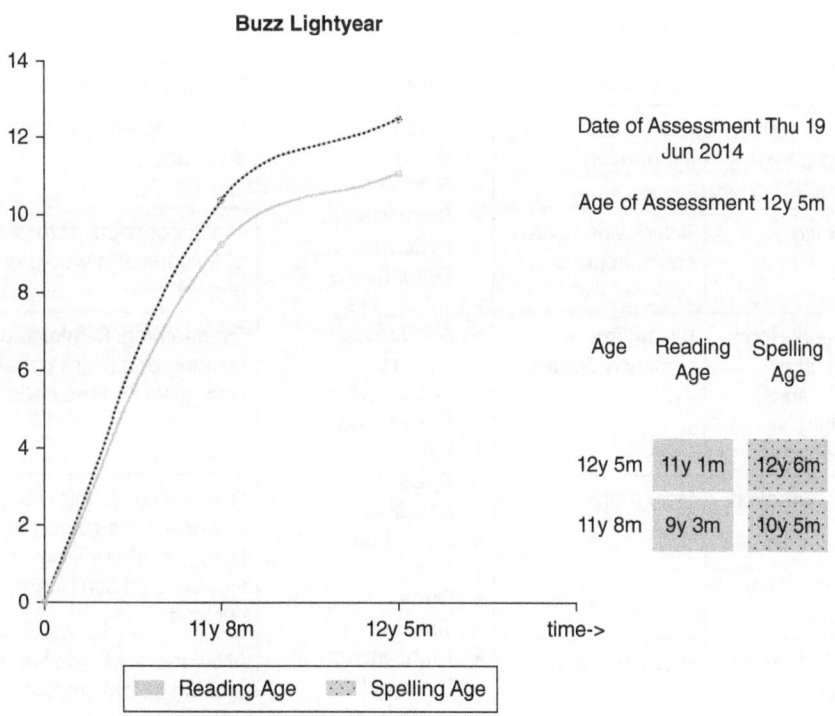

FIGURE 9.4 IDL literacy chart of progress

Source: IDL

Lexia (www.lexiauk.co.uk): For children Y1–Y8 who are reading two years below their chronological age, the intervention is for ten weeks for 20 minutes, two or three times a week. It is web-based and can be accessed at home. Lexia is a phonics-based intervention beginning at initial letter level and includes a comprehension element. Three studies published in *Reading Psychology* have shown that Lexia reading improves early literacy skills when used in conjunction with classroom reading (Macaruso and Rodman, 2009, 2011).

TABLE 9.4 Systematic review: Evidence-based approaches for dyslexia

Outcome	Approach	Researchers	Number of research studies reviewed/ dates
Phonics training has a positive effect on non-word reading accuracy and a moderate effect on word reading accuracy, word reading fluency, spelling, letter-sound knowledge and phonological output	Schools need to test poor word readers for a wide range of reading skills to determine if the have the difficulties that respond to phonics	McArthur et al., 2012 Cochrane Library	11/1990–2009

Table 9.5 (adapted from Irving and Martin-Denham, 2015; British Dyslexia Association, 2018a) highlights dyslexia-friendly practice. Note that not all strategies work for all children, so modify these to meet individual needs.

TABLE 9.5 Dyslexia friendly approaches

Presentation	Resources	Recording	Teaching strategies
Consistent approach agreed as a whole school	Highlighters for key information	• Audio • Video • Pictures • Discussion • Podcasts • Dictaphones • Talking tins • Mind maps • Posters • Drama/Dance • Presentations • Lists • Apps • Labelling • Flow charts • Music • Grids • Timeline • Highlighting • Bullet points • Speech bubbles • Cartoons • Drawings • Photographs • Sculpture • PowerPoint • Role play • Pictures/collage • Bar charts • Sorting • iPads, tablets, laptops and computers	Praise, motivate, engage and give feedback
1.5 line spacing	Tinted wipe boards, pastel paper and coloured overlays		Teach concepts across a series of lessons in a week, or as a project
Dyslexia friendly fonts (agree one) arial, calibri, comic sans, century gothic, verdana, trebuchet	Writing frames, sentence starters		Overlearning: Reinforce prior learning and revisit current themes with no written methods
Important information in **bold**	Story maps		Pre-reading discussions about the characters, the context and the blurb – read any tricky words together and don't insist they read out loud
Coloured transparency for board work	Post-it notes		Allow the child planning time and drafting before starting to formally write
No underline or italics	Learning walls		Unless the target is related to written recording, let them choose an alternative method (see recording column)
Important information in **bold**	Colour-coded timetables		Multi-sensory techniques across subjects
Coloured transparency for board work	A wide range of books related to their interests including comics; timers		Break down learning into small sequences of steps

Presentation	Resources	Recording	Teaching strategies
No underline or italics	Spares of stationery		Collaborative/cooperative learning project groups using multimedia materials
			Opportunities for ongoing verbal feedback
			Use of visuals to support memory and organisation
			Dimming the lights and electronic whiteboards
			Put any printed-off work onto pastel paper
			Give a longer response time as they may take longer to process and respond to your questions
			Pre-write the date and learning objectives in their books or have a date stamp

Source: Irving and Martin-Denham (2015); British Dyslexia Association (2018a)

www.callscotland.org.uk: This website includes 'a wheel of apps' for children with dyslexia, reading and writing difficulties; produced in 2017 it is the 6th version. The poster of apps can be downloaded and displayed in schools (see Figure 9.5 on the next page).

Google drive: If you go to 'tools' in a document there is a 'voice typing' facility. This is free and easy to use.

Irlen Syndrome

Irlen Syndrome is also referred to as Meares-Irlen Syndrome, Scotopic Sensitivity and Visual Stress. Those with Irlen are likely to have difficulty with glare and bright lights (particularly unnatural lighting). The child may experience physical symptoms such as tiredness, dizziness and/or headaches. The impact of this is that it is difficult to track text from word to word and line to line, it is easy to lose your place and causes frustration. Furthermore:

- Between 35–40% of children with dyslexic difficulties may experience visual disturbance when reading
- It is a visual perception difficulty
- Text can appear distorted and words or letters appear to move or become blurred
- White paper or backgrounds can appear too dazzling and make print hard to decipher, particularly when reading directly under a light source
- Natural lighting can help overcome some visual problems and in particular the avoidance of white backgrounds
- Coloured filters, overlays and glasses can reduce visual disturbance

Leading and Coordinating Provision

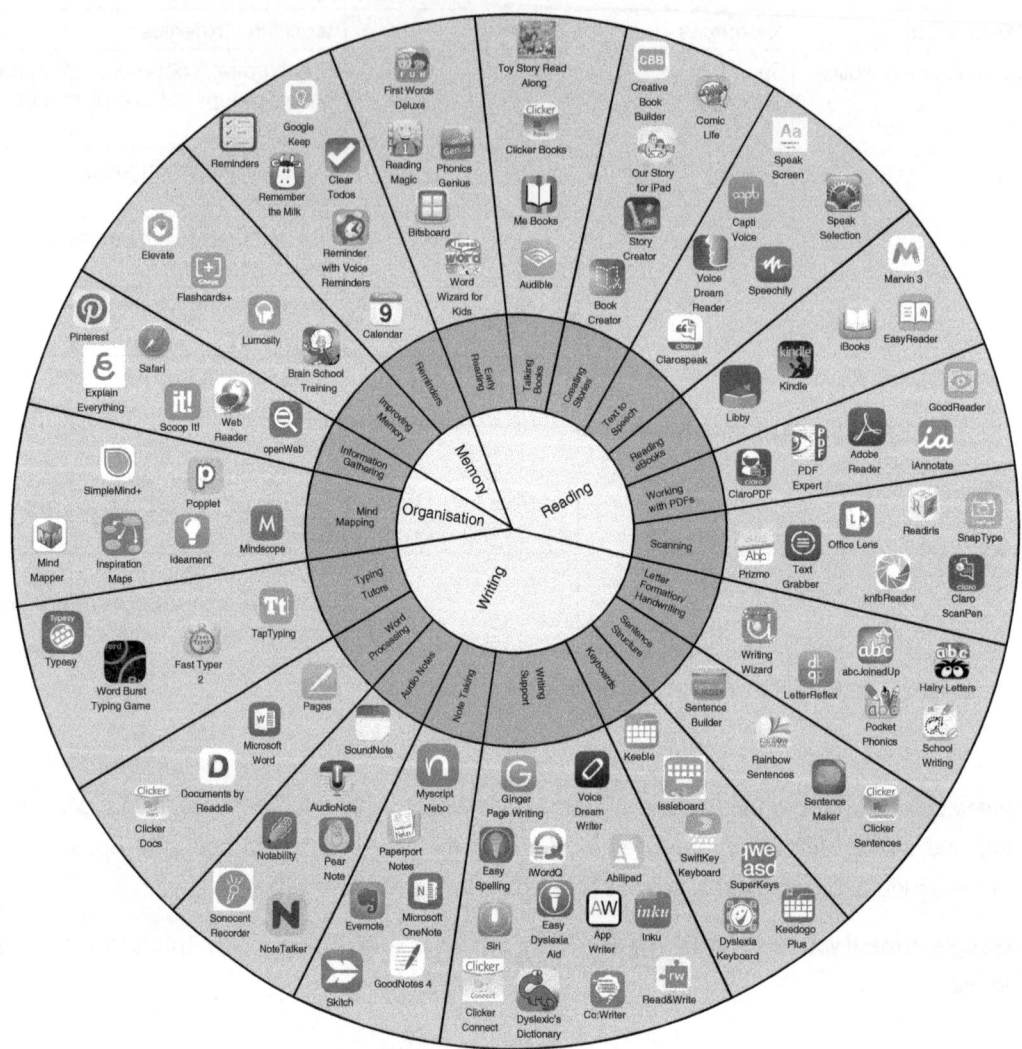

FIGURE 9.5 iPad apps for learners with dyslexia
Source: www.callscotland.org.uk

Dyscalculia

Definition

The term 'developmental dyscalculia (DD)' was coined by Cohn in 1968, to describe a learning difficulty in basic numerical and mathematical operations such as addition and subtraction. More recently, the American Psychiatric Association (2013) suggests DD is a specific learning disability characterised by persistent challenge in processing numerical information and learning arithmetic facts.

National prevalence

This is at around 5% though believed to be nearer to 25% in reality (BDA, 2018b). The BDA (2018b) highlights that diagnoses of DD are still in their infancy; this is largely due to a lack of awareness and specialism within educational psychology.

Co-existence

DD occurs alongside types of neurodiversity, in particular dyslexia and ADHD.

Known causes

The origins of DD are unknown but theories have suggested it is related to differences in cognitive functions; for example, magnitude representation (estimating and comprehending an amount), working memory, inhibition, spatial skills or phonological ability (Szucs and Goswami, 2013).

Indicators

Butterworth (2005) clarified that children with dyscalculia lag behind their peers in mathematical progress and attainment, but their general cognitive ability, reading and writing skills are at expected level.

It is important to remember that the indicators for DD will vary from child to child and their main barrier to learning may be not having their needs met in class, leading to anxiety and low self-esteem. Table 9.6 below provides some common indicators that a child with DD may display.

TABLE 9.6 Common indicators of dyslexic difficulties

Number	Time	Shape/estimation
Working memory		
Slower response time to problems and avoidance strategies (toilet, sharpening pencils)		
Difficulty with sense of number, visualising numbers and connections between them	Unable to tell the time from analogue clock, confused by 6:10 and ten past 6	Lack of number sense, to approximate (to know how many) without having to count
Difficulty counting from a given point, backwards or forwards	Unable to estimate time or lapses of time	
Counting 1 by 1 rather than groups of objects, confusion with the 100 square	Difficulty with the days of the week and months of the year	Problems remembering shape names
Forgets mathematical processes, for example division	Often late (for school and lessons)	Problems recalling the properties of shapes (cube/cuboid)
Difficulty recalling how to write numerals or recall number bonds or times tables	Difficulty with 24-hour clock	Difficulties with the spelling of shapes
Confused number direction (12 or 21)	Difficulty following timetables	Difficulty with spatial imagery between 2D and 3D shapes
Confusing and applying mathematical symbols × − + ÷	May find drawing shapes challenging due to recall	

Identification

DSM-5 and ICD-10 have a criterion for diagnosis known as 'specific disorder of arithmetic skills': the child must be significantly below the level expected for their age and it should not be due to a learning disability or inadequate educational provision. As with dyslexia, formal diagnosis will usually be made by an educational psychologist who specialises in DD.

Other routes to identification should be completed with the child to give an ***indication*** of DD.

TABLE 9.7 Dyscalculia checklist

Dyscalculia			
For each behaviour, please select either not at all, sometimes or often.			
Behaviour	**Not at all**	**Sometimes**	**Often**
Other family members with similar difficulties			
Problems with counting			
Confusion with number direction, e.g. 93 or 39			
Difficulty remembering how numbers are written			
Difficulties understanding mathematical symbols			
Difficulties with the concept of space and/or direction			
Takes a long time to complete mathematics tasks			
Problems with estimating			
Problems with planning activities			
Poor memory for basic maths facts			
High levels of debilitating anxiety related to maths			
Problems with orientation/direction			
Mixes up similar looking numbers (3, 8 and 6, 9)			
A poor understanding of place value and its use in calculations			
Problems remembering shapes			
Problems counting backwards			
Poor concept of time and difficulty reading analogue clocks			
Inability to subitise (instantly recognise number of items without counting)			

Source: Patoss (2018)

Evidence-based programmes, apps and resources

There are many apps and websites that offer games to develop number sense; below is a sample of some of these that have an evidence base indicating effectiveness.

Mathletics (uk.mathletics.com): This online resource follows the programme of study for England, the Scottish curriculum for excellence and the national curricula for Wales, Northern Ireland and the Republic of Ireland. It includes practice activities and provides pre and post assessments. Ingram et al. (2015) carried out a study of 13,000 schools that found that when schools made regular use of Mathletics children did significantly better on a range of measures compared to schools who did not use the programme.

Number Race (www.thenumberrace.com): For children 4–8 years to learn the basic concepts of number and arithmetic. The site states it is designed for children with DD, with evidence of impact in four research studies.

Number Catcher (www.thenumbercatcher.com): For children 5–10 years, it uses the same concepts as Number Race but for older children.

Dynamo Maths (dynamomaths.co.uk): The programme was reviewed by the University of Oxford with 3465 children in 368 schools for impact. The findings were that all age groups improved in the 8-week period (Dowker, 2017).

Numicon (www.numicon.co.nz): Numicon is a multi-sensory approach to children's mathematical learning that emphasises three aspects of doing mathematics: communicating mathematically, exploring relationships and solving problems in everyday life experiences.

Research studies by Devon Education Authority Maths Team, Wiltshire, Leeds and Brighton and Hove Local Authorities have reported the advantages of using the Numicon approach.

TABLE 9.8 Systematic Review: Evidence base for approaches to dyscalculia

Outcome	Approach	Researchers	Number of research studies reviewed/dates
Virtual environments with computer games are effective in motivating children with dyscalculia to improve mathematics proficiency	Use virtual environments that integrate thought, feeling and action, for example 'Tom's rescue'	Castro et al. (2014)	300 children between the ages of 7 and 10 years, in Brazil
Assisted or direct instruction supports basic numeracy competency that uses single-subject settings	Use computer programmes with direct instructions that teach the basic numeracy competency of +, ×, −, /	Chodura et al. (2015)	35/1992–2014

Developmental Coordination Disorder (DCD) / Dyspraxia

Definition

The Dyspraxia Foundation (2018) describes dyspraxia as a Developmental Coordination Disorder (DCD), which affects fine and/or gross motor skills and possibly speech. It is lifelong and is formally recognised by the World Health Organization. It is one of the most common movement difficulties in childhood and occurs across all intellectual abilities (Dyspraxia Foundation, 2018). More recently, health professionals are using the term DCD rather than dyspraxia.

National prevalence

The NHS (2018k) reports that approximately 10% of the population have DCD, adding that it is more common in boys than girls.

Co-existence

The NHS (2018k) reports that children with DCD have an increased likelihood of ADHD, dyslexia and autism.

Known causes

The exact cause is unknown but it is believed to be due to a disruption in the way messages from the brain are transmitted to the body, which then affects the ability to perform movements in a smooth and coordinated way. It is believed to run in families with the following risk factors:

- Being born prematurely
- Having a low birth weight
- A family history of DCD (but the specific genes are unknown)
- The mother drinking alcohol or taking illegal drugs while pregnant

(NHS, 2018k)

Indicators

Children with DCD will present differently, the commonality being that they will have fine and gross coordination difficulties, which are likely to impact on their participation, confidence, social skills and self-esteem. It is understood that children with DCD may be delayed, for example with: crawling, pulling up, walking, self-feeding, dressing, climbing, hopping, running, drawing, writing, using scissors and riding a bike. The challenges can include concentration, memory, sequencing organisation and time management. It can occur on its own or alongside other areas of neurodiversity. Henderson and Knott (2015) also report these additional signs:

- Difficulty chewing solid food
- Difficulty with pincer grip and holding a pen/pencil
- Taking longer to dress
- Falling over a lot or appearing clumsy
- Can have problems with establishing relationships and problems with social behaviour
- Anxiety and agitation
- Delayed language development

Identification

Children with DCD are usually referred through their GP or health visitor to a paediatrician, physiotherapist or occupational therapist for assessment and to address functional issues such as tip-toe walking, shortened tendons or muscle strength/control. In the UK it is likely that the assessor will use a method called Motor ABC, which tests gross and fine motor skills compared to the expected range for a child of their age and they will take into account their medical history and that of their family; as SENCO, you should get a copy of the report if the caregivers have given consent (NHS, 2018k).

INSET ACTIVITY

Using the areas of difficulty can you and your colleagues suggest solutions/reasonable adjustments to support children with DCD in Physical Education and classroom learning? Some have been started for you below in Table 9.9.

TABLE 9.9 CPD reasonable adjustments for DCD

Area	Indicator	Possible solution
Balance	Falls over, wobbles, can't stand on one leg	
Hand–eye coordination	Aim, predicting speed of moving objects	Begin with using a feather or scarves and build up to bean bags then balls, in close proximity to catch
Eye–foot coordination	Trapping a ball, kicking in right direction	
Motor planning	Difficulty planning movements, for example climbing on and off apparatus	
Stamina	Tires easily, has difficulty with long-distance running	
Self-confidence	Makes excuses to get out of the lesson, disengages or appears over-confident despite their difficulties	Don't let children pick teams; give each child a number instead, praise their efforts, participation and successes
Spatial awareness	Difficulty accurately predicting the movement of others, bumps into them or objects around them	Mark out areas with cones/markers to give a visual support for the use of space
Speed of processing	Difficulty coordinating their movements in to a timed response, may miss the ball	
Short-term memory	Remembering rules	Write them down concisely and refer to them
Fine motor skills	Changing for and after lesson in good time	Velcro shoes for PE
Self-organisation skills	Forgets and loses PE kit	

Evidence-based programmes, apps and resources

Health services will recommend the use of resources in school to support activities; these include writing slopes, pencil grips, velcro shoes (not slip-ons) and additional time to complete tasks. Teacher empathy is essential as a first approach as it will be hard for these children observing their peers to take part without difficulty; ask the child what will help them.

There are two main interventions classified as process- and task-oriented approaches:

Process oriented: use activity to address the underlying issues – improving function and structure, medical and focused on rehabilitation.

Task oriented: use activity to address the performance itself. In 2018, Smits-Engelsman et al. discovered that task-oriented approaches were more effective as they facilitate participation and are:

1. Child centred so meaningful
2. Goal orientated with specific activities and participation
3. Task and context specific
4. Involve the child taking part
5. Aimed at the child being functional
6. Aimed at caregiver involvement so learning is transferred to everyday contexts.

TABLE 9.10 Systematic review: Evidence base for approaches to dyspraxia

Outcome	Approach	Researchers	Number of research studies reviewed/dates
Activity and body-oriented interventions have a positive effect on motor function and skills (though caution noted due to varied quality of research)	Active video games, small group programmes, fitness-based programmes with repetition and intensity	Smits-Engelsman et al. (2018)	30/2012–2017

Attention Deficit Hyperactivity Disorder (ADHD)

Definition

There are three key features that define ADHD: persistent inattention (not being able to focus) and/or hyperactivity (excessive movement) and impulsivity (acting without thought), which impact on functioning and development (American Psychiatric Association, 2013).

National prevalence

The National Institute of Clinical Excellence (NICE) (2018) states that there are certain children with increased prevalence of ADHD, including those who are born pre-term, looked after and permanently placed, those with a diagnosis of oppositional defiance or conduct disorders, those with mood disorders and those with a family member with ADHD.

Co-existence

ADHD is most likely to co-exist with other areas of neurodiversity, in particular autism and mental health challenges.

Known causes

The exact cause is unknown but it has been shown to run in families; research also identifies differences in the brains of those with ADHD (NHS, 2018l).

Indicators

The ADHD Institute (2019) ICD-10 also lists symptoms characteristic of children with HKD, but not necessary or sufficient for diagnosis:

- Disinhibition in social relationships
- Recklessness in dangerous situations
- Non-adherence to social norms (interrupting, intruding on others, prematurely answering questions, difficulty in waiting in turn).

The NHS (2018l) also suggests there are issues that can impact on daily life, such as sleep disturbances, listening to and following instructions, organisation and concentration.

Identification

Within the revised guidelines NICE (2018l) recommends that when a child is suspected to have ADHD the SENCO should support the child with their behaviour, informing the caregivers about local training/education programmes. It is no longer the case that they should be referred straight to GPs until other pathways have been exhausted. Once within health services there are two options for clinicians: (1) a period of 'watchful waiting', which is 10 weeks and occurs where the child's behaviour is having an adverse impact on family life; (2) offering parents a referral to group-based ADHD focused support, which may be prior to a diagnosis.

Formal diagnosis

ADHD, symptoms of hyperactivity/impulsivity and/or inattention should be given by specialist psychiatrist, paediatricians or other appropriately qualified healthcare professionals through:

- a full clinical and psychological assessment including a discussion about behaviour and indicators using either ICD-10 (hyperkinetic disorder) or DSM-5 criteria
- the use of Conners' rating scales and the Strengths and Difficulties Questionnaire alongside observations to support judgements
- a full developmental and psychiatric history
- observer reports from school and assessment of their mental state.

For a diagnosis of ADHD, a strict set of criteria are followed. Children must have:

- been displaying symptoms for at least 6 months
- started to show symptoms before the age of 12
- shown the symptoms in at least 2 settings (home and school); this is to rule out reactions to caregivers or certain teachers
- symptoms that make their lives more difficult on a social, academic or occupational level
- symptoms that are not just part of a developmental difficulty or phase.

(NHS, 2018l)

> **Case study**
>
> Nial is in Year 4 and has many friends within the class and is able at mathematics and sport. He has difficulty maintaining focus during independent activities, particularly in tasks that involve writing. The father was called into school where the teacher said she was frustrated at repeating instructions and keeping him on task so the school decided to put him on SEN support. The father commented that completing homework was extremely challenging and often ends up in negotiations and bribes of what he can do next if he completes it. He also pointed out that his sister is dyslexic and dyscalculic and has working memory difficulties and problems concentrating. The teacher did not respond to this and continued by saying that he often turns around, fidgets and is distracted by the other children in his group and that work is mostly unfinished.
>
> - What does this tell you about the class teacher's knowledge and understanding of SEND?
> - Should the child be on SEN support?
> - How could the class teacher use Nial's strengths for learning?
> - How would you have led this meeting as SENCO?

Evidence-based programmes, apps and resources

Reasonable adjustments for children with ADHD will need to ensure that there has been a full assessment of individual needs. Teachers and those working with the child will need to understand how the ADHD impacts on the child and the family. As outlined below, exercise is a highly effective and evidence-based intervention to support children with ADHD.

Sport England (2018) advocates the benefits of exercise as improving:

- mental wellbeing
- physical wellbeing
- individual development
- economic development
- social and community development.

Exercise can be used as an incentive, in short bursts or throughout the school day; it benefits all children including those with ADHD. When introducing new physical education programmes, consider the following:

- any health needs and their triggers (asthma and cold weather)
- how you can gradually increase intensity and duration
- how exercise can be built into the daily routine, for example the daily mile
- how gaming and gyms can be used to support exercise indoors.

Therapies are another common intervention for children and wide-ranging examples include: psychoeducation (to discuss the impact of ADHD) behaviour therapies, tailored caregiver training programmes, cognitive behaviour therapy (to change the way the child thinks and behaves) and social skills training (lego therapy, for example).

If interventions are not effective, children may be given medication. The five that are licensed are:

- Methylphenidate
- Dexamfetamine
- Lisdexamfetamine
- Atomoxetine
- Guanfacine.

Medication should only be given as a last resort; they are stimulants and can have side-effects such as increasing blood pressure, heart rate, aggression, dizziness, diarrhoea, nausea, loss of appetite, headaches, stomach aches and mood swings. Atomoxetine is different to the others as it increases noradrenaline (a chemical in the brain); it is reported to have more serious side-effects such as liver damage and suicidal thoughts (NHS, 2018l).

TABLE 9.11 Systematic Review: Evidence base for approaches to AD(H)D

Outcome	Approach	Researchers	Number of research studies reviewed/dates
Physical activity has a positive effect on processing speed, working memory, planning and problem solving (outcomes vary depending on age)	20–30 minutes (40–75% intensity) exercise	Suarez-Manzano et al. (2018)	16/2004–2015
The clinical benefits of exercise of physical activity on neurocognitive function and inhibitory control	Moderate to intense activity	Ng et al. (2017)	30/1980–2016
The effect of mindfulness-based intervention to improve attention	Although improvement in attention is believed to be significant, it is unclear if it is effective for children with ADHD due to limited studies in this area	Lee et al. (2017)	9/2007–2016

INFORMATION-FINDING ACTIVITY

Find out the pathways that exist for assessment, diagnosis and intervention from your local NHS trust for autism and ADHD. Often, the NHS will have different pathways for the range of types of needs, for example autism and ADHD/ADD. Find out from your Local Authority (local offer) or Clinical Commissioning Groups what the local arrangements are and what voluntary

Support organisation

ADHD Foundation: Supports children, families and teachers by providing information and support, including training events; schools can apply for a ADHD-friendly schools award.

Website: www.adhdfoundation.org.uk

(Continued)

(Continued)

organisations are also available for support and guidance. It could be that there are different service providers and pathways for different ages of children; knowing this information will allow you to best advise and support children and their families.

Autism

Definition

Bakian et al. (2015) described autism as a neurodevelopmental disorder with a complex aetiology, which is characterised by challenges with social, communicative and behavioural functioning. It is lifelong and is characterised by variable challenges with social communication, social interaction and social imagination (Wing and Gould, 1979).

National prevalence

The current prevalence is believed to be one in 100 children in the UK (National Autistic Society, 2017). Farrell (2017) suggested possible reasons for an apparent increase in prevalence, which could include: widening of the definition; increased awareness; and differences in research methods used in studies (American Psychiatric Association, 2013). Autism is more prevalent in males than females; however, it needs to be noted that this could be due to a lack of under-identification in females (National Autistic Society, 2018).

The factors associated with increased prevalence of autism are:

- a sibling with autism
- dysfunction of the central nervous system during birth, including cerebral palsy
- a gestational age of less than 35 weeks
- a caregiver with schizophrenia
- a learning (intellectual) disability
- ADHD
- Down's Syndrome and other chromosomal differences
- genetic differences such as Fragile X
- muscular dystrophy
- neurofibromatosis
- tuberous sclerosis.

(NICE, 2016c)

Co-existence

Maskey et al. (2013) emphasised that co-existing secondary needs can include a range of emotional and behavioural challenges such as aggression, self-injury, issues with sleep, feeding, eating problems, sensory sensitivities, learning disabilities, epilepsies, ADHD, anxiety, obsessive thoughts and tourettes. Skokauskas and Gallagher (2010) and Steensel et al. (2013) further reported that there are other commonly occurring needs which are often identified in later childhood such as Oppositional

Defiant Disorder (ODD) and anxiety disorders, with the emergence of depression and obsessive compulsive disorder in adolescence/adult life.

Known causes

DeBooth and Reynolds (2017) highlighted that there is no single cause or biomarker that has been identified related to autism. Swartz (2016) highlighted that 'genome sequencing' has already found mutations in 65 genes that increase the likelihood of developing autism. He suggested that some are passed from the DNA of the mother, the father or, sometimes, from both caregivers to the child. The extensive research by SPARK (2017) discovered 'de novo' mutations occurring for the first time in a caregiver's sperm, egg or in the developing embryo, so appearing for the first time with the child. Others arise spontaneously, meaning they aren't present in either genetic makeup; to date, genetic causes have been pinpointed in only about 20% of autism cases. Farrell (2017) summarises that there are no definite causes of autism currently known. He suggests that the heritability of autism is thought to range from 37–90%, based on concordance rates in twins, and that there may be several genes which act with environmental factors.

Indicators

Health professionals will use the terminology 'disorder' as if it is an error of nature rather than an invaluable part of genetic human variability passed down through millions of years of evolution (Masataka, 2018). As schools, we need to challenge the use of derogatory language to describe variation and focus on the uniques skills; for example, having the ability to examine the finer detail of concepts and ideas. Molteni and Maggiolini (2015) recognised that children identified with autism often experienced limitations with interaction and communication. It needs to be noted that it is often adults who 'expect' children to socially interact even when the child is content with being on their own. Based upon the NICE (2016c) guidelines, the NHS produced tables that list the indicators of autism in pre-school, primary and secondary aged children. These highlight the expected features of development and are intended to alert professionals where there is a possibility of autism. These are useful for you as SENCO before discussing concerns with caregivers – they are not to be used as a diagnostic tool, as only health services can make a diagnosis.

Historically, it has been believed that children with autism are unable to attend to and process information from faces. Most evidence has concluded that this is not the case. In studies by Grossman et al. (2000) and Ogai et al. (2003), where photos were presented of people showing the emotions anger, fear, pleasure, surprise or disgust, the participants were asked which emotion the person was showing; there was no difference found between those with and without a diagnosis of autism.

Identification

Molteni and Maggiolini (2015) claimed that the majority of caregivers (71%) noticed the indicators of autism within the first two years of a child's life; in 72% of cases it was the mother who initially raised concerns. These findings have been echoed in international studies, which suggest worries being noted between 12 and 24 months of age, particularly when the child is not the first.

As Frenette et al. (2011) and the DfE (2015a) acknowledge, early identification of autism facilitates diagnosis, thereby allowing timely access to educational and therapeutic services.

The NICE guidelines (2016c) clarify that every autism diagnostic assessment will include the following:

- Detailed questions about the caregivers and child's concerns
- Details of experiences of homelife, education and social care
- Developmental history, consistent with ICD-10 or DSM-5
- Assessment (through observation and interaction) of social and communication skills and behaviours
- Medical history, including prenatal, perinatal and family history
- A physical examination
- Consideration of alternative diagnosis (mental health, ADHD, learning disability, language, dyspraxia, hearing and visual difficulties)
- Systematic assessment for other needs which co-exist with autism
- Developmental profile of strengths, skills, challenges to create a needs-based management plan
- Communication of assessment findings to caregivers and the child.

With caregiver consent, the assessment profile can be shared with you as SENCO, either through a school visit or as a report. This should then be used to contribute to planning and staff training in school, taking into account the individual interests and strengths to ensure their experiences are positive and promote wellbeing.

Evidence-based approaches

There have been a number of debates over recent years about the effectiveness of interventions, learning environments and approaches to learning and teaching for children with autism. There are extensive studies which have attempted to provide reliable knowledge about what interventions 'work'; the reality is that there is not enough evidence to promote one specific approach as often the evidence base is narrow and the sample size small (Howlin, 2010; Parsons et al., 2011). All children will react to the environment they are in; by seeing the world from their perspective, you will be better placed to create an 'autism-friendly' environment. A recent study examined the colour preferences of children with autism (Grandgeorge and Masataka, 2016). The study found that boys with autism were significantly less likely to prefer yellow (as it causes hyper-sensation and sensory overload) and more likely to prefer green and brown. As there is a scientific foundation to verify the effectiveness of green environments, consider the following approaches:

- Provide green and brown A5 and A4 overlays for classroom use
- Use colour sensitively in wall displays to create a sense of calm
- Utilise green spaces, for example field trips, outdoor learning, gardening.

Table 9.12 below summarises evidence-based interventions for children with autism based on findings from researchers who carried out systematic reviews of research studies.

TABLE 9.12 Systematic review: Evidence-based approaches to autism

Outcome	Approach	Researchers	Number of research studies reviewed/dates
The most effective cognitive, developmental and behavioural interventions	Music therapy to improve communication and social interaction	Su Maw and Haga (2018)	14/2001–2015
The most effective social skill intervention	Group-based social skills (developing social knowledge training) in older children	Gates et al. (2017)	18/2010–2014
Improvement in social interaction and behaviour	Equine-assisted interventions	Peters and Wood (2017)	33/2003–2015
Effectiveness of weighted vests to calm children and provide sensory input	Weighted vests are **not yet evidence-based practice** due to a lack of rigour in existing studies	Taylor et al. (2017)	13/2004–2011
Effect of early intervention in improving spoken language	Caregiver and clinician doing early language interventions together with clinician training caregiver for consistency	Hampton and Kaiser (2016)	26/1980–2014

As can be seen in Table 9.13, the use of weighted vests is not yet an evidence-based approach; however, this doesn't mean you shouldn't use them – if it supports the child then use the approach. All intervention and support offered must be in relation to the needs of the child rather than to make them 'fit' the classrooms and school communal areas. The starting point for achieving this is high-quality CPD for colleagues.

There are many approaches and programmes available; a model that may be useful is outlined below (Table 9.13):

TABLE 9.13 Understand behaviour by assessing the environment

Approach	Evidence base	The model
Positive Behaviour Support (PBS)	Department of Health policy – Positive and Proactive Care (2014)	Understanding of the behaviour of the child. It is based on assessment of the social and physical environment in which the behaviour happens and includes the child's views and those of everyone involved. This understanding is used to develop support to improve their quality of life and for those involved with them

REFLECTIVE TASK

Carry out an audit of the professional learning opportunities all staff in school have attended: what has the impact of this been? Consider carrying out a piece of action research to measure the effectiveness of training and the impact on day-to-day provision and practice.

Learning walks

It is likely that children will need specific approaches to support their social interaction, social communication, social imagination, information processing and sensory needs. The National Autistic

Society provides a useful framework (SPELL) for understanding and responding to the needs of children with autism – it provides values, practical elements and approaches to meet individual needs. These are identified as vital elements of best practice, emphasising changes to the environment and learning approaches:

- **S**tructure: for organisation, understanding tasks and what will happen next
- **P**ositive: developing strengths and interests to achieve goals
- **E**mpathy: understanding the perspective of the person
- **L**ow arousal: awareness of their sensory needs and the effect of these on stress levels
- **L**inks: the importance of communication with caregivers for consistency and stability.

To carry out a learning walk you need to decide a clear focus and consider the following questions:

- How will you decide which classes or children to visit?
- How will you let your colleagues know of your intentions?
- What will your focus be (inclusion, implementation of reasonable adjustments, participation, deployment of support staff, meeting of individual needs)?
- What will your role be?
- Will children accompany you? If not, how will you ascertain their views?
- How will you feed back findings to governors, senior leaders, colleagues, caregivers and children?

SPELL SENCO TASK

Carry out a learning walk using the checklist below:

- Do all staff know and apply the reasonable adjustments agreed for individual children? Is there evidence that these are effective?
- Are there low stimulus areas for those children who need them?
- Are the children with SEN and/or disabilities all participating and learning?
- Is the classroom physically accessible to all children?
- Are the teaching resources dyslexia-friendly?
- Is the noise level reasonable?
- Is there an adequate reason for any children who are working alone?

Sensory Processing Disorder (SPD)

Previously known as sensory integration disorder, SPD is neurological and is where the brain and nervous system have difficulty processing sensory stimuli. The impact of this is that the child can be overwhelmed by sensory input; as with other areas of neurodiversity, this is on a spectrum of severity. SPD is more prevalent in children with autism and ADHD but is not universally recognised as a standalone difficulty, though some NHS trusts provide guidance for families and schools.

Children can experience a range of sensory difficulties, which occur due to a range of stimuli or situations. There are five basic sensory systems, which are:

- Visual
- Auditory
- Olfactory (smell)
- Gustatory (taste)
- Tactile

Each child will be affected in a different way, so the environment will need to be considered to reduce the impact of SPD; for example, the lighting, distractions and noise.

Indicators

Children with SPD can present as over- or under-sensitive to the world around them. For example, some children may not enjoy touch, noises and smells while others actively seek them. You will need to find out the child's individual preferences and dislikes to adapt the learning environment.

> ### Support organisations
>
> **STAR Institute:** STAR aims to improve the quality of life for children, adolescents and adults with SPD. It is an international organisation that carries out research into the causes, diagnosis and treatment of SPD. The website has information for caregivers and professionals.
>
> **Website:** www.spdstar.org
>
> **Understood.org:** Understood is an American organisation that is a collaboration of 15 not-for-profit organisations, which aim to support caregivers of children 3–10 years of age with learning and attention challenges. It provides personalised resources, access to experts, an online community and practical tips.

> ### Chapter summary
>
> - Focus on the individual strengths and interests of children to ensure the experiences provided promote success and wellbeing
> - Encourage staff not to focus on the label as that tells you very little about the individual needs of the child
> - You will need to monitor and evaluate the effectiveness of the evidence-based interventions you provide
> - Only continue interventions that have a positive impact on progress and development; examine the value for money versus the time spent to secure the outcomes
> - Access to the curriculum for children who are neurodiverse depends on effective differentiation, planning and application of reasonable adjustments
> - High-quality staff training is needed to ensure needs are met effectively

10
Learning and Physical Disabilities

Sarah Martin-Denham

→ NASENCO outcomes: The statutory and regulatory context for disability equality and the implications for practice. Strategies for improving outcomes for children with SEND by addressing discrimination, stereotyping and bullying. Ensure appropriate arrangements are in place for national tests and examinations or undertaking other forms of accreditation. The potential of new technologies to support communication, teaching and learning for children with SEND. Ensure continuity of support and progression at key transition points for children.
→ Read alongside: Chapter 2: The Statutory and Regulatory Context; Chapter 8: Social, Emotional and Mental Health Difficulties

Chapter overview

The intention of this chapter is to develop your knowledge and understanding of a range of learning disabilities and their impact on participation and learning and mental health and wellbeing. It will also detail your legal duties and suggest best practice in meeting individual needs to promote the best possible outcomes.

The United Nations Convention on the Rights of People with Disabilities (UNCRPD)

In 2009 the UK ratified the UNCRPD, which includes:

- **Article 3:** Full and effective participation and inclusion in society; respect for the evolving capabilities of children with disabilities and respect for the right of children with disabilities to preserve their identities.
- **Article 7:** Includes all necessary measures to ensure the full enjoyment of children with disabilities of all human rights and fundamental freedoms on an equal basis with other children.

These UN articles are reflected in both the Children and Families Act 2014 and the Equality Act 2010. The definition of disability is **'a physical or mental impairment that has a "substantial" and "long-term" adverse effect on your ability to carry out normal day to day activities'**.

Models of disability

Models of disability move beyond the definition of disability and instead attempt to analyse where disability comes from, historically, socially and culturally and what it means for the individual and society. Health and education organisations label children as having special educational needs and/or disabilities (SEND) and often the discussion is around what is 'wrong' with them rather than considering it as natural human variation to be celebrated. The DfE (2014c) advised that the use of medical labels should be avoided as they say little about the individual but reinforce stereotypes of being patients, or unwell. They add that phrases such as 'suffers from' suggest discomfort, pain and hopelessness and that these terms should not be used. A disability should only be referred to when it is related to the context of the discussion; on all other occasions you would just use their name. Table 10.1 illustrates the appropriate terminology.

TABLE 10.1 Appropriate terminology

Avoid	Use
- The Downs boy in reception - Confined to a wheelchair - The wheelchair children - SEN Sarah - Able-bodied - The blind - Suffers from - Dwarf - Fits	- His name - Wheelchair user - Their names - Sarah - Non-disabled - Those with sight loss - Has - Restricted growth/short stature - Seizures

The use of medical labels in education can often lead to exclusion; an example of this is ADHD and autism, as behaviours that are a result of the physical environment are not understood and adjustments are not made. A diagnosis of a 'disability' ensures legal protection from discrimination within the Equality Act (2010), as it requires reasonable adjustments when a child with a disability would be at a 'substantial disadvantage'. An example is access arrangements, which are pre-exam adjustments for children based on evidence of need. This can include the entitlement to scribes, readers and Braille question papers but also other adjustments which may not be listed. Some children may also be entitled to 'special consideration'; this applies post examination and includes adjustments to grades or marks to reflect temporary injury, illness or other challenges at the time of the assessment.

For some children, their disabilities impact on their ability to participate and explore within their physical and social environment on a daily basis. The medical model of disability is a prevalent model where disability is seen as a 'problem' with the person's body or mind, a medical condition, which is in need of treatment to be cured or fixed so the person can be rehabilitated. With the medical model, a person is understood by their diagnosis – for example, cerebral palsy, autism, Fragile X – the disability is therefore medicalised and can be difficult to separate from the person, which can cause prejudice and discrimination (Dirth and Branscombe, 2017). In education, the social model is more prevalent, which is the view that disability doesn't lie within the individual's diagnosis but in their uniqueness; it is the environment and society that impose barriers to participation and acceptance. So, in education, there is usually an emphasis placed on how the environment can be adapted to enhance learning and outcomes.

For example, a child has a diagnosis of cerebral palsy and uses a wheelchair in school to move between classrooms throughout the school day:

1. **Medical model:** The child needs the wheelchair as they are disabled
2. **Social model:** The environment is inaccessible so the child has to use a wheelchair.

Case study

Mu has a diagnosis of Duchenne Muscular Dystrophy, which is genetic and degenerative. It causes muscle wasting due to a lack of protein called dystrophin, which is needed to keep muscles intact. He is 10 years old, with many friends and is doing well in school; he is due to start secondary school in September. Recently, he is finding walking and climbing stairs difficult and moving from sitting to standing.

What would the differing solutions be with the medical and social models of disability?

More recently, a cultural-historical model of disability has been proposed by Bøttcher and Dammeyer (2016), which recommends specific assessment of cognitive profile and considerations of adaptations to the environment to create specialised learning settings. This approach advocates working alongside educational psychologists who share their knowledge and understanding of individual needs and approaches to support. They also facilitate professional development to enable teachers and teaching assistants to integrate models of disability to ensure caregivers and colleagues understand the needs of the children (Rees, 2017). Clearly, this approach relies on the SENCO being supported at a strategic level to develop this approach to collaborate, to access funding and to commission effective educational psychologists.

Table 10.2 below offers a neurodiversity-based approach and aims to make use of emerging literature on the strengths of those with SEND (Mottron, 2011; Diehl et al., 2014)

TABLE 10.2 Deficit- versus strengths-based model

	Deficit-based model	Strengths-based model
Focus	Disability	Diversity
Assessment methods	Testing to detect deficits, disorders and dysfunctions	Assessing strengths and challenges
Teaching approaches	Remediating weaknesses	Building on strengths and using them to overcome challenges
Theoretical foundations	Genetics, neurobiology	Evolutionary psychobiology, social and ecological theory
View of the brains of those with SEND	In many cases, the brain is seen as damaged, dysfunctional or disordered	Part of the normal human variation of all human brains
Teaching goals	Meeting national objectives	Developing human potential
Child and young person goal	Learning to live with their disability	Learning to maximise strengths and minimise weaknesses

Source: Adapted from Armstrong (2017)

Learning disability

MENCAP (2018) describes a learning disability as reduced intellectual ability and challenges with everyday activities as it takes longer to learn concepts and skills. The NHS (2018m) clarifies that a learning disability affects the way a person learns during their lifetime, including how they understand information and how they communicate. They may have challenges with:

- understanding new or complex information
- learning new skills
- coping independently.

Learning disabilities can be mild, moderate or severe and in all cases they are lifelong. The Code (DfE, 2015a: 97) states in the broad area of 'cognition and learning' that

> learning difficulties cover a wide range of needs, including Moderate Learning Difficulties (MLD), Severe Learning Difficulties (SLD), where children are likely to need support in all areas of the curriculum and associated difficulties with mobility and communication, through to Profound and Multiple Learning Difficulties (PMLD), where children are likely to have severe and complex learning difficulties as well as a physical disability or Sensory Impairment.

Horridge (2018) states that each and every need must be accurately identified and described using consistent language if the best outcomes are to be achieved. If caregivers have given consent you should receive information from health services about any diagnosis or needs of children following consultations.

The British Institute of Learning Disabilities (BILD) (2011) clarified that internationally three criteria are required to be met before a learning disability can be identified or diagnosed. These are:

- they have a moderate, severe or profound learning difficulty
- IQ of less than 70
- early onset.

IQ is used by health professionals and educational psychologists to assess the presence and degree of learning disability, but it should not be used as a standalone measure. Norwich et al. (2014) agree and suggest that IQ scoring is outdated and is not referred to in the Code (DfE, 2015a). There should be a focus on assessing the child's preferred learning approaches, interests, strengths, knowledge, understanding and skills. It is also important to first assess for specific learning difficulties such as dyslexia, particularly when a child is diagnosed as having a 'moderate learning difficulty'.

In the UK 'learning difficulty' is used to describe Specific Learning Difficulties (SpLD), more recently known as neurodiversity, which includes dyslexia, dyspraxia, dyscalculia, ADHD and ADD, which often co-exist with autism. The distinction is that specific learning difficulties don't affect intellect but do affect the way information is processed and learned. Learning disabilities are applied to children where they have global not specific difficulties.

Causes of learning disabilities

There are many factors that are known to cause a learning disability. They can occur before, during or soon after birth.

- Before birth something can happen to the central nervous system (the brain and spinal cord) that can cause a learning disability
- The mother can have an accident or an illness or the unborn child can develop certain genes
- A lack of oxygen in childbirth, a trauma to the head or born prematurely
- Childhood illnesses, accidents and seizures.

(Adapted from MENCAP, 2018)

Diagnosis of learning disabilities

Diagnosis can happen at any time: at birth, during early childhood, or into adulthood, by a GP, a paediatrician or during a developmental check. In older children it can be diagnosed through physiological checks where a child's ability is compared with the development and cognition typical for a child of that age.

Many children will have more than one diagnosis and we know that there are particular needs that mean the child is more likely to have learning disabilities. Currently, there is no national data about how many children have disabilities or what their range of needs includes. Below is an outline of some common disabilities where it is likely that learning disabilities will occur (Table 10.3).

TABLE 10.3 Learning disabilities overview

Learning Disability	Cause	Associated Challenges	Useful Contacts
Down's Syndrome	Extra chromosome	Heart problems, sight and hearing, learning disabilities	The Down's Syndrome Association
Williams Syndrome	Rare genetic (missing chromosome)	Take longer to meet milestones, physical and mental health challenges	Williams Syndrome Foundation

(Continued)

TABLE 10.3 (Continued)

Learning Disability	Cause	Associated Challenges	Useful Contacts
Fragile X Syndrome	Rare genetic	Speech and language, social and emotional interaction, may also develop epilepsy and a few have autism	The Fragile X Society
Cerebral Palsy	Usually brain injury	Challenges with muscle control and movement, some may also have seizures, epilepsy or difficulty with speech and language	SCOPE

Source: Adapted from MENCAP (2018) and SCOPE (2018)

Thirty-six per cent of children with learning disabilities are likely to experience mental health problems (Youngminds, 2019). To identify if they are experiencing a mental health issue, consideration should be given to what is usual for the child in terms of their behaviour and what has changed to cause you to be concerned. There is also an increased likelihood of epilepsies, constipation and problems with swallowing. Any concerns should be raised with caregivers so they can seek support, diagnosis and intervention from health services.

In school, support could include the following:

- Increase opportunities for socialising.
- Change the activities to relate to their interests.
- Change staff if there are issues with relationships.
- Support transitions.

Moderate learning difficulties

Moderate learning difficulties (MLD) are the most common primary need overall at 21.6% of children with special educational needs (SEN) (DfE, 2018a). There needs to be careful consideration of the use of this category by SENCOs as often children are given this identification without a full understanding of how MLD is identified and assessed. The conflict is due to a lack of a current definition; the most recent one is from the DfES (2003: 8) which states: 'children with MLD will have attainments well below expected levels in most areas of the curriculum, despite appropropriate interventions. They will have greater difficulty than their peers in acquiring basic literacy and numeracy skills and in understanding concepts'. The concern is that schools need to eliminate any underlying specific learning difficulties, as there is overlap in challenges with literacy and numeracy. If you are dyslexic or dyscalculic, IQ questions are problematic as they are timed, are focused on the ability to estimate, calculate and comprehend, along with perception, effective working memory and information processing, which are barriers for those who are neurodiverse.

REFLECTIVE ACTIVITY

Examine the SEN register for your school. How many children have a moderate learning difficulty as their primary need? What is the evidence that they have a MLD? What do your colleagues understand by MLD in your school? Reflect on the basis and accuracy of this judgement.

Sensory and/or physical needs

Within this broad area of need, children will need special educational provision due to their disabilities (DfE, 2015a: 98). This includes those with a Vision Impairment (VI), Hearing Impairment (HI) or a Multi-sensory Impairment (MSI) – a combination of vision and hearing difficulties.

Physical disabilities will require ongoing support and equipment for the child to access and participate in opportunities available to their peers. Schools don't have to wait until a formal diagnosis to provide support; it should be in place as soon as the need arises. In some cases, children may have long-term and complex medical needs which require specialist care in school to keep them well or extensive monitoring and interventions in emergencies – their health will fluctuate over time. In addition, children with medical needs may have long-term absences, experience self-esteem issues and are more prone to mental health challenges, such as anxiety and depression.

The section below includes an overview of some of the physical disabilities that children can encounter. As with all special educational needs and disabilities, no two children will present with the same strengths, challenges or behaviours. The intention is simply to give you a general synopsis and evidence-based protective factors and approaches to learning.

Diabetes

Type 1 diabetes is due to the pancreas not producing enough insulin, which is needed to regulate blood glucose levels (Martin-Denham, 2015). Also, the body's immune system attacks and destroys the cells that produce insulin. If the levels become too high, organs, vessels and nerves can become damaged. This type of diabetes is not linked to age or being overweight and it is more common in children than type 2 diabetes (NHS, 2018n).

Indicators of type 1 diabetes

With children, the symptoms can happen quickly and it can be diagnosed from a urine sample:

- Feeling thirsty
- Weeing more than usual, particularly at night
- Tiredness
- Loss of weight
- Thrush
- Blurred vision
- Cuts and grazes that aren't healing.

(NHS, 2018o)

Management of type 1 diabetes

- Following diagnosis, the child will be looked after by a paediatric diabetes care team, who can also provide advice to schools.

- They will need to have their blood glucose levels regularly checked and most likely have to inject insulin four times or more a day using a syringe, pen device or insulin pump. They need to have a healthy diet and regular exercise.
- You will need to ensure the injection is on a different part of the body (stomach, thighs, bottom) each time.
- Provide emotional support and offer a comfortable and clean space to inject.
- Create an Individual Healthcare Plan.

Hypos

Most children and adults who have type 1 diabetes will have a 'hypo' (hypoglycemia or low blood glucose) at some stage. These are more likely to happen if they have:

- missed a meal/snack or lunch is delayed
- had insufficient carbohydrate intake
- done strenuous exercise
- an intercurrent illness such as a cold.

(Diabetes UK, 2018)

Common signs of a hypo are:

- feeling shaky, sweating and an increased heart rate
- hunger, tiredness or blurred vision
- pins and needles around the mouth
- feeling tearful and lacking concentration.

The signs will vary as everyone is different; not all children will have a hypo in the same way.

Type 2 diabetes

Type 2 diabetes is progressive and occurs when the body doesn't produce enough insulin, or the body's cells don't react to insulin (NHS, 2018p). This type of diabetes is caused by a poor diet coupled with a lack of exercise and in the UK 90% of adults with diabetes have type 2. The indicators are the same as for type 1 diabetes but it is less serious, with treatment usually in the form of tablets.

> **Support organisations**
>
> **DigiBete:** For those under the age of 18 and their caregivers to support the management of type 1 diabetes.
>
> **Website:** www.digibete.org **Helpline:** 07522 464 237 **Email:** hello@digibete.org
>
> **Diabetes UK:** Services to support the management of diabetes and has useful child-friendly resources.
>
> **Website:** www.diabetes.org.uk **Helpline:** 0345 123 2399

Many schools are now adopting the 'Daily Mile', which is a programme designed as a way of children improving health and wellbeing through daily physical activity. It is 15 minutes where children can run or jog at their own pace and has been acknowledged as reducing obesity and is within the government's 2018 Childhood Obesity Strategy.

Epilepsies

Epilepsies affect the brain and usually involve recurrent, unprovoked seizures; there are different types, which will be diagnosed by specialist paediatricians. During a seizure, electrical activity in the brain alters which causes a change in how the body behaves. Each seizure will vary from person to person, from trances to convulsions, they will change over time and can go away spontaneously (Martin-Denham and Horridge, 2015).

Management of epilepsies

- Anti-epileptic medication
- Healthy and balanced diet and exercise
- Awareness of common triggers which may include missing medication and meals, being tired, feeling unwell, flickering lights or images.

What to do when a child has a seizure

Tonic-clonic seizures are when a child goes stiff, loses consciousness and may fall, followed by jerking movements. It would also be likely that they have a blue tinge around their mouth due to irregularities in their breathing. Usually, the jerking will subside in a few minutes, but for the first seizure an ambulance must be called. For future seizures, there should be an Individual Healthcare Plan in place which has been agreed with health professionals, caregivers and where possible the child. Training must be arranged with the specialist epilepsies nurse for all staff in school.

> **Support organisations**
>
> **Epilepsy Action:** Provides expert advice, information to professionals and caregivers who are affected by epilepsy.
>
> **Website**: www.epilepsy.org.uk **Helpline**: 0808 800 5050

Foetal Alcohol Spectrum Disorder (FASD)

FASD is the most common, **preventable**, non-genetic cause of learning disability in the UK. It is a persuasive neurological difference that contributes to a wide range of disabilities (Kapasi and Brown, 2017). Prenatal exposure is caused by alcohol crossing the placenta, which can then cause physical, developmental, cognitive and behavioural challenges across the life course.

There are four diagnoses within the umbrella term FASD:

- Foetal Alcohol Syndrome (FAS)
- Partial Foetal Alcohol Syndrome (PFAS)
- Alcohol Related Neurodevelopmental Disorder (ARND)
- Alcohol Related Birth Defects (ARBD).

(FASD Network UK, 2018)

Leading and Coordinating Provision

TABLE 10.4 Approaches to learning

Potential challenges	Protective factors/approaches to learning
• Mathematics and working memory skills • Attention and/or hyperactivity • Challenging behaviour • Vision and hearing • Sensory integration • Coping with transitions • Lack of motivation • Regulating emotion	• A positive home and school environment • Building upon the child's strengths • Consistency, structure, routine and stability • Non-verbal, sensory and physical strategies • Short and precise sentences and instructions • Patience • Music to soothe and a therapy dog • Support networks for family and friends • Respite care

Source: Kapasi and Brown (2017)

Sight loss

SENSE (2018) states that vision loss can affect communication and access to information; some children are born with it and in others it develops over the life course. It can be full or partial loss of sight, temporary or permanent, and it can affect one or both eyes.

> **Support organisation**
>
> **FASD Network UK:** Provides training, consultancy and advocacy and support services for families and free resources online for caregivers and professionals.
>
> **Website**: www.fasdnetwork.org
>
> **Helpline**: 07743 380 163
>
> **Email**: fasdnetwork@mail.com

Congenital vision loss: When you are born blind or with partial vision loss.

Acquired vision loss: This usually happens later in life, often as a result of accident or illness.

Children with sight difficulties will have differing challenges, such as low visual acuities, varying visual fields and eye movement control, perception of movement, object recognition and visual perception.

Simultanagnosia: An inability to see more than a few objects at one time.

Optic ataxia: Difficulty with visual control, for example hand–eye coordination to a visual target.

Apraxia of gaze: Difficulty or inability to move eyes from one visual target to another.

Visual difficulties can be misinterpreted as ADHD as it can appear as a lack of attention and deemed to be a behavioural issue rather than due to visual difficulties. The impact of all types of sight loss is that children are often less physically and socially active than their sighted peers; it is important that the first response is an eye test. These children will find it hard to predict behaviour or emotions from facial expressions. Furthermore, they are more likely to experience anxiety and depression as they may be unable to access out of school activities, sports and community groups, which we know promote good mental health.

REFLECTIVE ACTIVITY

Review your after-school clubs on offer: how accessible are they to children with disabilities?

Approaches to learning

McDowell and Budd (2018) found that by reducing the amount of visual information in classrooms children are less distracted and concentration improves. They suggest the following: use black hubs by removing all information from the walls in specific areas of the classroom, add covers to open shelves to reduce clutter distraction, and remove unnecessary furniture, objects, displays on windows and hangings from the ceilings. These adaptations should result in less distraction and greater attention and focus.

Hearing loss

The National Deaf Children's Society (2018) uses the term 'deaf' to refer to all levels of hearing loss in children, including partial or full loss of hearing. Most children will have some level of hearing and this can be improved with the use of hearing aids. Deafness occurs when one or more parts of the ear cease to work effectively. The NDCS website recommends that if caregivers are concerned about hearing they should speak to their GP, though there is a free app which enables you to test a child's hearing.

Types of deafness

- **Sensorineural deafness:** This is nerve deafness, with hearing loss in the inner ear, and is permanent.
- **Conductive deafness:** Sound is unable to pass efficiently through the outer and middle ear to the inner ear, often caused by blockages such as wax or fluid (glue ear).
- **Mixed deafness:** A combination of those above.
- **Unilateral deafness:** Deafness in only one ear.

Approaches to learning

Well-fitting hearing aids reduce the risk of and protect against speech, language and communication difficulties. Children with mild to severe hearing loss are at risk of depressed language development; the risk increases with the severity of unaided hearing levels. Interventions for speech and language need to be in place as soon as possible.

> **Support organisation**
>
> **National Deaf Children's Society:** Support for caregivers and professionals who have children who are deaf through resources, factsheets and booklets.
>
> **Website:** www.ndcs.org.uk   **Helpline:** 0808 800 8880 and livechat service
>
> **Email:** helpline@ndcs.org.uk

Consider the seating plan and keep the classroom door closed to minimise distractions. Get advice from your local multi-disciplinary teams. Use audio technologies including FM systems (wireless audio systems), induction loop systems and microphones.

Deafblindness

Deafblindness is sometimes known as Dual Sensory Impairment or Multi-Sensory Impairment; it is a combination of sight and hearing difficulties, which affect communication and learning. A small number of children with deafblindness are totally blind and deaf but most will have some level of vision and/or hearing (Contact a Family, 2018). Children who are born deafblind (congenital deafblindness) may also have other physical disabilities, learning difficulties and challenging behaviour.

There can be many causes of deafblindness; there in no single or main factor. Some of these include:

- Being born prematurely
- Congenital genetic conditions such as CHARGE Syndrome or Joubert Syndrome
- Accident
- Illness such as meningitis and in-utero infection such as Cytomegalovirus
- Acquired deafblindness can include Usher Syndrome as a cause.

> **Support organisation**
>
> **SENSE:** Supports and campaigns for children who are deafblind or have progressive sensory challenges.
>
> **Website:** www.sense.org.uk **Helpline:** 0300 330 9256 **Email:** info@sense.org.uk

REFLECTIVE ACTIVITY

How do senior leaders ensure all staff know their legal responsibilities to children with disabilities?

How are the views of children with disabilities and their families captured and responded to?

Assistive technologies

SCOPE (2018) supports the use of computer technology as an alternative to written recording and the use of games for the development of literacy and numeracy skills. The technology provided should be led by the needs of the child with guidance from the family, not the budget or preference of the school. Simple adaptations can be made, such as the use of touchscreens, a joystick instead of a mouse or using accessibility settings on iPads. Keyboards have over 100 keys, which can confuse, intimidate and be hard to use. Adapted/coloured alternatives may be more accessible for some children; stickers are a cheap way to do this.

Switches are commonly used for children with profound and multiple learning difficulties to learn cause and effect; the effect needs to be a motivator for the child to relate to something they enjoy. Children will access them in different ways; for example, a child with cerebral palsy may use a mouth or head switch (Patterson and Roberts, 2015). The ACE centre online provides advice across the age range on overcoming communication challenges with computer aids and computer access.

What is a risk assessment?

A risk assessment is a tool used to examine potential harm to children and adults and is useful for children with complex needs starting school, during school and for off-site visits. A risk assessment must also be completed for children with medical needs such as Epilepsies and Anaphylaxis (nut allergy). It could be that the outcome is that some or all of the assessed activities are too high risk for the children. In these circumstances, refer to the guidance above on 'reasonable adjustments' (Equality Act 2010).

Risk assessment procedures

All schools will have risk assessment systems and procedures. Consider the following:

1. What are the possible hazards? (children, environment, security, safety, equipment)
2. Who might be affected and how?
3. What are the likely 'risky' behaviours that will arise?
4. What is the level of risk (low, medium or high) and what can be done as preventative measures?
5. Have I consulted with staff, caregivers and the child(ren)?
6. Have I produced a written plan?
7. How will the plan be evaluated?

TABLE 10.5 Risk assessment checklist*

Date of risk assessment:	Class/Tutor/Child(ren):
Review date:	Area of need:
Overview of the activity	
Hazard(s)	**Priority rating**
List all significant hazards (travel, groups or individual children, ratios, venue/site, equipment, personal care, trigger points)	Low, medium, high
Who might be harmed?	
List all the groups of children and staff who are at risk	
How is the risk to be managed?	
List all existing procedures/strategies to be used	
What further action is needed to manage the risk?	
List any risks which are not adequately managed and state the proposed action to be taken	
Risk Assessment Review:	
Headteacher Approval/Signature:	Date:

*see Appendix and online resources for assessment template

Reflecting on provision and practice

The following diagram (Figure 10.1) is adapted from the Council for Disabled Children (2015: 14) and is a useful tool for you to reflect on and challenge the ways you are working with children. This can be colour coded to support the process of review and action planning:

- Red: Not in place
- Amber: Review and consolidation are needed
- Green: In place with evidence

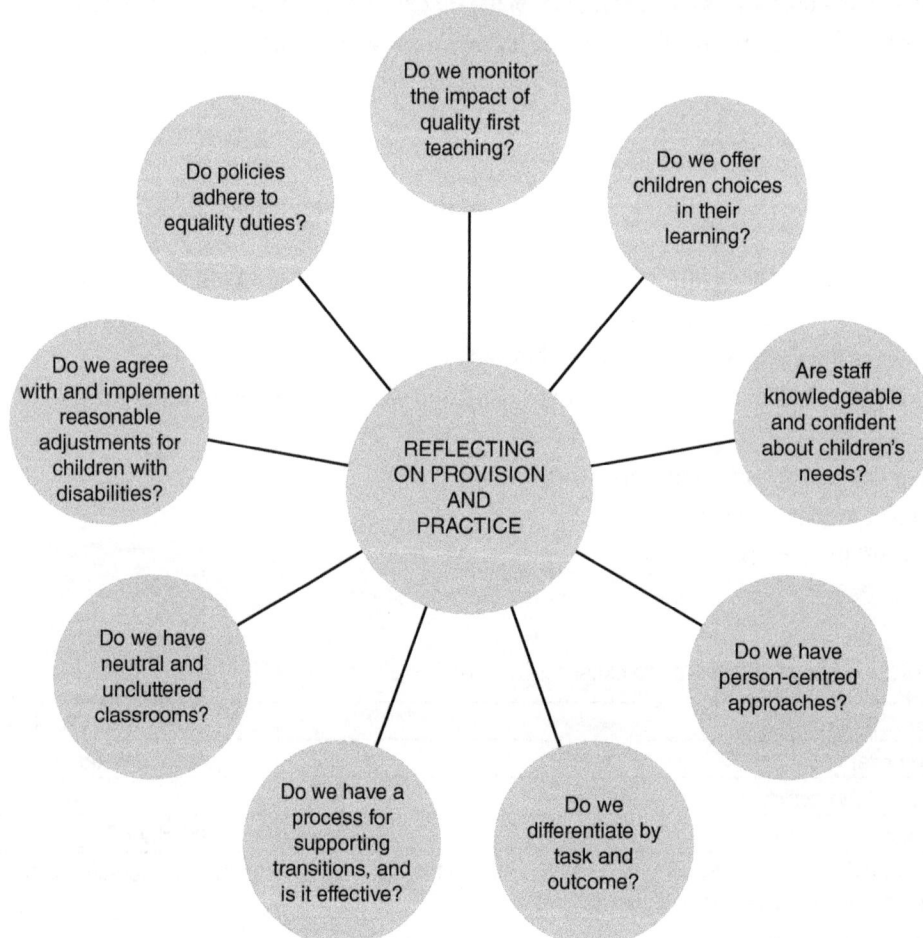

FIGURE 10.1 Reflecting on provision and practice

Supporting transitions

Transitions for both caregivers and children can provoke anxiety, stress and excitement – there needs to be preparation, planning and monitoring before, during and following the process. Most children will not be able to anticipate what challenges they will encounter, whether the move is a new timetable, teacher, taxi driver, year group or class, or moving to a new school. A generic transition plan will not work for all children; for some it needs to be bespoke to their needs. The key factors to successful transition are:

- Consulting with the child and caregivers about their views and suggested approaches
- Visits to open days, taster sessions where they can meet new staff and look around the building and local area

- Sharing of information with the next teacher/school such as photographs and timetables
- A visit to the new classroom/school (in school time or after school, whichever is most appropriate); some schools have virtual tours
- Reasonable adjustments, any accessibility arrangements and EHCP shared and agreed (if they have one) prior to start date
- Spending time in the new provision before officially starting
- A settling-in period, as it may not be in the best interests of the child to move from one setting to another full time in the first week.

Case study

Ali was in Year 2; he had a diagnosis of High Functioning Autism and needed support with changes in routine and forming friendships. In May, the SENCO, caregiver and Ali met to discuss the transition process to Year 3. The teacher was yet to be appointed and this was causing him anxiety, resulting in disruptive behaviour in class. Also, the junior school was a feeder school for four other local infant schools so he would have new children in his class.

How would you manage this transition?

What factors need to be considered/addressed?

Individual healthcare plans

The Children and Families Act (2014) Section 100 places a duty on governing bodies of maintained schools, proprietors of academies and management committees of Pupil Referral Units (PRUs) to make arrangements for supporting children with medical conditions (DfE, 2015b). Every school must have a medical policy so that an 'individual healthcare plan' (IHCP) is prepared for those with medical needs. Governors must ensure it is reviewed regularly and be readily accessible to caregivers and school staff. Most importantly, the policy must set out the procedure for when a school is notified a child has a medical need. Within the policy, the role of IHCPs needs to be included. The statutory requirements are that the medical policy includes:

- who has the responsibility to ensure sufficient staff are suitably trained
- a commitment that all relevant staff will be made aware of the child's medical needs
- cover arrangements in case of staff absence or staff turnover
- a briefing process for supply teachers
- a risk assessments process
- monitoring processes for IHCPs.

The benefits of IHCPs

- To reassure caregivers that you understand and are responsive to the ongoing support their child needs

Leading and Coordinating Provision

- To be clear about the complexity of individual health needs and the impact on the child's ability to learn
- To share systems to monitor a child's health and for any emergencies
- To show you have considered advice from healthcare professionals
- To put in place reasonable adjustments in accordance with your duties.

(Equality Act, 2010)

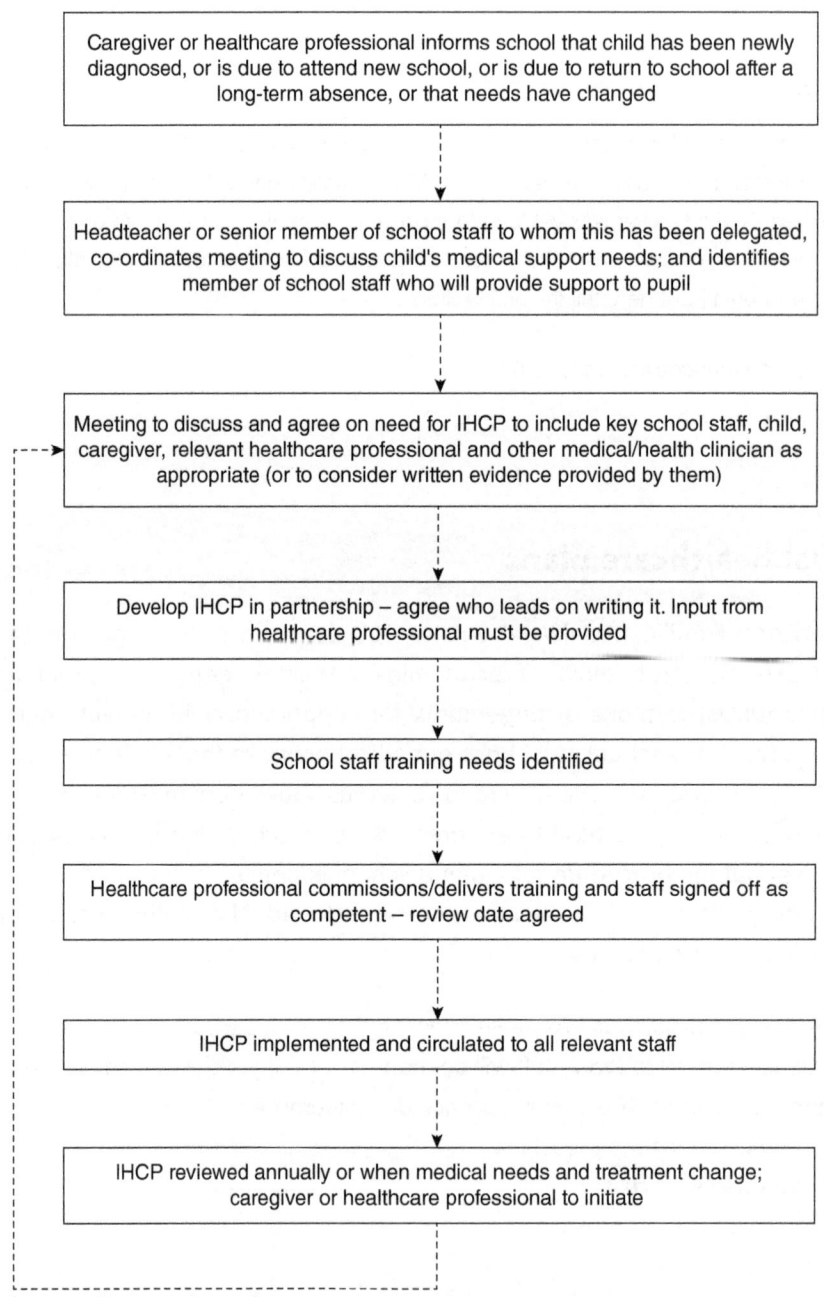

FIGURE 10.2 Model process for developing individual healthcare plans

Source: DfE (2015b)

Learning and Physical Disabilities

SENCO ACTIVITY
Who reviews the medical policy to ensure it meets statutory duties?

Not every child with a medical need will require an IHCP; the school will need to make a judgement depending on the complexity of their needs and support. The DfE (2014d) has IHCP templates you can use and adapt, which are entirely voluntary as you are free to design and use your own. Most charity websites have examples of IHCP templates for you to adopt in school. Examples include Asthma UK, Diabetes UK and Epilepsy Action.

A. What to include on an IHCP
B. Parental agreement for setting to administer medicine
C. Record of medicine administered to an individual child
D. Record of medicine administered to all children
E. Staff training record – administration of medicine
F. Contacting emergency services
G. Model letter inviting caregivers to contribute to individual healthcare plan development

Support organisations for families

SCOPE: Provides support from the point of diagnosis of a disability. They have resources to support knowledge and understanding of autism, cerebral palsy, challenging behaviour, communication difficulties, epilepsies, hearing and visual and learning difficulties.

Website: www.scope.org.uk **Helpline:** 0800 800 3333 (Weekdays 9am to 5pm)

Contact a Family: Provides advice and support for families, bringing families together to support each other.

Website: www.contact.org.uk **Helpline:** 0808 808 3555

Support organisation for professionals

Council for Disabled Children: The umbrella body for the sector in bringing together professionals, practitioners and policy makers to meet the needs of children with SEND.

Website: www.councilfordisabledchildren.org.uk

No child can be denied admission or be prevented from taking a place because arrangements have not been made (EA, 2010).

Equality Act 2010

The Equality Act (EA) 2010 brought together all the equality duties in a single legal framework. There are nine protected characteristics under the EA which apply to all schools and employers. These are:

- age
- disability
- gender reassignment

- marriage and civil partnership
- pregnancy and maternity
- race
- religion or belief
- sex
- sexual orientation.

The duties in Part 6 of the EA 2010 cover discrimination to:

- admissions
- the provision of education
- access to any benefit, facility or service
- exclusion of other forms of detriment; that is other forms of disadvantage.

As stated in Chapter 2, a child has a disability under the EA 2010 'if they have a physical or mental impairment and the impairment has a substantial and long-term adverse effect on their ability to carry out normal day to day activities'. A physical or mental impairment includes learning difficulties, mental health and medical needs, specific learning difficulties, autism and speech and language and communication difficulties. This legal definition is broad and will cover a greater number of children than you may realise. To be classified as a disability it has to be 'substantial', meaning more than minor or trivial and long term as a year or more.

The EA 2010 sets out the legal duties which apply to prevent unlawful direct or indirect discrimination, and these duties cover all aspects of school life including teaching, learning, lunchtimes and trips.

They must not:

- directly or indirectly discriminate against, harass or victimise children with disabilities
- discriminate for a reason arising in consequence of a child's disability (this is key when considering your behaviour policies)
- exclude a child from school because of a disability (whether permanent, fixed term or at lunchtimes).

They must:

- make reasonable adjustments, including the provision of auxiliary aids and services, so that children with disabilities are not at a substantial disadvantage compared with their peers – this is an anticipatory duty (you need to think in advance what they may require and what adjustments will need to be made to prevent disadvantage)
- have regard to the need to eliminate discrimination, promote equality of opportunity and to foster good relationships between those with and without disabilities.

(DfE, 2015a: 17)

All schools are duty bound to make reasonable adjustments for children with disabilities (EA, 2010). If a claim of discrimination was to be made it would be no defence that you did not know the child had a disability; you need to take steps to find out. The duty to make reasonable adjustments is anticipatory, meaning schools must plan and put in place in advance adjustments to prevent any disadvantage occurring prior to the child attending. Also, the Act does not say what is meant by 'reasonable'; this means that there is a degree of flexibility for different situations. The question is whether the adjustment is reasonable for the school to do. It is unlikely that there would be nothing a school could do for a child with a disability in a given situation. If it is decided not to make any reasonable adjustments for a child, then the caregivers must receive a letter setting out the reasons for the decision. The legal duties within the EA 2010 are there to ensure that children with disabilities are not treated less favourably than others and that they are not at a 'substantial disadvantage'. Caregivers can make a claim of disability discrimination to the SEND Tribunal; a claim against a College of Further Education or Local Authority is brought in the County Court.

Case study

Zac has dyspraxia and finds writing large amounts of text by hand tiring and frustrating. It varies in size and can be illegible; he finds it hard to read when revising. In geography and history, his teachers ask him to write paragraphs of text from the whiteboard. If Zac doesn't complete the writing in time he is given a 10-minute detention.

Zac is at a substantial disadvantage as he finds it hard to write large amounts of text due to his dyspraxia. In law, he cannot be given detention, as it is discrimination on the grounds of his disability.

It should be obvious whether or not the child is at a substantial disadvantage.

Case study

Lara has dyslexia and finds it hard to read black text on a white background. All teachers use a grey background on the interactive whiteboard and on handouts.

This is a reasonable adjustment.

Case study

Tia has cerebral palsy and is a wheelchair user; she is unable to access classes on the first floor of her new school as there isn't a lift. She wants to take GCSE physics but the labs are on the first floor. If this was another subject which did not need access to a lab her classes should be moved to the ground floor. However, this does not mean the school doesn't have to make reasonable adjustments; they would need to consider what else they can do to prevent her being at a substantial disadvantage compared to her peers.

CPD/INSET ACTIVITY

Which of the following scenarios require reasonable adjustments to be made to prevent substantial disadvantage?

(Continued)

Leading and Coordinating Provision

(Continued)

- On the newly revised seating plan a child with a hearing loss is sat at the back of the class.
- A child with chronic fatigue is timetabled to sit a mock mathematics exam on an afternoon.
- A child requires support with personal care needs such as toileting, washing and dressing; he has a learning support assistant in the school day. The school arranges a residential trip and he wishes to go, but the school says he can't unless his personal care needs are met.
- A secondary aged child who has autism is provided with transport after school. She wants to go to an after-school club but the school bus is unable to take her home after 3.15 p.m.

In law all of these children are at a disadvantage in comparison to those without disabilities.
In groups, identify 'reasonable adjustments' that could be made to avoid disadvantage.

....

The following section will guide you through making explicit the reasonable adjustments for children. This will focus on the use of 'one-page profiles', also known as 'pupil passports'.

One-page profiles

- Identify and record the child's strengths
- Engage the child and caregivers in their views
- Include notes on any involvement with external agencies
- Define any terms for colleagues and caregivers/carers
- Include teaching strategies and reasonable adjustments. I would recommend putting the reasonable adjustments in bold to make them explicit (these will become a legal entitlement in accordance with the Equality Act 2010 so ensure they are feasible).

See Figure 10.3* for an example of a 'one-page profile' or 'pupil passport' with reasonable adjustments for a child in Year 9 with a diagnosis of dyslexia and dyspraxia.

The following pupil passport was created for a fictitious child with a diagnosis of both DCD and dyslexia. This can be used as a template to show the reasonable adjustments that have been agreed with caregivers and child.

Name: Ioana   DOB: 10/05/2004   Year: 9
SEN support plan: Cognition and Learning – Dyslexia/Dyspraxia
Health: Occupational Therapy and Physiotherapy

Strengths and Interests: (always first and foremost)
Strengths
• I am a good friend and give good advice • I love art, it is my favourite lesson • Food tech is good because I work independently and I am trusted to get on with it
Interests
Swimming and art are my hobbies. I would like to look after animals in the future.

Difficulties:
• I need a blue reading ruler to help me read • I find it hard to copy from the board and being asked to do this causes me anxiety • I read best with 'calibri' and underline makes reading harder • I find it hard to read my own handwriting and this makes revising for tests hard • I don't mind where I sit in class as long as I am not distracted by another student • I get very worried about tests as I find it hard remembering things • I am shy, I won't ask you for help • I have difficulty getting ideas on paper, I have difficulties with organisational and planning skills, I need to work on a PC **Notes for teachers: DCD (Dyspraxia)** affects fine and/or gross motor coordination. Difficulties can include memory, perception and processing as well as additional problems with planning, organising and carrying out movements in the right order in everyday situations

Teaching strategies and reasonable adjustments (Equality Act 2010):
• Ensure she has a blue reading ruler available at all times • No copying more than 2 sentences from the board • Calibri 14, double space and no underline • Use of laptop for word processing • Provide alternative to written recording • Ensure that whiteboard presentation of text and diagrams is clear and uncluttered • Allow thinking and processing time to complete tasks

FIGURE 10.3 A pupil passport

*see Appendix and online resources for assessment template

REFLECTIVE ACTIVITY

Review and reflect on the processes and systems you have in place to find out information on the disabilities that children have in your context and how reasonable adjustments are agreed, shared, applied and monitored.

Disability discrimination

- Discrimination arising from a disability (when a school treats a child with a disability less favourably because of something due to their disability)
- Failure to provide reasonable adjustments for a child with a disability
- Direct discrimination (when a school treats a child less favourably that it would treat others because of a disability)
- Indirect discrimination (where the school has general policies or requirements which disadvantage those with a disability compared to those without)
- Harassment (inappropriate conduct which violates a child's dignity or creates an intimidating, hostile, degrading, humiliating or offensive environment for the child)
- Victimisation (the school does something disadvantageous to a child because they believe they are about to take action under discrimination law)

(HM Courts and Tribunals Service, 2013)

Accessibility plans

The accessibility plan can be a stand-alone document, part of your equality and diversity policy or school development plan. The plan would usually span a three-year period with an interim and annual review. It is not defined within the SENCO role that this would be your duty, though you may be asked to support the development; it would usually be the role of the Senior Leadership Team and governors.

There are three key areas to be addressed in the plan; these are to:

1. Increase the extent to which children with disabilities can participate in the **curriculum**
2. Improve the **physical environment** of schools to enable children with disabilities to take better advantage of education, benefits, facilities and services provided, and
3. Improve the availability of accessible **information** to children with disabilities.

Note: The plan should be produced in collaboration with children with disabilities and caregivers. The length of time allocated for the long-, medium- and short-term targets will be decided by individual contexts.

Promoting disability equality

The requirement for children with SEND to have their education in an inclusive setting has become increasingly established over the last two decades. The Sutton Trust Toolkit (EEF) indicates that setting children according to ability disadvantages those of lower ability in most cases. Schools need to promote disability equality in the ethos, curriculum content and materials to represent the diversity within society.

REFLECTIVE ACTIVITY

Do books and teaching materials include images of children and adults with disabilities in positive roles?

Inclusion in education involves:

- Valuing all children and staff equally
- Restructuring the cultures, policies and practices in schools so that they respond to the diversity of children in the locality
- Addressing barriers to learning and participation
- Emphasising the role of schools in building and sustaining communities, developing values as well as raising attainment
- Recognising that inclusion in education is one aspect of inclusion in society.

(Adapted from Booth and Ainscow, 2011: 7)

TABLE 10.6 Information to be included in the accessibility strategy/plan

Requirements and evidence	Action/targets	Staff/resource implications	Monitoring and evaluation	Review date
Requirement: To have an accessibility plan				
On school website	Long term: Full review January 2020	Lead: HT with SENCO	Annual reviews	Dec (2020)
Governor minutes	Medium term: Consultation with children and families	Lead: Chair of Governors, SENCO	Interim review	Jan–June (2020)
	Short term: Audit disabilities across school	Lead: SENCO, secretary	Interim review	July (2020)
Requirement: Increase the participation of children with disabilities in the school curriculum				
One-page profiles, observation feedback and learning walks	Medium term: Review visit policy and accessibility of planned school trips	Lead: SENCO, an additional 2 days of non-contact time	To be evaluated and fed back to SLT	June (2020)
Employment of specialist staff, auxiliary aids and equipment	Short term: Add reasonable adjustments to lesson observation pro-forma	Lead: SENCO	SLT to approve and circulate	Sept (2019)
	Short term: Purchase of adjustable desk and writing slopes	Lead: SENCO	Class teachers to introduce and monitor effectiveness	Sept (2019)
Requirement: Improving access to the physical environment				
Wheelchair access to all buildings and classrooms	Long term: Fit hoist in shower room and provide an EVAC chair for the first floor	Lead: SLT, Chair of Governors and Finance Committee	To be costed and evaluated and fed back in Governors' meeting	July (2020)
Widened electronic doors into reception	Long term: Develop a medical room on the ground floor	Lead: SLT, Chair of Governors and Finance Committee	To be costed and evaluated and fed back in Governors' meeting	July (2020)
Two parking bays and 4 drop-off spaces				
Requirement: Alternative formats for written information				
Reading books with buff paper for those with dyslexia/scotopic sensitivity/visual stress. Timetables colour coded	Long term: Audit library books to check for accessibility	Lead: English coordinator and SENCO, one day each	Fed back to SLT for action planning	July (2020)
VLE with audio and video content	Medium term: Explore assistive technology for neurodiverse children	Lead: Computing coordinator, one day	Fed back to SLT with costings and evidence base	May (2020)

Source: Equality Act 2010: Schedule 10

Chapter summary

- The meaning of disability has been understood in different ways, and you can have a disability at different times over a life course
- Accurate identification and assessment of disabilities to understand the child's primary and secondary needs
- Focus on addressing the needs rather than the label (diagnosis)
- Language used to describe those with disabilities can influence their aspirations, interactions and wellbeing
- Reasonable adjustments are a legal entitlement for children with disabilities
- Children need to have positive experiences of education

11
Preventing School Exclusion

Sarah Martin-Denham

→ NASENCO outcome: The breadth and complexity of the causes of underachievement and planning provision for children with more severe and complex SEN. There are high expectations for all children and young people with SEN and/or disabilities.
→ Read alongside: Chapter 6: Adverse Childhood Experiences; Chapter 7: Meeting the Needs of Looked After and Permanently Placed Children; Chapter 8: Social, Emotional and Mental Health Difficulties

Chapter overview

The purpose of this chapter is to support you as SENCO in identifying and supporting children and families where there is a risk of exclusion occuring. Key considerations for this chapter are to explore best practice in preventing school exclusions through effective approaches and solutions to promoting positive behaviour. It also aims to enable you to review your exclusion process and to consider interventions to meet the needs of these children, including support from health services.

Types of exclusion

The Education Act (2011) is the main statute that sets out the school's duties when excluding a child; the DfE (2017b) produced statutory guidance based on this legislation. IPSEA (Independent Parental Advisory Service) (2017) confirms that there are two lawful types of exclusion, which are: permanent and fixed-term. Only the headteacher of a school (or the teacher in charge of a pupil referral unit or the principal of an academy) can exclude a child. The legal stance is that a child is either in school full time or excluded. Informal or unofficial exclusions such as sending a child home for the afternoon following an incident are unlawful. If a caregiver is asked to keep a child off it is an exclusion: whether it is leaving early, at lunchtime or being part time, all exclusions must be recorded in school and reported to the Local Authority (LA). There is significant concern from local authorities and government about the rise in permanent and fixed-term exclusions.

What are permanent exclusions?

Permanent exclusions (PE) refer to a child who is excluded and who will not come back to that school (unless the exclusion is overturned) (DfE, 2016a). As the DfE (2017c) explains, a decision to exclude a child permanently should only be taken in response to a serious breach, or persistent breaches, of the school's behaviour policy; and where allowing the child to remain in school would seriously harm the education or welfare of the child or others in the school. The Education Act 1996 places duties on LAs to 'make arrangements for the provision of suitable education at school or otherwise'. The education provided must be full time and be in place from the sixth day.

A local and national concern is the number of PEs experienced by children with identified SEMH needs; in 2015–16, despite making up only 2.2% of the total population, they represented 28% of all PEs, an increase of 42% from the previous year. The inequity of this is that there is variability in what one school will exclude for (one swear word) compared to another (where no exclusion would occur due to swearing). Any exclusions need to be made with the knowledge that they are lawful, which includes ensuring there is no breach of the Equality Act 2010 and that the exclusion is rational, reasonable, fair and proportionate. Mills and Thomson (2018) provide evidence that children who

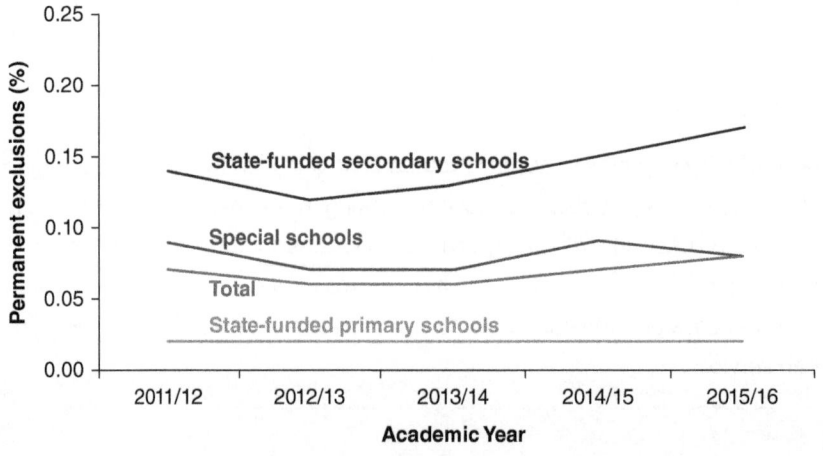

FIGURE 11.1 Annual number and rate of permanent exclusions from 2011/12 to 2015/16

Source: DfE (2018f)

are taught in alternative provision do considerably worse than their peers in mainstream. Only 4.5% achieve 5 GCSEs at grades 9–4 compared to 65% in state-funded mainstream schools.

What are fixed-term exclusions?

Fixed-term exclusions refer to children who are excluded from a school for a set period of time. This can involve a part of the school day and it does not have to be for a continuous period. A child may be excluded for one or more fixed periods up to a maximum of 45 school days in a single academic year. The DfE (2018f) clarifies that where a child has been subject to a fixed-term exclusion for more than five school days, schools must arrange alternative provision (AP) which is generally a form of pupil referral unit. AP can be provided full or part time with long or short placements. These are usually provided by AP academies, AP free schools and pupil referral units.

Alternative provision

Alternative provision (AP) is for children of compulsory school age who don't attend mainstream or special schools. This can be for a range of reasons, including:

- behaviour which has resulted in permanent or fixed-term exclusions, or an offsite direction by schools
- health reasons including physical or mental health needs
- where a child is awaiting a placement in mainstream school.

(DfE, 2018f)

Placements into APs are commissioned by LAs or schools and should take into account the views of caregivers and the child. Significant numbers of children in APs are boys from disadvantaged backgrounds; over 70% and 77.1% have SEN or disabilities. Also, more than 40% are eligible for free school meals, with a large proportion being from white British backgrounds, while other groups are over-represented including children who are black Caribbean; white and black Carribean; white and black African; Gypsy/Roma; Irish; and traveller of Irish heritage (DfE, 2018f). Mills and Thomson (2018) believe that it is the most marginalised children who experience exclusion, including males, those of lower socio-economic status, and those with maternal psychopathology, mental health and behaviour difficulties, communication difficulties, low caregiver engagement, poor relations with teachers, low attainment and SEN.

How many children are excluded from school and why?

> We know that excluded children are the most vulnerable: twice as likely to be in the care of the state, four times more likely to have grown up in poverty, seven times more likely to have a special educational need and 10 times more likely to suffer recognised mental health problems. Yet our education system is profoundly ill-equipped to break a cycle of disadvantage for these young people.

(Gill et al., 2017: 7)

In schools, there are some groups of children who are disproportionately more likely to be excluded compared to the whole school population. The DfE (2018f) clarifies that black Caribbean children are three times more likely to be permanently excluded than those who are white British. They add that white Irish traveller and Gypsy Roma children have by far the highest rates of both fixed and permanent exclusions. Looked after children are five times more likely to have a fixed-term exclusion and children with SEN are three times more likely than the general school population. The Timpson Review will explore the reasons why some groups are more likely to be excluded with the report published in Spring 2019.

We know that behaviour that schools deem to be in serious or persistent breach of the behaviour policy is most likely to lead to permanent exclusion. For these children, it ultimately results in admission to an AP unit of some kind. Recent analysis by Gill et al. (2017) implies that official data from the Department of Education does not show the full extent of exclusions. In 2016, there were 6,685 permanent exclusions but 48,000 were being educated in the AP sector which caters for excluded children.

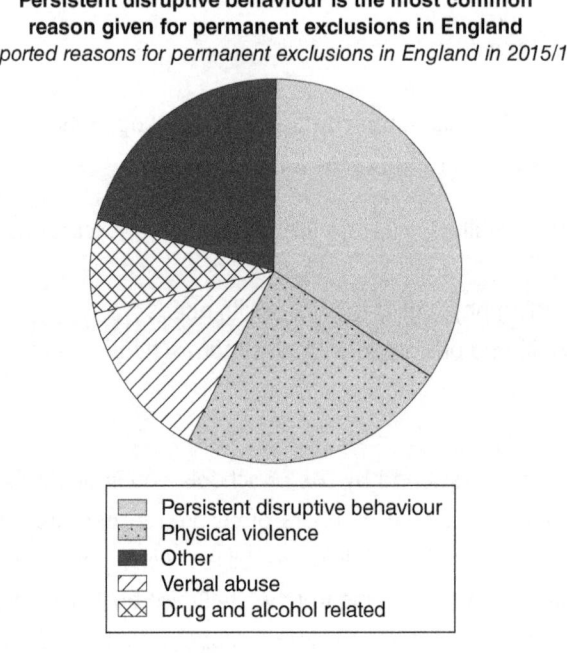

FIGURE 11.2 Reasons for permanent exclusions

Source: DfE (2017b)

What happens once a child is excluded?

The headteacher and governing body will have a number of options open to them. These are classified as official and unofficial exclusions:

Official Exclusions: These are recorded with central or local government and include fixed-period exclusions or permanent exclusions.

Unofficial Exclusions: These are not recorded as exclusions in the national data and include managed moves to a different school; a move into some form of alternative provision offsite; or illegal exclusions.

TABLE 11.1 Exclusions

Type of exclusion	Description	What happens next?
Official exclusion		
Permanent exclusion (expelled)	The child must permanently leave the school. This can only be used as a 'last resort in response to a serious breach … of the school's behaviour policy' and where the pupil is putting others at risk (DfE, 2017b).	The child usually becomes the responsibility of the Local Authority with education provided by a pupil referral unit (PRU) or another type of alternative provision (AP). This is supposed to be a temporary situation while the student waits to find a new place in a mainstream school or specialist provision. However, in practice permanently excluded children often remain in their PRU or other AP provider until they finish their GCSE exams.
Fixed-period exclusion (suspended)	The child's school attendance is temporarily suspended. This can occur on several occasions across the school year, for a maximum of 45 days within one year (DfE, 2017b).	A child can have a fixed-period exclusion for five days with no alternative education arranged, but on the sixth day their school must find alternative education for them. This may be in a PRU or another type of AP. Repeated fixed-period exclusions are often a precursor to permanent exclusion.
Unofficial exclusion		
Managed move	Instead of a permanent exclusion, headteachers and caregivers mutually agree to move the child from one school roll to another.	The child is taken off the roll of their original school, and becomes a child of the new school, which may be a mainstream school or a PRU.
Offsite Alternative provision	The school directs the child to be educated somewhere other than the school, full-time or part-time, if they believe it will 'improve his or her behaviour' or because, for 'illness or other reasons', they would 'not receive suitable education without such provision' (DfE, 2013).	The school will choose somewhere for the child to be educated offsite, in agreement with caregivers. This may be a PRU, an independent school or unregistered provision. The school will remain legally responsible for the child's education and safety.
Illegal exclusion	The school encourages caregivers to take their child out of school. This is illegal.	The parent may sign paperwork to home educate their child, or they may enrol their child in another school, as though they have moved house or made an independent decision to change local school.

Source: Adapted from Gill (2017)

SENCO TASK

- Ensure your behaviour policy includes a section on reasonable adjustments and has the flexibility to support vulnerable children. One-size-fits-all policies for behaviour will not work, neither will zero tolerance approaches. The response to behaviour should reflect individual circumstances.
- Have a system for logging behaviours so you can analyse patterns and to track the effectiveness of interventions. Support should increase during crisis and reduce once needs are being met; you can track this by using your school information systems to monitor behaviour. The starting point is assessing for any unmet need.
- Carry out 'reasonable adjustment audits' to ensure these are enforced by all staff.

Informing caregivers about exclusions

The DfE (2018f) states that schools must ensure caregivers have access to all relevant information about the circumstance of the exclusion and the process; headteachers are legally required to notify caregivers when the child has received an exclusion and the reasons for it, without delay. They must provide the following:

- The reason(s) for the exclusion
- The period of the fixed-term exclusion or for permanent exclusion the fact it is permanent
- The caregivers' right to make representations about the exclusion to the governors and how the child may be involved in this
- Information on how the representations should be made
- Caregivers have the right to attend the governors' meeting when they consider the exclusion, to bring a friend and to be represented.

The governing body can overturn a headteacher's decision. If governors support the permanent exclusion, caregivers can apply to the Local Authority or academy trust to request an Independent Review Panel to review the decision of the governing body not to reinstate their child. The panel can decide to uphold the decision, recommend they consider reinstating the child, or quash the decision and direct the governors to reconsider the reinstatement. They cannot direct them to reinstate the child.

> **Support organisations for caregivers**
>
> - Advisory Centre for Education for parents and carers (ACE) provides independent advice and information on state education in England.
>   **Website**: enquiries@ace-ed.org.uk
> - IPSEA offers free and independent legally based information, advice and support to help get the right education for children and young people with all kinds of special educational needs and disabilities (SEND).
>   **Website**: Caregivers can book a helpline appointment at www.ipsea.org.uk/Pages/Category/service-overview
> - The Coram Legal Centre promotes and protects the rights of children in the UK and internationally in line with the UN Convention on the Rights of the Child.
>   **E-mail**: info@coramclc.org.uk
> - The National Autistic Society also provides information on exclusions
> - The School Exclusions Service offers advice and information to parents of children and young people on the autism spectrum on all aspects of school exclusion in England.
>   **Telephone number**: 0808 800 4002.

Effective school policies to promote positive behaviour

Bennett (2017) shared the aims of education as revolving around:

- the academic education of the child
- the nurturing of their best interests
- the development of good character
- the training of the workforce and socialisation.

To achieve these aims, schools need to promote positive behaviour and the starting point for this to be achieved is by understanding and responding to the individual needs of children. If behaviour is not dealt with, learning cannot take place for either the child with the challenge or the other children in their classrooms. The DfE (2018d) asserts that the past experiences of looked after and permanently placed children can impact on their behaviour. It is important to remember this when considering how best to support the child or young person with their learning and the design and application of schools' behaviour policies.

As Booth and Ainscow (2011) discuss, developing inclusion involves reducing exclusionary pressures. They use the term 'disciplinary exclusion' as the temporary or permanent removal of a child for breaches of school rules. What needs to be understood is that for some children they have ongoing pressures which prevent them participating in school life, including dealing with previous or current trauma; learning challenges, for example specific learning difficulties; and ongoing unmet needs. The DfE (2018f) reported that the evidence for the Timpson Review highlights a rise in 'zero tolerance' behaviour policies, which is creating school environments where children are punished and excluded for incidents which could have and should have been managed within the mainstream school.

The purpose of a behaviour policy is to ensure all children are safe and are able to access the learning and teaching to enable them to achieve their full potential. Schools have the freedom to write their own behaviour policies and approaches to managing what they deem to be inappropriate behaviours. Currently, schools can use 'reasonable force', have searching powers, and impose same-day detentions. In examining behaviour policies it is clear that it is not made explicit how schools are meeting the Equality duties within the Equality Act (2010) for children with disabilities. If a school policy states that a child will get a detention if they forget their equipment for lessons on two occasions, there needs to be consideration of how this is applied to a child with a disability. In this circumstance, if a child has a diagnosis of dyslexia and challenges with their working memory this cannot be applied, as no reasonable adjustment has been made and the detention is not a proportionate means of achieving a legitimate aim. Instead, they should develop strategies to help the child to remember, such as text messages or a note in their planner.

Evidence-based approaches

Schools have varying approaches to how they manage behaviour; the effectiveness of these tends to be measured by the level of exclusions. It seems to be the case that isolation spaces/rooms are becoming increasingly common. Ofsted (2018) advises that separate isolation rooms should only be used when it is in the best interests of the child and other children and only for a limited time; their use needs to be made explicit in the behaviour policy. For a child to reach the point of needing an isolation space, it is clear that school policies, systems and/or processes have failed; it could also be due to ineffective teaching and/or a lack of quality staff training. There needs to be a shift from isolation processes to targeted specialist intervention to meet need and reintegrate the child back into school life.

TABLE 11.2 Systematic review: Evidence-based approaches preventing school exclusion

Outcome	Approach	Researchers	Number of research studies reviewed/dates
School-based interventions cause a small and significant drop in exclusion rates but effects are not always sustained	A focus on the child (enhancing academic skills, counselling, mentoring and monitoring) and a focus on the school (training for staff)	Valdebenito et al. (2018)	37/2003–2014

Children who display Challenging, Violent or Aggressive Behaviour (CCVAB)

The term CCVAB was introduced by Thorley and Coates (2018) to encompass a range of previous acronyms used to define children's behaviour: these included CPV (Child to Parent Violence), APVA (Adolescent to Parent Violence and Abuse), VCB (Violent Challenging Behaviour) and so on. They suggested more would be achieved in supporting these children and their families if these behaviours were not separated into a range of acronyms and consequently seen as 'different' categories. Children can display behaviour that is seen to be challenging, aggressive or violent by those who witness it and it can create disruption in the school or classroom. This can be difficult to predict, or it can be hard to determine how best to support children, families and colleagues; however, such support is crucial for the health and wellbeing of all concerned. These behaviours may arise due to trauma that they have or are experiencing, adverse childhood experiences, bereavement or identified/unidentified special educational needs or learning/physical disabilities. If staff are unable to understand or manage the behaviours they will continue or escalate, ultimately leading to both the teacher and the child having negative experiences and a relationship breakdown.

Children with autism may experience intense anxiety, which is the outcome of difficulties with communication and interaction with others. They could be over and/or under stimulated/undiagnosed or be suffering due to changes to school timetables or classroom routines or staffing. If you combine communication challenges with rising anxiety levels, the likelihood of stressed behaviours will increase which can lead to misunderstood behaviours, resulting in school exclusion. Support systems and processes will need to be put in place for colleagues to identify, predict and respond to the cause of the behaviour to prevent the child becoming distressed; these need to be agreed with the caregivers and the child. If there is not a clear system in place the behaviours will escalate, resulting in the child going into crisis, which unfortunately in some schools leads to restraint, punishment or isolation.

If a child goes into crisis or there has been an incident involving CCVAB, there must be a debrief to see how this could have been prevented. However, it must be remembered that attempting to debrief with children at the point of the behaviour can distress the child, causing further escalation of the situation; it is therefore important to *relate* before any attempt is made to *regulate*. When a child gets to the point of crisis it means school processes have failed, a need has not been met and this needs to be explored through debrief systems to plan to prevent future occurrences.

Debriefing processes following an incident

The process of debriefing should form an integral part of school processes to support learning and teaching where children are not meeting the requirements set out in the policy for promoting positive behaviour or when other critical incidents occur. This process will allow all stakeholders to continually develop and refine processes and allow an opportunity to reflect on the needs of individual or groups of children. The outcome may be that weaknesses in systems or training needs are identified and these will need to be followed up. The debrief should be carried out as soon as is feasibly possible; this is so that staff can learn from what happened and to prevent/identify triggers for the future. It is not to blame someone or a child but to collate views on what happened and why. This could be carried out by the SENCO or someone else who knows the child.

Types of debrief

A 'hot debrief' can be used immediately after an incident to capture key issues that led up to, during and following; however, it is essential the child does not feel further distress as a consequence and it may be that discussion with the child needs to wait until the child has regulated and is able to provide their thoughts and views. Formal debriefs have identified outcomes and follow a more formalised process.

The template below (Table 11.3) can be used for formal debriefs and can be used as a means to analyse causes for behaviours which result in children being removed from classrooms and then 'sent' to you as SENCO or other members of staff. By requiring a debrief staff will be incentivised to implement support strategies rather than complete forms and attend meetings. Remember, a requirement of teaching standard 7 is to maintain good relationships with children, exercise appropriate authority and act decisively when necessary (NCTL, 2011). It is important to remember that a good relationship is a two-way process; children cannot be forced into forming a good relationship and relationships take time, empathy, understanding and support. Such relationships cannot be seen to exist simply from a position held by an adult.

TABLE 11.3 Debrief template*

Description of the event: What happened   **Context: Where it started/ended**   **Children and adults involved:**   **Witnesses:**   **Date/time:**
Leading the discussion: (this should be a person who has a good relationship with the child and who the child trusts)   • Only begin if the child is calm, regulated and the caregiver is present   • Explain the purpose of the conversation and why it is necessary (to understand what happened and why)   • Ask if they have any questions   • Ask the child to think for a few minutes about what happened   • The child/adult should describe what they did, saw and experienced pre, during and post the event and how it made them feel (it may be in the best interests of the child to do this separately)   • Useful questions – Can you tell us what happened today? Do you know what made you feel that way? What are your ideas for making it better next time? What can I do to help you?
Note: If the child is in survival response fight/flight/freeze, they will have no memory of why they behaved in the way they did. It is important to remember that these subconscious occurrences are survival instinctive responses, not those of conscious thought, or if resulting from communication difficulties, the child may not be able to articulate the issue to you (see Chapter 6).
Analysis/reflection: With the evidence of the events, examine what happened and why   • Were there any warning signs? What were these and were they responded to?   • What did the behaviour look like and how often is it occurring? Does this occur elsewhere outside of school?   • What is the severity of the behaviour and how long did it last?   • What support do the child, family and colleagues need?   • How could the situation be prevented in the future?   • Are current processes/behaviour policy fit for purpose?   • How can any broken relationships be repaired?   • Are there any training needs?

(Continued)

Leading and Coordinating Provision

TABLE 11.3 (Continued)

Lessons learned and recommendations:	Actions	Review date/ outcome
• What was and was not managed well? • How can future incidents be prevented/managed? • Does the child appear to have unmet needs? • Does the child need referral to health/children's services? • What support needs to be in place for the child and family? • Are any risk assessments needed? • Is any staff training needed? • With hindsight, what could have been done differently/better? It may be appropriate for the child to develop a support plan with an adult to support them in sharing what their needs are to reduce future incidents. **Caregiver's response:** **Child's response:**		

*see Appendix and online resources for assessment template

Following the debrief process, a 'working together plan' should be created in collaboration with the child, family and other services involved in supporting the child. The purpose of the plan is to be proactive, giving the child strategies for home, school and in the community as an alternative to challenging, aggressive or violent reactions, and is for children where their behaviours are impacting on their daily life. The plan should be created in the interim and updated following recommendations from a full assessment of needs from a paediatrician, clinical psychologist, occupational therapist (for sensory needs assessment) or behaviour specialist.

> **Case study**
>
> Ben, 14, punches his chest with his right hand; he does this every day but it appears to happen more in certain lessons (mathematics and science). He will do this during independent work and it can last for up to 10 minutes; his teachers don't know what to do, so ignore the behaviour, as they know he stops eventually. Last week Ben hit another child; they were in the corridor moving between lessons and it seemed to come out of nowhere. The child he hit was hurt as he fell against the wall; the deputy head teacher wants Ben to be permanently excluded from the school. Ben lives with his birth mother, step-father and younger sister, who have shared that he has started to be violent towards his sister by hitting her; she also has some bruising to her arms. To date, Ben hasn't been referred to any services outside of school and his mother cannot understand the change in his behaviour.
>
> The 'working together plan' in Table 11.4 has been created for Ben.

TABLE 11.4 Working together plan

Green	
Support strategies	**What Ben will do, say and look like to show us he is calm and happy**
Pre-teach material for science and mathematics using the school VLE (share lesson content) and have a clear structure to the lesson	• I will make eye contact with you • I will look towards the front of the classroom • I will have my stretchy man in my hands • I won't be distracting other children by getting out of my seat

Give positive feedback and discreetly check he knows the task he needs to do	
Don't ask Ben to read out loud or answer questions in front of the whole class, he won't do it	
Allow Ben to use play with 'stretchy man' to keep himself regulated	
Allow Ben to leave the classroom 2 minutes before the lesson so he is not in a crowded corridor	
Amber	
Support strategies	**What Ben will do, say and look like in showing he is *becoming* anxious and agitated**
Discreetly check Ben understands the task with positive body language and supportive voice tone	• I will start to clench my fists • I will look distracted and will not want to make eye contact • I will fidget in my seat • I will rub my fist against my chest and I might put my head on the desk • I will drop equipment on the floor
Use 'talk partners' so he has peer support	
Check you have modelled the activity and provided manipulatives to support him	
Offer Ben a task to do outside of the classroom so he can go to the safe place or use the trampoline	
Red	
Support strategies	**What Ben will do when he is being challenging**
Stay calm and say you will help him	• I will be hitting myself in the chest • I will appear to be staring • I might pinch my skin • I will want to be left alone and for the class to go away • I won't be able to control my reactions if someone touches me
Ben regulates quicker when teachers talk to him about sport, ask him about what he has been doing in rugby, who he last played and what the score was	
If he starts hitting his chest, encourage him to stretch the 'stretchy man' or stamp his feet, give him something else to do with his hands (doodling), or suggest he works with his friend	
Don't let Ben leave the classroom without supervision if it is a transition time for the school	
Blue	
Support strategies	**What Ben does, says and looks like to tell us he is calming down**
Ben can quickly return to green (usually in a few minutes)	• I will begin to look at you • I might ask you a random question; I do this to check you are OK with me • I will stop hitting my chest and usually start to doodle on my notes
Ask him how you can help him; just knowing you care will help him regulate	
Check that the other children aren't staring at him as this can make the situation re-occur	

Source: Adapted from The Challenging Behaviour Foundation (2019)

Caregivers may need support to cope with and support children who are persistently non-compliant, violent and/or aggressive; this can include birth parents, step-parents, kinship carers, adopters or foster carers. Schools can support families by being understanding and listening to the challenges they are encountering and most importantly believing them. As Thorley and Coates (2018) suggest, there are costs with repair to damaged items and many of these caregivers are unable to work, which has economic implications. Unfortunately, there is little support available for families due to geography, or pressure on services, or lack of funding but mainly lack of awareness of CCVAB and any evidence-based interventions.

Approaches to support the child and their caregivers:

- Staff training so everyone who comes into contact with children understands the impact of CCVAB on the child and family
- School staff actively listen when caregivers raise the issue and find out the chronology of events over the child's lifetime
- SENCO/class teacher to create a working together plan for use in school
- Where there is violent and aggressive behaviour towards adults or children, a referral to a consultant paediatrician should be made in the first instance who will assess needs or refer onwards to CAMHS or CYPS
- Decisions made for the child based on evidence rather than presumption
- Interventions for children in school such as the internationally recognised FRIENDS programmes as well as alternative interventions specific to the child.

SNAP (Special Needs Assessment Profile) online

SNAP-Behaviour (SNAP-B) is an online diagnostic assessment and profiling tool that identifies and provides interventions for 17 social, emotional and behavioural difficulties. The three online questionnaires (Pupil Assessment Questionnaire, At Home Questionnaire and What I Feel Questionnaire) identify strengths and weaknesses and generate interventions based on the child's individual needs. There are 78 interventions to choose from for ages 5 to 16. Every term or twice yearly it is recommended schools repeat the assessment to quantify progress. The SNAP-B User's Handbook provides administration guidance, guidelines for interpretation and information about the development and rationale behind SNAP-B.

TABLE 11.5 RS Assessment

Relationship with self	Relationships with other children	Relationships with adults
Anxiety	Friendship deficit	Attention-seeking from adults
Explosive anger	Instrumental aggression	Defiance towards adults
Implosive anger	Attention-seeking from peers	Over-dependence on adults
Depression	Being hurtful towards peers	Being hurtful towards adults
Academic self-esteem	Relationships with other children at home	Relationships with adults at home
Social self-esteem		
Relationship with self		

Source: Dr Rob Long and Dr Charles Weedon, published by RS Assessment for Hodder Education

REFLECTIVE ACTIVITY

What systems are in place to support children and staff with CCVAB, such as strategies to diffuse, resolve and refocus children while finding out the reason for the behaviour(s)?

Chapter summary

- White British boys are most likely to be excluded
- Few excluded children achieve the equivalent of 5 GCSE passes
- Excluded children are over-represented in the criminal justice system
- To exclude a child the decision must be reasonable and fair and not discriminate against a child because of a protected characteristic (Equality Act 2010)
- Behaviour policies need to include reasonable adjustments for children with disabilities
- Schools need to develop systems to support children with challenging violent and/or aggressive behaviour
- Caregivers need to be involved in any provision planning to support children and in debriefs when an incident occurs

Part III

Personal and Professional Conduct

12
Person-Centred Approaches
Sarah Martin-Denham

- NASENCO outcomes: Advise on and influence the strategic development of a person-centred and inclusive ethos, policies, priorities and practices. Build upon and extend the experiences, interests, skills and knowledge of children, raise expectations and set challenging targets. The voice of children with SEN is heard and influences the decisions that are made about their learning and wellbeing. Family leadership is encouraged and caregivers are equal partners in securing their child's achievement, progress and wellbeing. Promote, facilitate and support effective multi-agency working for all children with SEND.
- Read alongside: Chapter 2: The Statutory and Regulatory Context

Chapter overview

The purpose of this chapter is to support you in ensuring the child and family are at the heart of the planning, assessment, review and transition processes in school. It will provide creative approaches to gathering child and family voice to prepare and enable them to contribute to decisions that affect them and to influence school improvement.

Person-centred approaches

Person-centred planning is the concept of moving the power from professions to the child and family, as they are best placed to understand their strengths, interests, preferences, challenges and to share future aspirations. Person-centred approaches (PCA) are advocated in the Code: 'a person-centred approach is where the views of children and caregivers are taken into account when decisions are made' (DfE, 2015a: 245). Adams et al. (2017) were commissioned by the DfE to survey caregivers and children with an EHCP to build a national and local picture of how they were experiencing the needs assessment, planning process and resulting EHCPs. Only half found the process easy and two-thirds were happy with the overall process. They were least positive about the child being given choices of how to take part in this process and about how they were supported to understand what was happening and why.

The UNCRC (1989) Article 12 makes it explicit that children have the right to participate in decisions that are made about their lives. It is required that all children have these rights upheld and that adults assist children to have their views, feelings and aspirations elicited and placed at the centre of plans for their future. This is strengthened in the Children and Families Act (CAFA) 2014 and stated in the Code that 'there is a clearer focus on the participation of children and caregivers in decision-making at individual and strategic levels' (DfE, 2015a: 14). It is therefore clear that there is a responsibility on adults to engage in creative and developmentally appropriate ways to facilitate children's communication (Hill et al., 2016).

Capturing the voice of the child

A key element of international and national policy initiatives is that they have focused on capturing the voice of the child with Special Educational Needs and Disabilities (SEND) (Children Act, 1989; United Nations, 2006; CAFA, 2014; DfE, 2015a). Although consulting children is expected in government policy, there is no guidance on how best to achieve this. For authentic voice to be achieved, children should be heard, asked for their preference on how they would like to share their views and with which supporting adult. This does not always happen in reality, as Palikara et al. (2018) found following the analysis of 184 EHCPs for depictions of children's voices; 26 of these could not be analysed as section A (the child's perspective) was either not completed, was limited or missing. They found high levels of variability in the way the voices of children were captured, including the methods used to ascertain their views.

Prior to gathering child voice for an EHCP you need to consider the individual child and their preferences. It may be that the SENCO or class teacher is not the person the child will talk to most freely, so consider other adults that the child has built positive connections with; for example, school crossing staff, taxi drivers, lunchtime supervisors. The environment is also important, as some children can find offices or formal approaches intimidating; maybe going for a walk or sitting in a familiar place would be more suitable. As SENCO, reflect upon the purpose of the information, what you will do with it and, most importantly, whether the children understand why their voice is important. As Adams et al. (2017) advocate, children first need to know what the process is and why it is needed. Once this is established, you need to find the most useful approach based upon the child's preferences, wishes and needs. It should never be tokenistic, as their voice matters to improve their experience and success at school, so think of the best way to achieve this. There will also be children who are non-verbal or have other communication challenges, so ways need to be sought to allow them to share their views; some children will ask to remain voiceless, and this also needs to be respected.

The following approaches are designed to gather child voice for section A of the EHCP:

- What they enjoy doing
- What their interests and hobbies are
- What they would like you to know
- What they are good at
- What they find difficult
- The places in school they feel happiest
- What they can help themselves by doing
- What is important to them for the future
- What they would like to be/do in the future.

Children's responses need to be shared with colleagues and other professionals to shape provision, practice and to produce relevant and realistic outcomes; they will also be used as the basis to formulate the graduated response for children on SEN support. There will need to be adaptations for the approach to gathering the child's views depending on the individual needs of the child, such as the use of technology, visual prompts, objects, pictures and makaton to explain and participate in the process. Creative and innovative approaches need to be developed, and some useful examples are given below:

Graffiti walls: This approach to elicit children's views and perspectives was recommended in the Save the Children study by Fajerman et al. (2004); it is considered to be an effective approach to use with all children of all abilities. It begins with the use of a stimulus – a video clip, an artefact – that leads to discussion about their experiences of school. They can then share their views on their experiences through access to a wall, large white board or sheet of paper, printed with a breeze-block pattern to record their responses to stimulus questions about their experiences (Hill et al., 2016). It is recommended that the children create the wall, as this is an opportunity to discuss their feelings about school in an informal manner; it creates a space for the child to talk and the adult to listen. This can be adapted through the use of post-it notes (one colour for positive aspects of school and another for what they don't like so much), and the child should then be supported to rank these in order of importance.

Mind mapping: This approach allows the child to share their views about school, learning and challenges they have in a personalised way, as with the graffiti wall. This is particularly useful for older children who can complete the mind map on paper or through an app such as LucidChart. The examples given below (Figures 12.1 and 12.2) are produced by Emily, age 15, who has a diagnosis of dyslexia.

iPads/tablets: These can be used to photograph or make a film of aspects of school life children like or dislike for discussion with their preferred member of staff; some children will be able to do this independently. These can then be incorporated into support plans or one-page profiles. They are particularly useful for children with speech, language and communication challenges and for children with learning disabilities.

Personal and Professional Conduct

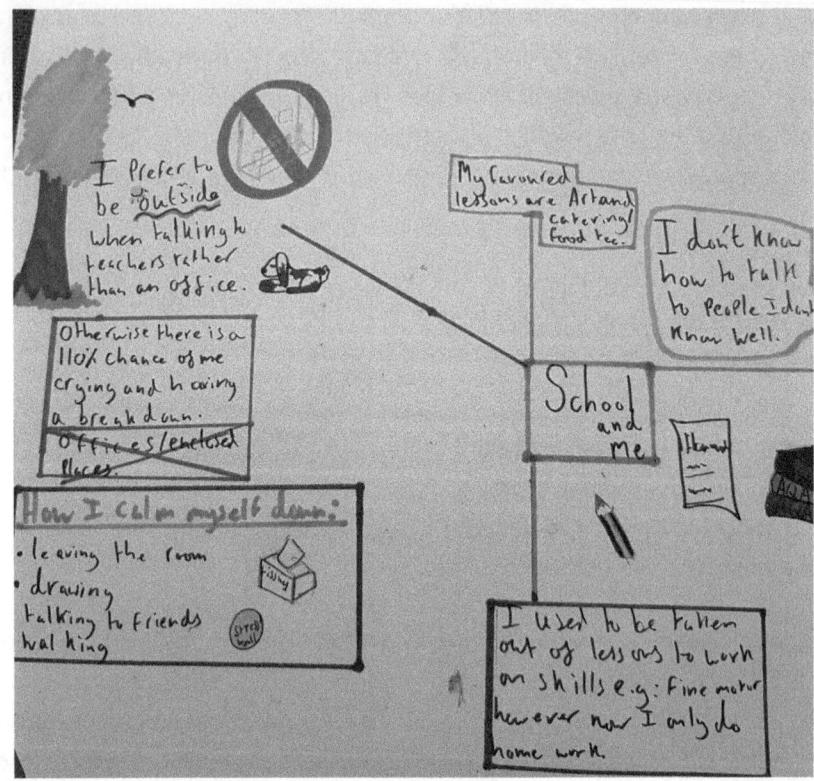

FIGURE 12.1 A mind map created in the child's chosen media

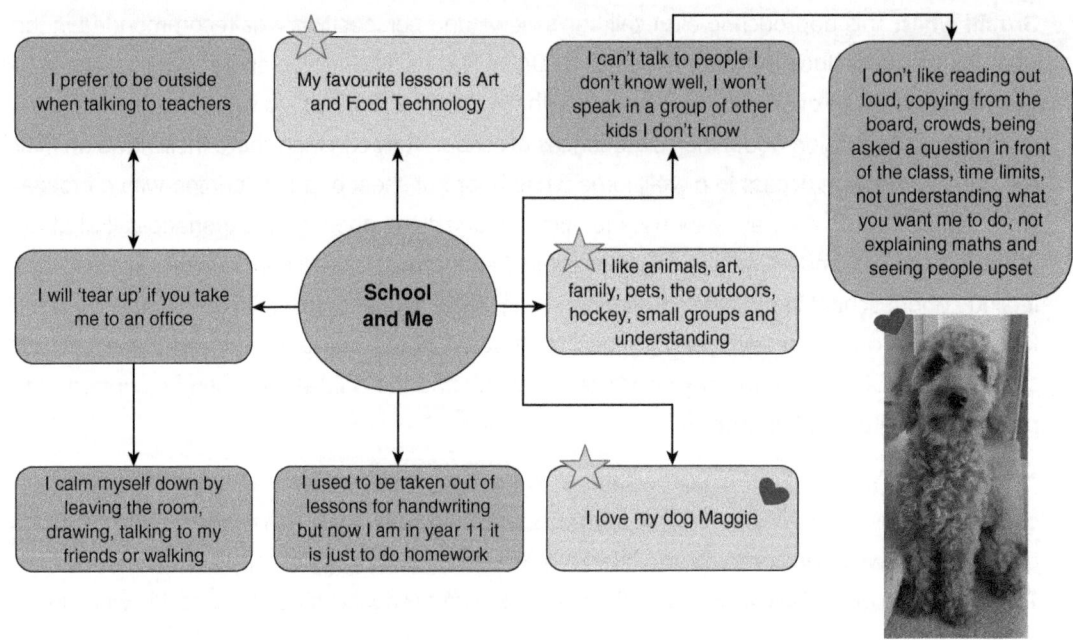

FIGURE 12.2 A mind map

Child voice checklist: This less creative approach is shared to allow you to compare the difference in the information you will gather using a checklist in comparison to a graffiti wall or a mind map. Checklists, although quicker to complete, are less child-centred and give less insight into the child's feelings, interests and aspirations.

TABLE 12.1 Child voice checklist*

Things that help me learn	Emoji	Child comment
Being told what to do		
Being shown what to do		
Watching a video clip of what I need to do		
My friend explaining		
Having new ideas explained		
Writing in my own words		
Copying from the whiteboard		
Designing and making		
Hot seating, role play, acting		
Using a mind map		
Asking questions		
Having a break		
Having longer to think		
Working alone/in pairs/in groups		
Using the computer		

*see Appendix and online resources for assessment template

Whole-school approaches

The voice of the child should not just be captured for the purpose of EHCP or SEN support but to inform provision and practice for all children. Estyn (2016) inspects quality standards in education and training in Wales and it produced a report for the Welsh government exploring characteristics of schools with effective capturing of child voice. It shared the benefits as enabling the building of positive relationships, contributing to school improvement and giving children skills to become active citizens. It recommends that a member of staff is responsible for coordinating child voice across the school and ensuring the participation of school leaders, governors and members of the local community. It outlines some innovative approaches, such as:

- **Associate child governors:** Two children are elected to represent views on the governing body; they attend full governing body and subcommittee meetings regularly
- **Child subject coordinators:** Children work alongside subject coordinators to feed back learning and teaching experiences in the curriculum. For example, a child with a particular interest in PE could support developments in this subject
- **School council:** Children contribute to the review of policies, in particular the behaviour/anti-bullying/marking and feedback policies based on the views of the school community; a governor attends this council
- **Suggestion boxes:** These are in various places around school and outside, which are followed up with a weekly meeting with senior leaders and children – the outcomes are shared in assembly
- **Provision and practice monitoring:** Children accompany the SENCO on learning walks and in observing lessons
- **The children's improvement plan:** In response to areas that they would like to develop, children from each year group work on this with governors and present to staff and the school community

- **Self-evaluation day:** School staff, governors, community representatives and children work collaboratively to make suggestions to improve teaching, quality of care, school buildings and the outdoor environment
- **A 'child voice group':** To gather views from the school community on their learning experiences and present their reviews at governors' meetings
- **A 'community council':** To look at ways the local community can be increasingly involved in school life
- **Circle time:** To share views at class level on feelings about school

REFLECTIVE ACTIVITY

Are the authentic voices of children a regular agenda item for staff, senior management and governor meetings?

Family leadership

The Code highlights the crucial role that caregivers play in taking part in their child's education. It reflects the findings of the Lamb Inquiry (2009) that suggested caregivers felt they were excluded or marginalised in decisions about their child and argued that caregivers should be equal partners with acknowledgement of their expertise; this Inquiry influenced the direction of the Code, placing caregivers and children at the heart of the process. The Code is explicit that schools need to have meaningful regard for the views, wishes and feelings of children and caregivers, providing them with information, advice and support to enable them to be partners in any decisions that affect them. Maher (2016) suggests that caregivers understand the needs of their children better than SENCOs and other educational professionals; they hold essential information on their health during pregnancy, their child's early development, strengths, interests, and can outline any support they have received from outside of school.

INSET/STAFF MEETING TASK TO INCLUDE CAREGIVERS:

In mixed groups, have governors, senior leaders, pastoral team, teachers, support staff and caregivers consider the following questions:

1. What approaches does the school use to encourage caregiver involvement?
2. How effective are these approaches?
3. What does your group perceive to be the barriers to engaging hard to reach caregivers?
4. What could you do differently?

Family leadership should be embedded in schools so that at the point a caregiver is made aware that special educational provision is being made, the positive relationship is already established. The CAFA (2014) does not say it is the SENCO who informs them about a child needing special educational provision but an 'appropriate authority' which is defined as the governing body (in a maintained school or nursery), the proprietor (in academies or alternative provision) or in a PRU the management committee. In reality, though, it is often the SENCO or class teacher who takes on this role.

Developing relationships with caregivers is complex as there can be several barriers to a two-way partnership developing due to factors such as work hours, feeling intimidated, experiencing their own difficulties or their previous negative experiences of school. Being told that your child has a special educational need is not easy; it is often unexpected and because of this you need to support caregivers in understanding the processes and how they work. Being informed that your child 'may' or 'does have' a SEN can cause a range of emotions from shock to relief; caregivers will have lots of questions and will need time to absorb the information. The priority of the caregiver may differ to yours; for example, their aspiration may be for their child to have friends, rather than academic attainment or passing an exam. There may also be cultural and language considerations, so ask if they would like to bring a friend or family member along to any meetings; record the meeting or take notes so they can revisit them later.

White and Rae (2016) carried out a study investigating caregivers' views of person-centred reviews and found the following:

- Caregivers are daunted by review meetings
- They are nervous about speaking out in front of professionals
- They feel unprepared for the meeting
- Caregivers liked that their views and those of their child were listened to

The caregiver must be party to the initial decision making about whether or not their child has SEND, they may need support preparing for any meeting, and if you don't need them to bring anything let them know in advance. A focus of any initial contact should be to build a positive relationship and trust by listening carefully to their views. The tool in Table 12.2 may be useful in ensuring you are meeting your statutory and recommended duties.

TABLE 12.2 Parental engagement checklist

Requirement (DfE, 2015a)	Considerations	RAG	Comments/action
Schools **must** provide an annual report for caregivers on their child's progress and for SEN support meet three times a year to set outcomes, review progress and discuss activities	How do you ensure caregivers can access the report? How do you get evidence they have engaged with it?		**Action:** To provide interim updates on progress by introducing progress texts termly
SEN support: set clear outcomes and review progress, discuss activities and support, identify responsibilities of school, caregiver and child	What is your process for this? Which approaches have you tried with hard to reach caregivers?		**Action:** SMART target training for all staff Introduce annual SENCO event for staff and caregivers in September
Discussions should be led by a teacher with good knowledge and understanding of needs and attainment	How can teachers securely access information on children's needs and attainment?		**Action:** SENCO review processes by September 2019 and present to senior leaders
Staff are supported in leading conversations with caregivers	This needs to be added to induction processes for NQTs and supply staff		**Action:** NQT training Autumn 2019 and review of induction by September 2019

(Continued)

TABLE 12.2 (Continued)

Requirement (DfE, 2015a)	Considerations	RAG	Comments/action
The views of the child should be included in discussions with caregivers	This is not consistent in all learning plans for SEN support		**Action:** Review of systems and processes to incorporate child voice by December 2019
School's management system records outcomes; action and support agreed for SEN support and shared with caregivers	It is unclear who has accountability for this and whether or not teachers access updates		**Action:** SENCO to embed through staff INSET December 2019

Source: Adapted from Campbell (2011)

Hellawell (2017) also points out that it is expected that caregivers engage in the co-production of aspirational targets, which they may find difficult or impossible to do; professionals need to be sensitive and explain what this means. Friswell (2014) makes a distinction between mere participation (expressing views, taking part in debates) and co-production (all agreeing outcomes, recommendations and actions are produced together). This aligns with the family partnership model way of collaborating, whereby professionals are 'helpers' ensuring consensual decision making, which is in the best interests of the child, relying on qualities such as respect. SENCOs should strive for the following:

- Working together with active participation/involvement
- Developing and maintaining genuine connectedness
- Sharing decision-making power
- Recognising complementary expertise and roles
- Sharing and agreeing aims and the process of helping
- Negotiation of disagreement
- Showing mutual trust and respect
- Developing and maintaining openness and honesty
- Communicating clearly.

(Davis and Day, 2010)

Case study

Lorna is the sole caregiver of Charlie who is 11 years of age. She was concerned that her child was not enjoying school and requested a meeting with his head of house. At the meeting she was told he started having additional support with his literacy and social skills 6 months ago and was on the SEN register. Lorna had not been told about this at the time; she was very cross and upset when she was told 'oops sorry you should have been told'.

What needs to happen next?
What processes should have been in place?
What would you do in this situation as SENCO?
How could you prevent this happening in the future?

Preparing for a meeting

- Prior to the meeting, explain the purpose to the child, ask them where they would like the meeting to take place, how they would like to be included and if they have any other special requests (music to be played, communication aids, visual aids, fiddle toys, comforters, snacks)
- Explain the purpose of the meeting to the caregiver and ask if they have any special requirements (leaflet/audio file with process, acronyms, advocate/supporter, translator, preferred drink) and how they would like to take part
- If the child doesn't share a preference, choose a less formal room with informal seating and provide refreshments
- Encourage the child to share their views or present their views through the creative approaches outlined in this chapter (the child's voice must be gathered prior to the meeting, not just before).

During the meeting

- Consider the seating so school staff are not opposite caregivers and child
- Discuss the child's strengths before any support needs
- Actively listen to the child and caregiver, noting responses
- Share the assessments that will happen in school or externally
- Share the immediate evidence-based interventions and support that will happen prior to any external assessments
- Discuss the outcomes each party hopes for
- Leave time for any questions, sharing of contact details and explanation of the local offer and other organisations given at the end of the chapter
- Find out the caregiver's preferred method of communication
- Agree a date for review
- Give thanks.

REFLECTIVE ACTIVITY

Can you think of any more ways to ensure the child and the caregiver feel at ease?

Supporting transitions

Any transition can provoke anxiety in children from entering school, changing for PE, queueing for lunch, to moving around corridors and going home. The transition to a new school is particularly difficult for some children and requires meticulous planning, information sharing, home–school and school–school liaison. The Code outlines that the school needs to share information with the provision the child is moving to (DfE, 2015a). As SENCO, you will need to use person-centred approaches to provide bespoke packages which focus on the holistic needs of the child to enable them to move from one activity or stage to another with as little disruption and anxiety as possible.

TABLE 12.3 Action plan template for SENCO: secondary transition 2019/2020

What we want to achieve	What we will do	The first steps	Who will be responsible and who will support?	SENCO support	How will I know I have been successful?	Date to be achieved
To identify training needs for staff for Y7 intake	Year 6 meetings with feeder schools to discuss learning and medical needs of Y6 children September 2019	Contact feeder schools to arrange meetings	SENCO/admin Admin to send and record responses	Admin to telephone/email	All schools meet and training needs identified	January 2020
		Make a question sheet for non-feeder schools to record outcome of meeting	SENCO	None required	Questionnaire complete/data gathered securely	March 2020
All staff know the varying barriers and approaches to learning for children with autism and cerebral palsy	Advice from consultant paediatrician, autism outreach team and school nurse	Review previous training of staff to identify gaps and audit specialisms within current staff	SENCO	School nurse, consultant paediatrician	All staff access and evaluate training to show increase in knowledge	September 2020

Case study

Shinji had been in the same primary school from the age of 4; he had a primary need of autism but his main challenge was coping with his anxiety. The school understood and had strategies in place to respond quickly to his emerging needs; he achieved national expectations and was generally happy. Shinji was moving to a large secondary school 5 miles from his home, a journey that would require using the school bus. His mother was concerned that the new school wouldn't understand his needs and that he would be unable to make the journey to school independently.

- As SENCO, how would you respond to the mother's concerns?
- What information do you need to share with the secondary school SENCO?
- How would you manage the transition to reduce anxiety for Shinji and his mother?
- How could you prepare Shinji for travelling by bus?

- Date of SEN review meeting with caregivers/carer/professionals:
- *If possible, copy of recent SEN plan/medical plans/pupil passport, EP report, etc.*

Transition documents provided by Clare Hornsby (SENCO) and Laura Reynolds (SENCO).

The following organisations will be able to provide support and advice to caregivers:

Support organisations for caregivers

Contact: www.contact.org.uk: Support for families and children with disabilities with guidance, information and support. They have online information on disabilities and signposting to parent forums

Independent Parental Special Education Advice (IPSEA): A registered charity offering free and independent legally based information, advice and support in relation to all aspects of SEND

National Network of Parent Carer Forums: www.nnpcf.org.uk: Provides information and advice to caregivers and supports their active participation locally and nationally; they also provide support to LAs and health partners

SENDirect: www.sendirect.org.uk: This site has been designed to support children and caregivers in finding activities and support which suit their interests, preferences, lifestyles and budgets

SEND Information, Advice and Support Service (IASS): This service provides free, impartial information, advice and support to children and caregivers about the SEND system

(Continued)

Personal and Professional Conduct

> (Continued)
>
> **The local offer:** This should be a comprehensive and accessible online resource provided by a Local Authority which sets out all locally available provision expected to be available for children with SEND
>
> **The Local Independent Support Service:** A person recruited by a local voluntary or community organisation to support families through the EHC needs assessment process. They are independent of the Local Authority.

TABLE 12.4 Individual transition plan*

Name:	Primary needs:	Cognition and Learning ☐
Feeder school:	Secondary needs:	Communication and Interaction ☐
Feeder SENCO:	Child Protection involvement:	Social, Emotional and Mental Health ☐
	Yes ☐ No ☐	Physical and/or Sensory ☐
SEN support: Yes ☐ No ☐		Caregivers actively involved?
Do they need/have an EHCP? Yes ☐ No ☐ Monitor ☐		Yes ☐
Annual review date for EHCP:		No ☐
Caregiver and child views: (Strengths, interests, aspirations, learning and challenges) Barriers to learning: Preferred approaches to learning: Effective interventions used to date: Approach to wellbeing: Diagnosed medical and/or learning needs:		Agreed reasonable adjustments with caregiver and child:
Professional involvement (AOT, paediatrician, CYPS, CAMHS, EP, language and learning, medical, Brain injury trust)		Available reports from other agencies:
Predicted SATS results Reading: Maths: Spelling, punctuation and grammar:		
Exam arrangements in place for SATS? (Small room, extra time, reader, prompt)		Primary SENCO actions:
Additional transition meetings/arrangements Additional meetings ☐ Visits ☐ Photography book ☐ Attendance at extra-curricular clubs ☐ Other ☐ (please specify)		Secondary SENCO actions:
Any Child Protection concerns? (Current or historic)		Review date:
Any other comments:		

*see Appendix and online resources for assessment template

Chapter summary

- The Code requires schools to seek and act upon the views of both child and caregivers to ensure they are involved in any decisions that affect them
- There are currently no national guidelines or standardised processes for capturing the child's or caregivers' voice
- Child and caregiver voice should be central to the school vision, ethos and policies
- There should be clear structures and response processes in place to gather child and caregiver views
- Child-centred and creative approaches must be used to allow children to influence decisions which affect them

13

Managing and Working with Support Staff

Dr Helen Benstead

→ NASENCO outcomes: To commission, secure and employ appropriate resources to reinforce the teaching of children with SEND and evaluate and report on their impact on progress, outcomes and cost-effectiveness. To deploy and manage staff effectively to ensure the most efficient use of resources to improve progress of children with SEND.

→ Read alongside: Chapter 3: Leading in the SENCO Role

Chapter overview

The aim of this chapter is to explore the factors that result in support staff being managed, deployed and supported effectively, leading to enhanced outcomes for children. For the purposes of this chapter, 'support staff' refers to members of staff whose role primarily involves assisting with learning; this includes Teaching Assistants (TAs), Higher Level Teaching Assistants (HLTAs) and Learning Support Assistants (LSAs).

Exploring effective management of support staff: A model of good practice

The role of support staff in schools is complex, in terms of responsibilities, thus often difficult to define and conceptualise (Devecchi et al., 2011). Support staff primarily work with children identified with Special Educational Needs and Disabilities (SEND), therefore there are significant links between the role of the Special Educational Needs Coordinator (SENCO) and the management and accountability for attainment and progress. Many SENCOs undertake positional responsibility within their role for coordinating and managing support staff, yet there are widespread ambiguities associated with the responsibilities associated with this role, as well as a lack of guidance on effective management of these staff members (Maher and Vickerman, 2018).

Due to the complexity and variance in the roles that support staff often undertake, managing them both as a group and individually can be very challenging. The model below (Figure 13.1) highlights an effective approach to successfully managing support staff, developed through an exploration of relevant literature and school-based research (Saddler, 2015). The model is presented as a useful tool through which to review the efficacy of support staff management.

FIGURE 13.1 Successful approaches to the management of support staff
Source: Saddler (2015)

Each component of the above model is discussed below:

1. **Consistent figurehead of management:** The staff member with positional responsibility for managing support staff varies widely; it can be the headteacher, deputy head, SENCO, or even an HLTA. A visible figurehead of management is likely to result in a better relationship between manager and support staff member, as the manager often appears more approachable.

2. **Status and respect:** Basford et al. (2017) suggest that a culture of equality between support staff and teachers is often lacking in mainstream schools across England. It is important to create a culture and ethos of equality between support staff and other teaching staff, stemming from the senior management team, in order that children view support staff as professionals who command respect. This culture of respect will support consistent behaviour management approaches and better teaching and learning practices.
3. **Access to training:** A lack of access to relevant training opportunities for support staff in mainstream schools has been widely acknowledged (Bowles et al., 2017). This research has indicated that support staff are likely to speak more positively about their Senior Leadership Team if/when they have accessed training opportunities that align with their personal interests and/or are of direct relevance to the responsibilities that they undertake within their role.

REFLECTIVE ACTIVITY

Reflect on the historic/current training opportunities that support staff have access to in your school. Are they directly relevant to their role? Do they take account of individuals' interests?
How is the impact of the training on outcomes for children evaluated and measured?

4. **Culture of high expectation:** A culture of high expectation is regarded as an effective approach to management of support staff, in encouraging staff to achieve their potential within their role. However, schools should be mindful that unreasonably high expectations can result in low levels of job satisfaction and excessive pressure in terms of staff accountability for children's progress.

REFLECTIVE ACTIVITY

Is there a culture of high expectation for all staff in your school? Reflect on a reasonable level of accountability for support staff versus teachers to ensure your expectations are fair for all.

5. **Clearly defined role descriptors:** In many schools, the lack of clear job descriptions for support staff is leading to 'role blurring' between teachers and support staff, which can be detrimental to the teaching and learning process. Schools should document clear role profiles detailing their specific professional responsibilities in that school.
6. **Contracts taking account of high-level qualifications:** In some schools, senior leaders have supported, and occasionally subsidised, additional qualifications for support staff, yet have not then provided promotional opportunities in their schools; for example, encouraging TAs to undertake HLTA status, but then not providing them with an HLTA role. Therefore, there can be some level of dissatisfaction amongst over-qualified staff members, as expectations have increased but pay and level of employment have stayed the same.

REFLECTIVE ACTIVITY

Identify the level of qualification of your support staff, e.g. Level 2/3/HLTA status. Reflect upon how reasonable the expectations are for individuals versus their level of qualification.

7. **Experience and autonomy:** These two areas of the model are discussed together, as they are interlinked. There is widespread evidence to suggest that more experienced support staff are better able to support children identified with SEND. Support staff often experience higher levels of confidence in their role when autonomy is afforded to them by senior leaders.

Education Endowment Foundation: 7 principles of effective practice in deploying TAs

In 2015, the Education Endowment Foundation (EEF) suggested seven recommendations for making best use of Teaching Assistants in UK primary and secondary schools (Sharples et al., 2015). These best practice principles provide a useful overview of the practical approaches that engender effective teaching and learning practices for children, but are also useful in ensuring support staff are managed effectively. SENCOs should use the information given under each principle as a tool for reflection.

In the classroom

1. *TAs should not be used as an informal teaching resource for low-attaining children*

Many TAs spend a significant proportion of their time implementing interventions and other structured programmes, yet research suggests that a significant proportion of their work is informal in nature (Sharples et al., 2015). This informality is less likely to result in high-quality learning experiences for children, therefore it is important that support staff are engaged in as many planned teaching and learning opportunities as possible.

2. *Use TAs to add value to what teachers do, rather than replace them*

Evidence shows that many schools have drifted into a situation where, arguably, the most in need children aren't getting enough time with the teacher due to being with TAs for a significant proportion of their time in school. This often does not provide optimum teaching and learning opportunities for staff and children (Lamb, 2009). TAs can be a vital aid to the children they support, but so are teachers, therefore the EEF recommends that schools do more to make sure that the most in-need children have access to 'quality first teaching' as well as support from TAs.

3. *Use TAs to help children develop independent learning skills and manage their own learning*

It is very important that the support TAs give to children encourages them to build the skills to work independently, otherwise children can become overly dependent on TAs and this can be difficult if/when they move classrooms or schools and can no longer work with the same adult; this is a situation known as 'SEN Velcro-syndrome' (Shevlin et al., 2008). Schools are encouraged to think carefully about the children that TAs work with across a given week, and to ensure that TAs' language during a task is thinking-orientated rather than completion-orientated.

4. *Ensure TAs are fully prepared for their role in the classroom*

TAs and teachers are required to find time to discuss expected teaching and learning approaches frequently. This will make sure that TAs are aware of what they need to say to children to support them and have the essential 'need to knows':

- Concepts, facts, information being taught
- Skills to be learned, applied, practised or extended
- Intended learning outcomes
- Expected/required feedback.

(Sharples et al., 2015)

Out of the classroom

5. Use TAs to deliver high-quality one-to-one and small group support using structured interventions

Evidence from the Sutton Trust shows that TAs' delivery of targeted interventions in a one-to-one or small group setting can add up to four additional months' progress for children. This finding shows the real impact that many TAs are having on outcomes for children. However, this impact is only observed when TAs are working in a structured group, with high-quality support and training. Therefore, making sure that TAs have had training on how to implement the intervention programme that they're delivering is essential.

6. Adopt evidence-based interventions to support TAs in their small group and one-to-one instruction

It is important that intervention programmes have evidence of impact behind them, so that schools know that they are likely to improve children's learning if they are implemented well. If the evidence behind an intervention programme is lacking, but it is still deemed appropriate for use, it is suggested that a school follows the 'good practice in running an intervention group' model, presented later in this chapter.

7. Ensure explicit connections are made between learning from everyday classroom teaching and structured interventions

If TAs can support children to see the connections between what they are learning in their intervention and what they are learning in the main classroom, then children are more likely to understand it. This is because children can more readily apply, demonstrate and consolidate new learning.

TA standards

In 2014, the DfE asked a panel of experts to draw up new TA standards. Although the DfE has not published these itself, a group of teaching unions were granted permission to publish these new, non-statutory standards in 2016. The standards document describes the primary role of TAs as:

> To work with teachers to raise the learning and attainment of children while also promoting their independence, self esteem and social inclusion. They give assistance to children so that they can access the curriculum, participate in learning and experience a sense of achievement. (Teaching Schools Council, 2016: 5)

SENCOs are advised to access these standards and use them as a reflection tool to explore the status and professionalism that the support staff in their school currently experience.

Personal and Professional Conduct

Modes of working associated with support staff: How to identify and utilise them

Support staff appear to work across three generalised 'modes' in the average educational setting: whole classroom, small group and one to one (Saddler, 2015). The three modes of working often require different approaches and skills, to maximise the teaching and learning experiences that children participate in. It is useful for SENCOs to be aware of these, to ensure that the skills, knowledge and understanding of individuals are considered in assigning responsibilities to support staff. The modes are explained below; effective support strategies associated with each mode are also presented. These support strategies can be used by SENCOs during observations, as a tool for highlighting areas of success and areas for improvement as well as in promoting effective teacher–support staff working.

Mode 1: Whole classroom

This mode is characterised by support staff undertaking the following:

- Usually spending time in the main classrooms of one or more teachers in the school
- Working with a range of children in the classrooms they spend time in
- Often supporting teachers with administrative duties, such as classroom displays and resources for lesson
- Choosing the children that they work with during lesson time by moving around the classrooms and identifying children that require support
- Being assigned specific groups/tables of children to work with during lessons but they will usually work with that group inside the main classroom.

Effective support strategies in whole classroom mode

Support staff and those they work with should take account of the following:

- *Try to work with children that have a range of needs:* It is often natural to go and support children of lower ability first, as they can be more vocal in their need for guidance and support. However, it is also important to support those children that are of other abilities, to ensure that they are experiencing stretch and challenge, as well as in maintaining high expectations of all.
- *Keep a time limit for each child:* Many children try to maintain the attention of an adult throughout a lesson. An appropriate approach to avoid this is to give each child that is being supported a time limit of 5/10 minutes, perhaps using a timer, so that the member of support staff can support multiple children throughout the course of a lesson. This ensures that children requiring support are noticed and helps to avoid over-reliance on support, as discussed earlier in this chapter.
- *Oversee:* One of the most effective ways for both teachers and support staff to identify who would most benefit from their support in whole class mode is to scan the room regularly. Often, scanning the room after the allotted 5/10 minutes with one child is the best way to identify the child that is off task/in greatest need of support; it is not always the child that is most vocal.
- *Use time wisely:* The relationship between a teacher and support staff in whole class mode is key to engendering effective teaching and learning experiences for children. While the teacher is engaging in whole class teaching, it is important that support staff engage in meaningful

activity, for example creating/giving out resources, working on a wall display, etc. However, in order to ensure that support staff hear the key learning needed for potential group work, it is often important that they stay within the classroom for this segment of the lesson.
- *Mirror the teacher's language:* To maximise children's understanding of a concept or task, it is important that support staff use the same language and terminology as the teacher at all times. It can be useful for support staff to note down key words and phrases used by the teacher during whole class teaching, so that children are not exposed to differing explanations and terms when it comes to group work.

Mode 2: Small group

This mode is characterised by support staff undertaking the following:

- Often implementing intervention programmes with small groups of children. This may be aligned to individuals' specialisms, e.g. pastoral interventions, booster groups for SATs/GCSEs or working with students identified with a specific SEND
- Supporting specific groups of children in a space outside of the main teaching classrooms in the school, e.g. the library or an intervention-focused room. However, staff in this mode may also spend some time working with small groups inside the main teaching classrooms
- Carrying out assessment of children in the small groups; this is often related to an intervention programme implemented by staff members in this mode
- Supporting children from across the school in different year groups
- Creating resources to use within the small groups of children they work with.

Effective support strategies in small group mode:

Support staff and those they work with should take account of the following:

- *Ensure familiarity with the content of an intervention programme before teaching it:* It will likely significantly increase the confidence of support staff if they can familiarise themselves with materials before implementation, which will, in turn, likely improve the efficacy of the intervention overall.
- *Promote opportunities for students to partake in discussion:* It can be difficult to encourage and facilitate opportunities for all children to contribute during small group work. An effective approach to this can be to question quieter students more frequently and subtly, ensuring you don't make them feel uncomfortable, to balance out the discussion regarding more dominant children.
- *Discuss assessment arrangements with teachers:* If support staff are asked to assess children in small groups, it is important that they are aware of the assessment arrangements before the lesson. Sharing these assessments with class teachers is often particularly effective, as it ensures all teaching staff are better able to understand individuals' learning needs.
- *Regularly review children's abilities:* Children in small groupings will progress at different rates. Support staff working with small groups should regularly informally/formally review individuals' progress regularly, throughout the course of an intervention.
- *Be aware of friendships:* Small groups containing particular friends can provide opportunities for learning but can also be problematic. Often, children that work with their friends can become distracted or may dominate the group.

- *Build upon learning outside of the group:* This suggestion is linked to recommendation 7 of the EEF's 7 best principles of effective practice, as explored earlier in this chapter. Effective support staff will often acknowledge and praise children that display an understanding of a taught concept outside of the small group context. For example, children may spell a word correctly in an English lesson, which has been taught to them during an intervention group, or they may demonstrate effective friendship skills in the playground, which they have learned during a social skills intervention.

Mode 3: One to one

This mode is characterised by support staff undertaking the following:

- Spending most of their time working with one child in the school
- The child the staff member works with will likely have been identified with a SEND that requires significant support most/all the time that he/she is in school. He/she is likely to have an education, health and care plan
- Attending review meetings regarding the support that the child receives in school
- Supporting learning in a space outside of the main classroom, or they may spend all their time in the main classroom
- Specific intervention programmes may be implemented with the child by the member of support staff
- May be asked to create/adapt resources to support the child(ren) they work with.

Effective support strategies in one-to-one mode:

Support staff and those they work with should take account of the following:

- *Engage in open and regular discussion with the class teacher:* Riviere (2016) indicated that some staff members find it difficult to facilitate an effective balance in responsibility for the child being supported on a one-to-one basis. An effective approach to ensuring appropriate levels of responsibility is for both the class teacher and the support staff member to engage in frequent and open discussion regarding the child's needs. This helps to engender a supportive and inclusive culture among staff and the children they support.
- *Support children to find the answer, don't give it:* All staff should encourage the children they're working with to look for or ask questions to find the answer independently. Failing to do this is often a significant contributor to over-reliance on adult support, particularly when working in one-to-one mode. Staff must become comfortable with children failing to achieve correct answers; getting things wrong is often the only way that staff can gain a true reflection of children's abilities.
- *Include the child receiving one-to-one support in the rest of the class:* It can be difficult for the child receiving one-to-one support to feel included within the rest of the class. Often, working in pairs or small groups can result in the child consistently solely working with the member of support staff assigned to them. Encouraging collaboration can often help with both social inclusion and academic achievement.
- *Know when to adapt materials:* Support staff working in one-to-one mode often better understand the abilities and learning preferences of individuals than teachers. Therefore, it is often appropriate for support staff to adapt materials; effective teachers should recognise the importance of this.

The role of the SENCO is often pivotal in assigning individual support staff to work across specific modes. Recognising the strengths and weaknesses of individuals will ensure that children are optimally supported and that support staff are utilising their skills, as well as given the opportunity to build skills in different modes. The template below (Table 13.1) is intended for use by SENCOs, in exploring individuals' skills and abilities to work across each of the three modes associated with the support staff role. It can be used during a review meeting to highlight areas of success and areas for improvement.

> **Case study**
>
> Jill is a TA working in a larger than average primary school that is inclusive in its admissions. She has worked in the school for 24 years and has always, in that time, worked in 'whole classroom' mode. Jill has been asked to work with Richard, a child that is new to the school, in 'one-to-one' mode for 3 mornings a week. Richard has severe learning difficulties, which means that he has challenges accessing content taught in the mainstream Year 3 classroom. He has an education, health and care plan that details all of Richard's needs, support strategies and expected outcomes. Jill has expressed to you, as her manager, that she doesn't want to move from working in 'whole classroom' mode to 'one-to-one' mode, as she feels that her skills are better used working in a familiar mode for her. You are keen that Jill builds skills in other areas and know that the school budget will rely on the TAs being adaptable in terms of their modes of working.
>
> **Questions for you to consider:**
>
> - What are the barriers to Jill wanting to work in a different mode?
> - Who should you discuss Jill's reluctance to her changing role with?
> - Should you involve the Senior Leadership Team in discussions around Jill's role?
> - How can you best support Jill to adapt to her change in role?
> - How will you proceed in ensuring that Richard's needs are met?

TABLE 13.1 Template: Assessing competency across modes of working*

Whole Classroom Mode		
Support Strategy	Prompts	Successes/Action points (Record your thoughts/discussion points in this column)
Working with children that have a range of needs	• Is the staff member able to consistently work with children that have a range of abilities? • Do they show the ability to provide adequate challenge for some children, as well as support those that require help to complete tasks?	E.g. Susan works across whole classroom and small group mode. She can differentiate materials to ensure that Josh is challenged in her Maths Mastery group, as well as provide adequate challenge for those of lower ability in the group.
Keeping a time limit for each child	• Is the staff member able to spend appropriate amounts of time with each child? • Can they move on to another child successfully after 5/10 minutes? • Does that child remain on task after having been supported?	

(Continued)

TABLE 13.1 (Continued)

	Whole Classroom Mode	
Support Strategy	**Prompts**	**Successes/Action points** (Record your thoughts/discussion points in this column)
Overseeing	• Can the staff member make accurate judgements regarding the engagement of a whole classroom of children? • Is the staff member able to make appropriate independent decisions about which child to support during a session?	E.g. Mohammad was observed moving on from supporting Jack after 5 minutes of input, leaving him with an achievable task to complete independently before returning.
Using time wisely	• Does the staff member consistently demonstrate effective use of their time in the classroom? • Are they always engaged in meaningful activity?	
Consistent use of language with children	• Does the staff member mirror consistent use in language/terminology with the children? • Can they provide accurate explanations of concepts when asked to by children?	E.g. Sarah clearly referred to the 'key word' board in the classroom to explain the meaning of apostrophes to the group she was supporting in the main classroom. This shows consistency in language between adults.

	Small Group Mode	
Support Strategy	**Prompts**	**Successes/Action points** (Record your thoughts/discussion points in this column)
Familiarity in programme content/ resource used	• Is the staff member adequately familiar with the materials used during the small group work? • Have they taken the time to explore/amend the materials as necessary before the group commenced?	
Allowing all children to partake in the session	• Is the staff member able to encourage quieter children to partake in the session? • Can they achieve an effective balance in the discussion?	E.g. Tia targeted all children with questioning, encouraging quieter members of the group to speak.
Assessment arrangements	• Can the staff member articulate the assessment requirements associated with the small group work? • Can they accurately complete assessments of the children and use these to inform future sessions?	
Regular review of abilities	• Is the staff member able to undertake effective informal review of individuals' abilities after each session? • Does this review result in effective differentiation of content?	E.g. John keeps a notebook in which he records key information about the successes and areas for improvement for every member of the group after each weekly session.
Effective grouping of children	• Can the staff member effectively group the children to ensure smooth running of the intervention? • Do they make good use of partnering/wider group organisation to facilitate learning?	

Small Group Mode		
Support Strategy	**Prompts**	**Successes/Action points** (Record your thoughts/discussion points in this column)
Building upon learning outside of the group	• Can the staff member refer to the concepts explored in different contexts? • Do they make good use of praise and reward to consolidate the learning outside of the small group?	E.g. Simon was observed praising one child in his group when they used addition effectively to count the number of mini-beasts they saw on the vegetable patch.

One-to-One Mode		
Support Strategy	**Prompts**	**Successes/Action points** (Record your thoughts/discussion points in this column)
Communication with class teacher/other staff members	• Is the staff member engaging in frequent and open discussion regarding the needs and abilities of the child they regularly work with? • Does this communication help to inform better teaching and learning approaches for that child? • Are the thoughts of the staff member listened to by other staff members?	E.g. Fiona and her class teacher have developed a system in which they use a shared notebook to record developments that occur during the day, regarding the child that Fiona supports. This helps to maintain a consistent dialogue between staff.
Supporting independent working	• Is the staff member mindful of the dangers of over-reliance? • Can they promote independent working during sessions? • Are they aware of how to avoid an unhealthy reliance between themselves and the child they support?	
Encouraging collaboration between the child and his/her peers	• Does the staff member encourage the child they work with regularly to build relationships with his/her peers?	E.g. Amin always ensures that another child works with Kate when she is asked to engage in paired working, rather than himself supporting collaborative working.
Knowing when to adapt materials	• Can the staff member successfully adapt materials so that they are appropriate to the abilities of the child they work with? • Do they share these resources with others and notify the class teacher when materials are adapted?	

*see Appendix and online resources for assessment template

Good practice approaches to leading an intervention group

As previously explored in this chapter, support staff often spend a significant proportion of their time in school implementing intervention programmes in small group or one-to-one mode. These programmes often include children of a range of abilities and in a range of curriculum areas. The advice in this section is useful for SENCOs in ensuring that the interventions implemented for children identified with SEND are effective, and in identifying appropriate support staff members to lead the implementation of interventions.

Personal and Professional Conduct

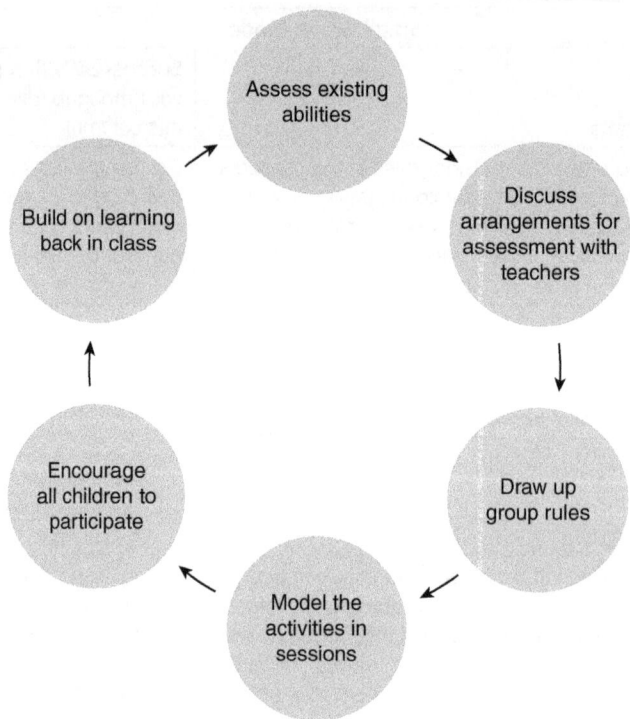

FIGURE 13.2 The effective intervention cycle

The following good practice approaches have emerged from the author's doctoral study and professional experience, also informed by relevant literature (Saddler, 2015). SENCOs should use these approaches to identify support staff members with the appropriate skills, knowledge and experience to run intervention groups, as well as identify appropriate training opportunities for support staff to gain these skills.

- *Conduct a basic analysis of children' existing abilities before commencing the intervention*: All staff implementing an intervention programme should endeavour to gain a basic understanding of children' existing knowledge and skills in the curriculum area explored in the intervention. This may involve simple observation of children during lesson time, reviewing children's prior work, or conducting a more robust baseline assessment.
- *Discuss assessment arrangements before the intervention begins*: SENCOs/class teachers should clearly communicate any assessment/monitoring expectations to support staff implementing interventions before the intervention begins. Capturing consistent indications of children's abilities not only ensures that the content is pitched correctly throughout the course of the intervention, but also allows staff to evidence that their approaches are supporting learning.
- *Draw up group rules:* An effective intervention in small group mode will be led by a staff member that is able to effectively communicate the basic rules associated with behaviour and participation within that group, during the first session. It is often very appropriate to involve children in the creation of these rules, as they support staff to gain 'buy in' from the children, which can better inform behaviour management approaches.
- *Model the activities required of children:* An effective implementer of intervention programmes consistently models all activities that children are requested to undertake. This ensures that

children better understand what they are being asked to undertake and can help to reduce children's anxiety towards sharing with the group/completing an activity.
- *Encourage all children to participate:* Children are likely to gain more from the intervention if they actively participate in the activities associated with it. Effective support staff will encourage participation through the use of praise and reward, being mindful not to expect unachievable levels of participation from individuals.
- *Build on learning on return to class:* If the intervention takes place outside of the main classroom setting, effective support staff will ensure that the learning taking place is built upon in other contexts, wherever appropriate. This links to a previous point regarding the efficacy of promoting children's transference of knowledge in different contexts to build sound understandings of concepts.

TABLE 13.2 Template: Assessing the efficacy of an intervention*

Cycle Stage	Observation Prompt	Areas of success/Action points
Assessing existing abilities	• Is the staff member showing signs that they understand individuals' abilities? • Can they differentiate the questioning used/task assigned to individuals? • Did they undertake any formal/informal assessment of individuals' abilities before the intervention began?	E.g. Kate made notes about how well individuals could add two-digit numbers before group began; Simon could have made better use of differentiated questioning during session.
Assessment during/at the end of the intervention	• Is the staff member aware of all assessment requirements during/at the end of the intervention? • Are they able to demonstrate effective use of the assessment tools?	E.g. Muhammad completed assessment form effectively, once the session had ended; Sarah appears unaware of the assessment requirements for this group.
Group rules	• Are there any group rules in place? • Were children involved in creating them? • How often are they referred to by staff member?	E.g. Action point for Sara to draw up group rules for this session, involving children; John clearly referred back to group rules during an instance of problematic behaviour as a way to reinforce behaviour expectations.
Modelling of activities	• Does the staff member model all activities children are expected to undertake? • How clear is the modelling process?	E.g. Tariq clearly modelled all activities in an accessible way, and children were aware of the expectations associated with the activity; Leah did not model the use of adverbs in a sentence in a clear and accessible way.
Participation of children	• Did all children participate in the session? • Does the staff member take appropriate measures to encourage quieter children to participate/reduce the input of more confident children?	E.g. Julia used targeted questioning to encourage less confident children to vocalise their thought processes; Kyle could have worked harder to reduce the input of some more confident and vocal students, as they overwhelmed the discussion at times.
Building upon learning in different contexts	• Did the staff member refer to concepts in different contexts to reinforce learning? • Have you seen them building upon learning in the group back in the main classroom?	E.g. Fiona was observed praising a child for using the good touch rule on the playground, making reference to the learning they completed in the group setting; Gavin could have extended learning in the main classroom by making reference to the spellings learned in the intervention during writing activity.

*see Appendix and online resources for assessment template

Personal and Professional Conduct

Presented above (Figure 13.2) is an 'effective intervention cycle', which serves as a visual tool for capturing the process of implementing an intervention programme effectively, summarising the bullet points explored above.

The above template (Table 13.2) is intended to be used by SENCOs/relevant staff members in exploring the effectiveness of current interventions. It will serve as a useful note-taking prompt during observations of intervention sessions.

> **Chapter summary**
> - The role of support staff is under increasing pressure and scrutiny from schools, children, Local Authorities and government. Yet, practitioners still regard the role of support staff as vital to providing effective teaching and learning experiences for some of our most vulnerable children (Fox, 2016)
> - There are three main modes that support staff work (across whole classroom, small group and one to one), as well as suggested supportive strategies within these three modes
> - Two practical templates have been presented and are intended for use by SENCOs in assessing the efficacy of the practices associated with the management and deployment of support staff in their settings

14

Coaching and Mentoring

Steve Watts

→ NASENCO outcome: Leading and Coordinating Provision. Part B: (Section 6) To model effective practice, coach and mentor colleagues.
→ Read alongside: Chapter 3: Leading in the SENCO Role

Chapter overview

The purpose of this chapter is to explore the origins of mentoring and coaching and their purposes, including the ways in which they are similar, as well as different. Guidance on how to set up a mentoring and coaching culture is provided, as well as the models and processes that can be adopted to mentor and coach colleagues and children.

Personal and Professional Conduct

Investing in staff development

Arguably the greatest resource a school has is its staff. As such, they need to be invested in if they are to develop over a long career. One of the ways in which schools can help this happen is through adopting a CPD vision that draws upon the tools, techniques and strategies of coaching and mentoring. These approaches are perceived to be expensive, however, because they draw upon staff time and quite often institutions shy away from them because they don't think the investment brings sufficient rewards. Equally, colleagues resist engaging in these approaches because they feel they are being imposed upon them and are being introduced for punitive reasons to measure and improve performance.

> **Case study**
>
> A mentor from a local college came to see me to discuss a dilemma they had been presented with. They had been tasked with mentoring an older and more experienced colleague who had been given an Ofsted grade 4 (unsatisfactory) for their teaching. The mentor, who had been graded 1 (outstanding) during the same inspection, was given three mentoring sessions to ensure that the mentee 'improved' sufficiently to be judged at least satisfactory (grade 3). What factors do you think contributed to the mentor's lack of success after the three mentoring sessions to improve the mentee's grade? How could this have been managed differently? Was mentoring the most appropriate approach to adopt?

When coaching and mentoring approaches are adopted by schools in an appropriate way through consultation and sharing of goals, aims and purposes, they can be extremely powerful tools to help develop ourselves, our colleagues and our children. They can also be, as the case study above illustrates, misunderstood and deployed inappropriately with unsatisfactory consequences for all concerned. Coaching and mentoring are different concepts and can be deployed for a variety of purposes, according to the context. What binds them together is the fact that they are both concerned with human development and share the need for good questions to be posed in order to be fully effective.

What is mentoring?

The word 'mentor' comes from the name of a character in Homer's *Illiad*, a story that is nearly 3000 years old. When Odysseus, King of Ithaca, left to fight in the Trojan War, he asked a trusted and experienced friend to look after his young son and heir, Telemachus, and prepare him for kingship. That trusted friend's name was Mentor. Thus, a relationship that involves a more experienced and skilled practitioner guiding and supporting a less experienced and skilled prodigy is often called a mentoring relationship. These can emerge organically and informally or be assigned through formal structures.

Mentors usually work with mentees over a sustained period of time with the mentee learning their skill or profession from their senior colleague. This is how apprenticeships are organised and how trainee teachers are prepared for the profession. It is the approach adopted for NQTs to support their transition into employment and, once this induction phase has been completed, it usually stops. It need not stop at this early stage in a teacher's career, however, but could continue as the newly qualified teacher progresses through the profession from NQT+1 onwards.

Working with a mentor can help an early career teacher prepare for a range of responsibilities, including a future role as SENCO. Equally, a newly appointed SENCO might benefit from a mentoring relationship as they transition into the role. The story of Mentor looking after the young Telemachus in Greek mythology helps serve as a powerful metaphor for the mentoring relationship in the twenty-first century. If more mentors were involved in supporting early career teachers then perhaps the drop-out rate from the profession would be lower. For example, the *Guardian* reported on 13 May 2018 that 9% of the workforce (40,000 teachers) left the profession in the UK in 2016.

REFLECTIVE ACTIVITY

Are you currently working with a mentor or have you been mentored in the past? Would you describe the experience as being positive? If so, what are the qualities that the mentor brought to their role? If not, then what could the mentor have done differently?

There are many definitions of mentoring. Megginson et al. (2006: 4–5) argue that 'mentoring is off-line help by one person to another in making significant transitions in knowledge, work or thinking'. Nemanick (2017: 2) suggests that mentoring 'in its simplest form is a relationship whereby an experienced senior is on a journey with a junior, helping the junior learn along the way'. Elsewhere Pask and Joy (2007) believe that a mentor is simply someone who helps another person think things through.

Definition of mentoring: Mentoring is a developmental process, which may in some forms involve a transfer of skill or knowledge from a more experienced person to a less experienced, through learning dialogue and role modelling; or in other forms may be a partnership for mutual learning between peers or across differences such as age, race or discipline. (EMCC, cited by Gray et al., 2016: 302)

Modern mentoring

The traditional process of mentoring, as identified above, is currently going through a transition as the expectations of the new workforce entering the profession require a much more flexible approach. This new workforce is sometimes referred to as Generation Y or Millennials (because they were born at the turn of the twenty-first century) and their way of working is challenging the traditional 9–5 workplace and the one-to-one senior to junior mentoring relationship that has dominated the work scene for at least half a century.

The key characteristics of Generation Y include an emphasis on collaboration, integrated use of technology, social responsibility, the desire for good leadership, professional development and coaching/mentoring. Millennials are less likely to see the traditional obstacles to mentoring and coaching, such as lack of time or appropriate location, as barriers to the process. They like to work flexibly and use new technology as a means to facilitate communication. Colleagues mentoring Millennials may need to adjust to these new circumstances. Some of the collaborative approaches outlined below would be better suited to Millennials' preferences rather than the traditional one-to-one approach. Millennials will also more readily learn from each other and be less bound by hierarchy, which could present difficulties in schools and colleges which are likely to be very hierarchical.

Julie Silard Kantor, president and CEO of Twomentor LLC, commented in the Huffpost (2.3.17) that 75% of Millennials (Generation Y) view being mentored as crucial to their professional success and most women leave their jobs because they do not have a sponsor (advocate/mentor). This reminds us that colleagues entering the profession now expect to be supported and developed through the involvement of a mentor and that such a mentoring relationship will be flexible and draw upon new technologies to facilitate it.

REFLECTIVE ACTIVITY

Have you experienced alternative approaches to mentoring beyond the traditional one-to-one meeting? For example, have you been involved in group mentoring, or have you used technology to facilitate mentoring, such as by being part of a closed group on social media? How would you feel being mentored this way or leading your mentoring using these approaches?

What is coaching?

Mentoring has existed for as long as we have needed to help people develop their skills and understanding. Coaching has also existed for a long time, but has only been formalised more recently. The word coach originates from the Hungarian town of Kocs where horse-drawn coaches were first built. The purpose of a wheeled coach is to move an individual from A to B and it is this process that the term *to coach* comes from. The process of coaching is goal driven to help people move from where they are now to where they want to be. Coaching relationships are usually shorter and more focused than mentoring relationships. The role of the coach is to help the coachee think through the potential approaches and solutions to the issues being discussed. This is usually done through the coach asking searching questions that help the coachee reframe the lens through which they view things and support a breakthrough in thinking that unblocks potential barriers to progress.

REFLECTIVE ACTIVITY

Have you ever been coached? What were the circumstances around which the coaching was set up? Did you ask to be coached in order to help you move forward, or was a coach assigned to you for a specific purpose? How did you feel about the coaching? Was it successful?

In the nineteenth century, coaching was viewed in a derogatory way because it was a process adopted by Oxbridge undergraduates who were 'coached' through their exams. In more recent times, while it still remains controversial, it has become much more accepted as a process to help people develop. Key to this was the publication in 1974 of Timothy Gallwey's book *The Inner Game of Tennis*. This seminal text shifted the emphasis in coaching away from skill development to supporting players in the management of the internal mental states that might be affecting their performance. Coaching was initially focused on sport, but following the principles of Gallwey's ideas it became increasingly adopted by the business community and then gradually by education. The origins in sport and business, and with an emphasis on performance improvement, mean that coaching is still perceived as a process based narrowly on performance rather than professional development. Even so, coaching is estimated to be a US$2 billion industry worldwide (Whittaker Dunlop, 2017).

Coaching has many definitions. Downey (2014: 39) suggests that 'coaching is the art of facilitating the performance, learning and development of another'. Van Nieuwerburgh (2014) believes that coaching is about empowerment, especially in relation to learning, growth and personal and professional development. Jones and Gorell (2018: 13) suggest that it is 'a conversation where the coach acts as a facilitator to the coachee, so that they learn, gain insight and take action toward a specific and agreed outcome'.

> **Definition of coaching:** 'Coaching is a collaborative, solution-focused, result-orientated and systematic process in which the coach facilitates the enhancement of work performance, life experience, self-directed learning and personal growth of individuals' (Greene and Grant, 2003: xiii).

What are the similarities and differences between mentoring and coaching?

There are many common elements to mentoring and coaching processes, but they do offer essentially different approaches to human development. Mentoring and coaching both require very good listening skills, with the emphasis on letting the mentee/coachee speak. They also both require time and space to be successful, but most importantly they depend upon the quality of the questions that the coach/mentor asks. The questions should be open-ended and support the coachee/mentee in thinking through solutions to the issues under discussion.

Equally, there are significant differences. Coaching tends to be a short-term, focused and non-directional approach to achieving a goal. Traditionally, mentoring usually takes place over a longer period of time and might include an element of the mentor showing and demonstrating skills that need to be mastered, as well as being an advocate for the mentee. Both of these traditional processes have, however, moved forward considerably in recent times, with the new dimensions being discussed below.

What is government policy on mentoring and coaching?

Mentoring of trainee teachers has been a process in operation since the nineteenth century, with the introduction of the 'pupil teacher' system. This was an approach that adopted the principles of the well-established apprenticeship movement and only over time has it transitioned to a process based on mentorship. There are statutory standards that trainee teachers must achieve in order to qualify, but there are no such benchmarks for the training of mentors, the assumption being that teachers are naturally able mentors given the nature of their role. With a few exceptions, mentors have not received any systematic training and have been provided with little time to carry out the role. There is no nationally recognised award for mentoring.

Significant steps have been taken recently, however, to improve the status of mentoring and coaching in schools and colleges, as well as the role of teachers' CPD. The process started in 2015 with the publication of The Carter Review, which set out recommendations to formalise mentor training. This was followed up the following year with the publication in January 2016 of the White Paper *Educational Excellence Everywhere* (DfE, 2016c), which advocated better investment in teachers' CPD. Later that year in July the Standards for Mentoring were published, outlining four standards that trainee teacher mentors should meet (see Figure 14.1 below):

Personal and Professional Conduct

Standard 1 – Personal qualities

Establish trusting relationships, modelling high standards of practice, and understand how to support a trainee through initial teacher training

The mentor should:

- be approachable, make time for the trainee, and prioritise meetings and discussions with them;
- use a range of effective interpersonal skills to respond to the needs of the trainee;
- offer support with integrity, honesty and respect;
- use appropriate challenge to encourage the trainee to reflect on their practice; and
- support the improvement of a trainee's teaching by modelling exemplary practice in planning, teaching and assessment.

Standard 2 – Teaching

Support trainees to develop their teaching practice in order to set high expectations of all pupils and to meet their needs.

The mentor should:

- support the trainee in forming good relationships with pupils, and in developing effective behaviour and classroom management strategies;
- support the trainee in developing effective approaches to planning, teaching and assessment;
- support the trainee with marking and assessment of pupil work through moderation or double marking;
- give constructive, clear and timely feedback on lesson observations;
- broker opportunities to observe best practice;
- support the trainee in accessing expert subject and pedagogical knowledge;
- resolve in-school issues on the trainee's behalf where they lack the confidence or experience to do so themselves;
- enable and encourage the trainee to evaluate and improve their teaching; and
- enable the trainee to access, utilise and interpret robust educational research to inform their teaching.

Standard 3 – Professionalism

Set high expectations and induct the trainee to understand their role and responsibilities as a teacher

The mentor should:

- encourage the trainee to participate in the life of the school and understand its role within the wider community;
- support the trainee in developing the highest standards of professional and personal conduct;
- support the trainee in promoting equality and diversity;
- ensure the trainee understands and complies with relevant legislation, including that related to the safeguarding of children; and
- support the trainee to develop skills to manage time effectively.

Standard 4 – Self-development and working in partnership

Continue to develop their own professional knowledge, skills and understanding and invest time in developing a good working relationship within relevant ITT partnerships

The mentor should:

- ensure consistency by working with other mentors and partners to moderate judgements; and
- continue to develop their own mentoring practice and subject and pedagogical expertise by accessing appropriate professional development and engaging with robust research.

FIGURE 14.1 The National Standards for School-Based ITT Mentors

Source: Teaching Schools Council (2016)

REFLECTIVE ACTIVITY

Have you been trained as a mentor? If so, how helpful was the training? Do you feel more confident about mentoring others? Do you feel you have the skills to carry out the role? If you haven't been trained, is there an opportunity for you to complete the training? Looking at the four standards outlined above, to what extent do you feel you demonstrate them in your work?

Implications of recent government policy

The recommendations of the Carter Review (2015) and the subsequent publication a year later of the National Standards for School-Based ITT Mentors (Teaching Schools Council, 2016) should be broadly welcomed. This is not the first time, however, that the government has attempted to bring the issue of ITT trainee mentoring to the forefront of the debate about the best way to train, induct and support teachers into the profession. In 2005, CUREE (Centre for the Use of Research Evidence in Education) established the National Framework for Mentoring and Coaching. The Framework never gained traction, however, because while it was research-based it did not carry the status of a Statutory Order. The National Framework contained ten principles, which still serve as an effective guide to establishing a school framework (Table 14.1).

TABLE 14.1 Principles of mentoring and coaching (CUREE, 2005)

	Principle	Explanation
1	A learning conversation	Structured professional dialogue, rooted in evidence, from the professional learner's practice, which articulates existing beliefs and practices to enable reflection on them.
2	A thoughtful relationship	Developing trust, attending respectfully and with sensitivity to the powerful emotions involved in deep professional learning.
3	A learning agreement	Establishing confidence about the boundaries of the relationship by agreeing and upholding ground rules that address imbalances in power and accountability.
4	Combining support from fellow professional learners and specialists	Collaborating with colleagues to sustain commitment to learn and relate new approaches to everyday practice; seeking out specialist expertise to extend skills and knowledge and to model good practice.
5	Growing self-direction	An evolving process in which the learner takes increasing responsibility for their professional development skills, knowledge and self-awareness.
6	Setting challenging and personal goals	Identifying goals that build on what learners know and can do already, but can not yet achieve alone, whilst attending to both school and individual priorities.
7	Understanding why different approaches work	Developing an understanding of the theory that underpins new practice so it can be interpreted and adapted for different contexts.
8	Acknowledging the benefits to the mentors and coaches	Recognising and making use of professional learning that mentors and coaches gain from the opportunity to mentor or coach.
9	Experimenting and observing	Creating a learning environment that supports risk taking and innovation and encourages professional learners to seek out direct evidence from practice.
10	Using resources effectively	Making and using time and other resources creatively to protect and sustain learning, action and reflection on a day-to-day basis.

It is interesting to note that the 2005 CUREE Principles of Mentoring and Coaching and the 2016 Mentor Standards both identify the importance of the benefits of mentoring and coaching for both coaches and mentors (e.g. Mentoring Standard 4 and Principle 8).

Thus, it could be argued that with the publication of the Mentor Standards we now have a basis upon which to engage in a national debate. The Standards were created by a fairly small working party quite quickly and, while consultation did take place with a variety of stakeholders, the research base appears sparse. The Standards to be met are non-statutory, though will most likely contribute to Ofsted Inspections of ITT provision, which makes them potentially statutory in all but name.

REFLECTIVE ACTIVITY

Have you ever acted as a coach or mentor to a colleague? If so, what benefits do you think you gained from carrying out the role? Were you surprised? Did you think it was a one-way process from you to the coachee/mentee? Why did you think this? If you are about to undertake the role for the first time, what benefits to you as mentor/coach do you anticipate receiving?

Mentoring of ITT trainees is only one part of the mentoring process that takes place in schools and colleges, but mentoring beyond the training phase is less likely to occur. It could be argued, however, given the high drop-out rate of teachers (Trapper, 2018) that mentoring is even more important during the early career development of teachers beyond the NQT year. Thus, the fourth recommendation of the National Standards for School-Based ITT Mentors (Teaching Schools Council, 2016: 9) is cautiously welcomed, though it remains to be seen what is meant by a 'more challenging teacher accreditation'. Here, the Report states:

> In light of the proposals set out about teacher accreditation in the White Paper, Educational Excellence Everywhere, the role of the mentor should extend beyond the initial training period to teacher accreditation and early career. Mentoring support is crucial in a system where we will move to a stronger and more challenging teacher accreditation.

What are the benefits of mentoring and coaching?

Mentoring and coaching can be defined as 'empowering' processes. Their purpose is to enable staff to become better teachers and leaders through supporting them to take greater ownership of, and responsibility for, their own professional development. A mentor, usually a more experienced colleague, would work with a mentee over an extended period to address a particular training need. A good example of this is the mentoring relationship that exists between a trainee teacher and their mentor. The brief of the mentor is wide-ranging, with ultimate responsibility to ensure the trainee transitions successfully to NQT. A similar relationship will exist between an NQT in their induction year and a mentor, as could a newly appointed SENCO, who is mentored by a colleague who has much greater leadership experience. In this latter example, the mentor might be a SENCO who has held the role for some time, but equally it might be a member of the school's middle or senior management teams with no experience of SEND.

This process involves considerable investment in time over a sustained period, both for the mentee and the mentor. This sometimes results in a decision not to proceed because the time to carry out the mentoring is not easily found in a busy school day. On occasion, there is scepticism about the benefits of mentoring and fear of a poor return on investment. If colleagues take a few minutes to think about the process and approach it with an open mind, they will find that the benefits are considerable and well worth the investment. This is because the mentor's accumulated experience and skill set essentially provides a 'sounding' board for the mentee as they grapple with unfamiliar issues during their transition. This is sometimes called 'capacity building' because the increased breadth and depth of experience gained as the mentee transitions into their new role serves to enhance the individual's, as well as the wider school's, capacity to move forward.

While many mentoring and coaching relationships are consensual, there are occasions when they are mandated. Such compulsory mentoring and coaching situations may not be fully effective because there might not be any commitment from the mentee/coachee and sometimes not even from the mentor/coach. There is evidence that mentors and coaches are allocated only to 'failing' teachers as a way of helping them improve (see case study on p. 258). Such an approach leads to wariness from colleagues about the purpose and value of mentoring and coaching. If the institution possessed a 'mentoring/coaching culture' (see below) where all colleagues' development was valued and mentoring and coaching were part of the day-to-day running of the institution, then being allocated a mentor or coach would be seen as something that all colleagues had access to.

Research suggests that in mentoring and coaching relationships it is not just the mentee/coachee who benefits, but that the mentor also gains insights into their own development and how the process can benefit the institution. This is something that the government recognises and has tried to address through the Mentoring Standards. For example, Standard 4 states that mentors should 'continue to develop their own mentoring practice and subject and pedagogical expertise by accessing appropriate professional development and engaging with robust research'. The implications of this Standard are huge because it reminds us that in a mentoring relationship it is not just the mentee who progresses in their development, but the mentor as well through their engagement with the wider issues.

Bush and Middlewood (2013) draw upon research by Luck (2003: 197), which shows that the mentoring process has a positive impact on both mentors and mentees. They also cite work by Hobson (2003: 2) who confirmed that all the major studies of formal mentoring programmes for new headteachers were effective. The main benefits for headteachers identified include:

1. peer support
2. gain confidence
3. reduction in isolation of the role
4. developing expertise in areas such as staff management and conflict resolution.

Bush and Middlewood (2013: 198) draw upon research by Bush (1996: 127) to confirm that the benefits for NQTs who have been supported by a mentor include:

5. listen and act as a sounding board
6. offer guidance and reassurance
7. are non-judgemental
8. can admit that they are also fallible.

The evidence for the benefits of mentoring for mentees is clear, but the benefits extend beyond the mentee to the mentor as well. Bush again refers to his research (1996: 128) to confirm that mentors of NQTs in his study also acknowledged the benefits; these included seeing the process as a learning partnership, a two-way interaction for mutual support and the benefit of both of us.

Bush and Middlewood (2013) refer to work by Barnett and O'Mahony (2008: 241) whose overview of mentoring and coaching demonstrated several benefits for mentors and coaches, including networking, professional development, increased self-esteem and the facilitation of communities of learning.

Mentoring and coaching programmes are introduced to support mentees and coachees and the evidence is clear that such programmes work. What is less understood or even expected is that the mentor or coach also benefits from being involved in the process because they have to think things through in the light of their own practice and experience. This might lead to the mentor or coach benefitting even more than the coachee or mentee. Thus, introducing such a programme might have a double benefit for what is probably seen as a single investment.

> **Case study**
>
> In a recent coaching session with me, the coachee presented a series of dilemmas that they were wrestling with. Negotiating with the coachee through the process of analysing these, it became clear that a coach, through their skilful questioning, patience and reframing of problems, is essentially a 'quandary buster', helping the coachee find a way through the morass of issues being grappled with.

Creating a coaching and mentoring culture

DEFINITION OF A COACHING CULTURE

'A coaching culture is one where people are empowered and where coaching happens at every level. And not only does it happen at every level, but it adds to bottom line performance. It is the recognised development tool that touches every part of the employee life cycle.' (Jones and Gorell, 2018: 16)

Ideally, schools and colleges will have a well-established mentoring and coaching culture that is embedded in the day-to-day operation of the institution. Where this is in place, developing a mentoring and coaching approach to work as a SENCO will be potentially more straightforward than if you are working in an institution where there is no such culture. Even so, such a situation does not prevent you as SENCO from introducing a mentoring and coaching culture among your SEND colleagues. One way to achieve this is through Jones and Gorrell's (2018: 158–66) four-phase strategy (see Table 14.2).

TABLE 14.2 Strategy for introducing a coaching and mentoring culture*

Phase	Purpose	Reflection
1 – Investigation	To investigate what is currently being done, when and by whom. What works and what does not. Check that culture will fit in with the wider organisation's strategic direction	
2 – Business Case	Link proposal to wider strategy, scope costs and investment, obtain buy-in from key stakeholders	
3 – Implementation	Implement proposals and monitor success/barriers	
4 – Review	Evaluate benefits for organisation and identify next steps	

*see Appendix and online resources for assessment template

TABLE 14.3 Ten-step approach to introducing a coaching and mentoring culture*

Phase	Stage	Explanation	Reflection
Empathise	1 – Understand organisation	Assess current reality	
Empathise	2 – Link to organisation's objectives/strategy	Validate need for change	
Define	3 – Identify vision and purpose	Define a destination goal for culture	
Define	4 – Gain stakeholder support	Focus on win-win	
Create	5 – Identify where to engage first	Identify low-risk area to trial	
Create	6 – Create measurements	Clarify what success means	
Experiment	7 – Introduce pilot	Identify learning and insights	
Experiment	8 – Evaluate results	Decide on how you will act on learning and insights	
Learn	9 – Introduce the next phase	Celebrate small wins	
Learn	10 – Maintain momentum	Implement actions from insights and improve	

*see Appendix and online resources for assessment template

As SENCO, you could 'mandate' such a culture, but without colleague buy-in the mentoring and coaching might have limited success. A more appropriate and successful approach would be to share your vision of a mentoring and coaching learning environment with your SEND colleagues at a staff meeting and open the vision to discussion (Phase 2 in Table 14.2 above). Colleagues may very well be wary of such an initiative, so sharing the vision as a developmental approach will be necessary in order to address staff reservations about the purpose of the initiative. If it is not possible to gain buy-in from all staff, then start with those colleagues who are willing to embrace the idea. It might be necessary to provide additional resources in order to support the introduction of mentoring and coaching. This would ordinarily involve finding time for colleagues to engage in the process, as well as an appropriate location for the colleagues to meet uninterrupted. Some colleagues may wish to register on mentoring and coaching training and accreditation courses and this may involve a request for both time and funding.

Some coaching and mentoring schemes require the outcomes to be measured, recorded and shared. This is a decision that will need to be made about the nature of the culture to be developed amongst SEND colleagues. There are examples of institutions allocating funding on the basis that there are measurable outcomes, such as improved Ofsted grades (see case study on p.258). Ideally, however, the outcomes of any coaching and mentoring scheme should be agreed at an open 'sharing' session where all colleagues contribute to a 'learning exchange'.

Jones and Gorrell (2018: 166–8) also offer a ten-stage model for introducing a coaching culture, which, if adopted, would support you as a SENCO in introducing a coaching culture (see Table 14.3).

By using a model, such as the four- or ten-stage models outlined above, perhaps with the support of a mentor, introducing a coaching/mentoring culture would be more structured in its approach, which would support you as SENCO enormously in the process.

Coaching and mentoring children

Most conversations about coaching and mentoring in schools and colleges refer to developing teachers. By virtue of the role they play, teachers are also mentors to the children they teach and engage in coaching on virtually a daily basis. Some teachers would not consider what they do as either coaching or mentoring. Being a role model to children, however, could be considered a form of mentoring, while working one-to-one with children to solve a problem where the emphasis is on the children working out the solution could equally be deemed a form of coaching.

While such processes go on all day, every day, with children in schools, they are usually informal and constrained because the opportunities to work one-to-one with children are severely restricted in school structures. Given the importance of developing positive relationships with children, it remains a frustrating fact that school buildings and school timetables are not usually organised to facilitate mentoring and coaching conversations with children. Two essential ingredients are quite often missing: the space to hold the conversations and the time to conduct them. A further difficulty is that if a child is assigned a coach or a mentor, it is usually because they are perceived to have some kind of difficulty, resulting in a stigma being attached to any children who receive such support.

Noam et al. (2014) propose the 'Cloverleaf' model for mentors to refer to when considering working with children. The model is so called because it replicates the four overlapping leaves of a clover. The leaves are thus not distinct entities, but overlap in a similar way to a Venn diagram and are not designed to be sequential. The four leaves of action, assertion, belonging and reflection are based on evidence accumulated from research, clinical work and school observations:

- Action – children, especially young children, are all about action, need to be active, and think better when active.
- Assertion – exploring their world is paramount for children and they do this by asserting themselves.
- Belonging – with a secure attachment a teenager will explore the world with ease, but a sense of belonging to a peer group can become magnified and override the family.
- Reflection – the teenager who has perspective can begin to reflect on ways in which they may differ from others in values, potential, interests and needs.

Noam et al. (2014) suggest that all children, no matter what their stage of development, will exhibit all of the characteristics identified above, hence the overlapping leaves. The purpose of using the overlapping leaves is to support professionals working with children to identify where each child is when mentoring them. Noam et al. (2014: 106) offer further explanation of the four clover leaves.

Noam et al. (2014) suggest that at each position on the clover, other leaves can take prominence for a brief or extended period or in specific relationships or contexts. Looking at the description of the four leaves should help support your approach towards working with young people.

TABLE 14.4 Scale diagram

Scale	Comments
10	
9	
8	
7	
6	
5	
4	
3	

In working with children as a coach, Tolhurst (2010) suggests using a scaling chart as a way of displaying the information visually, which helps with the coaching conversation. The child can locate themselves on the scale in terms of where they think they are now and where they would like to be. The coaching conversation then revolves around the best way to achieve the goal. The scale diagram can be used for a variety of purposes because it provides a helpful visual and tangible representation that can be annotated (see Table 14.4).

A helpful coaching model to use in conjunction with the scale is the LEAP model, which will support the coaching conversation when identifying where the coachee is now, where they would like to be and how to get there (Tolhurst, 2010: 238). The four steps of the LEAP model are:

Look at goals – start with the objective in mind – where the coachee wants to be

Explore reality – where the coachee is currently in terms of the reality of the situation

Analyse possibilities – consider what is possible and what is not

Plan action – the steps that would need to be taken to move towards the goal

Case study

Working with children in a school, the pupils were organised into groups and given school plans. Their task was to walk around the school and annotate their maps wherever they came across a space where they did not feel safe. The usual spaces cropped up, such as in unsupervised toilets and cloakrooms, but other areas included next to stairwells, corners, behind doors and anywhere that was badly lit. The maps were collated onto a master map and the children did a presentation to the school's SMT. As a consequence of this, modifications were made to the unsafe areas, including better lighting and the closing off of certain areas, such as the bottom of stairwells.

As can be seen from the discussion above, when embarking on a mentoring or coaching project with children it is important that we understand their developmental starting point before deploying the mentoring and coaching tools and processes that will help support the coaching and mentoring conversations within an open, caring and carefully scaffolded session.

Leading in coaching and mentoring

Coaching models

There is a plethora of coaching models available to draw upon. They are all based, however, broadly on the same principles and processes. The key purpose of the coaching relationship is to help move the coachee forward in an agreed area of their work or life. The process usually involves the identification of a goal or goals, followed by a discussion around the issues that have given rise to the coaching situation, what barriers might exist and how they might be overcome. The coach's role is to help the coachee reframe their attitudes towards, and perspectives on, the issue through thoughtful questioning of the coachee's assumptions and preconceptions.

The process normally involves around six coaching sessions over a period of approximately six months. The first session is usually focused on establishing a relationship with the coachee and identifying the issue(s) to be explored. The next four sessions revolve around developing strategies to address the issue(s) and potential barriers to progress, with a final sixth session a close-up meeting and reflection on progress.

There are many coaching models available, but possibly the most famous and popular is the GROW model, developed by John Whitmore in 1992 (see Table 14.5).

The GROW model is a very powerful tool, but it needs to be understood for it to be effective. I would advise that you develop your understanding of the model in conjunction with Whitmore's book. I have highlighted below some of the salient elements and these will get you started, but they are no substitute for the breadth and depth you will gain from reference to *Coaching for Performance*, now in its 5th edition (2017).

The intention behind any coaching process is that the coachee will achieve their goal(s) and in doing this will develop professionally and learn more about themselves. Thus, coaching could be described as a learning process and, in order to reflect on the learning that has taken place during the coaching process, it is important to review and evaluate. This makes the final review session potentially the most important phase of the model.

Mentoring models

Unlike coaching with its plethora of acronyms, mentoring is a less focused and normally longer-term process that does not lend itself so easily to straightforward models. One model that has been developed recently by Nemanick (2017) involves a process that is based on eight rules of effective mentoring:

1. Lead by following – the mentee needs to be the main driver of the process
2. Chart a course – goals should be set by the mentee
3. Create a safe place – encourage a culture of respect and trust
4. Know that good questions beat good advice – ask good questions rather than 'tell'
5. Balance empathy and action – connect with the mentee and help them move forward
6. Foster accountability – mentee to take responsibility for carrying out actions
7. Fill the toolkit – mentor won't have all the answers but will know where to go to find them
8. Honour transitions – mentoring relationships will come to an end and the mentor will support the mentee through the transition process.

TABLE 14.5 GROW model

GROW	Key Questions	Explanation
GOALS	What do you want?	It is important to start out with a goal(s) or outcome(s) because these give direction and focus to the coaching process.
REALITY	Where are you now?	This part of the process is important because it helps you identify the context in which you are seeking to achieve your goal(s).
OPTIONS	What could you do?	There is usually more than one option so this part of the process is important because it considers the choices you have.
WILL	What will you do?	This is often considered the most important part of the process because it is where the coachee commits to specific action(s).

Collaborative and alternative coaching and mentoring approaches

Most mentoring and coaching relationships are based on one-to-one dialogue, usually with a more experienced colleague (mentor) or facilitator (coach). The potential for a power differential to exist in such a relationship is high, leading to imbalances that might make the relationship less effective than it might be. To address this issue, collaborative approaches are becoming increasingly popular. These have the advantage of being non-hierarchical and non-mandated, with the benefit of sharing experiences within a wider peer group, where the group sets the agenda. There are many examples of such collaborative approaches, including peer-group mentoring and flash mentoring, both of which are discussed in detail below.

Peer-group mentoring for teacher development

This approach emanates from Finland (Heikkinen et al., 2012), where peer-group mentoring (PGM) aims to support teachers' coping both with work and their professional learning (p. 11). This makes it a very relevant approach for SEND departments because it goes beyond the traditional approaches to mentoring to offer an alternative approach based on constructivist principles. The authors compare traditional mentoring with peer-group mentoring as:

- Senior colleague mentors junior colleague v. mentoring is reciprocal and all can learn
- Usually involves 1-2-1 v. a group of between 5 and 10
- Knowledge can be transferred by telling v. knowledge is constructed out of social interaction.

> **Case study**
>
> The benefits of 'peer-group mentoring' are evident from a group of middle leaders I have been working with from three different schools. Drawing upon the 'Finnish model', each member of the group can act as a 'mentor' to other members of the group so they are not constantly reliant upon my interpretations as a facilitator, but can access advice, suggestions and guidance from each other. It is a self-managing group that shares ideas from across different boroughs and schools.

Heikkinen et al. (2012: 137) confirm that a key goal of PGM shared by all participants in the case study is the enhancement of wellbeing at work and it is this dimension that distinguishes the Finnish model from many others. They state that 'learning together, encouragement, confirmation, respect, active listening and trust are key factors in personal and professional development' (pp. 37–8) and feature prominently in PGM. The summary below of the processes and benefits is based upon empirical evidence drawn from the Finnish case studies:

Pre-requisites:

1. Open atmosphere and mutual trust
2. Ground rules and agreements

Benefits:

1. Time and space for reflecting and sharing experiences
2. Empowerment and increased self-confidence
3. Professional identity development
4. Conceptual change
5. Increased motivation and wellbeing.

(After Heikkinen et al., 2012: 140)

Peer-group mentoring provides a key opportunity to move away from the often solitary and individual nature of teaching. The authors confirm that from the case study evaluations many teachers mentioned 'the positive influence of mentoring on the individual teacher's wellbeing, mental stamina and workload experiences' and that 'mentoring is an effective way of preventing stress and burnout' (Heikkinen et al., 2012: 138).

> **Case study**
>
> The teachers in the schools mentioned in the third case study (p. 269) all engaged with their peers in a 'Lesson Study' approach which involved planning together, observing and feeding back in a process that involved early career teachers co-mentoring their more senior colleagues.

In particular, the case studies confirmed the importance of mentoring as teachers go through their professional stages of development:

- From trainee to NQT – evidence from case studies indicates that the level of support at this stage is inadequate
- Supporting NQTs – emphasis here through peer group mentoring is supporting NQTs through professional development and wellbeing at work
- Creating groups – groups can be either heterogeneous or homogenous in composition
- Selecting mentors – any mentor involved must be experienced in mentoring groups of professionals.

The evidence about peer and group mentoring, such as that identified by the Finnish study, indicates that as a SENCO this is an approach that should be given serious consideration because of the benefits to all those involved.

Flash mentoring

Scott Derrick, a US federal government employee knew that mentoring relationships between more experienced and less experienced workers were valuable, but was also aware that quite often those involved did not have the time to fulfil their commitments, so he came up with the concept of flash mentoring in 2007. The success of the idea soon spread and now many organisations use flash mentoring techniques, including York University in Toronto and Executive Women in Government.

The essence of 'flash' mentoring is that it is a one-time meeting or discussion through which an individual can seek guidance and learn from a more experienced person which requires limited commitment of time and resources from both parties. The meetings can be face-to-face, via telephone or through the use of telecommunication technologies such as Skype or social media. The intention is that it is a one-off mentoring engagement, but if both parties feel it would be useful to extend the meeting to a further session(s) then that is an option that can be agreed.

Variations on flash mentoring include sequential flash mentoring which involves the mentee holding conversations with several mentors over a period of time, which helps to broaden their access to expertise. Mentors have also been involved in group flash mentoring whereby one mentor works with a group of mentees, ensuring that a larger number of mentees gain insights from the mentor.

Flash mentoring is not intended to replace the more traditional long-term mentoring that colleagues value, but it provides an alternative approach in the tool box for those occasions when the need is urgent and time is short. Of course, colleagues have always met for one-off knowledge sharing opportunities, so in that sense flash mentoring is nothing new. By conceptualising the process as mentoring in a flash, however, we begin to think about alternative ways of carrying out mentoring.

Coaching and mentoring code of ethics

When coaching and mentoring colleagues we are in a very privileged position and because of this it is very important to adhere to a code of ethics. There are several codes available that are promoted by coaching associations, such as the Association for Coaching and the International Coaching Foundation (https://coachfederation.org/code-of-ethics). The codes all refer to similar issues. As qualified teachers and professionals working in a SEND environment, you will already be familiar with the principles of a code of ethics, so nothing in any of the codes would be a surprise. Even so, it is worth keeping these at the forefront of your mind. Further, depending upon the formality of the coaching/mentoring relationship it might be a valuable exercise to complete and sign a coaching agreement which essentially summarises the key ethical issues, as well as outlining the relevant contributions that both the coach and coachee will make in establishing the coaching/mentoring relationship (an example of a coaching agreement can be found in the online support materials).

> **Support organisations for coaching**
>
> Coaching organisations that support coaches include:
>
> International Coaching Federation – www.coachfederation.org.uk
>
> Association for Coaching – www.associationforcoaching.com
>
> European Mentoring and Coaching Council – www.emccouncil.org

Useful reading

Clutterbuck, D. (2014) *Everyone Needs A Mentor*. London: CIPD.

Chapter summary
- School staff are a key resource and need to be invested in
- Mentoring and coaching approaches provide appropriate tools to support staff development
- While mentoring and coaching have common elements, they are essentially different processes for different purposes
- To be fully successful, a mentoring and coaching culture that permeates the school or department will ensure greater success
- New approaches to mentoring and coaching, taking advantage of new technologies and ways of working, are changing the way we approach coaching and mentoring
- Children and young people can benefit from mentoring and coaching, both from school staff and each other
- There are ethical issues around mentoring and coaching and these must be addressed if the coaching or mentoring relationship is to be secure

15
Leading on Professional Learning

Steve Watts and Sarah Martin-Denham

- NASENCO outcomes: The principles and practice of leadership in different contexts. The role of leadership and professional challenge in supporting and promoting a culture of CPD linked to improvement. How children's development is affected by the quality of teaching they receive. To raise expectations and set challenging targets for children with SEND. To lead the professional development of staff so that all staff improve their practice and take responsibility for removing barriers to participation and learning.
- Read alongside: Chapter 4: Best Practice in Collecting and Using Data; Chapter 5: Practitioner Enquiry; Chapter 14: Coaching and Mentoring

Chapter overview

The purpose of this chapter is to identify the importance of continuous professional learning for practitioners. Guidance for SENCOs who lead on professional learning is provided in terms of conducting training audits, identifying needs and setting targets. The chapter shows how the performance review or appraisal process can support practitioners for the benefit of children, through setting clear targets and clarifying expectations. The chapter makes clear that practitioners are responsible for taking ownership of their professional development, which is often carried out through the process of reflection. The concept of the 'professional maturity spectrum' is introduced as a way of supporting SENCOs to audit their own development and that of their teams.

The nature of professional learning

Teachers and SENCOs continuously learn, reflecting on what works and what does not, as well as how to respond to challenges and opportunities. Teachers not only learn about the children they teach and the colleagues they work with, but most importantly about themselves. Thus, at the informal and intuitive level schools are not only places of learning for children, but also learning organisations where adults grow, learn and develop. Such professional learning should also be formalised which means that senior leaders in organisations, including SENCOs, need to be involved in their own professional development in order to demonstrate commitment to continuous improvement.

Carter (2015) suggests that the most effective professional learning programmes build upon the knowledge and skills needed to strengthen a practitioner's own teaching. He adds that schools need to note that Initial Teacher Education (ITE) is 'initial' and schools will need to provide the foundations on which NQTs can build their expertise and learning from more experienced others. It is a long-held view, as Burgess (2001: 87) argued, that in this way senior colleagues will be able to 'provide role models of good practice, arrange specific guidance and training, and encourage reflection in their staff'. It is this process of reflection that leads to advances in professional learning for colleagues.

REFLECTIVE ACTIVITY

As SENCO, how do you audit training needs in your school? Do your approaches vary for newly and recently qualified teachers and those with more experience? How can all colleagues share their training and wellbeing needs with you?

Reflective learning for professional development

Reflection has long been a process that teachers have engaged with in order to improve their practice. One of the first educational theorists in modern times to explore this process was John Dewey, an American educator and philosopher who worked during the first half of the twentieth century. Dewey introduced the concept of reflective practice, a concept that has been developed and adapted further by theorists such as Schon in the 1980s (Crowley, 2014: 127).

Reflecting 'on' action is a process that happens after the event and provides the practitioner with the opportunity to reflect on what happened, what the consequences were, what would be repeated in similar circumstances or what might be done differently. The learning taking place through this process allows the practitioner to move forward. Reflecting 'in' action concerns the point where automatic processes suddenly cease and the practitioner becomes conscious and aware of what is happening and, in the moment, changes direction as a result of that momentary awareness and reflection – the process commonly known as 'thinking on your feet'. Teachers will be familiar with the moment they realise that what they have planned is not working and they switch to a different approach (Hayes et al., 2014: 3). Whether it is possible to 'reflect in the moment' is still being debated, but the longer the gap between the event and the reflection the less clear it will be. Consequently, reflecting on action should take place as soon after the event as possible and ideally in a collaborative atmosphere with a colleague, group of colleagues, mentor or coach.

Burgess (2001: 87) suggests that 'the concept of a community of practice is based on a view of learning as a social process'. She argues that 'in a school that operates as a community of practice the progress of pupils will be paramount. However, teacher learning is crucial to pupil learning' (p. 89).

Not all organisations will be organised around a community of practice, but this should not prevent a SENCO from introducing the concept to the SLT.

SENCO ACTIVITY

Ask your colleagues to get into groups, ensuring there are senior leaders, teachers and support staff in each group. The focus of the activity is to get them to reflect on what provision is available and then to consider the following questions:

How effective is the universal, targeted and specialist provision?

How do we know it is having a positive impact on wellbeing and attainment?

Are there any gaps in our provision offer?

What are the training needs for the school and where can we access high quality training?

Universal provision	Targeted provision	Specialist provision
For all children – Quality First Teaching	Everyday approaches used for children with a range of SEND	This is bespoke support provided for individual children

In terms of SENCOs evaluating their practice as learners, before looking more closely at their colleagues, they could reflect upon where they would locate themselves on the spectrum of professional maturity (Crowley, 2014: 17). Crowley suggests that the spectrum contains at one end the 'technical rationalist approach which is primarily reactive and individualistic', while further along the spectrum 'we have an interactive approach to professionalism where we engage with a community of practice to enhance our professionalism'. At the other end of the spectrum, 'we have a community of exploration where perhaps the most innovative and critical approach to professional learning and teaching occurs and extends well beyond the confines of the organisation'.

On this spectrum, ranging from reactive to interactive to proactive approaches, one would expect to see senior staff, including SENCOs, being predominantly at the proactive end.

Reflective journals as professional development tools

What is important is that as SENCO you model good practice by taking responsibility for your own professional learning and development. One way to do this is through maintenance of a learning journal as a space to record reflections, notes, observations, goals and so on (Moon, 2001: 366). Moon suggests that through the process of writing 'unconnected areas of meaning cohere and a deeper meaning emerges'. Journal writing is a metacognitive process through which we reflect on and think about our thinking, a space where there are no boundaries and we can act freely without constraint. Journal writing does not come easily to everybody, however, so it is important to recognise that bullet point lists, dated diary entries, notes and so on are as acceptable as prose paragraphs. It is the process of putting thoughts, in whatever shape, onto paper that results in the deep learning, something that cannot be fully achieved if the thoughts and ideas remain inside the colleague's head.

Appraisal and target setting

Chapter 14 opens with the statement that the most important resource in a school is its staff and as such they need to be invested in. The argument in that chapter is that, through the effective deployment of mentors and coaches, staff development can take place to the benefit of all – the practitioner, their children and colleagues and the wider organisation and community. The appraisal process offers a similar opportunity to invest in the development of practitioners as an intrinsically valuable human resource that should be invested in because (a) it is a good thing for society to invest in people and (b) all involved in the organisation will benefit.

Thus appraisal, or performance review, should be seen as a professional entitlement for all practitioners. Storey (2001: 78) suggests that performance reviews provide an opportunity for professional dialogue, alongside the necessary support to achieve individual objectives. If framed in this way, it becomes a natural part of the professional learning process identified above. For example, as part of the preparation for the appraisal meeting the appraisee should spend some time reflecting on the achievements and challenges of the previous year by reviewing the targets they were set. The meeting itself should involve a celebration of successes, as well as a review of the challenges encountered and objectives met. Ashdown (2018: 3) draws upon Armstrong's definition of performance review as 'a systematic process for improving organisational performance by developing the performance of individuals in teams'. Ashdown (2018: 17–18) continues by sharing the outcomes of an interview with Martin Eves, a HR and Operations Director, who identified four key areas of effective performance in the workplace:

- The value of the employee – manager's role to enhance employee's value
- The importance of shared purpose – manager responsible for communicating
- Fit performance management to the context – targets are aligned with employee's aspirations
- Managing expectations – creating synergy through shared purpose.

How performance review or appraisal is carried out, will differ between schools, authorities and countries. It will almost inevitably be based on target setting and target review and these targets are likely to be closely aligned with measurable outcomes. These are important aspects of the process, as far as they go, but in the wider picture of the process it would be worth keeping in mind Martin Eves' four key imperatives outlined above (Ashdown, 2018: 17–18).

The psychological contract

The process outlined above relates specifically to the formal employment contract that exists between employer and employee in terms of reviewing the employee's practice as set out in the contract. There is another, unseen, unwritten and rarely discussed contract in operation, however, that exists alongside the employment contract. This is the 'psychological' contract, which exerts as much influence on a working relationship as the employment contract.

Ashdown (2018: 26–7) suggests that the psychological contract 'is fundamentally about the nature of the exchange relationship between employee and employer'. Ashdown draws upon Rousseau's work (1998, cited in Ashdown, 2018: 27) to define the psychological contract as being concerned with an individual's subjective beliefs that are shaped by the organisation, regarding the terms of exchange in the employment relationship. Thus, if an employee believes that a promise has been made and subsequently not met, then that situation could lead to negativity and a reduction in performance. In order to maintain a healthy relationship, performance review processes have a vital role in enabling an ongoing and two-way communication of expectations in the employment relationship (Ashdown, 2018: 27).

Ashdown (2018) identifies 'mutuality' and 'reciprocity' as two key concepts that contribute to a healthy psychological contract. In a healthy contract, both parties clearly understand the nature of the exchange and both parties feel that the perceived obligations are being met. Where there is a sense, however, that the obligations are not being met, there may be a breach in the psychological contract. If such breaches continue then an essential element of the psychological contract, trust, might be broken.

> **Case study**
>
> In a discussion with their mentor about a serious drop in an employee's performance, especially in terms of negative behaviour and motivation, the mentee indicated that, in working with the member of staff involved, they had suggested adding an additional check in a particular process. The mentee had intended this to act as a way of supporting the employee, but the employee perceived it as a lack of trust in their work and judgements. Feeling undervalued, the employee withdrew their goodwill, became critical and aggressive, indicating that the psychological contract had been broken. The mentee attempted to reassure the employee that this was not their intention, but to no effect. The mentor subsequently worked with the mentee to look at ways to re-establish the psychological contract, through focusing on alternative positive contexts rather than continuing to pursue the cause of the break. The strategy worked and the contract was restored.

Ashdown (2018: 28) suggests that 'a healthy contract is one where there is perceived fairness, high levels of trust and a perception that both parties are getting what they should from the employment relationship'. Ashdown (2018: 28) goes on to argue that 'when the contract is healthy, employees are more likely to have positive attitudes towards their employing organisation, demonstrated in valuable behaviours and valuable performance outcomes'.

REFLECTION

Reflecting on the discussion about the psychological contract above, can you identify any situations where the contract might have been breached, either with a member of the department, or with yourself? Can you identify what might have caused the breach? Was the contract restored? If so, what occurred to make this happen? Did you take any specific steps to help restore it?

How to share information with teams

There are different approaches to sharing information with teams; you will need to choose the processes that work best for you as SENCO. The important consideration is how you will ensure all staff employed by the school understand not only learning needs but also strategies to support the mental health and wellbeing of individual children. The school information system will be used to store key information on children's needs, attainment, SEN status and additional documentation including any agreed reasonable adjustments for children with disabilities. You will need to carry out an audit to ensure all staff are referring to and applying this information in their teaching.

There will be some information you will need to share that is a priority, for example a child with a new diagnosis, a newly arrived child with a particular need or if there has been a caregiver complaint. Consider the following:

- How soon do staff need to know?
- Which staff/senior leaders/external agencies need to know?
- What is the most efficient way to let them know? (Email: consider those who work part time.)
- GDPR – Is the information you are sharing secure? Do you have permission to share it?

Leading on and utilising CPD for improvement

The term CPD is used to describe the learning opportunities that professionals engage in to enhance their knowledge, understanding and skills. It can come in various forms, including conferences, events, workshops, e-learning through to accredited programmes of study at university from undergraduate to postgraduate level. CPD is important as it ensures that the workforce in an organisation is up to date.

There is a clear need to develop high-quality and successful training to develop teacher confidence in meeting the needs of those with SEND, which builds upon what they were taught and experienced through their Initial Teacher Education (ITE) provider (Carter, 2015). Carter shared that there is considerable variability in ITE course content, meaning newly qualified teachers may have significant gaps in their knowledge and understanding of behaviour management, and meeting the needs of children with SEND. The Code also reinforces the notion of high-quality teaching, directing the focus on the responsibilities of the teacher rather than the SENCO or teaching assistants. Furthermore, as explained by Florian and Spratt (2013), challenges with learning need to be viewed by teachers as dilemmas for themselves as teachers rather than within the child. To have an inclusive approach to learning and teaching, the teachers must have knowledge, understanding and confidence to teach the diversity of needs. The focus needs to be on building upon what teachers already know, developing inclusive techniques and approaches to removing barriers to learning and understanding behaviours that children may present with.

The DfE (2016b) defines effective professional development as a partnership between headteachers and other members of the leadership team, teachers and providers of professional development expertise, training or consultancy. The purpose of CPD is to develop knowledge, understanding and skill so that professionals continually develop their learning and teaching approaches. It needs to be carefully planned, based on an identified need and with clear outcomes and evaluation. Schools can have a tendency to front load staff training, usually in September and as a means to upskill new members of staff, share changes to processes and systems or to update safeguarding requirements and other legal obligations. CPD is most beneficial if it is high quality, robust, evidence based and embedded throughout the school year as a core requirement rather than 'opt in'.

The Department for Education (2016b) produced a framework that constitutes effective CPD as:

- developing practice and theory together
- linking pedagogical knowledge with subject/specialist knowledge, which draws on the evidence base, including high-quality academic research, robustly evaluated approaches and teaching resources
- delivered by those with expertise and knowledge to support participants in improving their understanding of evidence, and
- drawing out and challenging teachers' beliefs and expectations about teaching and how children learn.

Prior to planning for any training, you need to understand the pre-existing skills and qualifications of the team. As SENCO, is it useful to keep records of:

- which staff have attended which internal and external training, the cost, their evaluation of the event and the impact on provision and practice in school
- the skills, qualification and experience of the individual staff members and how this is used to inform who supports individual/groups of children and to identify training needs
- the training that Newly Qualified Teachers have attended and the impact of this observed in their classroom practice and confidence in meeting the needs of all children.

The Driver Youth Trust (2015) advocated that those leading provision for children with SEND should seek and receive support from colleagues in other schools. Greenwood and Kelly (2017) agreed, commenting that effective professional development could be brought about by encouraging schools to work locally, regionally and nationally to share good practice and to support each other's learning.

The DfE (2017d) launched a public consultation on 'strengthening Qualified Teacher Status and improving teacher career progression'. The government's aim was to ensure that teachers have the right support in place at the beginning of their careers and access to high-quality professional development. The outcome of this was the DfE (2018g) guidance on reducing workload and supporting teachers in the early stages of their careers. From this document consider the key advice and support you give to teachers, in relation to the following:

- How advice is reflected in policies, practice and expectations.
- How you ensure mentors have the time, capacity, expertise, knowledge and personal qualities required to undertake the role effectively.
- What you consider when giving colleagues mentoring positions.
- What opportunities you offer to early career teachers to collaborate and learn.
- Do you have a time management tool?
- Are colleagues encouraged to say when their workloads are unmanageable?

Recording CPD

There isn't one set approach to recording CPD but the following template may be useful to track who is accessing CPD, the impact and value for money (Table 15.1):

TABLE 15.1 Record of CPD

Date	Staff member	Title, provider and content	Development outcome	Impact on day-to-day practice, systems and processes
8/10/19	S.T.	Introduction to Adverse Childhood Experiences Company: Children experiencing trauma and loss	Key points shared in staff meeting, action plan activity led by SENCO	Changes to key person system (child stays in same form throughout school) Caregivers no longer expected to pay for local trips School released funding of £500 to purchase equipment spares for pastoral team
9/01/20	Whole school (J.S. absent)	Children who display Violent or Aggressive Behaviour Company: Children experiencing trauma and loss	Partnership with caregivers needs improving in Y7 and Y8	Caregivers' forums (targeted) Signposting to support services not on school website FRIENDS resilience programme (6 staff to be trained as facilitators)

REFLECTIVE ACTIVITY

'The quality of teaching for pupils with SEN, and the progress made by pupils, should be a core part of the school's performance management arrangements and its approach to professional development for all teaching and support staff' (DfE, 2015a: 93).

How does the quality of teaching and progress of groups of children influence the direction of your CPD?

Support organisations

The following organisations offer information, advice and training:

SEND Gateway: www.sendgateway.org.uk: developed by NASEN (National Association of Special Educational Needs), it provides easy-to-access information, resources and training to meet the needs of children with SEND

SEND training: www.oln.nasen.org.uk: a training course aiming to support teachers and support staff in working across the 0–25 age range to develop high-quality practice. They claim it is based on the evidence of what constitutes good CPD and takes a practice-led, enquiry-based approach

The Communication Trust: www.thecommunicationtrust.org.uk: this trust supports everyone who works with children in England to support their speech, language and communication. They have developed a wealth of information, resources and useful toolkits to support professionals in communicating more effectively with children with SLCN

Cowley (2014) argues that a learning culture can be facilitated through appropriate systems and protocols, but in the end it is about establishing trusting and respectful relationships. Cowley (2014: 144) suggests that in order to establish trust we may need to take risks, and suggests that practitioners:

- ask for and value the help and opinions of others
- admit our mistakes and share what can be learnt from them
- publicly acknowledge the capabilities of colleagues and consider how as practitioners we can learn from them
- ask others to comment on your practice as a practitioner with a view to improvement (including seeking feedback from children)
- share readings and links that you believe can inform practice.

In thinking about how this can be achieved, refer to the examples outlined in Chapter 14. In particular, consider introducing the Finnish model or adopting the 'lesson study' approach that Steve's mentees explored with each other. Only when we learn to work together and share understandings will we truly develop as the outstanding SENCOs and practitioners that we all have the capacity to be.

Chapter summary

- Continuous professional learning is the responsibility of all practitioners
- Newly qualified teachers need particular support to build upon their Initial Teacher Education (ITE)
- Continuous professional development or CPD comes in different guises, from the one-hour twilight session to the residential course
- CPD can be delivered in-house or through external bodies
- CPD can be internal and uncertificated, or part of a certificated external course or training
- Practitioners should use tools such as the professional development spectrum to audit where they are now and where they need to go
- Appraisal or performance review can be used to help with professional development through the identification of training needs and the setting of goals to achieve these
- Mentors and coaches can provide the support necessary to develop professionally
- Traditionally, teachers have worked mainly alone on reflecting on their professional learning, but increasingly such activity is becoming collaborative through, for example, the creation of communities of practice

It is by adopting the collaborative, sharing and reflection strategies outlined in this chapter that we will become outstanding SENCOs and practitioners.

Appendix

SEND: Assessment and Checklist Templates

The SEN and Disability Regulations (2014) Part 3 Duties on Schools

Example of a short note (possibility of SEN)

Example: SEN support plan

Audit for provision, practice and training

Self-analysis of key leadership attributes

Child's consent form

Relevance of intervention/teaching approach checklist

Self-assessment supporting children and families

A pupil passport

Risk assessment checklist

Debrief template

Child voice checklist

Individual transition plan

Template: Assessing competency across modes of working

Template: Assessing the efficacy of an intervention

Strategy for introducing a coaching and mentoring culture

Ten-step approach to introducing a coaching and mentoring culture

The SEN and Disability Regulations (2014) Part 3 Duties on Schools

Self-evaluation: SEN Information Report	
Requirement	Included
1. The kinds of SEN for which provision is made at the school	
2. Information about the school's policies for the identification and assessment of children with SEN	
3. Information about the school's policies for making provision for children with SEN, whether or not children have EHCPs, including:	
(a) How the school evaluates the effectiveness of its provision	
(b) The school's arrangements for assessing and reviewing the progress of children with SEN	
(c) The school's approach to teaching children with SEN	
(d) Adaptations to the curriculum and learning environment for children with SEN	
(e) Additional support for learning that is available to children with SEN	
(f) How the school enables pupils with SEND to engage in the activities of the school (including physical activities) together with children who do not have SEN; and	
(g) support that is available for improving the emotional, mental and social development of children with SEN	
4. In relation to mainstream schools and maintained nursery schools, the name and contact details of the SENCO	
5. Information about the expertise and training of staff in relation to children with SEND and about how specialist expertise will be secured	
6. Information about how equipment and facilities to support children with SEND will be secured	
7. The arrangements for consulting caregivers of children with SEND about, and involving them in, the education of their child	
8. The arrangements for consulting children with SEND about, and involving them in, their education	
9. Any arrangements by the governing body or the proprietor relating to the treatment of complaints from caregivers of children with SEND, concerning provision at the school	
10. How the governing body involves other bodies, including health and social services bodies, Local Authority support services and voluntary organisations, in meeting the needs of children with SEND and in supporting the families of such children	
11. The contact details of support services for the caregivers of children with SEND	
12. The school's arrangements for supporting children with SEND in a transfer between phases of education or in preparation for adulthood and independent living	
13. Information on where the Local Authority's local offer is published	

Table 2.2 reproduced from Martin-Denham, S. and Watts, S. (2019) *The SENCO Handbook*. London: Sage.

Example of a short note (possibility of SEN)

Short note		
Name	Date of birth	Date
Current attainment	Status: Looked after, English as an Additional Language, Pupil Premium	Attendance
Child's area(s) of strength and difficulties		
Child's views		
Caregivers' views/concerns		
Agreed outcomes		
Next steps		
Review date and time		
Caregiver and teacher's signatures		

Table 2.3 reproduced from Martin-Denham, S. and Watts, S. (2019) *The SENCO Handbook.* London: Sage.

Example: SEN support plan

Name:	All about me: (In child's voice)
DoB:	My strengths:
Attendance:	My interests:
	My aspirations:
What is important to me	What is important to my family
What is working well for me	What I would like to change
	What I need
Planned support/intervention	How long for

My targets	What we hope I will achieve	What I will need
1.		
2.		
3.		

Date of review:	Child's/caregiver's signature/comments:
	SENCO/Teacher signature comments:

Table 2.5 reproduced from Martin-Denham, S. and Watts, S. (2019) *The SENCO Handbook*. London: Sage.

Audit for provision, practice and training

Theme	RAG rating	Action
How well do colleagues understand their responsibilities to children with SEND?		
How well do colleagues understand the school's approach to identifying and meeting the needs of children with SEND?		
Do colleagues understand the process of how to raise causes for concern to the SENCO and caregivers? Do they have the confidence to initiate early intervention?		
How confident are staff in implementing the graduated response: assess, plan, do and review cycle?		
How well are children with SEND learning and making progress? Are outcomes good in all year groups with all members of staff?		
How well supported and trained are all staff employed by the school? Is the process for the induction of new staff and supply staff effective?		
How closely engaged are caregivers and how is their information/suggestions/concerns responded to?		
How well does the school liaise with external agencies and is this supportive to the SENCO in their role?		

Table 3.1 reproduced from Martin-Denham, S. and Watts, S. (2019) *The SENCO Handbook*. London: Sage.

Self-analysis of key leadership attributes

Attribute	Explanation	Reflection
Fair and efficient management	Do you manage resources effectively and maintain fairness and openness in decision making?	
Development and recognition	Do you recognise the contribution of others and support colleagues to develop their full potential?	
Interpersonal skills	Do you communicate clearly and give constructive feedback? Are you clear with your expectations and honest in your dealings?	
Strategy and vision	Do you work to create a shared vision and welcome new thinking?	
Transformational and collaborative leadership	Do you encourage participation, welcome questions, encourage the sharing of ideas and learn positively from mistakes?	
Leadership for teaching	Do you inspire respect as a teacher, and bring new ideas about evidence-based approaches to learning and teaching?	
Leadership for research	Do you encourage others to research and reflect on their own practice, to share their findings and experiences and engage in CPD?	

Table 3.3 reproduced from Martin-Denham, S. and Watts, S. (2019) *The SENCO Handbook*. London: Sage.

Child's consent form

Consent form

I have read/someone has read to me what _____ wants to know and the questions _____ will ask me

I know that when we talk _____ will record what we say, so that _____ can play this back later

I know that _____ may use some of my answers when _____ writes about _____ but _____ won't use my name

I know that _____ won't tell other people what I say unless _____ is very concerned that I might be harmed or in danger

I know that _____ will keep the chat that we have very safe

I know that I can say stop at any time even after we start to talk and that I do not have to answer any questions if I don't want to

I am happy to be part of _____ work

Not Sure   **Yes**   **No**

Figure 5.2 reproduced from Martin-Denham, S. and Watts, S. (2019) *The SENCO Handbook*. London: Sage.

Relevance of intervention/teaching approach checklist

Consideration	Evidence base/notes	Action
What is the evidence base that the intervention is necessary?		
What is the evidence base that the intervention or approach has a positive impact?		
Are colleagues including senior leaders supportive of a new intervention?		
What additional training is needed prior to beginning the intervention?		
How and when will you evaluate the impact of the intervention? Are monitoring systems in place and are they fit for purpose?		

Table 8.2 reproduced from Martin-Denham, S. and Watts, S. (2019) *The SENCO Handbook*. London: Sage.

Self-assessment supporting children and families

Self-assessment of knowledge and confidence of staff in supporting a child who has experienced bereavement. The second column to be used as an audit: Red (not in place and ineffective) Amber (in development) Green (in place and effective)		
	RAG rating	**Action to be taken**
There is an agreed procedure in place explaining processes the school will follow when a child is bereaved (including sudden bereavement)		
There is a named person responsible for the wellbeing and pastoral support of bereaved children		
1:1 in-school support is available for children and this person can be chosen by the child		
Staff have access to training on the complexities of grief and the impact of both natural and traumatic deaths on children (Archer, 2008; Attig, 2015)		
Support is available for the member of staff supporting the child and this is made explicit		
Peer support is available and the peers are chosen by the child		
There are age/culturally appropriate books in the library and classrooms which talk about bereavement and loss using appropriate terminology such as 'death' and 'dead' rather than 'lost' and 'gone'		
Bereavement and loss are part of PHSE		

Source: Adapted from Child Bereavement UK (2017b)

Table 8.9 reproduced from Martin-Denham, S. and Watts, S. (2019) *The SENCO Handbook*. London: Sage.

A pupil passport

Name: **DOB:** **Year:**
SEN support plan:
Health:

Strengths and Interests: (always first and foremost)

Difficulties

Teaching strategies and reasonable adjustments (Equality Act 2010)

Figure 10.3 reproduced from Martin-Denham, S. and Watts, S. (2019) *The SENCO Handbook*. London: Sage.

Risk assessment checklist

Date of risk assessment:	Class/Tutor/Child(ren):
Review date:	Area of need:

Overview of the activity

Hazard(s)	Priority rating
List all significant hazards (travel, groups or individual children, ratios, venue/site, equipment, personal care, trigger points)	Low, medium, high

Who might be harmed?
List all the groups of children and staff who are at risk

How is the risk to be managed?
List all existing procedures/strategies to be used

What further action is needed to manage the risk?
List any risks which are not adequately managed and state the proposed action to be taken

Risk Assessment Review:

Headteacher Approval/Signature:	Date:

Table 10.5 reproduced from Martin-Denham, S. and Watts, S. (2019) *The SENCO Handbook*. London: Sage.

Debrief template

Description of the event: What happened

Context: Where it started/ended

Children and adults involved:

Witnesses:

Date/time:

Leading the discussion: (this should be a person who has a good relationship with the child and who the child trusts)

- Only begin if the child is calm, regulated and the caregiver is present

- Explain the purpose of the conversation and why it is necessary (to understand what happened and why)

- Ask if they have any questions

- Ask the child to think for a few minutes about what happened

- The child/adult should describe what they did, saw and experienced pre, during and post the event and how it made them feel (it may be in the best interests of the child to do this separately)

- Useful questions – Can you tell us what happened today? Do you know what made you feel that way? What are your ideas for making it better next time? What can I do to help you?

Note: If the child is in survival response fight/flight/freeze, they will have no memory of why they behaved in the way they did. It is important to remember that these subconscious occurrences are survival instinctive responses, not those of conscious thought, or if resulting from communication difficulties, the child may not be able to articulate the issue to you (see Chapter 6).

Analysis/reflection: With the evidence of the events, examine what happened and why

- Were there any warning signs? What were these and were they responded to?

- What did the behaviour look like and how often is it occurring? Does this occur elsewhere outside of school?

- What is the severity of the behaviour and how long did it last?

- What support do the child, family and colleagues need?

- How could the situation be prevented in the future?

- Are current processes/behaviour policy fit for purpose?

- How can any broken relationships be repaired?

- Are there any training needs?

Lessons learned and recommendations	Actions	Review date/outcome
What was and was not managed well?		
How can future incidents be prevented/managed?		
Does the child appear to have unmet needs?		
Does the child need referral to health/children's services?		
What support needs to be in place for the child and family?		
Are any risk assessments needed?		
Is any staff training needed?		
With hindsight, what could have been done differently/better?		
It may be appropriate for the child to develop a support plan with an adult to support them in sharing what their needs are to reduce future incidents.		
Caregiver's response: **Child's response:**		

Table 11.3 reproduced from Martin-Denham, S. and Watts, S. (2019) *The SENCO Handbook*. London: Sage.

Child voice checklist

Things that help me learn	Emoji	Child comment
Being told what to do		
Being shown what to do		
Watching a video clip of what I need to do		
My friend explaining		
Having new ideas explained		
Writing in my own words		
Copying from the whiteboard		
Designing and making		
Hot seating, role play, acting		
Using a mind map		
Asking questions		
Having a break		
Having longer to think		
Working alone/in pairs/in groups		
Using the computer		

Table 12.1 reproduced from Martin-Denham, S. and Watts, S. (2019) *The SENCO Handbook*. London: Sage.

Individual transition plan

Name: Feeder school: Feeder SENCO:	Primary needs: Secondary needs: Child Protection involvement: Yes ☐ No ☐	Cognition and Learning ☐ Communication and Interaction ☐ Social, Emotional and Mental Health ☐ Physical and/or Sensory ☐
SEN support: Yes ☐ No ☐ Do they need/have an EHCP? Yes ☐ No ☐ Monitor ☐ Annual review date for EHCP:		Caregivers actively involved? Yes ☐ No ☐
Caregiver and child views: (Strengths, interests, aspirations, learning and challenges) Barriers to learning: Preferred approaches to learning: Effective interventions used to date: Approach to wellbeing:		Agreed reasonable adjustments with caregiver and child:
Diagnosed medical and/or learning needs:		
Professional involvement (AOT, paediatrician, CYPS, CAMHS, EP, language and learning, medical, Brain injury trust)		Available reports from other agencies:
Predicted SATS results Reading: Maths: Spelling, punctuation and grammar:		
Exam arrangements in place for SATS? (Small room, extra time, reader, prompt)		Primary SENCO actions:
Additional transition meetings/arrangements Additional meetings ☐ Visits ☐ Photography book ☐ Attendance at extra-curricular clubs ☐ Other ☐ (please specify)		Secondary SENCO actions:
Any Child Protection concerns? (Current or historic)		Review date:
Any other comments:		

Table 12.4 reproduced from Martin-Denham, S. and Watts, S. (2019) *The SENCO Handbook*. London: Sage.

Template: Assessing competency across modes of working

	Whole Classroom Mode	
Support Strategy	**Prompts**	**Successes/Action points** (Record your thoughts/discussion points in this column)
Working with children that have a range of needs	• Is the staff member able to consistently work with children that have a range of abilities? • Do they show the ability to provide adequate challenge for some children, as well as support those that require help to complete tasks?	
Keeping a time limit for each child	• Is the staff member able to spend appropriate amounts of time with each child? • Can they move on to another child successfully after 5/10 minutes? • Does that child remain on task after having been supported?	
Overseeing	• Can the staff member make accurate judgements regarding the engagement of a whole classroom of children? • Is the staff member able to make appropriate independent decisions about which child to support during a session?	
Using time wisely	• Does the staff member consistently demonstrate effective use of their time in the classroom? • Are they always engaged in meaningful activity?	
Consistent use of language with children	• Does the staff member mirror consistent use in language/terminology with the children? • Can they provide accurate explanations of concepts when asked to by children?	

Small Group Mode		
Support Strategy	**Prompts**	**Successes/Action points** (Record your thoughts/discussion points in this column)
Familiarity in programme content/ resource used	• Is the staff member adequately familiar with the materials used during the small group work? • Have they taken the time to explore/amend the materials as necessary before the group commenced?	
Allowing all children to partake in the session	• Is the staff member able to encourage quieter children to partake in the session? • Can they achieve an effective balance in the discussion?	
Assessment arrangements	• Can the staff member articulate the assessment requirements associated with the small group work? • Can they accurately complete assessments of the children and use these to inform future sessions?	
Regular review of abilities	• Is the staff member able to undertake effective informal review of individuals' abilities after each session? • Does this review result in effective differentiation of content?	
Effective grouping of children	• Can the staff member effectively group the children to ensure smooth running of the intervention? • Do they make good use of partnering/wider group organisation to facilitate learning?	
Building upon learning outside of the group	• Can the staff member refer to the concepts explored in different contexts? • Do they make good use of praise and reward to consolidate the learning outside of the small group?	

One-to-One Mode		
Support Strategy	**Prompts**	**Successes/Action points** (Record your thoughts/discussion points in this column)
Communication with class teacher/other staff members	<ul><li>Is the staff member engaging in frequent and open discussion regarding the needs and abilities of the child they regularly work with?</li><li>Does this communication help to inform better teaching and learning approaches for that child?</li><li>Are the thoughts of the staff member listened to by other staff members?</li></ul>	
Supporting independent working	<ul><li>Is the staff member mindful of the dangers of over-reliance?</li><li>Can they promote independent working during sessions?</li><li>Are they aware of how to avoid an unhealthy reliance between themselves and the child they support?</li></ul>	
Encouraging collaboration between the child and his/her peers	<ul><li>Does the staff member encourage the child they work with regularly to build relationships with his/her peers?</li></ul>	
Knowing when to adapt materials	<ul><li>Can the staff member successfully adapt materials so that they are appropriate to the abilities of the child they work with?</li><li>Do they share these resources with others and notify the class teacher when materials are adapted?</li></ul>	

Table 13.1 reproduced from Martin-Denham, S. and Watts, S. (2019) *The SENCO Handbook*. London: Sage.

Template: Assessing the efficacy of an intervention

Cycle Stage	Observation Prompt	Areas of success/Action points
Assessing existing abilities	<ul><li>Is the staff member showing signs that they understand individuals' abilities?</li><li>Can they differentiate the questioning used/task assigned to individuals?</li><li>Did they undertake any formal/informal assessment of individuals' abilities before the intervention began?</li></ul>	
Assessment during/at the end of the intervention	<ul><li>Is the staff member aware of all assessment requirements during/at the end of the intervention?</li><li>Are they able to demonstrate effective use of the assessment tools?</li></ul>	
Group rules	<ul><li>Are there any group rules in place?</li><li>Were children involved in creating them?</li><li>How often are they referred to by staff member?</li></ul>	
Modelling of activities	<ul><li>Does the staff member model all activities children are expected to undertake?</li><li>How clear is the modelling process?</li></ul>	
Participation of children	<ul><li>Did all children participate in the session?</li><li>Does the staff member take appropriate measures to encourage quieter children to participate/reduce the input of more confident children?</li></ul>	
Building upon learning in different contexts	<ul><li>Did the staff member refer to concepts in different contexts to reinforce learning?</li><li>Have you seen them building upon learning in the group back in the main classroom?</li></ul>	

Table 13.2 reproduced from Martin-Denham, S. and Watts, S. (2019) *The SENCO Handbook*. London: Sage.

Strategy for introducing a coaching and mentoring culture

Phase	Purpose	Reflection
1 – Investigation	To investigate what is currently being done, when and by whom. What works and what does not. Check that culture will fit in with the wider organisation's strategic direction	
2 – Business Case	Link proposal to wider strategy, scope costs and investment, obtain buy-in from key stakeholders	
3 – Implementation	Implement proposals and monitor success/barriers	
4 – Review	Evaluate benefits for organisation and identify next steps	

Table 14.2 reproduced from Martin-Denham, S. and Watts, S. (2019) *The SENCO Handbook*. London: Sage.

Ten-step approach to introducing a coaching and mentoring culture

Phase	Stage	Explanation	Reflection
Empathise	1 – Understand organisation	Assess current reality	
Empathise	2 – Link to organisation's objectives/ strategy	Validate need for change	
Define	3 – Identify vision and purpose	Define a destination goal for culture	
Define	4 – Gain stakeholder support	Focus on win-win	
Create	5 – Identify where to engage first	Identify low-risk area to trial	
Create	6 – Create measurements	Clarify what success means	
Experiment	7 – Introduce pilot	Identify learning and insights	
Experiment	8 – Evaluate results	Decide on how you will act on learning and insights	
Learn	9 – Introduce the next phase	Celebrate small wins	
Learn	10 – Maintain momentum	Implement actions from insights and improve	

Table 14.3 reproduced from Martin-Denham, S. and Watts, S. (2019) *The SENCO Handbook*. London: Sage.

References

Adams, L., Tindle, A., Basran, S., Dobie, S. and Thomson, D. (2018) *Education, Health and Care Plans: A qualitative investigation into service user experiences of the planning process: Research report.* London: DfE.

Adams, L., Tindle, A., Basran, S., Thomson, D., Robinson, D. and Shepard, C. (2017) *Experiences of Education, Health and Care Plans: A survey of parents and young people.* London: DfE.

Adelman, C. (1993) Kurt Lewin and the origins of action research. *Educational Action Research*, 1(1): 7–24.

ADHD Institute (2019) *Assessment and Diagnosis.* Available at: https://adhd-institute.com/assessment-diagnosis/diagnosis/icd-10/ (Accessed 7 June 2019).

Alloway, T. P. and Alloway, R. G. (2015) *Understanding Working Memory.* London: SAGE.

Altemueller, L. and Lindquist, C. (2017) Flipped classroom instruction for inclusive learning. *British Journal of Special Education*, 44(3): 1–19.

American Psychiatric Association (2013) *Diagnostic and Statistical Manual of Mental Disorders.* 5th edn. Arlington, VA: American Psychiatric Association.

American Psychological Association (2008) *Children and trauma: update for mental health professionals.* Washington: American Psychological Association.

Archer, J. (2008) Theories of grief: Past, present, and future perspectives. In M.S. Stroebe, R.O. Hansson, Schut, H. and W. Stroebe (eds), *Handbook of Bereavement Research and Practice: Advances in theory and intervention*, pp. 45–65.

Armstrong, T. (2017) Neurodiversity: The future of special education? *Educational Leadership*, 74(7): 10–16.

Ashdown, L. (2018) *Performance Management: A practical introduction.* 2nd edn. London: Kogan Page.

Attig, T. (2015) Seeking wisdom about mortality, dying and bereavement. In J. Stillion and T. Attig (eds), *Death, Dying and Bereavement: Contemporary perspectives, institutions and practices.* New York, NY: Springer, pp. 1–15.

Baddeley, A. and Hitch, G. (1974) Working memory. In G.H. Bower (ed.), *The Psychology of Learning and Motivation: Advances in research and theory* New York: Academic Press.

Bakian, A., Bilder, D., Coon, H. and McMahon, W. (2015) Spatial relative risk patterns of autism in Utah. *Journal of Autism and Developmental Disorders*, 45: 988–1000.

Barlé, N., Wortman, C. and Latack, J. (2017) Traumatic bereavement: Basic research and clinical implications. *Journal of Psychotherapy Integration*, 27(2): 127–39.

Barnett, B. and O'Mahony, G. (2008) Mentoring and coaching programs for professional development of school leaders. In J. Lumby, G. Crow and P. Pashiardis (eds), *International Handbook on the Preparation and Development of School Leaders.* New York: Routledge.

Barrett, P. (2010) *FRIENDS for Life: Group leaders' manual for children.* West End: Pathways Health and Research Centre.

Barumandzadeh, R., Martin-Lebrun, E., Barumandzadeh, T. and Poussin, G. (2016) The impact of parental conflict and the mitigating effect of joint custody after divorce or separation. *Journal of Divorce and Remarriage*, 57(3): 212–23.

Basford, E., Butt, G. and Newton, R. (2017) To what extent are teaching assistants really managed? 'I was thrown in the deep end, really; I just had to more or less get on with it'. *School Leadership & Management*, 37(3): 288–310.

BEAT (2019) *Help and Treatment.* Available at: https://www.beateatingdisorders.org.uk/recovery-information/help-treatment. (Accessed 7 June 2019).

Beaton, S., Forster, P. and Maple, M. (2012) The language of suicide. *Psychologist*, 25(10): 731.

Beecham, J. (2014) Annual research review: Child and adolescent mental health interventions – A review of progress in economic studies across different disorders. *Journal of Child Psychology and Psychiatry, and Allied Disciplines*, 55: 714–32.

Bellis, M.A., Hughes, K., Leckenby, N., Perkins, C. and Lowey, H. (2014) National household survey of adverse childhood experiences and their relationship with resilience to health-harming behaviors in England. *BMC Medicine*, 12(1): 72.

Bennett, T. (2017) *Creating a Culture: How school leaders can optimise behaviour. Independent review of behaviour in schools.* London: DfE.

Biesta, G. (2017) Mixing methods in educational research. In R. Coe, M. Waring, L.V. Hedges and J. Arthur (eds), *Research Methods and Methodologies in Education.* London: Sage, pp. 159–65.

Bomber, L. (2007) *Inside I'm Hurting.* Croydon: Worth Publishing.

Booth, T. and Ainscow, M. (2011) *Index for Inclusion: Developing learning and participation in schools.* London: Disability Equality in Education.

Bork, P., Harwood, D. and Bennett, S. (2014) Using play as a key to unlocking the silence for children with selective mutism. *Canadian Children*, 39(3): 24–33.

Bøttcher, L. and Dammeyer, J. (2016) *Development and learning of young children with disabilities: A Vygotskian perspective*, 13. Switzerland: Springer.

Bouck, E. and Park, J. (2018) A systematic review of the literature on mathematics manipulatives to support students with disabilities. *Education and Treatment of Children*, 31(1): 65–106.

Bowles, D., Radford, J. and Bakopoulou, I. (2017) Scaffolding as a key role for teaching assistants: Perceptions of their pedagogical strategies. *British Journal of Educational Psychology*, 88(3): 499–512.

Bowlby, J. (1969) *Attachment and Loss: Vol. 1. Attachment.* New York: Basic Books.

Bowlby, J. (1988) *A Secure Base: Clinical applications of attachment theory.* London: Routledge.

British Dyslexia Association (2017) What are specific learning difficulties? Available at: www.bdadyslexia.org.uk/ (Accessed 13 March 2017).

British Dyslexia Association (2018a) *Dyslexia guidance.* Available at: www.bdadyslexia.org.uk/educator/what-are-specific-learning-difficulties#Dyslexia (Accessed 1 November 2018).

British Dyslexia Association (2018b) *Dyscalculia guidance.* Available at: www.bdadyslexia.org.uk/dyslexic/maths-difficulties-dyscalculia (Accessed 1 November 2018).

British Educational Research Association (BERA) (2018) *Ethical Guidelines for Educational Research.* 4th edn. London: BERA.

British Institute of Learning Disabilities (BILD) (2011) Factsheet: Learning Disabilities. Birmingham: BILD.

Brodovsky, B. and Kiernan, K. (2017) How to talk to children about flight, fight and freeze. Available at: https://makingsenseoftrauma.com/wp-content/uploads/2019/05/8-How-to-Talk-to-Children-about-Freeze-Flight-and-Fight-Nov-2017.pdf (Accessed 22 May 2019).

Burgess, H. (2001) Working with others to develop professional practice. In F. Banks and A.S. Mayes (eds), *Early Professional Development.* London: David Fulton.

Burton, D. and Bartlett, S. (2009) *Key Issues for Education Researchers.* London: Sage.

Bush, D. and Middlewood, T. (2013) *Leading and Managing People in Education.* Los Angeles: Sage.

Bush, T., Coleman, M., Wall, D. and West-Burnham, J. (1996) Mentoring and continuing professional development. In D. McIntyre and H. Hagger (eds), *Mentors in Schools: Developing the profession of teaching.* London: David Fulton.

Butterworth, B. (2005) Developmental dyscalculia. In J.I.D. Campbell (ed.), *Handbook of Mathematical Cognition.* Hove: Psychology Press, pp. 455–67.

Campbell, C. (2011) *How to involve hard-to-reach parents encouraging meaningful parental involvement with schools.* Nottingham: National College for School Leadership.

Carter, A. (2015) *Carter Review of Initial Teacher Training.* London: DfE.

Castro, M., Bissaco, M., Panccioni, B., Rodrigues, S. and Domingues, A. (2014) Effect of a virtual environment on the development of mathematical skills in children with dyscalculia. *PLoS One,* 9(7): 1–16.

Centre for the Use of Research and Evidence in Education (CUREE) (2005) *National Framework for Mentoring and Coaching.* Coventry: CUREE.

Challenging Behaviour Foundation (CBF) (2019) *What is a behaviour support plan?.* Available at: https://www.challengingbehaviour.org.uk/understanding-behaviour/positive-behaviour-support.html (Accessed 7 June 2019)

Charlie Waller Memorial Trust (CWMT) (2017) *Depression: Let's get talking.* Reading: CWMT.

Child and Adolescent Bipolar Foundation (CABF) (2007) *Educating the child with bipolar disorder.* Wilmette, Il: Child and Adolescent Bipolar Foundation.

Child Bereavement UK (2017a) Impact Report: A year of rebuilding lives together. Bucks: Child Bereavement UK.

Child Bereavement UK (2017b) Schools Information Pack. Bucks: Child Bereavement UK.

Childhood Bereavement Network (2019) *National Statistics*. Available at: www.childhoodbereavementnetwork.org.uk/research/key-statistics.aspx. (Accessed 7 June 2019)

Childline (2018) Types of mental health issues. Available at: www.childline.org.uk (Accessed 26 March 2018).

Children and Families Act (CAFA) (2014) Available at: www.legislation.gov.uk (Accessed 22 May 2018).

Chodura, S., Kuhn, J. and Holling, H. (2015) Interventions for children with mathematical difficulties: A meta-analysis. *Developmental Dyscalculia*, 223(2): 129–44.

Cogmed (2018) *About working memory*. Available at: https://www.cogmed.com/about-working-memory. (Accessed 1 November 2018).

Contact a Family (2018) *Deafblindness: Background*. Available at: https://contact.org.uk/medical-information/conditions/d/deafblindness/ (Accessed 1 November, 2018)

Council for Disabled Children (2015) *SEN and Disability in the Early Years Toolkit*. London: Council for Disabled Children.

Council for Disabled Children (2017) *Education, Health and Care Plans*. London: Council for Disabled Children. Available at: https://councilfordisabledchildren.org.uk/sites/default/files/field/attachemnt/EHCP%20Exemplar%20Guide%202017.pdf

Couper, S. and Mackie, P. (2016) *Polishing the Diamonds: Addressing Childhood Experiences in Scotland*. Glasgow: Scottish Public Health Network.

Crenna-Jennings, W. and Hutchinson, J. (2018) *Access to children and young people's mental health services – 2018*. London: Education Policy Institute.

Crowley, S. (2014) *Challenging Professional Learning*. London: Routledge.

Data Protection Act 2018 (c.12). London: The Stationery Office. Available at: www.legislation.gov.uk (Accessed 30 May 2018).

Davis, H. and Day, C. (2010) *Working in Partnership: The family partnership model*. London: Pearson.

DeBooth, K. and Reynolds, S. (2017) A systematic review of sensory-based autism subtypes. *Research in Autism Spectrum Disorders*, 36: 44–56.

Department for Education (DfE) (2011a) *Green Paper: Support and aspiration – A new approach to special educational needs and disabilities*. London: DfE.

Department for Education (DfE) (2011b) *Teachers' standards guidance for school leaders, school staff and governing bodies*. London: DfE.

Department for Education (DfE) (2013) Alternative provision: Statutory guidance for local authorities. London: DfE.

Department for Education (DfE) (2014a) *The SEN and disability regulations*. London: DfE.

Department for Education (DfE) (2014b) *Assessment principles: School curriculum*. London: DfE.

Department for Education (DfE) (2014c) *Inclusive language: Words to use and avoid when writing about disability*. London: DfE.

Department for Education (DfE) (2014d) *Templates: Supporting pupils with medical conditions.* London: DfE.

Department for Education (DfE) (2015a) *Special educational needs and disability code of practice: 0–25 years.* London: DfE.

Department for Education (DfE) (2015b) *Supporting children with medical conditions.* London. DfE.

Department for Education (DfE) (2016a) *Mental health and behaviour in schools.* London: DfE.

Department for Education (DfE) (2016b) *Standard for teachers' professional development.* London: DfE.

Department of Education (2016c) *Educational excellence everywhere.* London: DfE.

Department for Education (DfE) (2017a) *Children looked after in England (including adoption).* London: DfE.

Department for Education (DfE) (2017b) *Exclusion from maintained schools, academies and pupil referral units in England: Statutory guidance for those with legal responsibilities in relation to exclusion.* London: DfE.

Department for Education (DfE) (2017c) *Behaviour and discipline in schools: Guidance for headteachers and school staff.* London: DfE.

Department for Education (DfE) (2017d) *Strengthening qualified teacher status and improving career progression for teachers.* London: DfE.

Department for Education (DfE) (2018a) *Special educational needs in England, January 2018.* London: DfE.

Department for Education (DfE) (2018b) *Data protection: A toolkit for schools.* London: DfE.

Department for Education (DfE) (2018c) *Working together to safeguard children.* London: DfE.

Department for Education (DfE) (2018d) *Promoting the education of looked-after children and previously looked-after children: Statutory guidance for local authorities.* London: DfE.

Department for Education (DfE) (2018e) *Outcomes for children looked after by local authorities in England.* London: DfE.

Department for Education (DfE) (2018f) *Creating opportunity for all: Our vision for alternative provision.* London: DfE.

Department for Education (DfE) (2018g) *Reducing workload: Supporting teachers in the early stages of their career – Advice for school leaders, mentors and appropriate bodies.* London: DfE.

Department for Education and Skills (DfES) (2003) *Data collection by type of special educational needs.* London: DfES.

Department of Health (DoH) (2014) *Positive and proactive care: Reducing the need for restrictive interventions.* London: DoH.

Department of Health (DoH) (2015) *Future in mind – Promoting, protecting and improving our children and young people's mental health and wellbeing.* London: (DoH).

Department of Health and Department for Education (DoH and DfE) (2017) *Transforming children and young people's mental health provision: A green paper.* London: DoH and DfE.

Devecchi, C., Dettori, F. and Doveston, M. (2011) Inclusive classrooms in Italy and England: The role of support teachers and teaching assistants. *European Journal of Special Needs Education*, 27(2): 37–41.

Dewey, J. (1933) *How We Think: A restatement of reflective thinking to the educative process.* Boston: D. C. Heath.

Diehl, J.D., Frost, S.J., Sherman, G., Mencl, W.E., Kurian, A., Molfese, P., et. al. (2014) Neural correlates of language and non-language visuospatial processing in adolescents with reading disability. *Neuroimage*, 101: 653–66.

Dirth, T. and Branscombe, N. (2017) Disability models affect disability policy support through awareness of structural discrimination. *Journal of Social Issues*, 73(2): 413–42.

Done, E., Murphy, M. and Bedford, C. (2016) Change management and the SENCO role: Developing key performance indicators of inclusivity. *Support for Learning*, 31(1):13–26.

Downey, M. (2014) *Effective Modern Coaching: The principles and art of successful business coaching.* London: LID Publishing.

Dowker, A. (2017) *Development of Components of Mathematics in 7 to 11 Year Old Children: A study using Dynamo assessment.* Oxford: British Society for Research into Learning Mathematics.

Dyspraxia Foundation (2018) Dyspraxia at a glance. Available at: https://dyspraxiafoundation.org.uk (Accessed 1 November 2018).

Education Act 1996 (c.56). London: The Stationery Office. Available at: www.legislation.gov.uk (Accessed 29 May 2018).

Education Act 2011 (c.21). London: The Stationery Office. Available at: www.legislation.gov.uk (Accessed 29 May 2018).

Education Endowment Fund (EEF) (2019) *Teaching and Learning Toolkit – An accessible summary of the international evidence on teaching 5–16 year-olds.* Available at: https://educationendowmentfoundation.org.uk/evidence-summaries/teaching-learning-toolkit (Accessed 24 February 2019).

Elliott, J. (1978) What is action research in schools? *The Journal of Curriculum Studies*, 10(4): 355–7.

El Zein, F., Solis, M., Vaughn, S. and McCulley, L. (2014) Reading comprehension interventions for students with autism spectrum disorders: A synthesis of research. *Journal Autism Developmental Disorders*, 44. 1303–22.

Equality Act (2010) Available at: www.legislation.gov.uk (Accessed 22 May 2018).

Equality and Human Rights Commission (2015) *Reasonable adjustments for disabled pupils: Guidance for schools in England.* Equality and Human Rights Commission.

Estyn (2016) *Pupil Participation: A best practice guide.* Cardiff: Estyn.

Fajerman, L., Tressander, P. and Connor, J. (2004) *Children are Service Users Too: A guide to consulting children and young people.* London: Save the Children.

Farrell, M. (2017) *Educating Special Students: An introduction to provision for learners with disabilities and disorders.* 3rd edn. Oxon: Routledge.

Felitti, V.J., Anda, R.F., Nordenberg, D., Williamson, D.F., Spitz, A.M., Edwards, V. and Marks, J.S. (1998) Relationship of childhood abuse and household dysfunction to many of the leading causes of death in adults: The Adverse Childhood Experiences (ACE) Study. *American Journal of Preventive Medicine*, 14(4): 245–58.

Florian, L. and Spratt, J. (2013) Enacting inclusion: A framework for interrogating inclusive practice. *European Journal of Special Needs Education*, 28(2): 119–35.

FASD Network UK (2018) *What is Foetal Alcohol Spectrum Disorder?*. Available at: http://www.fasdnetwork.org/what-is-fasd.html (accessed 7 December 2018).

Food and Agriculture Organization of the United Nations (FAO) (2016) *The state of food and agriculture.* Rome: FAO.

Fox, G. (2016) *A Handbook for Teaching Assistants: Teachers and assistants working together.* London: David Fulton Publishers.

Frank (2018) *Drugs A–Z.* Available at: https://www.talktofrank.com/drugs-a-z (Accessed on 7 June 2018).

Frenette, P., Dodds, L., MacPherson, K., Flowerdew, G., Hennen, B. and Bryson, S. (2011) Factors affecting the age at diagnosis of autism spectrum disorders in Nova Scotia, Canada. *Autism,* 17(2): 184–95.

Friswell, J. (2014) *Working with families and keeping parents and carers engaged in meeting the needs of pupils with SEND.* Available at: www.rnlcom.com/wp-content/uploads/2014/03/Jane-Friswell-PPoint.pptx.

Gallwey, W.T. (2015) *The Inner Game of Tennis.* London: Pan. (Originally published 1974)

Gates, J.A., Kang, E. and Lerner, M.D. (2017) Review: Efficacy of group social skills interventions for youth with autism spectrum disorder: A systematic review and meta-analysis. *Clinical Psychology Review,* 52: 164–81.

Gill, K., Quilter-Pinner, H. and Swift, D. (2017) *Making the Difference: Breaking the link between school exclusion and social exclusion.* London: Institute for Public Policy Research.

Goodman, R., Renfrew, D. and Mullick, M. (2000) Predicting type of psychiatric disorder from strengths and difficulties questionnaire (SDQ) scores in child mental health clinics in London and Dhaka. *European Child and Adolescent Psychiatry,* 9(2): 129–34.

Goodmon, L., Leverett, R., Royer, A., Hillard, G., Tedder, T. and Rakes, L. (2014) The effect of therapy balls on the classroom behavior and learning of children with dyslexia. *Journal of Research in Education,* 24(2): 124–45.

Grandgeorge, M. and Masataka, N. (2016) Atypical color preference in children with Autism Spectrum Disorder. *Frontiers in Psychology,* 7: 1–5.

Gray, D.E., Garvey, B. and Lane, D.A. (2016) *A Critical Introduction to Coaching and Mentoring.* Sage: London

Graydon, K., Jimerson, S. and Fisher, E. (2010) *Death and Grief in the Family: Providing support at school.* Bethesda, MD: National Association of School Psychologists.

Greene, J. and Grant, A.M. (2003) *Solution-focused Coaching: A manager's guide to getting the best from people.* London: Pearson Education.

Greenwood, J. and Kelly, C. (2017) Implementing cycles of Assess, Plan, Do, Review: A literature review of practitioner perspectives. British Journal of Special Education, 44(4): 394–410.

Griffiths, Y. and Stuart, M. (2013) Reviewing evidence-based practice for pupils with dyslexia and literacy difficulties. *Journal of Research in Reading,* 36(1): 96–116.

Grossman, J., Klin, A., Carter, A. and Volkamar, F. (2000) Verbal bias in recognition of facial emotions in children with Asperger syndrome. *Child Psychology Psychiatry,* 41: 369–79.

Hampton, L.H. and Kaiser, A.P. (2016) Intervention effects on spoken-language outcomes for children with autism: A systematic review and meta-analysis. *Journal of Intellectual Disability Research,* 60(5): 444–63.

Hayes, C., Duncan, M. and Whitehouse, A. (2014) *Developing as a Reflective Early Years Professional: A thematic approach.* Northwich: Critical Publishing.

Heikkinen, H., Jokinen, H. and Tynjala, P. (2012) *Peer-group Mentoring for Teacher Development.* London: Routledge.

Hellawell, B. (2017) A review of parent–professional partnerships and some new obligations and concerns arising from the introduction of the SEND code of practice 2015. *British Journal of Special Education*, 44(4): 411–30.

Henderson, R. and Knott, L. (2015) *Dyspraxia and Apraxia*. Leeds: Patient Platform Limited.

Higgins, E. and O'Sullivan, S. (2015) 'What Works': Systematic review of the 'FRIENDS for Life' programme as a universal school-based intervention programme for the prevention of child and youth anxiety. *Educational Psychology in Practice*, 31(4): 424–38.

Hill, V., Croydon, A., Greathead, S., Kenny, L., Yates, R. and Pellicano, E. (2016) Research methods for children with multiple needs: Developing techniques to facilitate all children and young people to have 'a voice'. *Educational and Child Psychology*, 33(3): 26–43.

HM Courts and Tribunals Service (2013) *How to claim against disability discrimination in schools – a guide for parents*. London: HM Courts and Tribunals Service.

Hobson, A. (2003) *Mentoring and Coaching for New Leaders*. Nottingham: NCSL.

Horridge, K. (2018) Variation in health care for children and young people with a disability. *Developmental Medicine and Child Neurology*, 60(8): 731.

Howlin, P. (2010) Evaluating psychological treatments for children with autism-spectrum disorders. *Advances in Psychiatric Treatment*, 16: 133–40.

Hung, S., Spencer, M. and Dronomraju, R. (2012) Selective mutism: Practice and intervention strategies for children. *Children and Schools*, 34(4): 222–30.

Independent Parental Advisory Service (IPSEA) (2017) *Exclusion from school*. Available at: www.ipsea.org.uk/pages/category/exclusion-from-school (Accessed 1 April 2018).

Ingram, J., Strand, S. and Sarazin, M. (2015) *The Use of Mathletics and the Relationship to Achievement at Key Stage 2 in England*. Oxford: University of Oxford.

International Dyslexia Association (IDA) (2018) Available at: www.dyslexiaida.org (Accessed 24 April 2018).

International Dyslexia Learning Solutions (IDL) (2019) Available at: https://idlsgroup.com/ (Accessed 7 June 2019)

Irving, H. and Martin-Denham, S. (2015) Specific learning difficulties, dyslexia, dyspraxia and dyscalculia. In S. Martin-Denham (ed.), *Teaching Children with Special Educational Needs and Disabilities 0–25 Years*. London: Sage.

Jones, A., Gallagher, B., Manby, M., Robertson, O., Schützwohl, M., Berman, A.H., Hirschfield, A., Ayre, L., Urban, M., Sharratt, K. and Christmann, K. (2013) *Children of Prisoners: Interventions and mitigations to strengthen mental health*. Huddersfield: University of Huddersfield.

Jones, G. and Gorell, R. (2018) *How to Create a Coaching Culture*. London: Kogan Page.

Kapasi, A. and Brown, J. (2017) Strengths of caregivers raising a child with foetal alcohol spectrum disorder. *Child and Family Social Work*, 18(1): 721–30.

Kennedy, C., McIntyre, R., Worth, A. and Hogg, R. (2008) Supporting children and families facing the death of a parent: Part 1. *International Journal of Palliative Nursing*, 14(4): 162–8.

Ko, B. (2015) Education health and care plans: A new scheme for special educational needs and disability provisions in England from 2014. *Paediatrics and Child Health*, 25(10): 443–9.

Kydd, L., Anderson, L. and Newton, W. (2002) *Leading People and Teams in Education*. London: Sage.

Lamb, B. (2009) *Lamb Inquiry: Special needs and parental confidence*. Nottingham: DCSF Publications.

Lee, C.S.C. et al. (2017) Review: The effectiveness of mindfulness-based intervention in attention on individuals with ADHD: A systematic review. *Hong Kong Journal of Occupational Therapy*, 30: 33–41.

Lee, F. (2016) 'Self-harm training in secondary schools: An educational psychology intervention using interpretative phenomenological analysis', *Educational and Child Psychology*, 33(2): 105–16.

Longfield, A. (2017) *Briefing: Children's mental healthcare in England*. London: Children's Commissioner for England.

Longfield, A. (2018) *Vulnerability Report 2018*. London: Children's Commissioner for England.

Luck, C. (2003) *It's Good to Talk: An enquiry into the value of mentoring as an aspect of professional development for new headteachers*. Nottingham: NCSL.

Macaruso, P. and Rodman, A. (2009) Benefits of computer-assisted instruction for struggling readers in middle school. *European Journal of Special Needs Education*, 24: 103–13.

Macaruso, P. and Rodman, A. (2011) Efficacy of Computer-Assisted Instruction for the Development of Early Literacy Skills in Young Children. *Reading Psychology*, 32(2): 172–96.

Maher, A. (2016) Consultation, negotiation and compromise: The relationship between SENCOs, parents and pupils with SEN. *Support for Learning*, 31(1): 1–12.

Maher, A.J. and Vickerman, P. (2018) Ideology influencing action: Special educational needs co-ordinator and learning support assistant role conceptualisations and experiences of special needs education in England. *Journal of Research in Special Educational Needs*, 18(1): 15–24.

Malloch, S. and Trevarthen, C. (2009) *Communicative Musicality: Exploring the basis of human companionship*. Oxford: Oxford University Press.

Martin-Denham, S. (ed.) (2015) *Teaching Children with Special Educational Needs and Disabilities 0–25 Years*. London: Sage.

Masataka, N. (2018) Implications of the idea of neurodiversity for understanding the origins of developmental disorders. *Physics of Life Reviews*, 20: 85–108.

Maskey, M., Warnell, F., Parr, J., Couteur, A. and McConachie, H. (2013) Emotional and behavioural problems in children with Autism Spectrum Disorder. *Journal of Autism Developmental Disorders*, 43: 851–9.

Maximising the Impact of Teaching Assistants (MITA) (2016) Professional standards for Teaching Assistants. Available at: http://maximisingtas.co.uk/assets/content/ta-standards-final-june2016-1.pdf (Accessed 25 February 2019).

McArthur, G., Eve, P.M., Jones, K., Banales, E., Kohnen, S., Anandakumar, T., Larsen, L., Marinus, E., Wang-Hua, C. and Castles, A. (2012) Phonics training for English-speaking poor readers. *Cochrane Database of Systematic Reviews*, 12.

McAteer, M. (2013) *Action Research in Education*. London: Sage.

McClatchey, I. (2018) Fathers raising motherless children: Widowed men give voice to their lived experiences. *Omega: Journal of Death and Dying*, 76(4): 307–27.

McDowell, N. and Budd, J. (2018) The perspectives of teachers and paraeducators on the relationship between classroom clutter and learning experiences for students with cerebral visual impairment. *Journal of Visual Impairment and Blindness*, 112(3): 248–60.

McNiff, J. (2013) *Action Research: Principles and practice*. London: Routledge.

McNiff, J. and Whitehead, J. (2011) *All You Need to Know About Action Research*. London: Sage.

Megginson, D., Clutterbuck, D., Garvey, B., Stokes, P. and Garrett-Harris, P. (2006) *Mentoring in Action: A practical guide for managers*. 2nd edn. London: Kogan Page.

Mencap (2018) *What is a learning disability?*. Available at: https://www.mencap.org.uk/learning-disability-explained/what-learning-disability (Accessed 7 November 2018)

Mills, M. and Thomson, P. (2018) *Investigate Research into Alternative Provision*. London: DfE.

MIND (2017) Available at: www.mind.org.uk (Accessed 17 February 2017).

Mohanna, K. (2007) Change management. In R. Chambers, K. Mohanna, P. Spurgeon and D. Wall (eds) *How to Succeed as a Leader*. Abingdon: Radcliffe Publishing.

Molteni, P. and Maggiolini, S. (2015) Parents' perspectives towards the diagnosis of autism. *Journal of Child and Family Studies*, 24(4): 1088–96.

Monei, T. and Pedro, A. (2017) A systematic review of interventions for children presenting with dyscalculia in primary schools. *Educational Psychology in Practice*, 33(3): 277–93.

Moon, J. (2001) Learning through reflection. In F. Banks and A.S. Mayes (eds), *Early Professional Development for Teachers*. London: David Fulton.

Moon, J. (2006) *A Handbook of Reflective and Experiential Learning: Theory and practice*. London: Routledge.

Mottron, L. (2011) Changing perceptions: The power of autism. *Nature*, 479: 33–5.

Muris, P. and Ollendick, T. (2015) Children who are anxious in silence: A review on selective mutism, the new anxiety disorder in DSM-5. *Clinical Psychological Science Review*, 18: 151–69.

Murphy, M.J., Madelaine, R., Abel, M., Hoover, S., Jellinek, M. and Fazel, M. (2017) Scope, scale, and dose of the world's largest school-based mental health programs. *Harvard Review of Psychiatry*, 25(5): 1–11.

National Association of Head Teachers (NAHT) (2018) *Providing Mental Health Support for Children in Schools*. London: NAHT.

National Association of Special Educational Needs (NASEN) (2014) *SEN Support and the Graduated Approach*. Available at: www.nasen.org.uk (Accessed 15 March 2017).

National Autistic Society (2017) *What is Autism?* Available at: www.autism.org.uk (Accessed 16 March 2017).

National College of Teaching and Leadership (2011) *Teaching Standards*. London: NCTL.

National College of Teaching and Leadership (2014) *National Award for SEN Co-ordination Learning Outcomes*. London: NCTL.

National Deaf Children's Society (2018) *What is deafness?*. Available at: https://www.ndcs.org.uk/information-and-support/childhood-deafness/what-is-deafness/ (Accessed 12 December 2018)

National Health Service (2016) Available at: https://www.nhs.uk/conditions/psychosis/ (Accessed 26 March 2018)

National Health Service (2017) Available at: https://www.nhs.uk/using-the-nhs/nhs-services/mental-health-services/child-and-adolescent-mental-health-services-camhs/ (Accessed 26 March 2018)

National Health Service (2018a) Available at: https://www.nhs.uk/conditions/stress-anxiety-depression/anxiety-in-children/ (Accessed 26 March 2018)

References

National Health Service (2018b) Available at: https://www.nhs.uk/conditions/stress-anxiety-depression/mindfulness/ (Accessed 26 March 2018)

National Health Service (2018c) Available at: https://www.nhs.uk/conditions/obsessive-compulsive-disorder-ocd/ (Accessed 26 March 2018)

National Health Service (2018d) Available at: https://www.nhs.uk/conditions/selective-mutism/ (Accessed 26 March 2018)

National Health Service (2018e) Available at: https://www.nhs.uk/conditions/post-traumatic-stress-disorder-ptsd/symptoms/ (Accessed 26 March 2018)

National Health Service (2018f) Available at: https://www.nhs.uk/conditions/clinical-depression/ (Accessed 26 March 2018)

National Health Service (2018g) Available at: https://www.nhs.uk/conditions/bipolar-disorder/ (Accessed 26 March 2018)

National Health Service (2018h) Available at: https://www.nhs.uk/conditions/self-harm/ (Accessed 26 March 2018)

National Health Service (2018i) Available at: https://www.nhs.uk/conditions/eating-disorders/ (Accessed 26 March 2018)

National Health Service (2018j) Available at: https://www.nhs.uk/live-well/healthy-body/talking-about-drugs-with-your-child/ (Accessed 26 March 2018)

National Health Service (2018k) Available at: https://www.nhs.uk/conditions/developmental-coordination-disorder-dyspraxia/ (Accessed 26 March 2018)

National Health Service (2018l) Available at: https://www.nhs.uk/conditions/attention-deficit-hyperactivity-disorder-adhd/ (Accessed 26 March 2018)

National Health Service (2018m) Available at: https://www.nhs.uk/conditions/learning-disabilities/ (Accessed 26 March 2018)

National Health Service (2018n) Available at: https://www.nhs.uk/conditions/diabetes/ (Accessed 26 March 2018)

National Health Service (2018o) Available at: https://www.nhs.uk/conditions/type-1-diabetes/ (Accessed 26 March 2018)

National Health Service (2018p) Available at: https://www.nhs.uk/conditions/type-2-diabetes/ (Accessed 26 March 2018)

National Health Service Scotland (2017) *Mental Health: Inequality briefing 10*. Edinburgh: NHS Health Scotland.

National Institute for Health and Care Excellence (NICE) (2005) *Obsessive-compulsive disorder and body dysmorphic disorder: Treatment*. London: NICE.

National Institute for Health and Care Excellence (NICE) (2011) *Generalised anxiety disorder and panic disorder in adults: Management*. London: NICE.

National Institute for Health and Care Excellence (NICE) (2014) *Bipolar disorder: Assessment and management*. London: NICE.

National Institute for Health and Care Excellence (NICE) (2016a) *Mental health problems in people with learning disabilities: Prevention, assessment and management*. London: NICE.

National Institute for Health and Care Excellence (NICE) (2016b) *Psychosis and schizophrenia in children and young people: Recognition and management.* London: NICE.

National Institute for Health and Care Excellence (NICE) (2016c) *Autism spectrum disorder in under 19s: Recognition, referral and diagnosis.* London: NICE.

National Institute for Health and Care Excellence (NICE) (2017a) *Depression in children and young people: Identification and management.* London: NICE.

National Institute for Health and Care Excellence (NICE) (2017b) *Self harm in children and young people: Identification and management.* London: NICE.

National Institute for Health and Care Excellence (NICE) (2017c) *Eating disorders: Recognition and treatment.* London: NICE.

National Institute for Health and Care Excellence (NICE) (2018) *Attention deficit hyperactivity disorder: Diagnosis and management.* London: NICE.

National Society for the Prevention of Cruelty to Children (NSPCC) (2012) *NSPCC Research Ethics Committee: Guidance for applicants.* London: NSPCC.

National Society for the Prevention of Cruelty to Children (NSPCC) (2018a) *Emotional abuse: Signs, indicators and effects.* Available at: www.nspcc.org.uk (Accessed 28 May 2018).

National Society for the Prevention of Cruelty to Children (NSPCC) (2018b) *Sexual abuse: What is sexual abuse?* Available at: www.nspcc.org.uk (Accessed 28 May 2018).

National Society for the Prevention of Cruelty to Children (NSPCC) (2018c) *Domestic abuse: What is domestic abuse?* Available at: www.nspcc.org.uk (Accessed 28 May 2018).

National Society for the Prevention of Cruelty to Children (NSPCC) (2018d) *Self-harm.* Available at: www.nspcc.org.uk (Accessed 28 May 2018).

Nemanick, R. (2017) *The Mentor's Way: Eight Rules for Bringing out the Best in Others.* Abingdon: Routledge.

Ng, Q., Ho, C., Chan, H., Yong, B. and Yeo, W. (2017) Managing childhood and adolescent attention-deficit/hyperactivity disorder (ADHD) with exercise: A systematic review. *Complementary Therapies in Medicine*, 34: 123–8.

Noam, G.G., Malti, T. and Karcher, M.J. (2014) Mentoring relationships in developmental perspective. In D.L. DuBois and M.J. Karcher (eds), *Handbook of Youth Mentoring*. Los Angeles: Sage.

Northouse, P.G. (2016) *Leadership: Theory and practice.* 7th edn. London: Sage.

Norwich, B., Ylonen, A. and Gwernan-Jones, R. (2014) Moderate learning difficulties: Searching for clarity and understanding. *Research Papers in Education*, 29(1): 1–19.

Nyatanga, B. (2018) Loss, grief and bereavement: An inescapable link in palliative care. *British Journal of Community Nursing*, 23(2): 1462–75.

Obsessive Compulsive Disorder UK (OCD-UK) (2018) *What are obsessions?* Available at https://www.ocduk.org/ocd/obsessions/ (Accessed 7 June 2019).

Obsessive Compulsive Disorder UK (OCD-UK) (2019) *Introduction to Obsessive Compulsive Disorder.* Available at: https://www.ocduk.org/ocd/introduction-to-ocd/. (Accessed 7 June 2019).

O'Reilly, M. and Parker, N. (2013) 'Unsatisfactory saturation': A critical exploration of the notion of saturated sample sizes in qualitative research. *Qualitative Research*, 13(2): 190–7.

Office for National Statistics (ONS) (2017) *Statistical bulletin: Suicides in the UK – 2016 registrations.* London: ONS.

Office for Standards in Education (Ofsted) (2017a) *School inspection handbook for inspecting schools in England under section 5 of the Education Act 2005.* London: Ofsted.

Office for Standards in Education (Ofsted) (2017b) *Ofsted inspections clarification for schools: Handbook for inspecting schools in England under section 5 of the Education Act.* London: Ofsted.

Office for Standards in Education (Ofsted) (2018) *Positive environments where children can flourish.* London: Ofsted.

Office for Standards in Education (Ofsted) (2019) *The Education Inspection Framework (Draft).* London: Ofsted. Available at: www.gov.uk/government/publications/education-inspection-framework-draft-for-consultation (Accessed 1 April 2019).

Ogai, M., Matsumoto, H., Suzuki, K., Ozawa, F., Fukuda, R., Uchiyama, I., Sucklin, J., Isoda, H., Mori, H. and Takei, N. (2003) FMRI study of recognition of facial expressions in high-functioning autistic patients. *NeuroReport,* 14: 559–63.

Oon, P. (2010) Playing with Gladys: A case study integrating drama therapy with behavioural interventions for the treatment of selective mutism. *Clinical Child Psychology and Psychiatry,* 15: 215–30.

Palikara, O., Castro, S., Gaona, C. and Eirinaki, V. (2018) *Capturing the voices of children in the education, health and care plans: Are we there yet?* London: University of Roehampton.

Parkinson, J. (2012) *Establishing a core set of national, sustainable mental health indicators for children and young people in Scotland: Final Report.* NHS Scotland.

Parsons, S., Guldberg, K., MacLeod, A., Jones, G., Prunty, A. and Balfe, T. (2011) International review of the evidence on best practice in educational provision for children on the autism spectrum. *European Journal of Special Needs Education,* 26: 47–63.

Pask, R. and Joy, B. (2007) *Mentoring–coaching: a handbook for education professionals.* Maidenhead: Open University Press.

Patoss and Department for Education (DfE) (2018) *Teaching for Neurodiversity.* Available at: https://www.patoss-dyslexia.org/Neurodiversity (Accessed 1 November 2018).

Patterson, J. and Roberts, C. (2015) Severe profound and multiple difficulties. In S. Martin-Denham (ed.), *Teaching Children with Special Educational Needs and Disabilities.* London: Sage.

Pearce, C. (2017) *A Short Introduction to attachment and attachment disorder.* 2nd edn. London: Jessica Kingsley Publishers.

Pedler, M., Burgoyne, J. and Boydell, T. (2007) *A Manager's Guide to Self Development.* 5th edn. Maidenhead: McGraw-Hill.

Perry, B.D. and Pollard, R. (1998) Homeostasis, stress, trauma, and adaptation: A neurodevelopmental view of childhood trauma. *Child Adolescent Psychiatry Clin N Am,* 7(1): 33–51.

Peters, B. and Wood, W. (2017) Autism and equine-assisted interventions: A systematic mapping review. *Journal of Autism & Developmental Disorders,* 47(10): 3220–42.

Pienaar, F. and Johnston, P. (2018) Mental health in schools: In the eye of the storm. *Every Child Journal,* 6.3/6.4: 1–6.

Public Health England (2018) *Severe mental illness (SMI) and physical health inequalities: Briefing.* London: Public Health England.

Ramsden, P. (1998) *Learning to Lead in Higher Education.* London: Routledge.

Rauh, S., Irwin, P. and Vath, N. (2016) Giving children hope: A treatment model for high-conflict separation families. *Canadian Journal of Counselling and Psychotherapy*, 50: 93–108.

Read, S. and Bowler, C. (2007) Life story work and bereavement: Shared reflections on its usefulness. *Learning Disability Practice*, 10(5): 45–53.

Rees, K. (2017) Models of disability and the categorisation of children with severe and profound learning difficulties: Informing educational approaches based on an understanding of individual needs. *Educational and Child Psychology*, 34(4): 30–39.

Rethink (2018) Available at: www.rethink.org (Accessed 26 March 2018).

Riviere, H. (2016) Using student engagement theory to explore inclusion for pupils with SEN in mainstream schools in England. In *Papers from the Education Doctoral Research Conference 2015*. University of Birmingham: Birmingham, pp. 115–21.

Rochford, D. (2016) *The Rochford Review: Final report – Review of assessment for pupils working below the standard of national curriculum tests*. London: Standards and Testing Agency.

Rogers, E.M. (1995) *Diffusion of Innovations*. 4th edn. New York: Simon and Schuster.

Saddler, H.J. (2015) Management of Teaching Assistants to Promote the Social Inclusion of Children Identified with Special Educational Needs in Mainstream English Primary Schools (Doctoral dissertation, University of York).

Schaffer, H. and Emerson, P. (1964) The development of social attachments in infancy. *Monographs of the Society for Research in Child Development*, 29(3):1–77.

Schofield, T., Donnellan, B., Merrick, M., Ports, K., Klevens, J. and Leeb, R. (2018) Intergenerational Continuity in Adverse Childhood Experiences and Rural Community Environments. *American Journal of Public Health*. 108(9): 1148–52.

Schmidt, J., Shumow, L. and Kackar-Cam, H. (2017) Does mindset intervention predict students' daily experience in classrooms? *Journal of Youth and Adolescence*, 46(3): 582–602.

Schreiber, J., Sands, D. and Jordan, J. (2017) The perceived experience of children bereaved by parental suicide. *Omega: Journal of Death and Dying*, 75(2): pp. 184–206.

SCOPE (2018) *Social Model of Disability*. Available at: https://www.scope.org.uk/about-us/social-model-of-disability/ (Accessed 7 November 2018)

Scrase, R. (1998) An evaluation of multisensory speaking computer based systems (Starcross-IDL) designed to teach the literacy skills of reading. *British Journal of Educational Technology*, 29(3): 211–24.

Sebba, J., Berridge, D., Luke, N., Fletcher, J., Bell, K., Strand, S., Thomas, S., Sinclair, I. and O'Higgins, A. (2015) *The Educational Progress of Looked After Children in England: Linking care and educational data*. London: Nuffield Foundation.

Selective Mutism Information and Research Association (SMIRA) (2019) *About Selective Mutism*. Available at: www.selectivemutism.org.uk/about-selective-mutism (Accessed 7 June 2019).

SENSE (2018) *Information and advice*. Available at: https://www.sense.org.uk/get-support/information-and-advice/(Accessed 8 November 2018)

Sharples, J., Webster, R. and Blatchford, P. (2015) *Making Best Use of Teaching Assistants: Guidance report*. London: Education Endowment Foundation.

Sharples, J., Albers, B. and Fraser, S. (2018) *Putting Evidence to Work: A school's guide to Implementation*. London: Education Endowment Foundation.

Shevlin, M., Kenny, M. and Loxley, A. (2008) A time of transition: Exploring special educational provision in the Republic of Ireland. *Journal of Research in Special Educational Needs*, 8(3): 41–152.

Shonkoff, J.P., Garner, A.S., Siegel, B.S., Dobbins, M.I., Earls, M.F., McGuinn, L., Pascoe, J. and Wood, D.L. (2012) The lifelong effects of early childhood adversity and toxic stress. *Pediatrics*, 129(1): 232–46.

Simmons, K. and Douglas, D. (2018) After the storm: Helping children cope with trauma after natural disasters. *Communique*, 46(5): 23–5.

Skokauskas, N. and Gallagher, L. (2010) Psychosis, affective disorders and anxiety in ASD: Prevalence and nosological considerations. *Psychopathology: International Journal of Descriptive and Experimental Psychopathology, Phenomenology and Psychiatric Diagnosis*, 43: 8–16.

Slack, K., Font, S. and Jones, J. (2017) The complex interplay of adverse childhood experiences, race, and income. *Health and Social Work*, 42(1): 24–31.

Smith, B. and Sluckin, A. (2015) *Tackling Selective Mutism: A guide for professionals and parents*. London: Jessica Kingsley.

Smits-Engelsman, B., Vincon, S., Blank, R., Quadrodo, V., Polatajko, H. and Wilson, P. (2018) Evaluating the evidence for motor-based interventions in developmental coordination disorder: A systematic review and meta-analysis. *Research in Developmental Disabilities*, 74: 72–102.

Söderqvist, S. and Nutley, S. (2016) *Cogmed Working Memory Training: Claims and Evidence*. London: Pearson.

SPARK (2017) *Autism Research*. Available at: https://sparkforautism.org/autism-research (Accessed 26 March 2017).

Sport England (2018) *Our Strategy*. Available at: https://www.sportengland.org/active-nation/our-strategy/ (Accessed 1 December 2018)

Steensel, F., Bogels, S. and Wood, J. (2013) Autism spectrum traits in children with anxiety disorders. *Journal of Autism Developmental Disorders*, 43: 361–70.

Stenhouse, L. (1975) *Introduction to Curriculum Research and Development*. London: Heineman Education.

Storey, A. (2001) *Performance Review: Opportunities for teachers in the early stages of their career*. London: David Fulton.

Su Maw, S. and Haga, C. (2018) Effectiveness of cognitive, developmental, and behavioural interventions for Autism Spectrum Disorder in preschool-aged children: A systematic review and meta-analysis. *Heliyon*, 4(9): e00763.

Suarez-Manzano, S., Ruiz-Ariza, A., De La Torre-Cruz, M. and Martinez-Lopez, E. (2018) Acute and chronic effect of physical activity on cognition and behaviour in young people with ADHD: A systematic review of intervention studies. *Research in Developmental Disabilities*, 77: 12–23.

Swartz, A. (2016) One big mystery, many autisms. *Newsweek Global*, 167(6): 46–9.

Szucs, D. and Goswami, U. (2013) Developmental dyscalculia: Fresh perspectives. *ScienceDirect*, 2(2): 33–94.

Tapper, J. (2018) Burned out: Why are so many teachers quitting or off sick with stress? *The Guardian*, 13 May. Available at: www.theguardian.com/education/2018/may/13/teacher-burnout-shortages-recruitment-problems-budget-cuts (Accessed 3 September 2018).

Taylor, C., Spriggs, A., Jones, M., Flanagan, S. and Sartini, E. (2017) A systematic review of weighted vests with individuals with autism spectrum disorder. *Research in Autism Spectrum Disorder*, 37: 49–60.

Teaching Schools Council (2016) *National standards for school-based initial teacher training (ITT) mentors.* London: HMSO.

Thapar, A., Collishaw, S., Pine, D. and Thapar, A. (2012) Depression in adolescence. *The Lancet,* 379: 1056–67.

The Dyslexia-SpLD Trust (2018) Available at: www.thedyslexia-spldtrust.org.uk (Accessed 28 October 2018).

The Mental Health Taskforce (2016) *The five year forward view for mental health.* London: NHS Taskforce.

Thomas, C. (2013) *Adoption for looked after children: Messages from research.* London: British Association for Adoption and Fostering.

Thomas, G. (2009) *How to do Your Research Project: A guide for students in education and applied sciences.* London: Sage.

Thorley, W. and Coates, A. (2018) *Let's talk about: Child to parent violence and aggression.* Amazon books.

Tolhurst, J. (2010) *The essential guide to coaching and mentoring* (2nd edn). Harlow: Longman/Pearson Education.

Townsend, H. (2017) *What survival looks like in school.* Inner World Work.

Tuffrey-Wijne, I. (2013) *How to Break Bad News: To people with learning disabilities.* London: Jessica Kingsley Publishers.

Turney, T. (2018) Adverse childhood experiences among children of incarcerated parents. *Children and Youth Services Review,* 89: 218–25.

UNICEF (2008) *Behind Closed Doors: The impact of domestic violence on children.* New York: UNICEF.

United Nations (2006) *Convention on the Rights of Persons with Disabilities.* Geneva: UN.

United Nations International Children's Emergency Fund (UNICEF) (1989) *The United Nations Convention on the Rights of the Child* (UNCRC). London: UNICEF UK.

United Nations Office on Drugs and Crime (2015) *International Standards on Drug Use Prevention.* Vienna: United Nations.

United Nations Office on Drugs and Crime (2017) *Executive Summary: Conclusions and policy implications, hard drug report 2017.* Vienna: United Nations.

Valdebenito, S., Eisner, M., Farrington, D., Ttofi, M. and Sutherland, A. (2018) School-based interventions for reducing disciplinary school exclusion: A systematic review. *Campbell Systematic Reviews,* 14: 1–13.

Valentine, C., Bauld, L. and Walter, T. (2016) Bereavement following substance misuse. *Omega: Journal of Death and Dying,* 72(4): 283–301.

van Nieuwerburgh, C. (2014) *An Introduction to Coaching Skills: A practical guide.* Los Angeles: Sage.

Viana, A., Beidel, D. and Rabian, B. (2009) Selective mutism: A review and integration of the last 15 years. *Clinical Psychology Review,* 29: 57–67.

Waring, M. (2017) Finding your theoretical position. In R. Coe, M. Waring, L.V. Hedges and J. Arthur (eds), *Research Methods and Methodologies in Education.* London: Sage, pp.15–20.

Wedell, K. (2017) Points from the SENCo-Forum: SENCos supporting parents. *British Journal of Special Education,* 44(4): 484–7.

White, J. and Rae, T. (2016) Person-centred reviews and transition: An exploration of the views of students and their parents/carers. *Educational Psychology in Practice,* 32(1): 38–53.

Whitmore, J. (2017) *Coaching for Performance* (5th edn). London: Nicholas Brearley Publishing.

Whittaker Dunlop, C. (2017) The Success and Failure of the Coaching Industry. Available at: www.forbes.com/sites/forbescoachescouncil/2017/10/05/the-success-and-failure-of-the-coaching-industry/#71b4e9246765 (Accessed 13th March 2019).

Wing, L. and Gould, J. (1979) Severe impairments of social interaction and associated abnormalities in children: Epidemiology and classification. *Journal of Autism and Developmental Disorders*, 9: 11–29.

World Health Organization (WHO) (2011) *Mental Health: A state of wellbeing*. Available at: www.who.int/features/factfiles/mental_health/en (Accessed 20 March 2018).

World Health Organization (2016) *Visual Impairment and Blindness*. Available at: www.who.int/mediacentre/factsheets/fs282/en (Accessed 10 March 2017).

World Health Organization (2018) *Mental Health Action Plan 2013–2020*. Geneva: World Health Organization.

Young, H. and Garrard, B. (2016) Bereavement and loss: Developing a memory box to support a young woman with profound learning disabilities. *British Journal of Learning Disabilities*, 44(1): 78–84.

Youngminds (2019) *Mental Health Statistics*. Available at: https://youngminds.org.uk/about-us/media-centre/mental-health-stats/ (Date accessed 1 June 2019)

Zakopoulou, V., Mavreas, V., Christodoulides, P., Lavidas, A., Fili, E., Georgiou, G., Dimakopoulos, G. and Vergou, M. (2014) Specific learning difficulties: A retrospective study of their comorbidity and continuity as early indicators of mental disorders. *Research In Developmental Disabilities*, 35(12): 3496–507.

Index

abuse, 85–87, **86**, *87*, 97
accessibility plans, 210, **211**
acquired vision loss, 198
action research
   data analysis and, 76
   different approaches to, 64–65
   dissemination and, 76–77
   ethical considerations and, 71–76, **72–73**, *74*
   origins and concept of, 63, *63*
   planning for, 65, **65–66**
   research methods for, 66–71, 75
   teachers and, 62
Adams, L., 230
ADHD Foundation, 181
ADHD Institute, 179
Adolescent to Parent Violence and Abuse (APVA), 220
adverse childhood experiences (ACEs)
   approaches to, 91–94, **92–93**, *93*
   concept of, 82
   impact of, 83–91, **84**, *85*, *87*, *91*
   survey on, 82–83, **82–83**
   See also looked after and permanently placed children
Advisory Centre for Education (ACE), 218
Ainscow, M., 219
Alloway, R. G., 163
Alloway, T. P., 163
Alternative Provision (AP), 215
ambivalent attachment, 103–104

American Psychiatric Association (APA), 172
American Psychological Association (APA), 98
Anorexia and Bulimia Care (ABC), 147
anorexia nervosa, 144. *See also* eating disorders
antidepressants, 135
anxiety, 124–127, **126**, 182–183
appraisal (performance review), 278
apraxia of gaze, 198
Armstrong, T., 162
Ascentis, 169
Ashdown, L., 278–279
assessment, 46
assistive technologies, 200
Association for Coaching, 273
atomoxetine, 181
attachment, 102–104, **103**
attention deficit hyperactivity disorder (ADHD)
   co-existence of, 166, 173, 176, 178, 182, 186
   evidence-based programmes, apps and resources for, 180–182, **181**
   learning disabilities and, 123
   overview of, 162, 178–180
autism
   CCVAB and, 220
   co-existence of, 176, 178, 182–183, 186
   evidence-based approaches for, 184–186, **185**
   mental health and, 123, 147–148
   overview of, 162, 182–184
avoidant attachment, 103–104

Baddeley, A., 163
Bakian, A., 182
Barlé, N., 147
Barnett, B., 266
Barrett, P., 125
Barumandzadeh, R., 89–90
Basford, E., 245
Beacon House, 94, 102, 112
BEAT, 146, 147
Beaton, S., 142
Bellis, M.A., 82, 83, 91
Bennett, T., 218
bereavement and loss, 89–90, 98–101, **99**, *100–101*, 104–106, *105–107*, 147–148. *See also* grief
Biesta, G., 70
binge eating disorder (BED), 145
bipolar disorder, 136–138
BipolarUK, 138
Blanchard, K., 36
Boettcher, L., 191
Bomber, L., 103
Booth, T., 219
Bork, P., 131
Bowlby, J., 103
Boxhall Profile, 121
British Dyslexia Association (BDA), 162, 165–166, 172
British Educational Research Association (BERA), 72
British Institute of Learning Disabilities (BILD), 192
Brodovsky, B., 100
Budd, J., 199
bulimia, 144. *See also* eating disorders
Burgess, H., 276
Bush, D., 265–266
Butterworth, B., 173

CALL Scotland, 171
CARE approach, 109–111, **110**, *111*
care orders, 96
caregivers
    children who display challenging, violent or aggressive behaviour and, 223–224
    exclusions and, 218
    family leadership and, 234–237
    parental divorce, separation or death and, 89–90
    support for, 29
    transitions and, 202–203, 237–240, **240**
    use of term, 3
Carter Review (2015), 261, 263, 276
Center for the Developing Child at Harvard University, 102, 113
Centre for the Use of Research Evidence in Education (CUREE), 263–264, **263**
change, 39–41, **40**
Change, Grow, Live, 159
Charlie Waller Memorial Trust, 135
child, use of term, 3
Child and Adolescent Mental Health Services (CAMHS), 120, 137
Child Bereavement Network, 155
Child Bereavement UK, 142, 143, 147–148, 149, 150–155
Child Death Helpline, 155
Child to Parent Violence (CPV), 220
Child Trauma Academy, 102, 113
child voice checklist, 232, **233**
Childhood Bereavement Network, 149
Childline, 119, 141, 159
Children Act (1989), 86, 96
Children Act (2004), 86
Children and Families Act (CAFA) (2014), 8–9, 14, 15, 73, 190, 230, 234
Children and Young People Service (CYPS), 121
Children Experiencing Loss and Trauma (CEL&T), 94, 102–103, 112
children in need, 96. *See also* looked after and permanently placed children
Children who display Challenging, Violent or Aggressive Behaviour (CCVAB), 220–224, **221–224**
Clinical Commissioning Groups (CCGs), 120, 128
Cloverleaf model, 268
coaching
    benefits of, 264–266
    children and, 267–269, **269**
    code of ethics for, 273
    collaborative and alternative approaches to, 271
    government policy on, 261–264, *262*, **263**
    mentoring and, 261
    models of, 269–270, **270**
    overview of, 258, 260–261
coaching culture, 265, 266–267, **266–267**
Coates, A., 220, 223
Cochrane Database of Systematic Reviews (CDSR), 165
code. *See* Special Educational Needs and Disability Code of Practice
Cogmed working memory training (CWMT), 164
cognition and learning, 16
Cognitive Behavioural Therapy (CBT), 125, 132, 139
Cohn, R., 172
Collier, J., 63
communication and interaction, 15–16
Communication Trust, 16, 282
community of practice, 276–277
conductive deafness, 199
confidentiality, 75
congenital deafblindness, 200
congenital vision loss, 198
Contact, 239
Contact a Family, 205
continuing professional development (CPD), 258, 261, 280–281, **282**
Coram Legal Centre, 218
Council for Disabled Children, 28, 201–202
Couper, S., 91–92
Crenna-Jennings, W., 120
Crowley, S., 277, 283
cultural-historical model of disability, 191–192

Daily Mile, 196
Dammeyer, J., 191
data analysis, 76
data collection
    child's progress and, 48–49
    comparative data and, 52–54, *53–57*, **55–56**
    Ofsted inspections and, 47, **47**
    overview of, 46–47
    provision management and, 49–50
    teacher accountability and, 57–58, *58*
data presentation, 50–52, **50**
Data Protection Officer (DPO), 59
data sharing, 58–59
deafblindness, 16, 200
deafness, 199
death, 89–90
DeBooth, K., 183
debriefing processes, 220–224, **221–223**

Department for Education and Skills, 194
Department for Education (DfE)
    on autism, 183–184
    on behaviour, 219
    on child abuse, 86
    on children with SEN, 10
    on continuing professional development, 280–281
    on curriculum, 46
    on designated teachers, 107
    on disability, 190
    on exclusions, 214, 215, 216, 218
    on Individual Health Care Plans, 205
    on looked after and permanently placed children, 103, 105
    on mental health, 116–117, 119
    national statistics and, 57
    on Ofsted, 47
    on outcomes, 21
    on privacy notices, 59
    on school finances, 92
    on SENCO, 34
    on TA standards, 247–248
    on virtual school heads, 106
Department of Health (DoH), 86, 117, 118–119, 124, 133
depression, 133–136, **135**, 138, 183
Derrick, S., 272
Designated Schools Grant (DSG), 31
Designated Senior Lead for Mental Health and Wellbeing, 117–118
designated teachers, 107–108
Developmental Coordination Disorder (DCD), 16. *See also* dyspraxia
developmental dyscalculia (DD), 172. *See also* dyscalculia
Dewey, J., 62, 276
dexamfetamine, 181
diabetes, 195–196
Diabetes UK, 196
DigiBete, 196
disability
    assistive technologies and, 200
    concept and definitions of, 10–11, 190, 206
    four broad areas of need and, 15–16
    models of, 190–192, **190**, **192**
    provision and practice and, 201–202, *202*
    risk assessment and, 201, **201**
    See also learning disabilities
disability discrimination, 209
disability equality, 210
disagreement resolution arrangements, 32
disorganised attachment, 103–104
dissemination, 76–77
divorce, 89–90
domestic violence, 87–88
Done, E., 34
Downey, M., 260
Driver Youth Trust, 281
drugs (substance misuse), 155–159, **157–159**
DrugWise, 156
Dual Sensory Impairment, 16, 200
Dynamo Maths, 175
dyscalculia, 16, 172–175, **173–175**
dysgraphia, 162
dyslexia
    co-existence of, 166, 173, 176
    evidence-based programmes, apps and resources for, 168–169, *169*, **170–171**, *172*
    overview of, 16, 162, 165–168, **166–168**

Dyslexia-SpLD Trust, 168–169
dyspraxia, 162, 175–178, **177–178**
Dyspraxia Foundation, 175

eating disorders, 144–147, **145–146**
Education Act (1996), 214
Education Act (2011), 214
Education Endowment Foundation (EEF), 122–123, 246
Education, Health and Care Plans (EHCPs), 25–30, **27–29**, 230–231
Education Support Partnership, 112
Educational Excellence Everywhere (DfE), 261
Edukey Provision Map, 23, 49–50, *49*
Elliott, J., 62
Emerson, P.E., 102
emotional abuse, 86, **86**
epilepsies, 197
Epilepsy Action, 197
epistemology, 66
Equality Act (2010), 9, 10–11, 162, 190–191, 205–208, 214, 219
Equality Act (2010) (Disability Regulations) (2010), 9
Estyn, 233
ethics and ethical considerations, 71–76, **72–73**, *74*, 273
exclusions
    caregivers and, 218
    children who display challenging, violent or aggressive behaviour and, 220–224, **221–224**
    as official and unofficial, 216, **217**
    prevention of, 218–219, **219**
    reasons for, 215–216, *216*
    types of, 214–215, *214*
Eye Movement Desensitisation and Reprocessing (EMDR), 132

Fajerman, L., 231
family leadership, 234–237, **235–236**
Farrell, M., 182, 183
FASD Network UK, 198
Felitti, V.J., 82, 83
fixed-term exclusions, 215
flash mentoring, 272–273
Florian, L., 280
focus groups, 69
Foetal Alcohol Spectrum Disorder (FASD), 197–198
Food and Agriculture Organization (FAO), 88
Food Insecurity Experience Scale (FIES), 89
Fostering for Adoption (FfA) placement, 96
FRANK, 159
Frenette, P., 183–184
FRIENDS resilience, 125
Friswell, J., 236
funding, 30–32

Gallagher, L., 182–183
Gallwey, T., 260
Garrard, B., 153, 154
gatekeepers, 73
General Data Protection Regulation (GDPR), 47, 58–59, 75
generalised anxiety disorder (GAD), 124–127, **126**
Generation Y (Millennials), 259–260
Gill, K., 215
Gorell, R., 261, 266, 267
graduated approach, 17–19, **18–19**, *18*
graduated exposure therapy (systematic desensitisation), 130

graffiti walls, 231
Greenwood, J., 281
grief, 148–155, **149–150**, *151–152*, **154**. *See also* bereavement and loss
Grossman, J., 183
GROW model, 270, **270**
growth mindset, 126
guanfacine, 181

Harmless, 141
Hearing Impairment (HI), 16
hearing loss, 199
Heikkinen, H., 271
Hellawell, B., 235–236
Hersey, P., 36
Higgins, E., 125
Hitch, G., 163
Homer, 258
Horridge, K., 192
hunger, 88–89
Hutchinson, J., 120
hypos (hypoglycemia or low blood glucose), 196

IDL Literacy, 169, *169*
Illiad (Homer), 258
Independent Parental Special Education Advice (IPSEA), 214, 218, 239
Individual Health Care Plans (IHCPs), 119, 203–205, *204*
Information, Advice and Support Service (IASS), 239
informed consent, 73–74, *74*
Ingram, J., 174
Initial Teacher Education (ITE), 276, 280
The Inner Game of Tennis (Gallwey), 260
Inner World Work, 94, 102, 103, 113
insecure ambivalent attachment, 103–104
insecure avoidant attachment, 103–104
insecure disorganised attachment, 103–104
intelligence quotient (IQ), 192–193
International Coaching Foundation, 273
International Dyslexia Association, 165–166
International Statistical Classification of Diseases (ICD), 116, 134
intervention programmes, 246, 247, 249–250, 253–256, *254*, **255**
interviews, 68–69, 70–71, 73–76
Irlen Syndrome, 171

Jones, A., 90
Jones, G., 261, 266, 267
Joy, B., 259

Kantor, J. S., 259–260
Kelly, C., 281
Kennedy, C., 148
Kiernan, K., 100
Kydd, L., 35

Lamb Inquiry (2009), 234
leadership
    change and, 39–41, **40**
    concept and models of, 35–37, **36**
    self-analysis of, 37–39, **37–38**
    teamwork and, 41–42
LEAP model, 269
learning disabilities
    mental health and, 123, 147–148
    overview of, 192–195, **192–194**
    See also neurodiversity; sensory and/or physical needs; specific learning disabilities
learning walks, 185–186
Lewin, K., 63
Lexia, 169
lisdexamfetamine, 181
literature review, 67
Local Authority Interactive Tool, 53–54, *53–54*
local offer, 15
Longfield, A., 117, 120, 160
looked after and permanently placed children
    attachment and, 102–104, **103**
    CARE approach and, 109–111, **110**, *111*
    concept and statistics on, 96–98, *96–97*
    designated teachers and, 107–108
    resources for, 112–113
    trauma and loss in, 98–101, **99**, *100–101*, 104–106, *105–107*
    trauma-informed approaches and, 108–109
    virtual school heads and, 106, 108
    See also adverse childhood experiences (ACEs)
loss, 89–90, 98–101, **99**, *100–101*, 104–106, *105–107*, 147–148. *See also* grief
Luck, C., 265

Mackie, P., 91–92
Maggiolini, S., 183
Maher, A., 234
management, 35, 38–39
Maskey, M., 182
Mathletics, 174
McAteer, M., 77
McDowell, N., 199
McNiff, J., 63, 64, 65
Meares-Irlen Syndrome, 171
mediation, 32
medical model of disability, 191
medication, 135, 137, 139, 181
Megginson, D., 259
MENCAP, 192
Men's Advice Line, 88
mental health, 116. *See also* social, emotional and mental health (SEMH) needs and difficulties
Mental Health Act (1983), 159
Mental Health Taskforce, 119
mentoring
    benefits of, 264–266
    children and, 267–269
    coaching and, 261
    code of ethics for, 273
    collaborative and alternative approaches to, 271–273
    government policy on, 261–264, *262*, **263**
    models of, 270
    overview of, 258–260
mentoring culture, 265, 266–267, **266–267**
methylphenidate, 181
Middlewood, T., 265–266
Millennials (Generation Y), 259–260
Mills, M., 214–215
MIND, 138, 140, 155
mind mapping, 231, *232*
mindfulness, 125
The Mix, 127
mixed deafness, 199
mixed methods, 70
moderate learning difficulties (MLD), 2, 16, 194
Mohanna, K., 39–40
Molteni, P., 183

Moon, J., 277
Motor ABC, 176
Multi-Sensory Impairment (MSI), 16, 200
Muris, P., 129
Murphy, M.J., 125

National Association of Head Teachers, 120
National Association of Special Educational Needs (NASEN), 282
National Association of Virtual School Headteachers (NAVSH), 103
National Autistic Society, 218
National Award for Special Educational Needs Coordination (NASENCO), 2–3, 34, 71–72
National Centre for Eating Disorders (NCFED), 147
National Deaf Children's Society, 199
National Domestic Violence Helpline, 88
National Framework for Mentoring and Coaching, 263–264, **263**
National Health Service (NHS)
  on adverse childhood experiences, 91
  on anxiety, 124–125
  on attention deficit hyperactivity disorder, 179
  on autism, 183
  on bipolar disorder, 136
  on depression, 133
  on dyspraxia, 175–176
  on eating disorders, 145–146
  on learning disabilities, 192
  on mental health, 118, 120
  on obsessive compulsive disorders, 127
  on psychosis, 138–139
  on PTSD, 131
  on selective mutism, 129
  on self-harm, 140–141
  on substance misuse, 156
National Institute for Health and Care Excellence (NICE)
  on anxiety, 124–125
  on attention deficit hyperactivity disorder, 178, 179
  on autism, 183, 184
  on bipolar disorder, 136
  on depression, 133
  on eating disorders, 145–146
  on Obsessive Compulsive Disorders, 127–128
  on psychosis, 138–139
  on self-harm, 141
National Network of Parent Carer Forums, 239
National Society for Prevention of Cruelty to Children (NSPCC), 72, 73, 87, 141
National Standards for School-Based ITT Mentors, 263–264
national statistics, 57
natural bereavement, 147
neglect, 86, **86**, 97
Nemanick, R., 259, 270
neurodiversity
  concept of, 162–163, *162–163*, 193–194
  cultural-historical model of disability and, 192, **192**
  general learning and teaching approaches for, 165, **165**
  systematic reviews of, 164–165
  working memory and, 163–164, **164**
New Mental Health Support Teams, 117
No panic, 127
Noam, G., 268
non-participant observation, 67–68
Norwich, B., 2, 193
Number Catcher, 175

Number Race, 175
Numicon, 175
Nyatanga, B., 148

observation, 67–68
Obsessive Compulsive Disorders (OCD), 127–129, 183
OCD Action, 129
OCD-UK, 127–129
official exclusions, 216, **217**
Ofsted, 42–43, **43**, 47, **47**, 219
Ogai, M., 183
Ollendick, T., 129
O'Mahony, G., 266
one-page profiles. *See* pupil passport (school passport)
ontology, 66
Oppositional Defiant Disorder (ODD), 182–183
optic ataxia, 198
O'Reilly, M., 122
O'Sullivan, S., 125
other specified feeding or eating disorder (OSFED), 145

PAC-UK, 103
Palikara, O., 230
parents. *See* caregivers
Parker, N., 122
Parkinson, J., 116
participant observation, 67–68
Pask, R., 259
Pearce, C., 109
Pedler, M., 38–39
peer-group mentoring (PGM), 271–272
performance review (appraisal), 278
permanent exclusions (PE), 214–215, *214*
person-centred approaches (PCA)
  concept of, 230
  family leadership and, 234–237, **235–236**
  transitions and, 237–240, **238**, **240**
  voice of the child and, 230–232, *232*, **233**
  whole school approaches and, 233–234
personal budgets, 31–32
Personal Education Plans (PEPs), 108
physical abuse, 86–87
Physical Disability (PD), 16. *See also* sensory and/or physical needs
pilots, 70–71
Place2Be, 120
placement orders, 96
Post-Traumatic Stress Disorder (PTSD), 131–132
practitioner enquiry, 62. *See also* action research
prison, 90–91, *91*
privacy notices, 59
process-oriented approaches, 177
professional learning, 276–283, **277**, **282**
profound and multiple learning difficulties (PMLD), 16
psychological contract, 278–279
psychosis, 138–139
psychotherapy, 132, 137, 139
pupil passport (school passport), 23, 208, *208–209*
Pupil Premium Plus (PP+), 108
Pupil Referral Units (PRUs), 203

questionnaires, 70–71

Rae, T., 235
Ramsden, P., 37
Rauh, S., 90
reflection-in-action, 276

reflection-on-action, 276
reflective diary, 71
reflective journals, 277–278
reflective learning, 276–277
reflective practice, 62
Relate, 90
research methodology, 66
research methods, 66–71, 75
resilience, 91–92
Rethink Mental Illness, 139, 143
Reynolds, S., 183
risk assessment, 201, **201**
Rochford Review (2016), 46

Samaritans, 136
Save the Children, 231
Schaffer, H.R., 102
schizophrenia, 123, 138
Schmidt, J., 126
Schofield, T.J., 92
Schön, D.A., 276
school, use of term, 3
School Exclusions Service, 218
school passport (pupil passport), 23
SchoolBeat, 159–160
Schreiber, J., 142
SCOPE, 200, 205
Scotopic Sensitivity, 171
Sebba, J., 104
sectioning, 159–160
secure attachment, 103–104
selective mutism (SM), 129–131, **131**
Selective Mutism Information and Research Association (SMIRA), 130, 131
Selective Serotonin Reuptake Inhibitors (SSRIs), 125
self-evaluation tools, 11, **12–13**
self-harm, 140–142, **140–141**
semi-structured interviews, 68
SEN information report, 11–14
SEN register, 19–20
SEN support, 17–25, **18–19**, *18*, **22–23**
SEND Gateway, 282
SENDirect, 239
SENSE, 198, 200
sensorineural deafness, 199
sensory and/or physical needs, 16, 195–200
Sensory Processing Disorder (SPD), 162, 186–187
separation, 89–90
severe learning difficulties (SLD), 16
Severe Mental Illness (SMI), 119
sexual abuse, 87, *87*
shaping (vocalisation ladder), 130
Shonkoff, J.P., 83, 84
sight loss, 198–199
simultanagnosia, 198
Singer, J., 162
situational leadership II (SLII), 36–37
Skokauskas, N., 182–183
sliding in technique (stimulus fading), 130
Sluckin, A., 129
SMART outcomes, 26, 27, **27**
Smith, B., 129
Smits-Engelsman, B., 177–178
SNAP-Behaviour (SNAP-B), 224
social, emotional and mental health (SEMH) needs and difficulties
 anxiety and, 124–127, **126**
 assessment tools for, 121
 bipolar disorder and, 136–138
 Children and Young People Service and, 121
 concept of, 16, 116–117
 depression and, 133–136, **135**, 138
 Designated Senior Lead for Mental Health and Wellbeing and, 117–118
 eating disorders and, 144–147, **145–146**
 evidence-based interventions and approaches to, 122–123, **122–123**
 grief and, 148–155, **149–150**, *151–152*, **154**
 health and wellbeing agenda and, 120–121
 loss and, 147–148
 Obsessive Compulsive Disorders (OCD) and, 127–129
 Post-Traumatic Stress Disorder and, 131–132
 prevalence and indicators of, 118–119, *118*, **119**
 psychosis and, 138–139
 range of challenges in, 123
 sectioning and, 159–160
 selective mutism and, 129–131, **131**
 self-harm and, 140–142, **140–141**
 substance misuse and, 155–159, **157–159**
 suicide and, 142–144, **144**
 See also attention deficit hyperactivity disorder (ADHD); autism
social model of disability, 191
SPARK, 183
special educational needs (SEN)
 concept of, 9–10, *10*
 four broad areas of need and, 15–16
 SEN information report and, 11–14
 SEN register and, 19–20
 SEN support and, 17–25, **18–19**, *18*, **22–23**
Special Educational Needs and Disability Code of Practice
 on caregivers, 234
 on child's progress, 48
 on evidence-based practice, 165
 on high quality teaching, 10, 280
 on interviews with children, 73
 on learning disabilities, 192
 on mental health, 116–117
 overview of, 8
 on person-centred approaches, 230
 on SEN support, 17, 20, 24
 on SENCO, 34, 41
 on social, emotional, mental health difficulties, 16
 on teacher accountability, 58
 on transitions, 237
Special Educational Needs and Disability Regulations (2014), 8, 9, 11, **14**, 15
Special Educational Needs Coordinator (SENCO)
 Ofsted inspections and, 42–43, **43**
 role of, 34–35, **35**, 41. *See also* leadership
 self-evaluation tools for, 11, **12–13**
 See also National Award for Special Educational Needs Coordination (NASENCO)
Special Educational Needs (Personal Budgets) Regulations (2014), 9
Special Educational Provision (SEP), 10
special guardianship, 96
specialists, 41–42
specific learning difficulties (SpLD), 16, 162. *See also* neurodiversity
Speech, Language and Communication Needs (SLCN), 15–16
SPELL framework, 185–186
Sport England, 180

Spratt, J., 280
staff development, 258, 278. *See also* coaching; mentoring
STAR Institute, 187
Steensel, F., 182–183
Stenhouse, L., 62
stimulus fading (sliding in technique), 130
Storey, A., 278
Strengths and Difficulties Questionnaire (SDQ), 121
stress, 84, 91–92, 98–101
structured interviews, 68
substance misuse (drugs), 155–159, **157–159**
suicide, 142–144, **144**
Support and Aspiration (DfE), 8
support staff
  effective management of, 244–246, *244*
  intervention programmes and, 246, 247, 249–250, 253–256, *254*, **255**
  modes of working with, 248–251, **251–253**
  principles of effective practice for, 246–247
  standards for, 247–248
Sutton Trust, 210, 247
Swartz, A., 183
systematic desensitisation (graduated exposure therapy), 130
systematic reviews, 164–165

tablets, 231
task-oriented approaches, 177–178
teacher accountability, 57–58, *58*
Thomas, G., 67
Thomson, P., 214–215
Thorley, W., 220, 223
THRIVE, 125–126
Timpson Review (2019), 216, 219
Tolhurst, J., 269
toxic stress, 84, 91–92
transactional leadership, 35–36, **36**
transformational leadership, 35–36, **36**
transitions, 202–203, 237–240, **238**, **240**
trauma, 98–101, **99**, *100–101*, 104–106, *105–107*. *See also* Post-Traumatic Stress Disorder (PTSD)
trauma-informed approaches, 108–109
traumatic bereavement, 147
Trussell Trust, 88, 90
Type 1 diabetes, 195–196
Type 2 diabetes, 196

Understood, 187
unilateral deafness, 199
United Nations Children's Fund (UNICEF), 87
United Nations Convention on the Rights of People with Disabilities (UNCRPD), 190
United Nations Convention on the Rights of the Child (1989), 230
United Nations Office on Drugs and Crime (UNODC), 155–156
unofficial exclusions, 216, **217**
unstructured interviews, 68–69

van Nieuwerburgh, C., 260–261
violence, 87–88
Violent Challenging Behaviour (VCB), 220
virtual school heads (VSH), 106, 108
Visual Impairment (VI), 16. *See also* sight loss
Visual Stress, 171
vocalisation ladder (shaping), 130
voice of the child, 230–232, *232*, **233**

Waring, M., 66
White, J., 235
Whitehead, J., 63, 64
Whitmore, J., 270
whole school approaches, 233–234
Winston's Wish, 155
working memory, 163–164, **164**
Working together to safeguard children (DfE), 86
World Health Organization (WHO), 116, 125, 175

Young, H., 153, 154
YoungMinds, 131, 136

Zakopoulou, V., 162